MICHAEL JORDAN ON:

THE PRICE OF FAME

"Sometimes I've told people there's no reason to be nervous [around me]. I want to joke with them and tell them that I go to the bathroom, I eat, I'm just like they are."

DOWN TIME

"Sometimes I'll just sit in a chair and look out the window and try to clear my mind. I find it peaceful, and I wish I could do it more. But then something always comes up."

FANS

"I think they stand up when I come out. The sense of respect I get from the people . . . I get chill bumps. Sometimes I'm misty-eyed, and it doesn't have anything to do with whether it's a big game or not. It just happens."

THE COMPETITION

"I like to play with their confidence and piss them off a little bit. I do it so that I get into their heads, because as soon as I'm in a guy's head, then I have him beaten."

GRACE UNDER PRESSURE

"The basketball court for me, during a game, is the most peaceful place I can imagine. When I'm out there, no one can bother me, I worry about nothing. It's one of the most private parts of my life."

OUTSTANDING PRAISE FOR
BOB GREENE'S *HANG TIME*:

"Fascinating . . . Greene's book is not just another saga of a superstar. What elevates it is Jordan himself, who, unlike a number of famous people, is a man of real introspection."
—*Baltimore Sun*

"A slam dunk of a book."
—Rita Mae Brown

"Far from a typical sports-hero bio . . . On-court heroics and megabucks play little part; instead, Greene seems to enter Jordan's psyche in a simple, personal way. Engaging and likely to sell very big."
—*Kirkus*

"Greene truly knows the art of the interview. Jordan's comments are not sensational, just unusually candid and heartfelt. He does, however, speak out. It is Greene's ability to stretch and see beyond basketball that allows him and Jordan to connect. And because he does, we do too."
—Armen Keteyian,
Chicago Tribune

"Jordan sensed he could trust Greene with at least one corner of his heart . . . Greene discovered private things about Jordan."
—*The New York Times*

"Fascinating . . . Not your average sports book . . . This is the Michael Jordan that you probably won't find on the sports pages."
—*Chicago Heights Star*

"Personal, anecdotal, and human, filled with the sounds of Jordan's voice . . . Destined to become one of the handful of books about sports that will still be read decades after the moments they recount have passed."
—*Beverly Hills Today*

HERE'S WHAT READERS SAY ABOUT *HANG TIME*:

"I am an avid reader, yet I have never before felt compelled to express on paper my feelings and my gratitude about a book. *Hang Time* is wonderful, it is amusing, it is touching—I actually cried a few times while reading it. Thank you for letting someone like me into Michael Jordan's world for a little while."
—Sandy Workman, Julian, WV

"I have just completed *Hang Time,* and I didn't want it to end. I am eighty-six years old—the book had such a fascination for me, and it will be a great and lasting satisfaction."
—Jeannette Grogan, Chicago, IL

"Only a very good writer can capture the essence of the person he is writing about. Thanks for giving me the chance to get to know Michael Jordan."
—Pat Brantly, Umatilla, FL

"I tell everyone I know what a great book *Hang Time* is— but I won't loan them mine! I'm taking no chances that I won't get it back."
—Tim Kelly, Springfield, VA

"*Hang Time* is just wonderful. The prose pleases the eye and stimulates the mind and heart."
—James R. Miller, St. Charles, IL

"I was moved deeply from the first page. I have a deeper appreciation for who Michael is, and how the world looks through his eyes."
—Linda Howard, Washington, D.C.

Other Books by Bob Greene

ALL SUMMER LONG (1993)
TO OUR CHILDREN'S CHILDREN: PRESERVING FAMILY
HISTORIES FOR GENERATIONS TO COME
(with D. G. Fulford) (1993)
HE WAS A MIDWESTERN BOY ON HIS OWN (1991)
HOMECOMING (1989)
BE TRUE TO YOUR SCHOOL (1987)
CHEESEBURGERS (1985)
GOOD MORNING, MERRY SUNSHINE (1984)
AMERICAN BEAT (1983)
BAGTIME *(with Paul Galloway)* (1977)
JOHNNY DEADLINE, REPORTER (1976)
BILLION DOLLAR BABY (1974)
RUNNING: A NIXON-McGOVERN CAMPAIGN JOURNAL
(1973)
WE DIDN'T HAVE NONE OF THEM FAT FUNKY ANGELS ON
THE WALL OF HEARTBREAK HOTEL, AND OTHER REPORTS
FROM AMERICA (1971)

HANG TIME

**Days and Dreams
with Michael Jordan**

BOB GREENE

ST. MARTIN'S PAPERBACKS

Published by arrangement with Doubleday

HANG TIME

Library of Congress Catalog Card Number: 92-26494

ISBN: 0-312-95193-0

Printed in the United States of America

Doubleday hardcover edition/November 1992
St. Martin's Paperbacks edition/December 1993

10 9 8 7 6 5 4 3 2 1

FOR NICK

NEW FOREWORD
FOR THIS EDITION

When the hardcover edition of *Hang Time* was released in November of 1992, Michael Jordan was in the midst of a period of great triumph. Yet if you listened to him closely enough in private moments, it was abundantly evident that he had already begun thinking seriously about the possibility of leaving basketball.

The Chicago Bulls had just picked up the championship rings commemorating their second consecutive National Basketball Association title. Some people were saying there would not be a third. The team was complacent, these observers said; their play was suddenly lackluster, their attitude appeared jaded. The Bulls and Jordan were destined to become just another NBA team that fell apart on their way to a third championship that would not happen. So the informed word had it.

Among the people who were hearing all of this was Jordan himself.

"I'm a person who thinks we can do it," he said to me one morning as we sat in his hotel room in Atlanta. "I really do. We're actually underdogs, which always drives me. Everyone's talking about the New York Knicks. Isn't that wild? I love it— it's like we're still being challenged by the [Detroit] Pistons, but they're wearing different uniforms."

The isolation in Jordan's life that is depicted in *Hang Time* had only intensified in the months following the book's release. He had reached such a level of fame, his celebrity had become so immense, that he was going out in public less and less, and choosing to keep to himself virtually all of the time on the road. On this day, he had returned to his room from the team's customary morning shootaround, and would stay here until it was time to get on the bus for the evening's game against the Atlanta Hawks.

"I'm feeling like an old guy, if you want to know the truth," he said as a steady rain pounded against the sixteenth-floor windows. "I've been through all of this so many times. Nothing on the basketball court really fazes me anymore. Not that I don't still have the enthusiasm to do the job. I do. But I'm wiser now. I'm preparing for the end. The end of my life in basketball. It's not a bad feeling at all. It's that wise old man feeling. The hungry young kid is still inside me, and I can find him when I need him, but these days it's mostly the wise old guy who I find."

When Jordan talked like that, it made me more sure than ever that he was starting to make up his mind. The years chronicled in *Hang Time*—all the basketball, all the personal and public pressures, all the extraordinary and often disorienting details of the singular life he was living—all of that was present tense as I watched it unfold. Now Jordan was giving every conceivable signal that it would soon enough shift dramatically and inexorably into something that used to be, that it would disappear into the vapors of time.

So his announcement, less than a year later, that he had chosen to retire from the NBA, should not have shocked anyone. The death of his father in August of 1993 certainly had an enormous effect on the timing of his decision; whatever troubles Jordan faced in his life prior to his father's murder, whatever adversities he prided himself on overcoming, this was in a different universe of pain.

Just when Jordan appeared to be managing to steel himself against the seemingly endless litany of ways in which his life was tossed about, something terrible beyond imagining happened. He always tried to stay a step ahead of trouble, as if by guessing what it would be, he could dilute the effects. The killing of his father, though, was so cruel, so awful, that no one who knew Jordan could do anything but wonder how he would weather the loss. On this day as I sat with him in Atlanta, it had yet to happen; on this day in Atlanta, as he talked on the sixteenth floor about the pressures of his life, the numbing news about his dad was still months away, and the pressures on his mind were things he could intellectualize, and at least try to make sense of.

"In terms of the icon thing, I don't think I can ever get any higher than what I was before," he said as he fiddled with the remnants of one more hotel breakfast on one more room-service tray. "I was in everyone's house, on everyone's TV screen, probably on everyone's wall. That's going to stop one of these days. People only want to see you so much. Maybe they get bored with you. Maybe they're getting tired of seeing my face so much. If that's true, I don't blame them at all. It's human nature, and when they get tired of me I'll accept it and try to find some kind of regular life for myself."

He was fully aware that such a thing might turn out to be impossible, even after he left basketball. During the course of the new season he had been hospitalized for a severely infected foot. If ever there was a person unsuited for a hospital stay, it was Jordan—he is a person who hates to sit still for more than a few minutes at a time, he is a man who despises being told what to do.

"Yeah, I really didn't like being there," he said. "It was like I was in . . . I wouldn't say prison, but close. I couldn't control things in the hospital, and I need to be in control all the time.

"For one of the few times in my life, I was vulnerable. I didn't sleep well at all. They had to put an extension on the bed because of my height, and the hospital pajamas weren't big enough for me, so I wore my sweats in bed most of the time. Being there made me feel very exposed, and I don't like to feel exposed."

And the hospital routine of nurses and doctors coming in at all hours of the night to check vital signs. . . .

"Yes, and they were getting autographs," Jordan said. "Interns, residents—they'd come in and take a look at my foot, and then they'd ask me for autographs, and I'd never seen them before and I never saw them again. I know for a fact that some of them, they weren't assigned to my foot. They just wanted to come in.

"I guess I should have challenged them, but they all had doctors' outfits on. . . . I was in a vulnerable situation. When you're in a hospital bed, you don't challenge someone in a doctor's outfit. You do what you're told. I just hate being so vulnerable."

I told Jordan that many people who had read *Hang Time* had said to me that when they read about his days behind double-locked doors and do-not-disturb signs, it sounded like a lonely existence. I didn't think that was quite true; I understood why they could think it, but "lonely" did not sound entirely accurate to me.

"I don't think it's lonely," he said, looking out the window at the downpour. "I think it's peace. I like this. I'm very happy being by myself. There will be plenty of people at the arena tonight. I'll see them and hear them tonight. Being by myself doesn't bother me at all. It's OK. It's fine. It's as peaceful as my life gets. At least for now."

He said again that he thought the Bulls could win the third straight championship. "To have gotten to the mountaintop," he said, "and then to get knocked off, and to have to start all over again—that would be a very fatiguing feeling. To start all over again as losers."

To hear Jordan use that word—"losers"—was jarring, dissonant. It was as if he had decided that it just wasn't acceptable—to allow himself to become regarded as a loser.

"There is nothing I love more than proving people wrong," he said. "There is nothing I love better than people telling me that something can't be done.

"And then doing it."

I left Jordan's room that day convinced he had decided that it would be less trouble for him to win the third championship than to lose it and have to contend with the lethargic, frustrating feeling the loss would bring. Other athletes, to be sure, could will themselves into displaying that kind of confidence, but with Jordan it never seemed like a pose—it never seemed like an artificial goad he was using on himself. It was almost a business resolution. He had determined that it would be prudent to win the third championship.

Which, of course, he and his teammates did, defeating the Phoenix Suns in a remarkable six-game series for which Jordan was chosen (for the third consecutive NBA Finals) Most Valuable Player. Something else Jordan said to me that morning—almost as an aside—stuck in my mind, too.

"They're digging up the gambling stuff again," he said.

He didn't have to explain what he meant.

"New stuff?" I said.

"New stuff, old stuff," he said. "They're digging it up. Sometimes I think this is just never going to end."

Jordan's troubles with gambling had first surfaced during the years in which *Hang Time* was being reported; some of his comments that appear in this book *(Was I gambling with goons who had bad reputations? Yeah, I was. Should I not gamble with goons anymore? Yeah, I shouldn't gamble with goons.)* made national news. To me, the specifics of Jordan's alleged transgressions—who he might have gambled with, how much he might have lost—while certainly the stuff of headlines, was not ultimately as interesting as how it fit into his prophecy for himself. For Jordan always seemed to be convinced that he was eventually going to make a terrible mistake, and lose everything.

"I am not a perfect person, and I have flaws," he would say to anyone who asked. Yet any time his imperfections became evident, any time his flaws became public, it was international news. Jordan told me many times that he was convinced that some mistake he would make would have the potential to bring him down. He didn't limit it to gambling; he seemed coldly aware that the tradeoff he had made for his unique position in contemporary American society was that all of his success was fragile, was just waiting to be taken from him. At least that was his belief.

Sometimes I think this is just never going to end. When, during the playoffs in the Bulls' pursuit of their third championship, fresh gambling allegations against Jordan were made public, I sensed that his anguish and consternation were not because of the specifics of what was being charged, but rather because he knew that such things indeed never would stop. As long as he was a dominant public figure, he knew that any area of his life that anyone might find lacking, any weakness anyone might discern, could and would be used to embarrass him. Knowing this and accepting it did not lessen the pain and humiliation it brought him. And the pain that would come the following August, with the news of his father, was of a magnitude that rendered the other bad news all but insignificant.

When I think about the third championship season, though, and all of the events that would follow, it is not Jordan's troubles that stand out, nor the fact of the championship itself. Rather, what moves me now, as it moved me during the writing of *Hang Time,* is how complicated it is to be Michael Jordan, how the human aspects of what he is going through—one man trying to figure out how to deal with the particulars of a life the rest of us can barely imagine—are infinitely more compelling than even the basketball superlatives.

In January of 1993, just after Christmas, a twenty-six-year-old Chicago attorney named Tim Brandhorst wrote a letter to his family and friends. It was the kind of holiday letter that many Americans mail to their loved ones—a summing up of what has happened in the year just past, run off in multiple copies but intended to convey a sense of personal warmth and heartfelt regard.

One of Brandhorst's relatives sent me a copy of the letter. It contained such a lovely sketch of an unexpected and pure moment that I have decided, with Brandhorst's permission, to include it here. I have spoken to officials of the health club which forms the background for what is told in the letter; they corroborate that the story happened just as Brandhorst records it. Somehow, among all the headline news about Jordan and his life, and especially in light of the retirement decision that he would within the year announce, the story in Tim Brandhorst's holiday letter is one that speaks about who Jordan really is, and that has the power to teach something essential about him:

Greetings from Chicago. Hope your Christmas was great and that your new year is off to a good start.

A good year here for me. Graduated from law school. Passed the bar exam. Finished my second consecutive Chicago Marathon in October. Got a job —with the Chicago City Law Department, a pretty good place to start. I get to work in City Hall and get to be in court a lot.

No major calamities, no scientific breakthroughs or earth-shattering inventions to report, didn't win the lottery (though the Publishers Clearinghouse Sweepstakes is coming up), took some good trips, had my car stolen outside the new Oriole Park at Camden Yards in Baltimore, got mugged outside my own apartment building, family's doing fine, a little older, no wiser, trying to enjoy it all.

So anyway, the Friday before Christmas I decide to go over to my health club after work and get in a quick workout before the weekend starts. The first thing I do when I get there is start shooting some baskets, just shooting around, waiting to play. There's a couple of teams playing, maybe ten or twelve guys waiting on the side, the regular after-work crowd on this court.

And Michael Jordan walks in.

Michael wanders over to one end of the court, just

standing there, watching. The place starts buzzing. As the guys on the court realize who's there, the game picks up, and pretty soon guys are trash-talking and woofing and trying to dunk (this court has some *players* on it). Nobody really bothers Michael, certainly nobody asks him for an autograph or anything like that, and pretty soon he wanders away to go lift some weights. The buzz, the excitement in the air, stays behind.

My team gets called next, and we start playing. Tonight I get lucky. My team includes a former pro and a former college ballplayer. Another guy on my team walks up to me and tells me that I should clear out and let those two guys take over. I don't touch the ball much, which is just as well and the way it often goes on this court. We win, which means we get to stay on the court.

As we're playing the next game, Michael wanders back. He sits down at one end of the court, grabs a ball, and just starts to watch the game. Michael Jordan is watching me play basketball! Another guy and I agree that we have never played under pressure like this. Halfway though the game, when we're at the other hoop, he strolls out on the court and starts launching rainbow three-pointers, like he's trying to hit the ceiling with his shots, every one of which swishes. My team wins again, so again we get to stay out on the court and play the next team.

Michael hasn't stopped commenting on our game since he came back to the court. He has a low voice, and tends to repeat himself, especially when he gets a laugh or a reaction. He walks under the basket and says, None of you can do this. He then does a flat-footed, no-step, three-sixty slam. There are a couple of guys there who are taller than him, and they immediately step up and insist they can—and, of course, not being Michael, they can't.

Michael then says, Gimme four.

It takes me a split second to fully comprehend those two words and everything they imply. Gimme four. Gimme four players. Wait a minute—GIMME FOUR? You don't mean—

And I start playing against Michael Jordan. I *said*, I start playing against *Michael Jordan*.

At first, he stays outside, passes to the other guys on his team, swishes a couple long shots. Which makes sense—of course the guy isn't going to jeopardize everything and take the chance of breaking an ankle or blowing out his knee in a pick-up game. I realize this as we're playing, and try to stay as far away from him as possible—I can just picture him coming down on my foot and twisting his ankle, having it be me, a gravity-bound, no-talent, small town *lawyer*, for heaven's sakes, who ends Michael's career.

Except, Michael can't just take it easy. He continues to talk trash, mostly to the ex-pro on my team who's trying to guard him. And before long, he's driving the lane, he's going inside for rebounds, he's blocking shots. He's playing like he has to prove to us that he's the best player out there. And, well, maybe that's how he got that good, by always feeling like he has to prove it. Or, from watching him, maybe that's the way he has his fun—he looked and sounded like he could not have enjoyed himself more out there. Or maybe it has something to do with the playground ethic of walking the walk to back up your talk, of the only important thing, the thing you judge others by and are judged on yourself, being what you do on the court, what you produce, how you perform—not what you've done in the past, not reputation, not history, not anything but what can you do *now*.

Word travels through the rest of the health club that Michael is not only in the building, but that he is actually playing, and people start to ring the basketball court. There's a running track overhead, and people line that as well. A couple hundred people are now watching. I'm having fun, just watching Michael, not really in the flow of the game because there's so much else to think about.

Someone on my team takes a long shot from the right side, and suddenly the long rebound is in my hands. I'm about eight feet from the hoop on the left baseline. Somewhat stunned, I look for an open man to pass to.

Oooh, take your shot, that's your shot, oooh, take your shot, oooh comes from everyone on the court, including Michael, and from everyone crowded around the court.

I throw up a shot.

Swish.

It doesn't matter that Michael was on the other side of the lane. It doesn't matter that, if he had wanted to, Michael could have walked over and swatted my shot away. Hey, he chose not to. It doesn't matter that the shot was a heave, a brick, a throw that just happened to go in. And it doesn't matter that his team whipped mine.

What *matters* is that *I scored on Michael Jordan.*

So you see, Christmas came early for me this year. The best Christmas present I could ever get. One I'll never forget.

Hope your new year is a tremendous one.

P.S.—As we were walking off the court I came up from behind him and patted him on the butt. Good game, I said. He didn't even acknowledge me. *As it should be.*

"As it should be." Meaning: Let the moment be. Meaning: It happened—don't step on it or overanalyze it or try to extend it. Brandhorst and the other men on the health club basketball court that day were privileged to see a Jordan that the rest of the world seldom does. Jordan as a person—Jordan as a man in the act of being himself.

When, ten months later, he announced his intention to retire from the NBA, the speculation immediately began about whether he would ever return. Within minutes of his announcement, people were starting to predict that he would come back the next year, or the year after. Many of the people doing the guessing had a hopeful tone to their voices; as much as they were thinking about Jordan and his life, they may have been thinking about their own. For with Jordan, whatever your troubles, whatever was worrying you in your own daily life, on a game night you could push all of that aside and watch something wonderful, and the night would suddenly be less cold. That's why so many people were wishing so fervently that his retirement would not truly be a retirement at all, and why their wishes were so understandable: They did not want to give up that warmth on all those winter nights.

One night Jordan said to me, "Sometimes I feel like I'm watching all of this along with everyone else." He, too, is a spectator taking in the Michael Jordan story; as exhilarating and confusing—and sometimes terrifying—as it appears to the rest of us, we ought to keep in mind that often he reacts the same way. It unfolds in front of him, and he watches, wondering what can possibly happen next.

For those of you who are reading *Hang Time* for the first time in this paperback edition: Thank you for choosing to come along on the trip.

BOB GREENE

I

"I DO DREAM," he said one night.

We had been talking about that word—the word "dream"—and how often people seemed to use it when referring to him. The word came up so frequently in conversations when strangers were discussing him, it was almost as if the usage was involuntary. People would use it when trying to explain how he inspired young boys and girls: "Michael Jordan teaches children to dream." People would use it when endeavoring to make the point that no goal should be considered unreachable: "Michael Jordan shows that you should never give up on your dreams." It had become a part of his job, really—he stood constant visible sentry as living, public proof that dreams can come true.

Not that he was entirely comfortable with it; who would be? And anyway, the dreams that were always talked about when his name was mentioned—dreams as inspirations, dreams as goals—were not literal dreams. A dream is something that happens when you aren't in control; a dream is what takes over when you have finally fallen asleep for the night, and you have had to temporarily give up the task of attempting to direct your life. A dream is not yours to determine.

"Most of the time I'll sleep right through the night," Jordan said. "But on the nights when I do have dreams, I wake up remembering them."

Most of the people who speak about Jordan and dreams are people who don't know him; that's another aspect of being who he is. We'd been talking about this, and I had brought up the subject of real dreams. Dreams like the rest of us have, two-o'clock-in-the-morning dreams that sneak into our heads when we're lost to the world and can't help it.

"I have very few sports dreams," he said. "It's not very often in my dreams that I'll be playing sports. Usually when I dream it will be about problems."

He stopped, but I knew not to interrupt. With Jordan, so often people will not allow even a few moments of silence to form during a conversation. It's as if they fear he will walk away—as if they assume he is so busy and so constantly behind schedule that if a bubble of emptiness is permitted to build, he'll be gone. That's not how you would behave with anyone else. Think about it—think about talking to a friend and not permitting the conversation ever to take a breath. It's something else Jordan had reluctantly become accustomed to: knowing that he had given up the luxury of pausing in wordless contemplation.

I waited for him to continue.

"What would happen if I had a bad problem," he said. "What I would do about it. In the dreams there will be negative things. I've had dreams in which I'm an alcoholic. What would I do? I'm an alcoholic in the dream, and because of it all the things I've worked so hard for will be taken away. I wake up numb after those dreams. Those are the kind of dreams when you want to make yourself wake up, because they trouble you so badly. In the dreams I'm making bad mistakes, and I'm not perfect, but I don't know what to do about it because I might lose everything."

What about good dreams? The kind of dreams that make you wake up with a smile on your face?

"Not really," he said. "Oh, sometimes I'll have a baseball dream."

Baseball?

"I'll dream I'm a baseball pitcher," he said. "In the dream, I'm all alone on the pitcher's mound. I'm a pitcher, but I also want to hit the ball. I'm not a pitcher who has to bat ninth. I'm a pitcher who bats third. And in the dream I will hear the crowd cheering for me, but the cheers are different than the cheers I hear every night on the basketball court.

"In the baseball dream, everyone has been saying that I can't do it—that I'm not good enough to be a good pitcher. And the cheers I hear are from the people in the stands who are feeling: 'I hope he'll do well.' "

So in the dream he can actually discern a sound that's different from the sound he has grown accustomed to hearing in basketball arenas around the globe?

"In the baseball dream, they're more cheers of hope than cheers of expecting me to be good. They're cheering for me even though they don't know that I'll be good. No one knows if I'll do well, but they hope that I might. In the baseball dream, when I'm at the plate I don't hit home runs, but I don't strike out, either. I'm just a baseball player who always connects with the ball. Or when I'm pitching in the dream, I won't be pitching a no-hitter, but I will always protect my team's lead. And the crowd is on my side because they don't know much about me, but they hope I'll do okay."

Is that the only sports dream he has? Is there any dream in which he's a basketball player?

"I don't dream about basketball anymore," he said.

2

SOMETIMES IN YOUR LIFE, when you least expect it, something wonderful comes along.

I am not a sportswriter. Before all of this happened, I was not even much of a basketball fan—at least I hadn't been since I was a kid. In my adult life, though, I had never become one of those people who feel obliged to spend every weekend watching sports on television. I watched the big games and matches that everyone in the country was talking about: the Super Bowl, the World Series, Wimbledon. If I was with friends and a game that mattered to them was on, I'd sit with them and enjoy it. But sports as something that consumed me —sports as something that had the power and resonance that sports have when you are a child—had gone away. I took it for granted that, at least for me, sports would never feel the way sports had felt when everything is new to you, and you are filled with wonder, and you are a boy to whom sports played by the great athletes you read about in the morning paper make a difference in your life. I knew the names of the famous contemporary athletes, and I admired their skills during the nightly highlights segments on the late-evening newscasts. But whatever connection the great athletes have with you when you are a child—whatever it is that makes your world sweeter because of them—that was gone. The loss of that was just one more inevitable aspect of growing older, or so I thought.

Then, quite by happenstance, I met Michael Jordan. What came to pass in the months and years that have followed was nothing I planned in advance; it just happened, and there is no explaining it except by recounting for you what it has been like. My life is better for having lived this time. I know that's a curious thing to say out loud. It's true, though, and perhaps the best way to tell you the story is simply to take you along on the journey.

I had been finding myself in the midst of some pretty grim professional times. I had been writing a newspaper column for almost twenty years. As a part of my work I had seen some of the darkest and unhappiest aspects of human nature, and I had written about them. It was beginning to get to me; at the start of my career I seldom used to lie awake at night wondering about the stories I was covering, but now, more and more, I was. I knew that a reporter was not supposed to allow himself to become affected by what he was seeing as part of his job, yet I couldn't help it. For only so many years can you exult in such ephemeral rewards as front-page bylines and healthy numbers of syndication clients. Eventually you come to the realization that when you move on to the next story tomorrow, the people you've written about today remain behind. You may have come quickly in and out of their lives, but after your story is finished the problems they are having stay just as real.

There were nights when I would go home from work and question the very nature of humanity, and wonder if there was any answer to the unremitting cruelty I was observing and writing about so often. Part of this had to do with a particular case I had been covering. The case involved one of the worst crimes I had ever encountered.

A beautiful, bright-eyed, four-year-old boy named Lattie McGee had been systematically tortured over the course of a long Chicago summer. He had been beaten, he had been starved, he had been hanged upside down in a locked and darkened closet for nights on end. That was how his mother and her boyfriend made him sleep—with his mouth taped shut, with his feet tied to a closet rod as he was hung up for the night like a bag of filthy laundry.

All that summer his life dwindled agonizingly away in that closet, and no one knew he was there; no one heard his muffled cries. After his death, when the police discovered what had been done to him, I wrote column after column about the people who had murdered him. So many cases of impoverished children from forgotten neighborhoods get lost in the courts system. I wanted to make sure that Lattie McGee, even though he would never know it, received justice, or something close to it.

His mother and her boyfriend went on trial and were sentenced to life in prison, but still I could not go to sleep at night without thinking of him. With all the public interest in Lattie because of the columns, the story of his brother, whose name was Cornelius Abraham, did not receive as much attention. Cornelius was six during the summer that Lattie was tortured and killed; the same things that were done to Lattie—the beatings, the starvation, the burning with an iron, the nights of being hung in the closet—were done to Cornelius, too. Somehow he survived. He watched his brother slowly being killed and was unable to stop the killers. Cornelius' brave testimony in court is what helped to convict them.

By the end of the trial Cornelius had just turned nine. He was a thin, extremely quiet boy; with his little brother dead and his mother and her boyfriend in prison, he was living with other relatives. The two great loves of his life were reading and basketball.

After the judge had sentenced Lattie's killers, I had gone to Florida for a short break. I wanted to try to think about something else for a change. But I ended the vacation early and flew back north, because an opportunity to do something for Cornelius had arisen.

In one of the columns I had written about Lattie, I had mentioned Cornelius' passion for basketball. Steve Schanwald, a vice president of the Chicago Bulls, had read the column and left a message at my office: Though tickets to Bulls' games were harder to get than virtually any other ticket in Chicago—they were without exception sold out—Schanwald said that if Cornelius would like to come to a game against the Miami Heat on a Sunday afternoon, he would be sure there were tickets available.

So I flew up from Florida, and on an April afternoon in 1990 a Cook County assistant state's attorney named Jim Bigoness and I took Cornelius to the Chicago Stadium. Bigoness was the prosecutor who had put Lattie's killers in prison; it had been his delicate and difficult job to prepare Cornelius for testimony.

Cornelius had the wide, all-seeing eyes of a frightened doe. It was not hard to figure out why; those eyes had seen things that no human should ever have to see. On this day he seemed almost unable to believe that he was really in the

Stadium. To every Chicago youngster who follows basketball, the Stadium is a shrine. Think of where Cornelius once was, locked up and tormented and hurt. And now he was in the Stadium, about to see his first Bulls game.

He said nothing. He just looked around.

Bigoness and I stood with him, and after a few minutes we said that we had somewhere else in the building we had to go. We asked Cornelius to come with us.

We walked down a stairway, until we were in a lower-level hallway. Cornelius stood between us. Then a door opened and a man came out. Cornelius looked up, and his eyes filled with a combination of wonder and awe and total disbelief.

Cornelius tried to say something; his mouth was moving, but no words would come out. He tried to speak and then the man helped him out by speaking first.

"Hi, Cornelius," the man said. "I'm Michael Jordan."

Jordan knelt down and spoke quietly with Cornelius. He made some jokes and told some stories about basketball and he didn't rush. You have to understand—for a long time the only adults Cornelius had any contact with were adults who wanted to hurt and humiliate him. And now Michael Jordan was saying, "Are you going to cheer for us today? We're going to need it."

Jordan went back into the locker room to finish dressing for the game. Bigoness and I walked Cornelius back upstairs to the court. There was one more surprise waiting.

Cornelius was given a red shirt of the kind worn by the Bulls' ball boys. He retrieved balls for the players from both teams as they warmed up.

Then, as the game was about to begin, he was led to Jordan's seat on the Bulls' bench. That's where he was going to sit—right next to Jordan's seat. During the minutes of the game when Jordan was out and resting, Cornelius would be sitting with him; when Jordan was on the court, Cornelius would be saving his seat for him.

I try not to be a vengeful person. But as I watched the game, I hoped I could be forgiven for thinking: The two people who killed Lattie McGee and tortured Cornelius were in prison on this afternoon. I hoped they understood that they were going to spend every day for the rest of their lives in prison. They were going to die in those stinking cells.

Nothing could bring Lattie back, and nothing could undo what had been done to Cornelius. But the killers were in prison, and Cornelius was in the Stadium, sitting on the wooden surface of the court right next to Michael Jordan's chair. At one point late in the game Jordan took a pass and sailed into the air and slammed home a basket. And there, just a few feet away, was Cornelius Abraham, laughing out loud with joy.

After the game was over—after the teams had left the floor, after Jim Bigoness and I had talked with Cornelius about the last few marvelous hours, after Bigoness and Cornelius had departed the Stadium for Bigoness' car and the drive home to where Cornelius was living—I didn't feel quite like leaving.

I wasn't sure what it was that was keeping me there. Part of it, of course, was the residual good feeling of Cornelius' day. There was a kind of glow to the moment that I didn't want to end.

But it was that and it was something else at the same time. In all my years in Chicago, I had never seen a Bulls basketball game before that afternoon. I had watched games on television over the years, and I had read newspaper coverage of the various annual incarnations of the teams. Somehow, though, I had never gotten around to coming out to the Stadium.

Jordan on the court had been even more than I had expected, and I had expected plenty. He had scored forty-seven points during the Bulls' victory over Miami, but more impressive than that number was the feeling that he was involved almost in a separate activity from the other men who shared the playing surface with him. I had heard all of the superlatives about his skills—the most oft-repeated comparison was to a ballet dancer, the point being that a person would not even have to know the rules of basketball to be in veneration of Jordan, just to watch him move on the court was sufficient explanation of his singularity—but it went beyond that. There had been certain moments during the game when it appeared that the other nine men on the court were schoolyard players, and that Jordan was a professional athlete somehow set down among them by mistake. The reality, of course, was that any player good enough to make the NBA was one of the most gifted athletes on the globe. They were all that good, they had all reached that pinnacle, and still Jordan had the ability to fuel the illusion as he moved through them that they were children, that they were just learning the sport.

While Cornelius had been sitting next to Jordan's seat on

the Bulls' bench, Bigoness and I had been up in the stands. I had noticed a number of parents with their young sons and daughters in the seats around us; the parents were pointing to Jordan as a parent might point to the Eiffel Tower or the Venus de Milo. I know that sounds overheated, perhaps comically so, but that's what it was like. Because of the extreme scarcity of Bulls tickets, some of these parents were undoubtedly thinking that this might be the only time in their lives they would be able to provide their boys and girls the opportunity to see Jordan in person. The parents were like tour guides, not wanting the children to miss a nuance. I had watched this and wondered what it must possibly be like to be the person on the other end—to be the person on the receiving end of all this hope and desire.

I wanted to thank Jordan for taking the time to be so nice to Cornelius. The meeting between them, I had learned, had been something that Jordan had volunteered for; he had been aware of the Lattie McGee case, and when he had heard that the Bulls were giving Cornelius tickets to the game, he had let it be known that he was available. Now I asked directions back down to the locker room, and within minutes found myself in front of the same basement-level door from which Jordan had emerged before the game. A security guard let me go inside.

The twelve members of the Bulls were at their dressing cubicles, and surrounding Jordan's cubicle were ten or fifteen reporters and cameramen. He was almost hidden by them. To eavesdrop on the postgame interviews was instructive; the beat reporters—the people whose job it was to cover the Bulls every day—were asking Jordan nuts-and-bolts questions, variations of questions that have been asked in tens of thousands of locker rooms over a century of big-time American sports: how Jordan had tailored his play against a certain Miami defender, why he thought that Phil Jackson, the coach of the Bulls, had decided to keep him in the game for a certain number of minutes. It was the job of the sportswriters to elicit such information, they would need it for their game stories that would appear the next morning, and Jordan answered each question patiently. I knew that for each of the sportswriters there must have been a first time that they had seen Jordan perform—a time when they had thought not of game strategies and statistics, but of the overriding miracle they had just observed. By now, though, this was one game out of an eighty-two-game season that the beat reporters had to cover, and this scene in the locker room did not seem to strike them as at all curious—this business of asking a miracle for a logical explanation of being miraculous.

One by one the sportswriters, having received the quotes they needed, peeled off to meet their deadlines. After the last writer had left, Jordan got up to retrieve his gym bag and head for home. As he walked toward the door of the locker room he saw me and stopped, and I said, "I just wanted to tell you how much Cornelius appreciated what you did for him."

For a second, I had the strange but undeniable impression that perhaps this was a man who didn't get thanked all that often—or at least that there were so many people endlessly lining up to beseech him for one thing or another that all he was accustomed to was the long file of faces in front of him wanting an autograph, a favor, a moment of his time, faces that would immediately be replaced by more faces with more entreaties. He stood there waiting, as if he was so used to ceaselessly being asked for things that he thought my thanks on Cornelius' behalf might be the inevitable preface to petitioning him for something else.

When I didn't say anything, he said, "That's why you came back down here?"

"Well, I don't think you know how much today meant to Cornelius," I said.

"No, I'm just surprised that you came back down to tell me," he said.

"My mom would kill me if I didn't," I said, smiling. "She tried to raise me right."

He smiled back. "Mine, too," he said.

We shook hands and I turned to leave and I heard him say, "Do you come out to a lot of games?"

"First one," I said.

"Well, you ought to come back," he said.

And so it began.

In my time as a reporter, I have witnessed some important, moving and emotional things. I have watched the country responding to politicians, to personalities, to events. I had never seen anything like what I was about to see with Jordan. Although it is often said that he is very likely the best basketball player who ever lived, the sports part of this at times seemed almost secondary.

We are coming out of an era of cynicism and self-indulgence. We are just discovering that there is a different way to look at the world than through a jaded sneer. Part of my willingness to see what I saw in the company of Jordan was undoubtedly based upon an eagerness I probably didn't even know I was harboring—an eagerness to take a step back from a society that seemed to have turned bitter and cold, and to step toward something hopeful. I didn't know that at first, at least not on any conscious level, but clearly it was there. The harshness I was seeing in the stories I so often covered was indicative of a growing meanness that had somehow crept into our national life; later, when I looked back over my time with Jordan, I would understand that much of what I sought was an escape from that meanness.

During the spending of the time, though, all I was really aware of was what a remarkable thing I was seeing. I thought about what it must have been like to spend 1927 with Babe Ruth, watching him perform every day, talking with him about it before and after the performances, both of you filled with wonder at the scope of what was transpiring. I thought about what it must have been like to spend 1956 with Elvis Presley, both he and you beginning to sense that decades later people would look back and say: This was it. This was the seminal time.

Because that's what the days and nights with Jordan turned out to be. For whatever reason, it was a period during which a man and a nation's yearnings were coming together. Decades from now the athletic record books will note that it was the same time during which Jordan and the Bulls won the NBA championship for the first time, and then repeated that feat, the time during which Jordan ascended to the ultimate heights not only of American sports, but of American culture. To me, though, the fact that it was a time of championships is an interesting backdrop to what took place, but ultimately incidental. There are champions in every sport every year; few things are more transitory. At least for me, what the days and nights with Jordan felt like is something that will outlive any memories of a win-loss record or a playoff run.

It was this remarkable moment out of time; it was this slice of something I had almost given up hope of recapturing, but it happened. Jordan the basketball player has been dissected and analyzed and held under a microscope; his motives and his intentions and his style have been criticized and debated and argued over. Likewise, Jordan the icon has been taken apart and inspected and displayed under the light, his value as a marketing commodity evaluated, his corporate partners' strategies broken down into increments in an effort to understand why he has the power in the commercial marketplace that he does.

I wasn't interested in any of that, and I probably wouldn't have had the expertise to evaluate it if I had set out to. But I didn't set out to do anything; I went to a basketball game with a lonely little kid one April afternoon, and I saw something that moved me, and Jordan said "You ought to come back" and I did, just about every night. The time since then is something I would never trade, not for anything; the time since then gave me back something I wasn't even fully aware I had lost. All my life, all I have ever known for sure is what I see for myself and hear for myself. That's what this book is a record of: What I have seen and what I have heard during a time that I will never forget.

3

S OON AFTER THAT DAY with Cornelius at the Stadium, the Bulls' 1989–90 season drew to a close and the members of the team went their separate ways for the summer months. Baseball took over the sports pages, and I went on with my daily professional life, writing my newspaper columns and covering stories that had nothing to do with athletes or athletics. In June an envelope arrived from Jim Bigoness; he had taken a snapshot of Jordan with Cornelius outside the locker room, and he sent me a copy. In his note he said that Cornelius was doing surprisingly well; the day with Jordan seemed to have lifted his spirits in a way none of us could have predicted. Bigoness had been out to visit him. Cornelius had his own copy of the snapshot taped above his bed, and in his room he kept a miniature basketball that Jordan had signed and presented to him that afternoon.

In the snapshot, Jordan was crouched, almost down on his knees, so that he and Cornelius could both fit into the frame of the photograph. Both the man and the boy were smiling broadly. What I found notable about the photo was how drab and dingy that corridor outside the locker room was. I did not remember it being that way; if I'd had to describe it from memory, I would have said that it was bright and modern and newly appointed. The picture proved otherwise, though; it was a very old and very beaten-up hallway in an ancient, dismal arena that had been standing since before the Great Depression. What had lighted it up in my recollection was the same thing that had lighted up Cornelius' smile.

Jordan's name appeared regularly in the papers during the summer; it didn't take much for him to make news, and as basketball practice began in October he soon became a daily presence for readers again. So, too, his televised image once again became inescapable. One piece of video in particular caught my attention. Jordan had been at a meeting somewhere, and the word had gotten out that he was in the building, and as he left a crowd of several hundred people that had gathered began screaming and shoving toward him as they might toward a rock star. It was a jarring sight; athletes, while among the most famous people on earth, do not generally draw that kind of response, and in the video footage Jordan had to run through them to get to a waiting car. I thought once more about what it must be like to be the person on the receiving end of that.

As November began the first home game of the new 1990–91 season was played. I didn't go. Back on that April Sunday the Bulls' management people who had arranged for Cornelius' ticket had explained to me the procedures for requesting a credential for press row, and had made it clear that I was welcome to come out and visit. To me, though, even after all my years as a reporter, the mechanics and logistics of the sportswriting craft remained mysterious and implicitly exclusionary, something that seemed restricted to members of a close-knit club of which I was not a member. I knew how to cover a federal courtroom or a political news conference or a murder scene; I didn't really know how the sportswriters did their jobs. They always seemed to be traveling in groups, beat reporters and sports-page columnists and TV sports anchors who covered all the teams and knew the ropes.

One of the things I did know how to cover was an election night. The following Tuesday, the first Tuesday in November, was election day in Illinois. I had written about so many election nights over the years; the early returns would begin to come in just after the dinner hour, and they would accumulate quickly, and starting around eight or eight-thirty the various candidates would make their initial appearances behind lecterns in hotel ballrooms. It was a dreary and entirely predictable routine, familiar to anyone who has ever watched an election night on television; in the winners' ballrooms the bands would play loudly and the inebriated crowds would holler and the victorious candidates and their families would stand grinning on makeshift stages. In the losers' ballrooms the bands would continue stalwartly even though there was no one left who wanted to dance, and the candidates' press secretaries would say that no statement would be available until at least midnight. There was a time when covering nights like these had seemed exciting to me, had seemed important. But over the years the election nights had all blended together; in the end they were all the same night with the same scripts and the same actors, and on that Tuesday night, as I considered which contest I should cover—governor of Illinois? Cook County state's attorney? Cook County sheriff?—I realized there was another contest in town. Out at the Stadium it was the Bulls versus the Boston Celtics, Jordan versus Larry Bird, second home game of the new season, and I decided that election night would certainly not miss my presence or even notice I wasn't there. I grabbed a cab for the Stadium.

Gate 3½ is on the west side of the Stadium, a single doorway protected by a high fence surrounding a small parking lot. The doorway is where the players, arena staff, and sportswriters enter the building. The Stadium itself is in one of Chicago's most depressing and dangerous neighborhoods. Some cities boast of brand-new domed convention center arenas in the heart of downtown; some cities feature architecturally flawless stadiums located on rolling acres of suburban land. The Chicago Stadium, constructed in 1929, is a massive gray barn rising indifferently into the night in the midst of urban desolation all around.

The chain fence is no coincidence; the few thousand square feet of blacktop inside the fence, patrolled by yellow-jacketed sentries, allows the players to leave their cars in presumed safety during the hours they are in the building. The TV broadcast trailers, too, are parked here; at least for five or six hours on the day of a Bulls game, this little hemmed-in patch of the city is secure. It is a false and fleeting security; it is the same kind of security you feel at a roped-off crime scene after the shots have been fired and the bodies have been rushed to the hospital and the police have swarmed in to gather evidence.

I walked across the little parking lot and headed toward Gate 3½. Inside the doorway a young man at a wooden table checked my name against a typed list, then handed me a round red sticker, which he instructed me to affix to my shirt. He pointed toward a tunnel; I followed his directions and within a few moments I was standing by the court.

More than eighteen thousand people apparently shared my willingness to wait until later in the night, or even until morning, to find out the election results. If the basement locker-room area was dark and moldering, the arena itself was glaringly bright, jacked up to full candle power for television, the floor a gleaming, brilliantly polished yellow and red. I walked down to the far basket, under which two long rows of press tables were set up. Each reporter or news organization had a card bearing his or her name or affiliation taped to the tables, like place cards at a highly unusual party.

A card with my name was next to the seat occupied by Jackie MacMullan of the *Boston Globe*. She was already typing away at her laptop computer; because her newspaper was in the Eastern time zone, she would lose an hour of deadline time, so she was drafting the column of sidebar notes that would run beneath her game story. I settled into my seat as the players ran through their warm-up drills.

It's difficult to imagine a better vantage point from which to watch a game. Maybe not for the sportswriters who have to be attuned to every move at either end of the court; for them, a press box high in the building might better suit their needs. And indeed, there was a balcony-level press box on the other end of the Stadium to provide a panoramic view for those writers who preferred it.

Here, though, under the basket, we were within several feet of the players. Had we stood up and walked a few steps forward, we would have been on the court. When the action was down at the other end, at the other basket, everything was mainly a distant rumor. But when the ball was in play at our basket, every expression on the faces of the Bulls and the Celtics, every sound they made, every frustration that flashed through their eyes, was right there. This was not so much like watching a basketball game as wandering into one.

The noise level in the building was at a constant and furious peak as the teams went at each other. It was a game that the Bulls would lose in the final seconds, by a single basket, with Jordan scoring thirty-three points, Bird scoring twenty-four. For me, though, one of the most memorable scenes of the night took place when the game itself was not in play.

The first half had ended; Jordan had left the court, his face betraying the knowledge that this was only the beginning of a long season, and that much arduousness lay ahead. Bird and his team also exited. These were two men who had become so accomplished at their craft that their names and faces were instantly recognizable in every corner of the globe. At some level, though, they were traveling salesmen, carrying basket-balls instead of sample cases, and this was one more night at the office.

On the court during that first half, they had barely looked at each other. If the eighteen thousand–plus had come to see them do battle, the eighteen thousand–plus were being amply rewarded. But except for the relatively few moments when Jordan and Bird were going head-to-head, when you looked in their eyes you saw no more emotional connection between the men than if they were two commuters on the 5:22 heading home.

During the halftime intermission, the Bulls' management sponsored a promotion: Some two hundred youngsters were allowed to walk onto the court, and each was allowed to shoot a ball toward the basket. Those who managed to sink their shots were presented with a gift.

The gift was a hand-held video game. It was called "Jordan versus Bird, One-on-One." On the cover of the cardboard package was a color photograph of Jordan and Bird reaching for a basketball as it bounced off a hoop. The package promised "7 Game Options—Sound On/Off—High Score Retention." The product itself, manufactured in China, consisted of a screen upon which two tiny, electronically simulated images in the approximate shapes of basketball players, one black and one white, could be maneuvered via plastic buttons toward a tiny, electronically simulated hoop.

This was true fame. All of the other professional basketball players in the Stadium this night were superb athletes, but Jordan and Bird had reached the pinnacle. They were so famous that they had been repackaged in China as electronic blips. In our contemporary world, few things could be considered more flattering.

So the lucky youngsters whose shots went into the basket at the Stadium were given their "Jordan versus Bird" video games. And with a few children on the court still waiting their turns, the Bulls and the Celtics emerged from their locker rooms.

The teams were just half a minute or so early. Thus Jordan, in the company of his teammates, waited at the side of the court for the children to finish. Bird, too, with his own team-mates, waited. It was impossible for these two men to be invis-ible anywhere, and especially in a basketball arena.

For those few seconds, though, they were bystanders. They

were international stars and they were human beings and they were electronic blips, not necessarily in that order, and they watched as the children tried to win the toys. Then, with the noise in the Stadium rising again, they went back to work.

When the game ended and the Bulls were leaving the floor on their way to the stairs that led down to their locker room, I saw for the first time what I would later see every time I was in Jordan's company.

Several hundred people had gathered just to look at him. They were being held back by ushers and security guards, and they weren't yelling. They were just staring. It was a permutation of what I had noticed at that first game the previous April, when the parents in the stands had been pointing him out to their children and describing him as if he were a museum piece. This, though, was up close; these people were within feet of him. As he walked quickly by with the rest of the Bulls, all of those eyes bored right into him. Every set of silent eyes.

It gave me the chills. It was almost creepy. Later in the year, when I knew him better and we were talking on a regular and casual basis, when I felt comfortable enough to ask him about things like the eyes, he would say that there was seldom a moment when he wasn't aware of them.

"You can feel the eyes," he would say. "I don't want to make too much of a point of it, but it's like the eyes are burning into you. It never goes away, not even for one second. If I'm sitting on the bench during the game, I don't want to touch my nose, even if my nose itches or something, because I know that a lot of people are looking at me even though I'm not in the game."

So he assumes that there's never a moment when he isn't being watched?

"Any time I'm not completely by myself, I know that people are watching me. The only time I'm not aware of it is when I'm playing."

But that's when everyone is watching.

"I know it, but for some reason when I'm playing it doesn't matter. The rest of the time, when they're looking at me, I think they're trying to figure me out or something. It's like if they look at me hard enough, they'll be able to figure out what I'm thinking, or who I really am."

And the people who gather to stare at him when he leaves

the court—during that rapid walk through their midst, does he shut them out?

"I see it even if they don't think I see it. Sometimes they'll say something about you, as if they don't think you can hear them. Even though you're so close to them. It's as if they're trying to connect their personality to yours, or something. I just keep walking and don't stop. It's a very strange feeling. All those eyes, all the time, and it never stops. I just have to walk right through it."

On this night, though, I could only wonder what he was thinking. I didn't know whether it was because the Bulls had lost the game that the people were stone silent, or whether it was simply their involuntary response to being so close to him, but every eye was on him and there was scarcely a sound and soon enough he disappeared down the stairs.

The Stadium after a game becomes extremely chilly extremely fast; the basketball court is laid directly over an ice rink that is used for Chicago Blackhawks hockey games, and as often as not there is a hockey game scheduled for the next night. So even as the fans are leaving, workers are already taking down the backboards and pulling up the floor.

I hung around for a while, and by the time I left the building most of the fans were long gone. I was walking off the floor area, heading for the same narrow tunnel I'd come in through. Approaching the tunnel from another part of the court was a person who looked vaguely familiar. He was a gray-haired man with a craggy, distinguished appearance and grace in his step, and he seemed tired, and when I figured out who he was I had a sudden flash of what sports used to mean to me when I was young, when the stars seemed so far away.

Back then, when I was eight or nine years old, I never gave any thought to the idea I might ever meet an athlete whose talents had thrilled me on television, or whose face I had seen smiling out at me from the full-color cover of *Sports Illustrated* or *Sport.* Growing up in central Ohio, my friends and I never saw any professional athletes play in person. Columbus had no big-league teams, which made the world of the national stars seem all that much more distant. The big-league stars were like movie stars to us; it was as if they weren't real, a Mickey Mantle was like a Kirk Douglas, a Stan Musial was like a Humphrey Bogart. They were delivered to us out of the air, or onto the newsstand down at Rogers' Drugstore on

Main Street. Their lives had no true-life intersections with ours.

Tonight had been heady yet within the realm of expectation; tonight, walking into the Stadium and sitting at the press table, had been something out of my adult life as a newspaperman. It had been something that the eight-year-old me never could have imagined. The eight-year-old me, and all my eight-year-old friends, did do one thing in an effort to connect with the stars whose names thrilled us, though.

We had heard a rumor. According to the rumor, if you sent a stamped, self-addressed postcard to the big stars in care of the stadiums where they played, they just might open the envelopes before a game, see your postcard, scrawl their signatures, and drop the cards into a mailbox. The key to this, or so the rumor had it, was to make it easy on the stars. Make it so all they had to do was autograph the card.

So we sent the cards off—to Mantle in care of Yankee Stadium in New York, to Musial in care of Busch Stadium in St. Louis, to Jim Brown in care of Cleveland Municipal Stadium. Mostly the cards would not come back; mostly we would check our mailboxes and find nothing.

Once in a while, though, it would happen. Once in a while someone would come through. I remember the day I rushed to the mailbox, and there, nestled among the letters and magazines addressed to my parents, was a postcard—a postcard I had sent off. On the front of it was my name and address, in my own handwriting. And on the back—I can still see it—was: "To Bobby. Best wishes, Bob Cousy."

Bob Cousy—the most exciting guard and playmaker in the National Basketball Association, the great Bob Cousy of the Boston Celtics—had somehow opened the envelope I had sent him, in care of the Boston Garden, and had somehow decided not to throw the card away. He had sent it back. I don't know whether he had just been in a good mood that day, or whether he did it for kids all the time—but he did it.

Tonight, as I walked toward the tunnel, the man who was approaching from the other side of the arena—Bob Cousy—looked weary and ready for some sleep. He was in his sixties; he worked as a broadcaster for Celtics games, and he was on the road with the team. There was no way he could ever have remembered signing a postcard all those years ago. Today, of course, so many big-league stars in every sport charge money for their autographs. They get appearance fees to come to card shows, and they set a certain fee per autograph. Children and their parents hand over cash in order to walk away with a signature. It has become the accepted way.

Which may make financial sense for the athletes; the money is there for the taking, and they take it. I wonder, though, what those bought and paid for autographs will mean to the children when they grow up. Will the autographs seem special? Will the grown-up children save the autographs and look at them some day and feel anything approaching warmth?

Cousy tonight was a fatigued working man on the road. But I remembered; I remembered how special and how exhilarated and how grateful I had felt that day at the mailbox, I remembered how a moment's courtesy by a famous star had made me feel happy. It was cold in the Stadium, and we walked through the tunnel and then toward Gate 3½, alone in that section of the building save for a swing-shift maintenance worker or two and an occasional cop.

4

JORDAN, IN THE MOST PECULIAR WAY, sometimes seemed as if he did not belong on the court.

That's what began to strike me as I found myself returning to the Stadium in the ensuing nights. There was a draw to the place that was hard to resist; on the morning following the Celtics game I went to the office, and it had the feel of a cold and sober New Year's dawn after an exultant New Year's Eve. The fun was over. So the pattern commenced. I would work a full day at the newspaper office, and then I would set out for the Stadium. And what I noticed as I watched the Bulls playing the NBA opponents who flew in and out of Chicago was that Jordan, on the court, seemed to be an outsider.

Not in the literal sense; no one belonged on a basketball court more than Jordan did, and far from being a true outsider on the Bulls, he was the central fact of the team. But he had the look of an outsider in a what's-wrong-with-this-picture sense, like a find-the-item-that's-different puzzle in a children's book. He was so famous—so photographed, so televised, so ubiquitous in milieus as expansive as network TV commercials and as intimate as posters on suburban bedroom walls—that the sight of him running down the court among the other players always took a moment to click in.

It reminded me a little bit of the first time I saw the Rolling Stones. They were international celebrities, at the very apex of worldwide adulation, but they were still very young and this was still in the mid-1960s, before rock concerts moved to football stadiums with million-dollar pyrotechnics and lighting directors available to mythologize each move of each performance with a computer-board wash of color. The stagecraft had not yet caught up with the frenzy, so the night I saw them

on a bare wooden stage there had been several opening acts—
a blues singer, a young guitar whiz—and then, onto that same
stage, came the Rolling Stones, and it didn't seem like they
should be there. After seeing the bluesman singing his dirges
on the stage, after seeing the young guitarist standing there at
the microphone, the sight of Mick Jagger almost would not
register. Same cruddy stage, same microphones and amplifiers
and speakers, yet now it was the Rolling Stones. They were in
the same business as the others who had used the stage, but
they were in a completely different business, too, and the shift
was so jarring that it distracted from the performance. It
didn't diminish the performance—it just changed it. At the
same time I watched the band work, I couldn't stop thinking:
How odd. Those five men are the Rolling Stones.

So, too, with Jordan. The court may have been crowded
with nine other players and three referees, but Jordan might
as well have been outlined in glowing neon. He was in the
game but he was separate from the game; there were two
connected but distinct things going on. You could look up at
the scoreboard and remind yourself which team was winning;
that was the information that would go out over the wire services after the game had ended, and that would appear in
agate type the next morning on sports pages all over the
world. But you could also watch the Jordan concert.

This was why the Stadium was filled every night; if the team
won, that was fine, a bonus. Regardless of the score, though, a
ticket bought a promise of an indelible memory. For hard-
core basketball fans, an NBA season was now underway. For
them and for anyone else, there was a second and concurrent
drama. You could lose track of the game and still walk away
gratified from this loud old building full of light and life. Like
the other eighteen thousand–plus under the roof, I leaned
forward and took in the two parallel shows.

Tim Hallam, as director of the Bulls' press operations, was in
charge of shepherding the sportswriters in and out of the
locker room on game nights. NBA leaguewide rules dictated
that the locker rooms would be open to the press ten minutes
after the final buzzer of each game. For beat writers on morning papers, and for TV reporters trying to get postgame comments on videotape in time for inclusion on their late-evening
newscasts, gaining access to the players as rapidly as possible
was important. The writers knew precisely when the ten-min-

ute waiting period had passed. "Tim, it's been twelve minutes," I would hear a voice among the reporters in the
basement corridor call out.

But the decision on when to open the door wasn't Hallam's;
Phil Jackson was the team's head coach, and not until he was
finished talking privately with his players each night would
Hallam be free to signal the reporters that they could come in.
Some nights it was ten minutes; some nights it was fourteen;
some nights it was sixteen.

There was a certain dynamic at work in the locker room, a
dynamic that had no direct correlation to the way human beings in the real world relate to each other. The door would
open, and the reporters—who had stood single-file in the narrow hallway as they had waited—would stream in. In front of
each cubicle would be the players who had only minutes before finished performing upstairs.

Jordan would not always be at his cubicle at first; he generally changed out of his uniform and into his street clothes in
an anteroom, so that he would be dressed by the time the
cameras focused on him. The reporters would glance quickly
at Jordan's deserted cubicle, and then turn to the other players for comments until he arrived.

That is when the curious dynamic kicked in. The players
and the sportswriters were people who dealt with each other
on a nightly basis; not only did they know each other, but they
all depended on each other, to some degree, in the execution
of their livelihoods. The writers depended on the players for
quotes and information and, on a more essential level, for
playing the game and thus being the basis for what they reported in the papers each day. And the players depended on
the writers and photographers and broadcasters to keep their
names and pictures and electronic images in front of the fans.

So they knew each other. Yet when the game ended each
night, and the reporters stepped up to the cubicles, there was
seldom even the briefest exchange of pleasantries or greetings. The members of the Bulls' starting lineup would be sitting on folding chairs: Scottie Pippen, the wary, reticent
forward who always wore the expression of a man ready to
believe that someone was eager to do him wrong; Horace
Grant, much softer up close when his ready smile broke out
across his playful-eyed face than he appeared on the court,
where his wraparound goggles and stoic countenance combined with his six-foot-ten-inch frame to form the requisite

picture of an NBA power forward; Bill Cartwright, the center, who as the oldest man on the team appeared always resigned to the fact that this was one more late evening in a steamy locker room in a life that had included thousands upon thousands of locker-room nights just like it; John Paxson, Jordan's running mate at guard, the only white player among the starters, looking like a hundred other shyly grinning, sandy-haired Dayton, Ohio, sharpshooters who come into the city's high schools as freshman dreamers and graduate four years later as all-league local heroes—except that all of the Paxson lookalikes were back in Ohio in insurance offices or factories or on family farms, their basketball dreams hidden away forever like old varsity letter jackets in basement storage closets, and Paxson was the one among them who had made it to the NBA, and had stuck.

A writer would approach a player—Cartwright, Pippen— and the first words would be a direct, unadorned question, demanding of a direct answer. "Why did you guys have so much trouble stopping Hardaway tonight?" the words might be. Or: "Why does Parish always seem to have such a good night against you?" It wasn't a matter of the questions being rude; rudeness, or lack of it, had nothing to do with this; any basketball question was fair game, and rightfully so. Rather, it was the abruptness of how the exchanges began. Usually no hello, no small talk, no banter at all, just a series of unprefaced questions and limited-eye-contact answers between people who no longer even seemed to expect the pretense of conventional pleasantries.

I didn't detect any particular bad feelings here. This was just the way these things were done. The deadline pressure could conceivably provide a handy excuse for this—with the copydesk back at the office waiting, who had time for wasted words?—but it doesn't take much time at all to say "hello." Rather, the brusque initiation of the questions to the players seemed an implicit affirmation that the athletes on the one hand, and the writers and broadcasters on the other, lived in totally different universes, and always had, and that everyone in the room knew it. That's what this felt like—like a room filled with people who, except for the professional circumstances that had brought them here, would never in their lives end up spending time together. No animosities, or at least not many, on either side—just the unspoken acknowledgment that this was strictly business for everyone involved. If I'd had to jump to a conclusion, I would have guessed that it felt safer that way, all around.

On one of my first visits to the postgame locker room, I had seen something that had made me inquisitive. Once Jordan would arrive at his cubicle, the reporters would halt their previous interviews and flock to him, sometimes leaving the other players in mid-sentence. The room at that moment would suddenly have the ambience of a high school prom at which the other Bulls had become wallflowers.

There was a pecking order of sorts in the way the cubicles were assigned. The veteran, more established players had no desire to sit near Jordan's locker; it wasn't so much a matter of being chagrined at all the attention he received as it was something more practical. With so many sportswriters and camera crews gathered in a deep semicircle sticking microphones and miniaturized tape recorders at Jordan, the cubicles next to his were not very comfortable places in which to attempt to get dressed. So the players with the least seniority were given those spaces. To the outside world it might have seemed like an honor of sorts—being put next to Jordan. The reality was quite different.

One of the players whose cubicle was in Jordan's vicinity was B. J. Armstrong, a twenty-three-year-old sure-handed reserve guard who, because of his startlingly youthful appearance—there were moments when his face literally could have passed for that of a twelve-year-old—and his physical stature as the smallest Bull, was rapidly becoming a favorite with fans at the Stadium. I had come into the locker room and had taken in the tableau of all the reporters and video crews pressing toward Jordan. I had seen Armstrong looking cramped-in as he put his street shoes on in their wake.

He had his gym bag open on the floor. The stereotype of traveling professional athletes is that they watch a lot of TV on the road, and listen to a lot of Walkman music. Especially with the exhausting pace of the NBA, with teams always flying off to the next city in the middle of the night after a game, you wouldn't necessarily expect the players to have a lot of time or inclination for serious literary introspection.

What I had seen in Armstrong's gym bag was a hardbound copy of John Irving's 1978 novel *The World According to Garp*. That particular book is hefty in size alone—it would make a good doorstop—and it is not a book that would seem to make for quick browsing during red-eye plane flights. I found myself wondering about it. So after a game against the Charlotte Hornets I went down to the locker room again, introduced myself to Armstrong, who was alone at his cubicle, and asked if he'd mind a non-basketball question.

"Go right ahead," he said.

"Are you reading *Garp*?" I said.

He laughed and asked me how I knew. I explained about his open gym bag. I assured him I hadn't intentionally been checking out his possessions; that book jacket is just unmistakable.

"A friend told me that she thought I'd like this," he said. "Any time I get a good recommendation, I try to pick the book up." He said that the team had a long series of road games looming ahead. "A really well-written book is good to have with you on a long trip."

I asked him if that was his custom on the road. "You have so much free time," he said. "You have to make the choice of what to do with it. There are a lot of things I don't know about. I look at my time on the road as the opportunity to learn some things."

Did he do the reading on the team plane?

"That's a pretty noisy place," he said. "But I'll read just about everywhere else. I'll read on the bus to the hotel, and then when I get to my room, a lot of times I won't be able to sleep. So I'll order room service and read until I'm tired."

Often, he said, he will read early on the day of a game. "It helps me to relax. I'll bring whatever book I'm reading to the arena where we're playing, and I'll read right up until game time."

He could read in the confusion of a locker room?

"I'm so used to locker rooms," he said. "I've been in them all my life. I don't have any problem blocking everything out and reading."

The hardback edition of *Garp* was such a large book to be lugging around. Wouldn't it be more convenient to carry a paperback? Didn't the hardback book take up a lot of space in his gym bag?

"I have two books in there," he said.

Two?

"What, you didn't see the other one?" he said, smiling again.

He reached inside the gym bag and moved some clothes aside.

There, resting at the bottom of the bag, was a Bible.

Off to our side there was a sudden rustling and a rise in the noise level and a turning on of portable lights. Jordan had once again arrived, in a suit and tie, at his cubicle.

Later on, I would understand better; later on, I would realize that this nightly locker-room scene was just a variation of the separateness that was both Jordan's blessing and his burdensome fate, the same separateness that made him appear to be a person apart on the crowded court. Whether he welcomed it or not, it was a fact of his life.

As soon as Jordan, fresh from his shower and dressed as if on his way to a corporate board of directors meeting, sat down, the questions began. This was a part of his job the same way that scoring thirty points a night was a part of his job. On all of the local television stations, within the hour, the coverage of the Bulls-Hornets game would consist of three elements. First the sports anchor, on the set, would say that the Bulls had defeated the Hornets 105–86; then there would be video footage of Jordan making two or three spectacular shots; then there would be a few seconds of him sitting here at his cubicle, saying "We're starting to come together as a team, but it's still very early in the season," or whatever other snippet of Jordan's voice the videotape editors decided to select. The precise words that Jordan said would not matter; the truth was that virtually all of these postgame comments in front of massed reporters were boilerplate, they were intentionally bland and general.

What mattered, then, was not the content of the interview, but the existence of the interview. A few seconds of Jordan speaking was a staple of those late-evening sportscasts; for those few seconds not to be included would be something that would leave viewers, at least on some level, confused and feeling something was missing. It would feel vaguely akin to a story about a White House event without any footage of the president talking. So Jordan offered his comments about the game, while his teammates finished getting dressed.

He and I had talked briefly at the Boston game, the first time I'd seen him since the day I had brought Cornelius Abraham to the Stadium. I had been more than surprised when he had approached me and said, "Thank you very much for that nice article. I appreciated it." I assumed he had been referring to something I had written when I had wrapped up the Lattie McGee case; in that story I had referred to Jordan's generosity to Cornelius. So few people you write about ever take the trouble to respond, unless they hated the story; it was just a reality of the business I was in, a reality I had learned to accept over the years. And Jordan, of all people, could have been excused not only had he neglected to respond to a story in which he was mentioned, but had he not even been aware the story had been written. Literally hundreds of stories about him appeared in newspapers and on TV all over the country every week, thousands if you counted the game reports. He was a fixture on the cover of *Sports Illustrated,* in the national papers, in the pages of *Time* and *Newsweek* and countless other publications that endeavored to chronicle the country.

So at the Boston game, I had not expected it when he had walked over to offer his hand and say thanks. The story had appeared months before—and besides that, Jordan was in his official territory here, he was on the court, on his way to work as it were, and presumably busy or even preoccupied; there just was no need for him to bother. Later on I would understand that this was part of his attempt to defeat his separateness. I was not alone in wrongly presuming that he reveled in it; I would come to see how hard he worked to push it out of the way so that he could try to live his life.

John Paxson understood this. Paxson, as the other starting guard on the Bulls, was in the unique situation of making his living directly next to Jordan on the court. No one could be expected to have quite the same perspective on Jordan that Paxson did; Jordan and Paxson were, in a grandly elevated sense, like two men who worked next to each other on a factory assembly line.

So later in the year, when I had gotten to know Paxson and I found myself thinking about this incontestable separateness of Jordan's, I would ask Paxson about it.

"The whole atmosphere of being around him is something that I've gotten used to," Paxson would say. "To people who see it for the first time, it's amazing, but because I play beside him every night, to me it's the norm. The only way I'd be surprised is if I *didn't* hear all the noise when he was in public, and if people *didn't* push to be near him."

And all the superlatives that sportswriters routinely used to describe Jordan's basketball skills—was that greeted with a secret wink or a furtive rolling of eyes by fellow players? Did they privately think that Jordan was a pretty good player, but in truth not all that much better than they were?

"He is the best basketball player I have ever seen," Paxson would say. "There's just no comparison with anyone else. I've watched a lot of guys—after all, I grew up wanting to be a basketball player. I don't know every move he can make, and I still see new things, but he's so good that the only time he surprises me on the court is when he doesn't do something great. If he'll miss a dunk shot or something, that's what will amaze me—not when he'll make a great move. When I see him make a mistake, I'll be on the court and I'll tell myself: 'That did not happen.' "

So there wasn't any impulse to play down Jordan's skills? After all, Paxson and every other athlete in the NBA were in the same business that Jordan was. Wouldn't human nature dictate that there would be a certain inevitable tendency for Jordan's fellow players to tell themselves that he wasn't really as hot as all that?

"This is the sixth year that I've been playing beside him," Paxson would say, "and I really don't think it will be until later in my life that I understand just what that means. If I had to go out now and coach in high school or in college, I would probably have a tough time judging the kids. Because playing next to Michael I have seen everything you can do on a basketball court be done the best it has ever been done. I see that every night, and I think I would judge the kids too hard—I would forget that no one can achieve what Michael can do.

"I play basketball for a living, obviously, but I'm smart enough to know that I can't do the things that he can do. When my playing days are over, this is going to be something to look back on. I've played beside him for so long—probably longer than anyone in the world. To be able to say that I was his backcourt partner—that's going to be something, twenty or thirty years from now."

And the separateness? Paxson, of all people, might be expected to be able to get through that. Jordan and Paxson were, in Paxson's own word, partners. They brought the ball down the court together in arenas all over the country. No one else worked that closely with Jordan. Did that carry over after the games?

"I would never want to infringe on his privacy," Paxson would say. "Because I see what he has to go through every day, with everyone wanting part of his time. We don't socialize, and part of that is because I don't want to call him up. I've called him twice in these six years."

Two phone calls?

"Both times he wasn't home," Paxson would say, and then smile. "But he called me back both times."

That conversation with Paxson, though, was something he and I would have months later, when I had seen all of this night after night. Tonight, after the Charlotte game, I was still a newcomer to this world, and Jordan was giving the writers and broadcasters in the locker room what they needed, and the semicircle they formed around him might as well have been a barricade, keeping him in and keeping everyone else on the other side, including eleven professional basketball players, John Paxson among them, eleven men who by now were putting on their overcoats at the end of their day's work.

The pure athletic feats of Jordan were well documented. I was sitting at the press table one night with an old friend who had been covering sports all over the world for more than thirty years. He had seen everything. He said: "I have never seen anything like this."

There were so many things to observe on the court. Some of them were almost silly; every kid who ever played basketball at any level—and that must be almost every one of us—is familiar with the line drill, in which half the team lines up to shoot layups while the other half lines up to rebound. It is the simplest and most elementary of basketball warm-up drills. On the occasions when Jordan did this, you had to sit back and grin. What was he practicing? Michael Jordan doing the line drill . . . it was something to see.

Other things were strangely stirring. Jordan's presence in the arena surpassed the importance of the final score of an individual game; whether the Bulls won or lost on a given night had little to do with what the world thought of him. But to watch him at near range during a close contest was instructive. He might be clear to receive a pass; Scottie Pippen might have the ball. Jordan knew that if he were to wave, or even gesture, the opening would be gone. So he did it with his eyes and his mouth; he tried to will his teammate into seeing him by the strength of the passion in his eyes and the silent plea on his face. He still cared; after mastering his game as perhaps no one ever before, he still cared about doing his best.

With all that, though, sometimes something unforeseen would happen, something that made all the athletic heroics fade away. Jordan had become a lot of things; if I had noticed the Babe Ruth/Elvis Presley parallels early on, the parallels were becoming more evident with each new game night. People wanted to see in him a combination of athletic perfection and show-business magnetism and personal goodness—it was as if he was expected to be an amalgam of the Babe and Elvis and Santa Claus. That's why the Bulls no longer played to empty seats, either at home or on the road; even people who didn't follow basketball wanted to be able to say they had once seen him.

After a game, to walk out the players' entrance of the Stadium with Jordan was a remarkable experience. It was stunning to hear the people scream at the sight of him—just at the sight. On that cold night after the Charlotte game he emerged out of Gate 3½, and as soon as the waiting crowd saw him it was as if the Beatles had bounded onstage in some long-ago news clip.

Jordan approached his car, which the security guards had readied. There were so many people, and so much noise. And about twenty feet away was a little boy in a wheelchair.

This was not something that had been arranged by the team. The boy's father had brought him there, just so the boy could get a close glimpse of Jordan. The boy's affliction had caused his neck to form at an unnatural angle; his eyes could not look directly forward. He was quite small.

Jordan clearly was in a hurry. Strangers were screaming—and Jordan had his own son with him.

So he opened the door to his car, and somehow he saw the boy in the wheelchair. Jordan would have had every excuse not to notice; the boy did not have the ability even to motion to him. But he did notice. Something about Jordan—maybe it was the peripheral vision that served him so well on the court, or maybe it was something else, a kind of compassionate radar —made him notice.

He walked over to the boy and got down on the ground beside him and spoke. The boy was so excited that he began to come out of his chair. Jordan comforted him and talked softly. The boy's father had a camera; he tried to snap a picture. The camera didn't work. Jordan noticed. He didn't have to be asked; it was freezing outside, but he stayed beside the boy until the father was able to make the shot.

Only then did he return to his car. You can't set out to learn how to do this; no one can tell you how or advise you on it. It comes from something inside you, and you can't fake it. All Jordan did by seeing that child and stopping to spend time with him was make that little boy's life. If nothing else good ever happens for that little boy, he will always know that on one night Michael Jordan included him in his world.

The boy's head was still off at that angle, but his eyes were glistening. His dad was already replaying the moment with him. Jordan got into his car and drove into the night. I headed out the gates, toward home. Something very rare was happening here, and I knew once again that I must pay close attention.

5

"**Y**OU'RE GETTING HERE BEFORE I DO," Jordan said late one November afternoon.

"I know it," I said. It was still light out, and I was walking toward Gate 3½ at the same time he was. He had arrived alone, more than two and a half hours before tipoff.

"Do you get a ride out here early or something?" he said.

"No," I said. "I take a cab."

"Is it harder to get a cab from downtown closer to game time?" he said.

"Not that much harder," I said. "I just like it out here before everyone else shows up."

"Me, too," he said. "But I have to be here."

"So do I," I said.

"But for what?" he said.

"I'm not exactly sure yet," I said. "That's what I'm trying to figure out."

In my newspaper work there was an essential aspect of isolation, some of it endemic to the task any writer performs, some of it particular to the specific circumstance in which I found myself.

I had gotten professionally lucky very early. By the age of twenty-three I was writing a column that was distributed nationally; it was a piece of good fortune that seems almost impossible to me now, but at the time I did not consider it to be all that much out of the ordinary. I know that the people with whom I worked back then thought I was driven with ambition; clearly that was true, but I think the ambition was probably fueled much more by a sense of fear than by a sense of anything being due me. When I was starting off it was as if I was afraid that if I didn't try very hard every second, I'd be overlooked or ignored by the older editors and reporters around me; I was afraid that if I didn't take charge of my own career, then there would be no career.

I'm not quite sure where that impulse came from, but things developed quickly. I traveled throughout the country and the world, and I expanded the scope of what I tried: I wrote books and I worked in network television and I appeared regularly in magazines, maintaining the newspaper column all the while. Some people apparently thought I was okay at what I did, and others went out of their way to let me know that they didn't, and there were years when I was routinely working seven-day weeks and when I took no vacations or time off at all. It was everything I had dreamed of when I was a boy hoping to become a newspaperman, yet as the years went by it became clear that the dream had one big hole in it, and it was a hole no one but I could have been aware of.

One of the biggest lures of newspaper work, one of the things that drew me to it so strongly in the first place, was the casual warmth and camaraderie that I had always associated with city rooms. I'm not sure whether that was an image that came from old movies, or from my first experiences as a seventeen-year-old copyboy back at the Columbus *Citizen-Journal* in Ohio, but to me the joy of newspapering had a lot to do with a big old room where everyone was loose and laughing, where the sound of typewriter keys banging away was a day-long symphony and no one seemed as if they were grown-up or serious or worried about much at all. It was a promise of eternal adolescence, although I could not have put it in those words at the time, and it was everything I wanted.

When I got my first full-time reporting job at the Chicago *Sun-Times* that promise was much fulfilled. The big old room was there, the company was raucous, and it felt as if I had ended up in some unlikely study hall that somehow had been populated with itinerant adults of all ages. All of us seemed to be rushing around the city all the time, traveling with staff photographers and reporters from other papers and TV and radio stations to press conferences and federal trials and crime scenes, all of us in a continual mob, the observers and not the observed, doing work that mattered but having fun. No one was making a lot of money, and no one held out any realistic hopes for fame or glory. At the end of every day we all went to one bar or another and replayed the events of the last eight hours as if they had all the lasting, winking resonance of an old Ben Hecht–Charles MacArthur screenplay.

That's what I gave up, without even knowing I was doing it. Maybe everyone gave it up; there are no more typewriters, and newspaper city rooms no longer feel like day camps for a willfully grungy parallel universe of men and women who could not fit in anywhere else in the working world, and from what I understand most reporters don't even go to bars together after work. But my leaving the close society of the city room had nothing to do with changes in the business, or changes in the world; my leaving had to do with my getting lucky. At least it seemed like luck at the time.

For as the column started and then grew, and the other opportunities increased, I noticed that more and more I was working alone. I moved from the Chicago *Sun-Times* to the *Tribune;* instead of going each morning to a crowded city room, I set my own schedule and did my writing in a private office with a door to keep out noise. I was freed from having to cover the routine stories of the city; I was encouraged to travel widely, and I did, invariably by myself, checking into hotels at midnight and spending my days in places where I knew no one. My circle of professional companions shrunk; when my newspaper day was done and the column completed, maybe they were out together and maybe they weren't, but I was back at the keyboard after a quick meal, putting in a second full day trying to meet whatever book or magazine deadline was upon me.

It was the kind of success I had always longed for, and only occasionally did I stop to notice that the sole sound I was hearing as I worked was the lonely clacking of keys echoing off the walls of a room where I sat by myself.

When I was twelve my parents gave me season tickets to see Ohio State University basketball games.

It was a thoughtful present that turned out to be something more than that. Ohio State had three sophomores on its team that season—this was during an NCAA era during which freshmen were not permitted to play varsity sports, the theory being that they could better use their first year in college to study and get accustomed to university life—and the three sophomores, by the end of that season, would lead Ohio State to the national championship. They were Jerry Lucas, John

Havlicek, and Mel Nowell, and in the happiest recesses of my memory I can still see Nowell lobbing a soft pass over the rim to Lucas; can still see Lucas leaping high in the air to tip it in; can still see Havlicek positioning himself in case he needed to grab a rebound. They were three teenagers from three Ohio towns, and along with their older teammates in the starting lineup, Larry Siegfried and Joe Roberts, they became the finest college basketball team in America.

What I remember much more vividly than the details of all those winning games on winter Columbus nights, though, was the big, brilliantly lit, welcoming building that was St. John Arena on the Ohio State campus. When you're a twelve-year-old kid your world inevitably seems small and unimportant; your neighborhood and your school are as familiar as your bedroom at home, and whatever drama there might be in your life is drama with built-in limits. That's good, in many ways; that's the way things are supposed to be.

But on all those game nights during the winter of 1959–60, I was allowed to become a citizen of a larger, livelier, immensely more pleasing world, a world of exactly 13,497 people who gathered in St. John Arena to sit in the stands and watch that fabulously talented group of young basketball players work their way toward the NCAA title. Whatever ambition that might have revealed itself later in my life had to be forming then; I laugh when I think of the gall it must have taken to approach Jimmy Crum, and to volunteer my services.

Jimmy Crum was the television play-by-play broadcaster for WLWC, Channel 4 in Columbus; he was the voice of the Buckeyes, and he sat at a table halfway up the mezzanine section of the arena, calling the action. Sitting next to him was a harried fellow who wore a perpetual expression of consternation; this was Gary Taylor, Jimmy Crum's statistics man. It was Taylor's duty to keep track of all the numbers—points, shooting percentages, fouls, free throws, rebounds—for both teams, Ohio State and visitors. It was a lot of work for one man in a pre–pocket-calculator era, and Gary Taylor seldom had time to look up for even a second and just enjoy the games.

I knew this because my seat was within view of Jimmy Crum's and Gary Taylor's seats. One night early in the season —I cannot believe I did this—I purposefully started to keep track of the visiting team's statistics on a piece of paper. At halftime, when Gary Taylor was frantically scrambling to prepare his numbers sheet for Jimmy, I walked over and, without saying a word, handed my statistics to Gary. He peered up at me, peered down at his watch, knew that his time was running out, and tossed two sheets to Jimmy—his sheet bearing the Ohio State statistics, my sheet bearing the visiting team's. He must have been praying I was right.

Fortunately I was—at least I was close enough. When the official halftime numbers were delivered later on—too late for Jimmy to use on the air (this was why Gary Taylor was present, to give Jimmy unofficial numbers in time to intone into the microphone), they bore me out. And so my career as Jimmy Crum's other stats man was launched. After the game I introduced myself to Gary Taylor, who motioned me with his head in Jimmy's direction, and I approached Jimmy and told him that I already had season tickets, I wanted neither passes nor money from him, I just wanted to help. I just wanted to be a part of this.

Thus a third chair was pulled up to the table. We were the WLWC broadcast team—Jimmy Crum and, as he referred to us on the air each halftime and during each postgame report, "the men with the pencils, Gary Taylor and Bobby Greene." We were never seen on camera, so there was no way for anyone in Columbus outside my family and friends to know that the third man on Channel 4's esteemed broadcast crew was twelve years old.

I was in love with that job and I was in love with that team and I was in love with what it all represented. On game days I would sit in my seventh-grade classes, impatiently looking out the windows at the snow-covered streets, listening to my teachers and answering questions by rote and staring at the clock. I knew that, just hours away, something great was waiting for me. It was bigger than me and it was better than me and somehow I was allowed to be inside it, every night; there was never an empty seat, and Lucas and Havlicek and Nowell and their teammates were on their way to the championship, and against all odds I was watching them do it. That was the promise on every game day—school might have seemed small and chilly and constricted, but soon after the sun went down I would be walking into that bright, teeming place where the band played and the fans shouted their encouragement toward the court and something was forming, something I couldn't be sure of except that I knew it was good and I knew that I loved it. I was brand-new to this, I was brand-new to everything, I was a beginner, and I loved that place like I had loved no other place before.

But it had been years since I had been a beginner at anything.

So as I traveled to the Chicago Stadium every game night, even though I was venturing into a milieu that was unfamiliar to me, I was aware that I was a guy who had been around the newspaper world for more than twenty years, and that when you've done anything for twenty years you are no longer permitted to be a wide-eyed boy who goes home at the end of each day with your head buzzing in wonder and enthusiasm at what you've seen. That's something you do when you're still brand-new; that's something you do when everything is fresh to you.

I think I missed that feeling more than I knew. No matter what you do for a living, there comes a time when you cross over an invisible line, a line you're not even aware is there. Suddenly you're no longer the person who was once new on the job, the person who didn't know his way around and had to ask a lot of questions about the daily routine and was always a little nervous that he might do something wrong. Suddenly you're a different person—you're one of the people who is supposed to have the answers, who is supposed to have seen everything and be beyond surprise. When you cross over that line you leave the wide-eyed boy behind forever, and usually the approaching and crossing of the line is such a gradual and inevitable process that by the time it happens and you've crossed over to the other side the boy is gone and you didn't even have time to say goodbye.

At the Stadium, I didn't feel that I knew everything. I didn't feel that I had seen everything. During the daytime, as I did my reporting and wrote my columns, I was accustomed to and conversant with all the conventions and professional minutiae of the job. But as soon as I arrived at the Stadium in that early part of the season, I was once again the boy who had not yet crossed over. At least a part of me was: I looked around me every night and I didn't know what I would find.

There was a grimness to so many of the stories I covered during the daytime hours, and it took on almost a life of its own, urging me to distance myself from the stark and merciless subjects I was writing about. The last thing I needed in my life was that distance; distance was something I was all too familiar with because of the solitary nature of the way I too often did my work.

At the Stadium it wasn't like that. At the Stadium, I was starting to realize, the distance disappeared as soon as I walked through Gate 3½. It was happening every night: No matter how on my own and hemmed-in I might have felt during the day, by the time I got to the Stadium that feeling had lifted. At the press table I was surrounded by the beat reporters, and by the TV and radio people who also gathered there for every game. They may have been used to this, but I wasn't, at least I hadn't been for many years; they may have taken for granted the atmosphere of covering something together, all of them here to witness the same contest with the same sustaining cast of players, contest after contest over a long and tapestried season, but it was new to me, it was something I wasn't accustomed to, and I welcomed it without ever revealing out loud just how much I welcomed it.

"Was that Grant or Pippen?" Dave Hoekstra said to me one night. Hoekstra, who covered the Bulls for the Chicago *Sun-Times,* was often assigned the seat next to mine at the press table. I had known his name from his byline; he had arrived at his current assignment in an unconventional way: He had covered rock and roll and the nightlife scene before being given the Bulls beat, and now he was chronicling the games full-time.

Because of where we sat, directly underneath the one basket, at some moments it was difficult to be sure of exactly what had gone on during a jammed-up play at the other end. That was what had just occurred; the Bulls had the ball down at the other end of the court, and Horace Grant and Scottie Pippen had both gone high in the air after a rebound, and the ball had banked off the glass backboard and into the net.

So Hoekstra asked, "Was that Grant or Pippen?", and it was a simple question, the kind of question that might be asked a dozen times a night at the table. For me, though, it was more than that; for me it represented the essential change this place was having on my days and nights. It had been a long time since I had gathered with the same constant group of people on a regular basis, all of us experiencing the same world together. It was what I had always longed for in a city room, it was what I had liked so much when I had first broken into the business, and this was pretty close to that, this was close enough.

And it was close to something else, too. It was starting to seem very close to those winter nights in St. John Arena, when everything was new to me, and a basketball game could serve as a provider of comfort and the best kind of heat, and as long as I was a kid in that central Ohio fieldhouse the cold ordinary next morning was long hours away. Now, in the Chicago Stadium, I felt like a beginner again. Whatever I might have managed to accomplish in my professional life, whatever distance might have accrued because of it, here I was the new guy, here I was the person who was learning as he went along. I was a beginner in this building, and I was a little surprised at just how much I liked that.

"It was Grant," I said to Hoekstra over the screaming wash of cheers from the Stadium crowd.

"Are you sure?" he said, raising his voice to be heard.

"I'm sure," I said, and he wrote something down on his score sheet, and I remembered Gary Taylor handing my piece of paper to Jimmy Crum, remembered how fiercely I'd hoped that my numbers were right.

Those moments at the press table would come well into the evenings, though, when the games were in full progress. For me, the night at the Stadium would have begun much earlier, when the place was silent.

Right around four o'clock on game days I would be at work, and I would start to feel like I was running late for something. I would be in my office, and the afternoon would almost be over, and a sense that I was behind schedule would begin to kick in. Even though the game would not be scheduled to start until 7:30, I would usually head out for that hulking old arena on West Madison Street.

When I arrived the temperature inside would be uncomfortably cold. The lights would not be all the way up; parts of the interior of the Stadium would be in shadows.

The vendors would be there, and the ushers, and maybe a few uniformed Chicago police officers. They would all be getting ready for their night of work.

And in this setting—frigid and dimly lit and quiet—Jordan would emerge from the stairs that ran up from the basement and, usually by himself, he would walk onto the court, dribbling a ball to test the surface.

He would do this almost every night. That was why he arrived so early; for him to practice after the building had been opened would be impractical, because too many people would crowd around to call to him and ask for autographs and take pictures.

In these moments Jordan would not be wearing the famous Bulls uniform with the numeral 23 on the front and back. In these moments he was just a person in a pair of gym shorts and a T-shirt. And he would start shooting. One. Two. Three. Four. Five. Six. Seven. Eight.

He would switch to a different position on the court. There would be no fooling around. He was up here in the empty arena for a reason. He was aware of something: All of the endorsements, all of the television commercials, all of the magazine covers, all of the interviews . . . all of that was absent in these moments, and paradoxically it was these moments that made all of that possible. Sometimes—considering the apparent ease with which Jordan dominated opponents—it was tempting to temporarily lose sight of just how skilled those opponents were. That Jordan could so often leave those superlative professional athletes flat-footed and embarrassed as he glided past them was merely testament to just how singular he was.

And he knew that everything that had come to him in his life stemmed from this, from moments like these moments in the locked arena. Once they were all kids learning how to loft a basketball into the air. Nine. Ten. Eleven. Twelve. Thirteen. Jordan, by himself in the empty Stadium, would fire the ball. The best basketball player in the world. In all likelihood the best basketball player who ever lived. Fourteen. Fifteen. Sixteen. Seventeen. The ball would keep dropping through the net.

Much has been made of the story that, as a sophomore in high school, Jordan was cut from his school's basketball team. It's part of the legend. But think about it for a minute. It wasn't a legend for him then. He was a boy who was told that he wasn't good enough. Eighteen. Nineteen. Twenty. Twenty-one.

Often Jordan would ask one of the Bulls' ball boys to help him in these moments. Jordan would stand near the out-of-bounds line, with his back toward the basket. The ball boy, cued by a nod from Jordan, would fire him the pass. Jordan, catching the pass, would wheel and jump and face the basket and shoot. The ball would come down. Jordan would already be facing the ball boy again. Another nod. Another throw.

Jordan, with not a sound from the vacant stands, would go into the air. I found myself hoping that the ball boys realized how important their memories of these late afternoons would be to them some day.

When it was time for the building to open up, Jordan would head back downstairs to the locker room. The next time he would emerge, he would be in the familiar clean white Bulls uniform, and the music would be playing, and the arena would be packed with a standing-room-only crowd, and the voices would be screaming in tribute from the moment of the first communal glimpse of him.

For me, no matter how exciting the game might turn out to be on a given night, the trip to the Stadium would already have been well worth it. By the moment of the tipoff, I would already have seen things to make me glad I was there. Probably it was because of this:

In the course of my work I saw so much of the world that was low-spirited and mean and shoddy and common. I saw so much that was wretched. But in these hours in the deserted Stadium, watching Jordan in solitude honing his craft, I saw something that was almost beyond excellence. It was like nothing I had ever seen in my life, and it was changing the way I looked at the world, and each game day before the sun went down I headed off to witness it anew.

6

"**I** WENT TO MY ROOM and I closed the door and I cried," Jordan said. "For a while I couldn't stop. Even though there was no one else home at the time, I kept the door shut. It was important to me that no one hear me or see me."

We were sitting alone together in the Stadium one late-November night in those hours before the doors to the outside world opened up. I had been thinking a lot about the story of him being cut. Now his likeness and his electronic image were everywhere; sometimes it seemed as if he was as much logo as he was human. I kept wondering how it must have affected him at the time it happened.

We talked about it that night, and it turned out to be the first of many long conversations. Soon I would come to value these conversations every bit as much as I valued the games; the conversations, I know now, will last in my memory well beyond the final scores of the basketball contests. This night was the first, though, and initially I was surprised that Jordan remembered every detail of something that had happened to him long ago. But then I understood: Of course he remembered. How could he not? Back then he didn't know that someday he was going to be Michael Jordan. Back then, all he wanted was the chance to play with the others.

"For about two weeks, every boy who had tried out for the basketball team knew what day the cut list was going to go up," he said. "We knew that it was going to be posted in the gym. In the morning.

"So that morning we all went in there, and the list was up. I had a friend—his name was Leroy Smith—and we went in to look at the list together.

"We stood there and looked for our names. If your name

was on the list, you were still on the team. If your name wasn't on the list, you were cut. Leroy's name was on the list. He made it. Mine wasn't on the list."

As we talked, other members of the Bulls walked past us, arriving at the Stadium. Pippen came by, and then Grant, and then Paxson and Cartwright. Jordan's voice was soft, and he nodded hello to each of them and continued with his recollections. The juxtaposition of his words and this setting—an NBA arena on game night—was something you could never invent.

"I looked and looked for my name," he said. "It was almost as if I thought that if I didn't stop looking, it would be there."

I asked him if the list had been in descending order of talent. Were the best players at the top of the list, with the marginal players at the bottom?

"No," he said, as if envisioning the list anew. "It was alphabetical. I looked at the H's, and the I's, and the J's, and the K's, and I wasn't there, and I went back up and started over again. But I wasn't there.

"I went through the day numb. I sat through my classes. I had to wait until after school to go home. That's when I hurried to my house and I closed the door of my room and I cried so hard. It was all I wanted—to play on that team.

"My mother was at work, so I waited until she got home, and then I told her. She knew before I said anything that something was wrong, and I told her that I had been cut from the team. When you tell your mom something like that the tears start again, and the two of you have an aftercry together."

I asked him if he had stayed away from the varsity team that whole year. He said no; as the regular season was wrapping up, he said, he went back, but not to request a tryout.

"At the end of the season, I worked up the nerve to ask the coach if I could ride along on the bus with the team to the district tournament," he said. "I just wanted to watch the others.

"The coach told me no. But I asked again, and he said I could come. But when we got to the tournament gym, he said he didn't know if I could go in. He told me that the only way I could go in was to carry the players' uniforms.

"So that's what I did. I walked into the building carrying the uniforms for the players who had made the team. What made me feel the worst about that was that my parents had come to watch the tournament, and when they saw me walking in carrying the uniforms, they thought I was being given a chance to play.

"That's what hurt me. They thought I was being given a chance. But I was just carrying the clothes for the others."

There can't be many professional athletes in any sport who were cut from their high school teams. The men who make it to the pros have always been the best on every playground, the best in every class, the best in every school. The men who make it to the pros don't go through things like that.

"It's okay, though," Jordan said. "It's probably good that it happened."

"Good?" I said.

"I think so," he said. Soon it would be game time in the Stadium, to that constant soundtrack of shattering, overwhelming, adoring noise.

"It was good because it made me know what disappointment felt like. And I knew that I didn't want to have that feeling ever again."

The Bulls were playing well but not spectacularly—they were 7–6 after the first 13 games of that '90–'91 season—and the denizens of press row were beginning to tease me not only about my constant attendance, but about my rapidly evolving attitude.

"I thought you were just out here because of the Michael Jordan Show," said Paul Sullivan, a young sportswriter from the *Tribune*.

"Yeah, I am," I said. When people asked me, I said that it really didn't matter to me who won the games; Jordan was going to do enough spectacular things on any given night that the final score was secondary.

"Well, listen to yourself sometime," Sullivan said.

"What do you mean?" I said.

"You just said 'Shot clock, B.J.,' " Sullivan said.

"No, I didn't," I said.

"You did," Sullivan said.

I knew he was probably right. I was surprising myself—and amusing myself a little bit—by how swiftly I was becoming a person who cared about how this team did. B. J. Armstrong would have the ball with the twenty-four-second clock winding down, and I would find myself thinking that he'd better take a shot before the horn sounded. I didn't know I was saying it aloud, though.

" 'Shot clock, B.J.'?" I said to Sullivan.

"You just said it," he said. "On that last possession."

And that wasn't even the half of it. I would turn to Dave Hoekstra after John Paxson had made a long jump-shot in the opening minute of play and say, "You ever notice that Pax always makes the first shot he tries?"

"Pax." I heard my voice referring to Paxson as "Pax."

Will Perdue, a reserve center for the Bulls, would grab a crucial rebound and I would turn to my neighbor and say something about Perdue being an effective role player. I had no idea what a role player was. It was just a term I had always read on the sports pages. When the Phoenix Suns came to town and their star guard, Kevin Johnson, drove to the basket in front of us and attempted to bank in a shot, I heard myself saying: "Well, where have we seen *that* before?"

I said it with a really stupid chuckle in my voice. It was the kind of stupid chuckle that know-it-all sports fans always used when they were bringing up some obscure bit of lore that no one with any sense would care about. What I was referring to was a similar shot that Johnson had made at the buzzer when the Bulls had played them on the road a couple of weeks before. The road game was one I had watched on television (I was watching all Bulls road games on TV, it seemed), and now the Suns were in the Stadium, and from somewhere deep in my newly addled brain that shot was recalled. Such a lame comment: "Well, where have we seen *that* before?" I never used to chuckle.

But the Stadium was a place for chuckles, it was a place for smiles and full-fledged laughter, and it was a place where for a few hours you could care about things like that. Walking into the Stadium was like exhaling; for me, at least, walking into the Stadium was like letting every muscle and nerve relax.

"So are you planning on missing any games at all this year?" Paul Sullivan said to me.

But I wasn't looking at him; I was looking out onto the court, where the clock said that there were only twenty seconds left in the quarter.

"Are you?" Sullivan said.

"Play for one shot," I said in the general direction of Scottie Pippen.

* * *

And the laughter was not limited to those of us who weren't on the court.

During warm-ups before a game against the Washington Bullets, Cliff Levingston, a forward who had come to the Bulls in a trade with the Atlanta Hawks, was standing under the basket. Jordan was dribbling the ball behind the foul line, not doing much more than killing time, and Levingston called to him: "Come on!"

Jordan looked around to see who had said it. "Come on!" Levingston repeated. "Try me!"

Levingston had a big grin on his face, as well he should have; one of the things that a basketball player with standard gifts—one of the things that *any* basketball player—should be advised never to do is to challenge Michael Jordan. Levingston knew it, and Jordan knew he knew it, and Levingston called "Come *on!*" one more time, this time with more urgency, and Jordan drove toward him, Levingston blocking the path to the basket, and Jordan leapt high in the air to try to dunk over him while Levingston jumped as high as he could to push him away. It was for fun and it was for real and they went at each other over and over, these moments meaning nothing and meaning everything, two men laughing out loud and trying hard all the while in this game before the game.

One night just before the teams were introduced an usher approached me and said, "There's a man in the stands who wants to talk with you."

I looked over in the direction the usher had come from. A trim, white-haired man in his fifties was standing in the aisle waving at us. He looked like a vibrant young grandfather in one of those *Modern Maturity* magazine recruitment ads. I figured that maybe he had a column idea for me or something.

So I walked over to see what he had on his mind, and he said, "We grew up in the same town, and I wanted to introduce myself." I shook his hand and I asked his name, and he said, "I'm Sandy Shkolnik."

My amazement was instantaneous; it didn't even take a full second to register. "I used to watch you play," I said.

"You watched me play?" he said, clearly puzzled.

"If your name's Sandy Shkolnik and you went to Bexley

High School, I watched you play," I said. "Correct me if I'm wrong, but you were All-CBL your senior year, weren't you?"

"I believe I was," he said. "But that was a long time ago."

Only one person can be Michael Jordan, but a lot of boys, early in their lives, get at least a hint of what it must be like. Even before my nights in St. John Arena, I had my basketball heroes, and they were the Bexley High School Lions. All of us elementary-school children would buy tickets to the Bexley games (the high school was right next door to Cassingham Elementary), and on Friday nights we would go to see the Lions play. The co-captains were two dark-haired seniors: Mike Benis and Sandy Shkolnik. The cheerleaders would form a circle in the gym before the start of each game, and they'd hold up a big hoop covered with white paper bearing the painted face of a Lion, and the team, to the strains of "Onward Bexley," would come tearing through the paper hoop, led by Benis and Shkolnik.

As we talked in the Stadium the crowd noise rose as Jordan, warming up for the game, favored the fans with a reverse dunk. Horace Grant followed him with more of the same, causing the crowd to erupt.

"Do you hear much from Mike Benis?" I said.

"Not really," Sandy Shkolnik said. "Like I say, it's been a long time."

One night during their senior year—I'm sure Mike Benis doesn't have any memory of this—he and his girlfriend drove me to the Bexley game. Mike Benis' parents were friends of my parents, and they all knew what a fan of the high school team I was. So on Mike's way to the game, he and his girlfriend swung by our house on Bryden Road and gave me a lift. It was about as prestigious an entrance as a ten-year-old could make: arriving at a Bexley game in Mike Benis' car, and walking into the gym with him and his girlfriend.

Mike Benis was Michael Jordan for a time, and so was Sandy Shkolnik, and so are thousands upon thousands of kids all over America, in every city and every town, every year. That's the beauty of the dream—so many thousands, when they are young, can know the feeling at least briefly before it goes away, and I sensed this pleasant and personable white-haired man standing in the Stadium aisle would think I was joking if I were to say to him that I planned on telling Jordan that he—Sandy Shkolnik—was actually in attendance tonight.

I did plan on telling Jordan that, because I knew he'd fully understand. But what I said to Sandy Shkolnik right now was, "You definitely made All-CBL that year. I remember."

And he had. He and Mike Benis, too. Both of them first-string selections on the All–Central Buckeye League basketball team in the Midwestern winter of 1957.

During a time-out in a game against the Indiana Pacers a fan was selected to participate in a shooting competition. This was a regular part of game-night activity; no time-out was permitted to go unfilled. The action in the NBA contest might come to a stop, but in an effort to make an evening at the Stadium a "total entertainment package" for ticket-holders, fast-tempo promotions were held on the court every time the teams went to the benches.

So the fan was led onto the hardwood, and the music was jacked up to earsplitting level, and the public address announcer told the eighteen thousand-plus that if the man did well enough, he could win one thousand dollars—or even a new car.

The man started shooting. The crowd yelled its encouragement as his first two shots went in the basket. He ran toward the net to grab the ball as it dropped to the floor, and he turned around to position himself for his next shot, and I saw him freeze.

Just like that. Even with all these people observing him, even with the money and the prizes at stake, he had been remarkably cool. But now he seemed temporarily paralyzed, and as I followed the path of his eyes I saw why.

Standing watching the man get set to shoot was Jordan. Whatever Phil Jackson might be telling his players as they gathered around him on the bench, Jordan was watching the guy in the shooting contest. A thousand dollars was a lot of money for the man to be thinking about; a car was more valuable still. This, though, was real pressure.

The shooter saw Jordan looking at him. He turned and aimed at the basket. Good again. The crowd bellowed, and he saw he was the winner of a thousand dollars. His next shot, the shot for the new car, fell short. There was a prolonged groaning from the stands. A member of the Bulls promotion staff escorted the shooter off the court. His friends were congratulating him on his good showing. He didn't appear to be listening.

Instead, even as they talked to him, he turned around to

where he had just been. The game had started again. Ten professionals were now running along the same surface where, moments before, the shooter had starred as the main, if momentary, attraction. The shooter stared at Jordan, but by now the clock was ticking and the shooter had passed forever in and out of Jordan's consciousness. It was safe to assume that many years would go by before the shooter would forget the time Michael Jordan watched him play basketball. But now, as the shooter took one more long look before being led back to his seat, Jordan was facing the other way, waiting for a pass from Horace Grant.

I was still new enough at the Stadium that all of this was first-time stuff for me; it was easy to forget that whatever was going on here had been under way for a long time before I ever started showing up.

But for the people who had been game-night regulars for many years, this was all a chapter in a continuing story. In the basement of the building was an area that was set aside for a buffet dinner before each contest; coaches, broadcasters, sportswriters, security personnel, and other arena workers gathered there just after sundown to grab a quick meal before the tipoff. This was something I hadn't known about; I guess I always assumed that the people who worked in stadiums and ballparks simply bought hot dogs from the vendors.

To the veterans of Stadium life, though, the nightly basement buffet was part of the scenery, no more noteworthy than the updated scoresheets that were handed to them at the press table after each quarter, or the colored stickers they wore on their shirts or jackets allowing them access to the locker rooms and courtside areas. There were all kinds of back rooms and cubbyholes in this interior, hidden part of game night; when one of the official scorers would look up from his dinner plate and say "I think the snapper is new this year," it was not intended as humor or offhanded irony. He meant just what he said. He did not recall eating red snapper in the basement last year.

So while I at first thought it odd to be walking up the narrow stairs from the basement twenty minutes before game time and to find myself sharing the steps with Kurt Rambis of the Phoenix Suns, dressed in his warm-up clothes, to everyone else it was just a function of Stadium logistics. The basement buffet was a few feet away from the visitors' locker room.

Dinner was served every night around the time the opposing team came up to warm up, causing a traffic jam on the steps. When the Suns, or whatever team was in town to play the Bulls, reached the top of the steps and were spotted by the fans, the arena would burst into a cascade of boos. On the steps, Rambis—a six-foot-ten-inch man in purple satin—was polite and even courtly as he offered to wait. "After you." "No, after you." Maybe he just wanted to delay those boos a few more seconds.

And while often the details of the interior game night were trivial—an usher listening to the overamplified rock music that punctuated the action of each contest and saying to his partner, "The songs they're playing aren't as good this year"; a referee glancing at Indiana coach Dick Versace and re-marking, "New suit"—sometimes they were enough to invite contemplation.

The previous season, the Bulls had employed a backup for-ward by the name of Ed Nealy. Nealy, while not a star, had gained great favor among fans during the playoffs, when he had come off the bench game after game to furnish muscle and brute force. Anyone who had watched the playoff games at home on television—and I had been one of those viewers—knew of this because the announcers always used variations of the same words to describe Nealy. Their descriptions went something like this: "He's pure Chicago—he comes to work with a hard hat and a lunch bucket. There's nothing fancy about Nealy, but these Chicago fans love him because he puts in a day's work for a day's pay. He's a blue-collar ballplayer."

It was the kind of thumbnail sketch guaranteed to endear Nealy to the hometown crowds, and they did, indeed, delight in him. After the Bulls were eliminated from the playoffs that previous spring and the season ended, Nealy, an unrestricted free agent, cut himself a better deal with Phoenix and moved to Arizona. So this game, when the Suns came to town to play the Bulls, was the first time Nealy was back in the Stadium. The fish dish in the basement was different, the music had changed, and Nealy, in the same building where he had been held in such fond regard, was wearing a different uniform.

What surprised me was not the crowd's reaction to Nealy, but the lack of it. The fans did not welcome him back as an old friend, or jeer at him as a turncoat who had spurned them. If they had loved him back in June, now, in early December, most of them didn't even seem to realize he was here.

I was a few yards away from where he sat on the Phoenix bench. At one point his coach, Cotton Fitzsimmons, motioned to him and told him to go into the game. Nealy took his place on the painted line perpendicular to the basket in preparation for a Horace Grant free throw. B. J. Armstrong was in the vicinity; when their eyes met there wasn't even a flash of anything, and they did not speak. Less than a year ago, in this same arena, they were Bulls teammates basking in the same frenzied applause.

Tonight Nealy might as well have been a stranger passing through, and after he'd played his assigned minutes Fitzsimmons sat him down on the Phoenix bench again, on the opposite end of the court from the bench where he'd been a working-class hero. As he mopped his face, a thirty-year-old with first a bus ride, then a plane ride to the next city ahead of him after the game was over, I wondered if he had presumed residual loyalty or even the pretense of a kind welcome when he had anticipated the evening.

Later I asked B. J. Armstrong about that moment on the court when they had not said a word to each other.

"He was a nice guy last year," Armstrong said. "I enjoyed knowing him when he was here. But you just have to treat it as work."

Was there an etiquette to all this—was there an unwritten rule that you don't let on if you used to like a player who's no longer your teammate?

"On the court, he has to be an enemy, and I don't mean that as anything personal," Armstrong said. "When I'm playing the game, I'm playing the game. It's not the time to think about friendship or talk about old times. I don't have any friends when I'm playing."

Armstrong was such a pleasant, thoughtful young man. The words seemed vaguely foreign, like something that had been ingrained in him as a professional athlete rather than like a reflection of any true coldness. "Is this just how you feel about it?" I said. "Or would welcoming back someone like Nealy be violating some sort of players' code?"

"It's just not done," he said. "It's not a very cool thing to do."

"If you walked up to a guy you used to play with, and you shook his hand during a game, would that make you look bad to your fellow players?" I said.

"It's not the thing to do," he said.

* * *

The tension of playing in a professional basketball game seemed as if it would provide just about all the stress a man might ever need. When you added the knowledge that network television cameras sometimes broadcast the games live to as many as forty million people at home, the thought occurred that ruminating about the cameras might have the potential to just about immobilize a player.

"When you're at the free-throw line, does that ever cross your mind?" I asked Jordan one evening. We had started having these conversations on just about a nightly basis.

"The cameras?" he said.

"Not so much the cameras as the people who are out there watching because of them," I said. "When you're getting ready to shoot a free throw, do you think about those millions of people at all?"

"I can't," he said. "I couldn't."

"You just block it out?" I said.

"I concentrate on knocking in the shot," he said. "If I thought of the number of people who were watching me as I got ready to shoot, I'd miss it. I'm serious—I would be unable to make it. If I thought about what those cameras represented—who's watching in all the cities, how many people are sitting looking at a TV screen and paying attention to a shot I haven't even tried yet—if I thought about that, I couldn't do it."

"So how do you ignore it?" I said.

"I just go through my ritual," he said. "I walk up to the line. I spin the ball in my hands. I dribble until I feel comfortable. That will usually be from three to five bounces. Then I spin the ball again, and then I shoot after that second spin. When I'm doing that, I don't see anyone. I turn around to look for a signal from Phil Jackson to tell me what we're doing on defense after the shot—so I do see someone. I see Phil."

"But the TV cameras are just machines as far as you're concerned?" I said. "While you're getting ready to shoot, the camera lenses don't represent tens of millions of people to you?"

"They didn't until about sixty seconds ago," he said, laughing. "Thank you very much. Now I'll probably never make another free throw."

* * *

No matter how many times I saw it, the swift transformation of the Stadium after a game was something I never quite got used to. The prying up of the basketball court, the erection of the ice hockey walls, was almost like a taunt, a reproachful reminder of just how ephemeral all of this was. The itinerant basketball players were wealthy heroes now, their names were known to people all over the world, but in ten years they would be fuzzy and uncertain memories, if that. They would be replaced by newly minted heroes, who in turn would be replaced when their few years of brilliance were over, and meanwhile the crews would lift up the floor to reveal the ice, wood to water to wood to water, again and again and again.

There would be only one certain exception, and everyone knew it. Of all the people who ever passed in and out of this building, forevermore it would be associated with one. There was nothing architecturally remarkable or truly lovable about the Stadium; as an edifice it was dank and forbidding and without grace or beauty. The only thing it had to offer were the lingering echoes of the people who performed within its aged walls.

And after it had emptied for the night, after the fans had departed, the power of Jordan's presence became even more evident. During the hours of the game, the noise and light gave the illusion that this was eternally a place of excitement and joy. Afterward, though, in the basement hallways, in the cracked, damp corners, the building looked and felt like what it was: an ungainly concrete barn in a dying and desolate part of an old city.

Because of Jordan's presence, all the others came. He was why it was constantly full, he was why it was brimming with life and energy. In the year before Jordan arrived in town, there had not been a single sellout. Some nights there had been scarcely three thousand souls rattling around the cavernous structure.

What that must have felt like was easy to sense after the games were over and the fans had left for home. To walk around the Stadium then, as the floor came up, was to know why in the pre-Jordan years few had wanted to venture out this way on a frigid basketball night. It was not a place that readily invited company.

Jordan was always one of the last of the Bulls to depart. On nights when the team and staff flew out to another city, he would emerge from the basement in a long overcoat, on his way, with his teammates, to a private air terminal where a chartered jet waited.

That part of the NBA regimen was one of the most difficult to identify with. The sight of basketball players sprinting up and down a court incessantly was so commonplace that you almost had to stop and remind yourself about the reality of the inherent physical exhaustion. The players didn't seem like us; they didn't seem like they were supposed to grow weary. But to watch them do it, and then to try to imagine what it must feel like in your lungs and in your legs and in your throat, gave pause. And then, immediately after the game was over, for them to fly after midnight to a different city, where hotel keys would be handed out at 2:00 A.M., and practice would be held at 11:00 A.M., and a game would begin at 7:30, after which another flight . . .

Jordan would come up the stairs with his gym bag in one hand. He would say goodnight to the workers yanking at the floor.

"I just sleep most of the time," he told me. "It truly doesn't bother me."

He said he was so accustomed to the late-night flights after the games that they no longer seemed unusual to him. After all that exertion, after all that pressure and concentration, to leave the Stadium and head directly off for another arena in another town was something he didn't question.

"Once I'm in the hotel room in the next town, it takes me maybe thirty minutes to fall asleep," he said. "I'll watch a movie on the hotel room TV, and I'll be tired within half an hour, and then I'll be asleep. Sometimes when I wake up the next morning the TV set is still on."

He would walk past the work crews and out of the building, and every time he did it the place suddenly felt like it had to offer an excuse just for being there.

7

IF THE PREDOMINANT MOOD of the Stadium on game nights was one of boisterous, full-throated exuberance, I was spending many of my days in a building as far removed from that happiness as any place I could ever imagine.

The Cook County Juvenile Court was a low-slung structure on South Hamilton Avenue in Chicago, less than ten minutes away from the Stadium. I was covering the story of a child who through governmental and judicial indifference and incompetence had been uprooted from the love-filled foster home where she had spent the first five years of her life and handed over to a woman who, addicted to heroin and cocaine and working as a prostitute, had given birth to her and abandoned her. At the age of five the little girl was forced, sobbing and pleading not to go, to leave the foster parents she considered to be her true mother and father, and to go live with the birth mother and her boyfriend, in a house where the child had never before slept a night.

The judicial reasoning behind this decision was that, by virtue of having given birth to the child, the birth mother had an absolute right to her. It didn't matter that the birth mother had walked away from the newborn five years before; it didn't matter that for those five years the child had grown up in a fine and caring home, content and full of good feelings, making friends in her neighborhood and going to church and taking dancing lessons and thriving in school. It didn't matter that the child was terrified of the idea of leaving her home, and that she was begging to stay. It didn't even matter that, astonishingly, the judge who sent her away from the home she cherished had never laid eyes on her, had never spoken to her, and would not have known her had she been permitted to walk into his courtroom. In his eyes none of that was relevant; in his eyes, because a woman had once had intercourse and conceived, she was the owner of this child. Years later she could decide that maybe she had been wrong in abandoning the baby. Even though the baby had grown to be a girl with a life of her own, in the opinion of the judge all the woman had to do was complete a drug rehabilitation program and demonstrate that she wanted the child now, and the child would be presented to her. The prize at the end of drug rehab was not a ribbon or a certificate of completion—the prize was a five-year-old human being.

The story haunted my nights, and I kept going back to that Juvenile Court building because going there and reporting on what was happening seemed to be the only way to keep governmental attention on the case. I went to every hearing and every progress report and every continuance, and I was filled with fury and shame each time I saw what the children of the county had to contend with as they entered what was supposed to be a hall of justice.

The building was filthy. Sinks and water fountains overflowed; there was not enough room for families to wait to go into the courtrooms, so in the hallways parents and children were forced to sit on the floors. No one appeared to be in charge; children waited for hours and no one called their cases. Angry sheriff's deputies screamed obscenities in front of frightened toddlers. Graffiti marred the walls. Robberies took place on the premises. And thousands upon thousands of the children whose lives depended on what went on in this building were not delinquents charged with crimes, but neglected, abused, or abandoned boys and girls whose only transgressions were having been born to people who did not love them.

I would spend a full day in the courthouse, and I would go back to the newspaper to write up what I had seen, and then, as darkness fell, I would head west again, toward the Stadium. If, at first, I had not been quite certain of why it was so important for me to go there, now I was beginning to understand. I thought of the famous line of verse by Edgar Allen Poe. The one about searching for surcease of sorrow.

On days when the court sessions had been especially tormenting, and when I had been writing my column right up until deadline, I would still be filled with the ache of the courthouse as I arrived at the Stadium. If I was using the Stadium as some sort of medicine for what I was feeling, as some sort of pain reliever it had been my good luck to discover, there were often ten- or twenty-minute spans at the beginning of the evening, after I had arrived, when even the bright lights and the music and the noise weren't enough to do the trick.

One freezing December night the New York Knicks were in town, and I got to the Stadium right before the team introductions and the national anthem. There was yet another child in a wheelchair off to the right of where I sat at the press table. The presence of the disabled boys and girls, I was to learn, was a constant; for whatever reason, they seemed to have faith that they could take some sort of fulfillment and encouragement away from watching these marvelous, healthy athletes who could effortlessly do things that would forever be beyond their own reach.

The boy who was off to my right was with his dad. The father had bought a cup of ice cream, and he was patiently spooning it into his child's mouth. The child took a long time to swallow. The father waited between bites, determined to make this a memorable night.

The public address announcer asked the crowd to rise for the national anthem. The father stood up; the child, of course, could not. The singer at center court began the song.

The Knicks were standing directly in front of me. I looked at them, and then I looked over at the boy. He was trying so hard. His head was bent, and he was singing every word, and he was doing his very best to keep up with the rest of the people in attendance. I saw his lips moving: "What so proudly we hailed . . ."

This was so important for him. This was such a big night. I turned around toward the Knicks, and there was Patrick Ewing, standing impassively, not singing, not moving his mouth, appearing bored. I looked at the boy: ". . . gave proof through the night . . ." I looked back at Ewing, who was stifling a yawn. I had read in the newspaper that the Knicks had offered him a contract extension worth more than four million dollars a year; that was less than Ewing wanted, and he was quoted as saying that he was "insulted" by the offer.

This was one of those nights when I couldn't shake the day. It probably wasn't Ewing's fault; it was probably just my residual rage from the Juvenile Court. But on this night it was too much. I watched that boy, so determined as he tried to sing the song properly, and I looked at Ewing again, and I just wanted to grab him. I just wanted to say: Look, I know you do this eighty-two nights a season, and I know you're on the road, and I know you're tired. But try, damn it. Make the effort. Go through the motions. A night like this means something to some people. Would it kill you to sing the song? Would it kill you to at least pretend to care?

But it wasn't Ewing's fault. It came from somewhere else, and soon enough the horn sounded to begin the game and the teams were on the floor and running.

The athleticism of the men on the court was so consistently eye-popping that, paradoxically, the sight of it could become deadening. To see on a nightly basis people this good at what they did was to risk taking it for granted. And Jordan, of course, was the best of all.

He would twirl under the basket, grab a rebound, take the ball downcourt by himself, fire a no-look pass to Pippen, seem to stop, then suddenly appear leaping toward the rim where Pippen would hit him with a lob; Jordan would catch it, turn in mid-air, hold the ball behind his head, and drop it into the basket while seeming to look in the opposite direction, up toward the second balcony. And that would just be one eight-second sequence; he'd set up and then complete little dramas like that all night.

While, all around the Stadium, a certain number of people were seeing their first National Basketball Association game in person. Those were the people I envied each night—the people who would go home absolutely buzzing at what they'd just witnessed. I asked Jordan what he had thought on the day he'd seen his first NBA game.

"The first NBA game I ever saw was one I played in," he said.

"What?" I said, thinking he was kidding.

"I had never seen a professional basketball game before I became a professional basketball player," he said. "In North Carolina there was no NBA team, so I didn't have a chance to see a game when I was growing up."

He said he'd seen some on television, of course. But that unique feel and look and sound of an arena on game night—that amazing tableau of athletes routinely doing the seemingly impossible—was a treat he'd never had. Even during high school and college.

"Do you think that deprived you of any kind of head start?" I said. "Not having seen what you were reaching for?"

"Actually, it probably worked in my favor," he said. "I really didn't know very much about professional basketball. I kept my dreams so much in reach, rather than dreaming about something so far ahead. In a way, I think it was a blessing that I never saw an NBA game."

"You see kids on the playgrounds now, it seems that's all they're thinking about," I said. "You hear kids who are seven or eight years old, and they're seriously thinking about playing in the NBA some day."

"That's what I mean," he said. "I never walked into an NBA arena as a fan, or as a child who hoped to be there some day as a player. I kept my dreams closer to me, and more realistic. One step at a time. So when I finally did see an NBA game, I was seeing it from on the court."

"It seems like a fairly rare thing," I said.

"I can't imagine a better way to do it," he said. "Can you?"

Sometimes there would be singers at the Stadium; sometimes there would be jugglers; sometimes there would be dance teams. They would perform at halftimes and during time-outs, all of them a part of the Bulls' management's attempt to make a night at the arena a nonstop amusement.

In truth, these additional attractions weren't necessary, at least not now. All the acts and promotional gimmicks kept things moving, but with Jordan in the building nothing else was required. The place would be filled to standing room if the sole activity going on was him practicing free throws under a forty-watt bulb.

Everyone involved in the Bulls' front office knew, though, that some day Jordan would be gone. Some day the sellouts would not be a given, and the team would have to solicit customers once again. So in preparation for the inevitable post-Jordan era, the sideshows were built in as a regular part of game nights, getting the fans accustomed to the idea that no matter if the team won or lost, there was excitement and thrills on West Madison Street.

One of the attractions was something called the Bulls Brothers. The act consists of two men dressed as Jake and Elwood, the old John Belushi–Dan Aykroyd Blues Brothers characters. This was one of the most popular sideshow features at the Stadium—the Bulls Brothers came back again and again, the fans loved them—and I found their success at the games both fascinating and, in one way, vaguely disturbing.

I had known Belushi a little bit when we were both young and just getting started in Chicago. He was a novice performer at the Second City nightclub, I was a novice newspaper columnist, and although we were not close friends, we'd stop and talk whenever we ran into each other. The rapidness of his rise to the pinnacle of national celebrity seemed to disorient and, somehow, even anger him; there were times when he gave the impression that he believed the tens of millions of people who knew him only from "Saturday Night Live" were being fooled, that they were buying into a product that was far removed from who he really was.

I always thought that the Blues Brothers act was a reaction to that by him and Aykroyd. Dressed in those baggy black suits, porkpie fedoras, and sunglasses, it was as if they were making fun of everything they had become. The "Saturday Night Live" characters that had made them famous—the bees, the Samurai variations, all of them—were one level of fiction. The Blues Brothers were another layer removed. Here was John Belushi, from Wheaton, Illinois, and the world knew him as a jolly costumed bee on national television, and on top of that he added the Blues Brothers persona, and it didn't matter how many layers he added on, at the time the public would take whatever he offered them. "Saturday Night Live" was the number one television program among young Americans, *The Blues Brothers* was the number one record album, the Blues Brothers movie was a box-office hit, and even as everyone was laughing, there was a nagging feeling that maybe they didn't get the joke.

When Belushi died in March of 1982, people began to understand for the first time that essential parts of him were desperately troubled. Now almost a decade had passed, and here at the Stadium the Bulls Brothers pranced out at halftime or during breaks in the game, looking for all the world like Belushi and Aykroyd in their Jake and Elwood getups. They lip-synched old Blues Brothers songs, and they danced around with beautiful female assistants, and their every move mirrored the Belushi-Aykroyd routine. And the crowds at the Stadium accepted them as celebrities. Not parodies of stars; not carbon-copy jesters. But legitimate game-night heroes.

I looked up in the stands during one of these performances, and there was Jim Belushi.

John's younger brother was sitting with a baseball cap yanked down on his head. He was in town filming a movie, and apparently he had gotten hold of some Bulls tickets. On the court the Bulls Brothers were doing a slapstick routine—the man who played the Belushi character had stripped off his suit jacket to reveal a Bulls jersey over his thick torso—and the crowd was ecstatic.

Jim Belushi wasn't looking. Every other eye in the Stadium may have been on the Bulls Brothers, but John Belushi's brother was staring determinedly down at his game program, not looking up, choosing not to see the show in front of him.

At the end of their routine the Bulls Brothers sprinted to the far end of the court and the man made up to look like John pounced on a trampoline, was propelled toward the basket, and at the top of his mechanically enhanced leap he stuffed a miniature basketball into the hoop. The Bulls Brothers left to sustained applause, and the horn sounded to signal the recommencement of the game. Fame in America is the most ambiguous and enigmatic of commodities. Jordan walked slowly to the center of the floor, and John Belushi's brother put his program down, disposed again to watch.

Every night there were many fans who brought signs to hold up in the air. This was a standard part of big-time sports, of course; if there was ever a time when you could go to a stadium or arena and not see hand-lettered banners, that time was long gone.

To think about the signs and the sign-bearers, though, was sometimes an exercise in bewilderment. I saw a man one night, for example, carrying a sign upon which the words "When Jordan Cooks, the Bulls Heat," had been drawn. There was nothing off-color about the sign, or objectionable. And in the atmosphere of the Stadium, it was not remarkable; no one took much note of it.

But where did the man get that specific idea? Apparently he had taken the time to sit down in his kitchen or living room at home; he had put together the requisite materials; he had thought up that slogan; and he had carried the sign to the game. "When Jordan Cooks, the Bulls Heat"? Where does that come from in your brain? The Bulls weren't playing the Miami Heat, so that wasn't it. So where does the instinct come from? At what point does a man decide: "Here's one worth expending some effort on—'When Jordan Cooks, the Bulls Heat' "?

"What do you think makes a man think that up?" I said to Paul Sullivan, sitting in the next chair at the press table.

"Watch the game," he said, making notes on his pad.

"I'm serious," I said.

"I don't know, Bob," he said. "Why don't you go ask the guy?"

"I think it's a very interesting question," I said.

"I'm sure you do," he said.

Jordan never appeared undressed in the locker room. Other players did; one of the annoyances of being a professional athlete is that strangers wearing press credentials are permitted to wander around the room where you change clothes, and some of the Bulls players dealt with this inconvenience by simply undressing whenever they felt they ought to. Questions of modesty aside, it was difficult to blame them. Having to plan their dressing and undressing schedule around the timetables of the reporters must have been a pain.

But in a room where naked people were seen all the time, Jordan was not seen without his clothes.

"I never do that," he told me. "Out of respect for myself. It's not that I disapprove of women in locker rooms—that's not it. My feelings about it are the same for men as for women. Out of respect for myself, and for other people, I could not appear undressed in front of them."

"Some of the others don't seem to be bothered by it," I said.

"I know that a lot of athletes have no problem being naked in front of people, but I would just not feel comfortable talking to people without my clothes on," he said. "I get dressed before anyone can see me, and I would never be able to feel relaxed any other way."

"So you don't get dressed and undressed out in the main locker room?" I said.

"I usually go get dressed somewhere else," he said. "And if I'm not dressed by the time the reporters are supposed to come in, sometimes I tell Tim Hallam to keep the doors closed until I am dressed. That's the reason the reporters sometimes have to wait—because I don't want them to see me without my clothes on. I just think it's a question of dignity. I can't do it any other way."

"Are you afraid someone would take pictures or something?" I said. "I guess that could happen to you—someone could snap a picture of you undressed and sell it to some magazine."

"Maybe that's a part of it," he said. "But that's not the main reason, or even a big reason. The reason is one of respect, and of an attempt to be dignified."

The sportswriters had to deal with a different set of circumstances than I did: They had to talk with professional athletes every working day of the year, all year round, and they had to depend on the athletes to cooperate, to give them quotes for their stories. I suppose I had always assumed that the athletes in various sports were all pretty much the same. But I was told different.

"These guys are the best," a sportswriter said at the table one night down in the basement press buffet. "Basketball players are great to talk to."

"Better than baseball players?" I said.

"Are you kidding?" another sportswriter said. "Baseball players are the worst. They're the worst pricks in the world."

"Football players are just as bad as baseball," a third reporter said.

"Yeah, football players are terrible," the second writer said. "But baseball players are worse."

"What's wrong with baseball players?" I said.

"They're stupid, they're uneducated, they're rude, they hang together in schoolyard cliques, they play juvenile jokes—I can't stand them," the first writer said.

"Why do you think they're like that?" I said.

"Most of them never went to college," the second writer said. "All they've ever been exposed to is other baseball players. I despise going into their clubhouses."

"Hockey players are the best," the third writer said.

"Hockey players and NBA basketball players," the first writer said.

"So hockey players are good and football players are bad?" I said. "That doesn't make any sense. They're both violent sports. Why would hockey players treat you better?"

"Canada," the third writer said. "Canada's more civilized."

"But you said that NBA players are just as polite to you as

hockey players," I said. "It can't be Canada. The basketball players aren't Canadian."

"Trust us," the second writer said. "Or go to some locker rooms in other sports and see for yourself. Basketball and hockey players are generally princes. Baseball and football players are generally scum."

One of the greatest tributes to Jordan's skill was something that would never end up on a scoresheet, in a record book, or in a newspaper account of a game.

Occasionally he would make a blatant error. Someone would throw him a pass, and it would slip through his hands and roll out of bounds. Or he would be clear for a layup and would simply miss the shot. Once in a while he would try for a long shot that he plainly wasn't in position to make, and it would bang off the backboard.

When this happened, there would be not a sound in the Stadium. Not one boo. Not one groan. Not one shout of reproach, or even of encouragement. To hear that kind of silence in a building that was normally so clamorous was extraordinary.

It was as if, in eighteen thousand throats, sounds had begun to form—and then, instantly, before they could emerge, had been extinguished. It was as if eighteen thousand people had started to do what spectators at athletic events customarily do —involuntarily vocalize their reactions to a play—and had quickly made eighteen thousand reflexive decisions that this was not the time.

If they had explained their quietude, the reason would most likely be this: Jordan did so many things so spectacularly— things no one had any right to expect him to do—that to chastise him for an error, or take any overt notice of the error at all, even a forgiving notice, would be improper.

A sports arena is not necessarily a place where you will find generosity of spirit. But in the Stadium, every Jordan error seemed to be weighed instantly against eighteen thousand emotional bank accounts, into which Jordan had made so many deposits. One or two unexpected debits were automatically absolvable, no questions asked. Or so it seemed during those flashes of stillness, when Jordan would stop in his tracks, turn around without looking at anyone, and prepare for play to continue.

       *   *   *

In a game against the Portland Trail Blazers, during December, one of the referees called a traveling violation, and made that revolving motion with both arms, almost like bicycle wheels turning, that all of us remember from the first organized games we played as kids: "You're walking with the ball!"

Moments like those gave the temporary illusion that what the players on the court were going through wasn't all that much different from what we once experienced. But there are so few men who make it this far. There was a brief exchange in that same game, in the fourth quarter, when Scottie Pippen of the Bulls and Danny Ainge of the Blazers found themselves standing together. They were on opposite teams and they were competitive people and they obviously both wanted to win. It was a close game—the Stadium crowd was in full voice, it was one of those nights when things were so loud that your eardrums seemed to be pressing inward. And in the midst of that Pippen and Ainge spoke briefly, back and forth, and laughed a little.

It was a small signal, yet all the signal you'd ever need, that their lives were so different from the lives of anyone in the stands. There are fans who love the game, and there are sportswriters who know the game, and there are broadcasters who disseminate the game to millions of viewers and listeners. But regardless of the hue of their uniforms, the ten men on the court, although they are on the payrolls of different teams, are on the same team. They are on the team that made it here, and the rest of us aren't; the fans on a given night, in a given arena, may cheer for Pippen or boo at Ainge, but Pippen and Ainge are teammates in the one way that ultimately counts, and whatever joke they may have shared on the floor, it was a joke for their ears only. For members only.

With all the games, night after night in city after city, I wondered whether many of the details of what happened on the court stuck in the minds of the players. By the time the newspapers hit the streets the next morning with the report of one game, the team would very likely be in another city, thinking about the coming evening's game. One night I asked Jordan about this. Did he remember specific games?

"No," he said. "But I never forget teams. I might have forgotten about a game we played three weeks ago, but when we play the team again, I'll remember things."

"Do you have to be reminded?" I said. "Do the coaches have to show you films and go over strengths and weaknesses?"

He began to laugh.

"What's the matter?" I said.

"Nothing," he said. "It's just that every night before a game we have our pregame meeting in the locker room. The coaches will be standing at the blackboard, or showing us something on the VCR. And I never follow along. I'm never paying attention."

"Never?" I said.

"My whole life, I never did," he said. "They'll be diagramming plays on the board and going over the scouting report. I don't think the coaches are aware I'm not listening. I'm looking at them and sitting there, but my mind is totally somewhere else."

"Why wouldn't you listen?" I said.

"I know what to do," he said.

"But there's no information that might help you?" I said.

"I know what to do," he said. It wasn't so much that he was trying to be cocky as that he was stating what he perceived to be a simple fact.

"What if the coach asked you to repeat what he had just been talking about?" I said. "What if he pointed at the diagram and asked you for the right answer? What would you do then?"

"There are only a certain number of ways you can do a certain play," he said. "I could look up at the board and figure it out and get the answer. There are only certain possibilities, so I'd probably get the right one if I was asked."

"But even if it wouldn't help you to listen, it wouldn't hurt you, would it?" I said.

"I guess it wouldn't," he said. "But I don't want to hear it. I want to go out and play. Just go play the game. That's when it's time for me to pay attention."

"So none of the pregame stuff would help you at all?" I said.

"I know what I'm doing," he said, as if to doubt him was to challenge him. "I know the answer to how I should play. *I know what I'm doing.*"

"Jordan hurt his heel," someone at work said to me one day. "I heard it on the radio. He hurt it around the house."

The last phrase—"around the house"—was said in an almost accusatory manner. The tone of voice conveyed the kidding-on-the-straight message that Jordan should not be allowed to be wandering around his house without a specific purpose in mind. The person who was speaking was a big fan of the Bulls; he never missed a telecast of a game.

Like so many people, he listened to news bulletins about Jordan's health with extravagant concern. And it was understandable; Jordan had become so much a part of public life that a pain in his foot had the power to distress some people more than if the pain was in their own feet.

So when the radio reported that Jordan's heel was hurting, there were going to be a certain number of people who would think: See? The guy doesn't even bother to take care of himself properly. He should be in bed resting all the time when he's not playing. Why exactly does he feel he has to walk around his house, anyway? Doesn't he have someone who can do that for him?

I got to the Stadium earlier than usual. Not many people were there, but Jordan was, warming up alone. Every night, regardless of the strength of the opposing team, he knew he had to prove himself all over again, as if he'd never played a game before. He knew that every night the people on the other side would like nothing better than to make him look inadequate.

He shot and the ball bounced off the rim and rolled over to where I was sitting. I picked it up; he came over to retrieve it and sat down for a moment.

"So your foot's hurt?" I said.

"Yeah, I heard that on the radio on the way in," he said.

"You're going to play tonight?" I said. I was like everyone else; if he didn't, I was going to be let down.

He raised his eyes briefly and shook his head, as if to say: Will everybody please relax? I always play, don't I?

He scored thirty-five points to lead both teams and in the morning his name was in cheerful headlines.

8

THE RIDE TO THE STADIUM every night had a strangely small-town feel to it. It shouldn't have; the stretch of Chicago from downtown to the West Side is about as quintessentially urban a patch of property as you'll find in the United States.

But I always asked the cabdrivers to take Randolph Street west. Randolph, in the blocks outside of the downtown business district, is a part of the city that most people either take for granted or never see. The meat purveyors, the fruit and vegetable wholesalers, the produce marketers have their brick buildings and cement-block warehouses on Randolph Street. It's the kind of street that comes to life well before dawn each day, and shuts down early.

So by the time I would head for the Stadium, Randolph Street would be closed for the night. The stereotype of a big city is centered on brawniness—high rises and international airports and superhighways and construction cranes. A city has to eat, though, and Randolph Street is the place where the American food-chain passes through on its way to the people of Chicago.

It was an oddly peaceful feeling, riding by those buildings every night. I began to look forward to seeing the signs: Olympic Meat Packing, C & S Vegetables, Dino's Produce; Manny's Meat, LaQuinta Food Products, El Rey Seafood; Chuck Meats, Randolph Dairy, Crown Sausage. I got used to the presence of those buildings; they started to feel familiar and welcoming to me, even though no one was inside. They looked nothing at all like the homes and stores I used to pass on my way up to St. John Arena on game nights when Ohio State was playing, when I would be hurrying so that I could help Jimmy Crum—the streets and suburbs of central Ohio thirty years before were considerably less gritty, considerably less gray. The two routes might as well have been on different planets.

But something good was waiting on the other end, both back then in Columbus and now in Chicago. Riding past the food warehouses on Randolph Street, just like riding past the houses and stores on Olentangy River Road in central Ohio, brought on a sense of anticipation and glad expectancy that had nothing to do with the landscape itself. The streets were the pipelines; the streets became warm streets because of where they led. The daytime hours were done and I was on my way to something better in the dark. On Randolph Street I would pass Mid Town Meats and United Wholesale Provisions and the Schwartz Pickle Company, and it was like running a friendly gauntlet where there was a guaranteed prize at the other end. It rarely felt anything but lovely, that ride, even on the coldest nights.

The Los Angeles Clippers were in town for a Friday night game, and during the Bulls' early warm-ups Bill Cartwright was practicing layups. Just as Cartwright put the ball against the backboard, John Paxson took a long shot from the outside. Paxson's ball came down right on top of Cartwright's, knocking it off course.

"Got you that time!" Paxson, grinning, called to Cartwright. The banter itself was unremarkable. Yet the context—these two men joking about a warm-up-drill incident on a basketball court—was worth taking note of. How many years had Paxson been doing precisely this before playing a game? He was thirty, so it would be safe to bet that, on some level, he had been warming up in gyms from junior high school to high school to college to the NBA for just about two decades. That he would even think to say anything at all when his ball hit another ball—"Got you that time!"—and that he would sound like he meant it was attestation to just how intertwined were the players and the game they played.

What a sweet piece of knowledge for them to have. Other men might go to work and deal with computer spreadsheets or detailed blueprints or inventory checklists; other men might say a perfunctory "Good morning" to their colleagues at the office coffee machine, or complain to the guy in the next cubicle that the Xerox room was out of paper again. "Got you that time!" John Paxson, happy, called to Cartwright at the beginning of their shift at work, even as Cartwright ran to retrieve his ball.

Will Perdue joked with them as he warmed up. The newspapers that week had been reporting that Phil Jackson was displeased with Perdue's performance as a backup center; there was speculation on the sports pages that he was in the front office's bad graces. But a newspaper was only a newspaper, and words were only words. Here, Perdue was getting ready to do what he liked best—play in a game that counted, in the company of some of the best athletes in the world—and no matter what the next day's paper might report, that would have to wait until morning.

All of the players were paid extremely well; because the NBA was so lucrative for the men who made it into the league, the salary numbers were well publicized. Big salaries or not, though, part of the treasured compensation was clearly this: the chance to play basketball with your friends for a living, and not have to do anything else.

Had any of these players been even 6 or 7 percent less gifted than they were—had they been wonderful basketball players, the best in their high schools, the best in their colleges, but not quite good enough for the NBA—their lives, of course, would be completely different. They would still be marvelous athletes, but had they fallen short of reaching this ultimate level of talent—of being among the 324 men employed to play 82 games each regular season in the National Basketball Association—their lives would likely bear no resemblance to the lives they had come to know now.

Horace Grant, as a starting forward, was paid in excess of one million dollars a year for playing with the Bulls. Born in Augusta, Georgia, he now lived with his wife and baby son in an affluent northern suburb of Chicago. He told me one night that, had he not gotten this far with his basketball ability, he knew what he'd be doing.

"I had a regular thought about being in the Marines," he said. "I'd sit there and watch TV all day, and the Marines commercials would come on. The ones about looking for a few good men. I guess I liked the sound of those words. Or what the uniforms looked like."

I had no idea whether the Marines accepted recruits who were six foot ten, but the important thing was that the military was the one occupation to which Grant was drawn. A million dollars a year for being this good in basketball; a government paycheck had he been just the slightest bit less accomplished.

"Did you think about joining out of patriotism?" I asked him.

"That wasn't really it," he said. "It appealed to me as a way to do something good that would get me out of town. I think I would have tried to get in. I wanted to travel and I really did like the way that uniform looked, so that's what I would probably be doing."

"Did you ever give any thought at all to the world of business?" I asked.

Grant was a usually sunny person, but as he considered the question he had a solemn look on his face. "No," he said. "I think the business world would have treated me too cruelly."

One person the business world had unquestionably treated anything but cruelly was Jordan. No one outside his family and his circle of financial advisers really knew just how much money he made from all of his endorsements and commercial sponsorships—his basketball salary was almost insignificant when factored into his gross earnings—but informed guesses ranged up to twenty-eight million dollars a year.

Figures like that simply won't compute in the mind—you can't look at a fellow human being and fathom that he is being paid twenty-eight million—and at least for me, it was easier not to think about it. It was a joy to watch Jordan work and a constant pleasure to spend time talking with him, and as we grew friendlier as the weeks went by I began to realize that regardless of the precise amount of money he made—for most of us, how would we understand the difference between ten million and twenty-eight million, anyway?—it was probably healthier to just let all thoughts about that go. However much he was paid had nothing at all to do with why I enjoyed his company, and I was sure he had more than enough people spending more than enough energy dwelling on the fiscal part of his life.

Still, there were times when it was impossible not to consider the exceptional and inevitable contrast his good fortune had created between his circumstances and everyone else's, including those of his fellow players. I'd think about it during seemingly minor moments. Sometimes, for example, when Jordan arrived at the Stadium for the evening and headed toward the stairs that led down to the locker room, he checked to see if Tim Hallam or one of Hallam's assistants, Joyce Szymanski or John Diamond, had left the game notes on the press tables yet.

The nightly notes consisted of a thick, stapled sheaf of statistical data, mostly about the Bulls and that night's opponents, but also about the whole league. The notes were arcane and specialized—if you ever wanted to know how many rebounds the Atlanta Hawks as a team were averaging on the road, you could find it in the notes—and they were intended to help the sportswriters do their jobs.

On the nights that the notes had been stacked early on the press tables, Jordan would reach out for a set and begin to read them even as he walked the final few dozen feet toward the stairs. It made sense on an obvious level—he was a basketball player and these were basketball statistics, naturally he'd be interested. At the same time, though, I'd see him perusing the notes, and I'd wonder: Do these numbers really have any relation to what he does? They're necessary after the fact—they accurately sum up, in the driest and most passionless terms, what has happened up until tonight—but do they help explain in any meaningful way, either to him or to the rest of the world, the unique turn his life had taken?

He'd read them as he walked. And as much as I liked sitting with him and hearing him try to make sense out of the real-world aspects of his life—the things that had happened to him because of basketball—there were times that to hear him expound on basketball itself was an education into just what it was that made him care.

Like this:

There was something that regularly happened as the clock was running down at the end of a quarter, when there were 28 or 30 or 32 seconds left, and the Bulls got the ball. There was time for one full possession—the twenty-four-second clock would expire just before the buzzer sounded to send the teams to the benches.

So the Bulls would know that they had time to run one play. And almost every time, the four other Bulls would spread themselves around the court, while Jordan, all alone, would stand midway between the back of the free-throw circle and center court, and, almost tauntingly, cradle the ball to his chest.

Everyone in the Stadium knew what was going on. He was going to wait until the last possible moment, and then he was going to make the play. Whether he would shoot from outside, or drive in in an effort to score while drawing a foul, or find someone else who was open—that was in question. But whatever the specific outcome, it was always an electrifying sequence. The noise level would rise with each tick of the clock, and there he would stand, in no hurry at all, not moving, not even dribbling. He was like a commuter patiently waiting for his bus to come, but he was Michael Jordan, and every eye was on him.

This was the kind of basketball moment I loved hearing him talk about—not just for the information his words provided, but for the animation in his voice, the verve behind the specific phrases. He would explain the basketball strategy, and he would sound like a young kid in the throes of his first romance.

"See, what I'm doing when I'm standing there is looking at the defense," he said. "I'm looking to see if they're going to double-team me, or if they're going to try to come at me and get the ball out of my hands. So while I'm standing back there, I'm watching for them to send two men at me, and at the same time I'm looking up at the clock as well. I know that I have until the clock runs down to ten seconds before I have to do anything."

"Ten?" I said. "Always?"

"Ten is the number," he said. "Phil wants me to do something when it gets to ten. When it hits ten, that's when I'll run the play.

"Sometimes the other team will see me standing out there, and they'll send two men at me. When that happens, I'll know I can do one of two things. I can go for the shot myself, hope to make it, and give us a chance for an extra shot with time on the clock. Or I can get rid of the ball right then. Because someone's going to be open when they decide to double-team me. So when they send two at me, I'm already looking to see who they've left."

"A lot of the time, Paxson," I said.

"Paxson will be open a lot in that situation," he said. "So I have to decide right at that moment: Do I get the ball to John? Do I take an outside shot myself? Do I drive and draw the foul? Do I see an opening to take the ball to the basket? And all the time I'm watching the clock, to see when it hits ten."

"And then?" I said.

"At ten, I go," he said. "If it's ten or below and there are two men on me, I have to determine in that instant who can get the easiest shot off. Sometimes I purposely try to get one of the defenders on the other team to come at me, so he'll leave his man open. Or I'll decide that I can make the long shot. Or I'll know that they probably can't stop me if I take it to the basket myself."

"Is that any more or less nerve-wracking than any other point in the game?" I said. "Because the clock is winding down and everyone has their eyes on you?"

"I'm not nervous at all in that situation," he said. "Because I feel like I'm in total control. Whatever's going to happen out there, it's not going to happen until I start it. And everyone in the building knows it. Moments like that make me happy."

"Happy?"

"It really does make me happy," he said. "When you're standing out there in control like that, everyone knows that you've got to do something. The other team, and everyone else in the arena. They know that you've got to do something, but no one but you knows what the something is going to be."

Beyond the obvious satisfaction of getting these Basketball 101 lectures from Jordan—he never seemed to mind walking me through the various scenarios, and I never got tired of listening to him explain what went on in his mind during the diverse situations in which he found himself on the court—I was constantly struck by the recognition that these things still and genuinely buoyed him. I don't think even he realized how much the tone of his voice came to life when he went into detail about how he did his job.

"So in those last few seconds of the quarter," I said, "are you aware of how noisy the crowd becomes?"

"Oh, yeah," he said. "And I can see the other team looking at me, and they know what I'm going to have to do and their job is to stop me, and my job is to make sure they don't stop me. So all of that is going on while I'm standing back there— the noise, and the defenders looking at me, and me looking at my teammates, and keeping my eye on the clock at the same time. And even though everyone in the whole place knows that I have to try to score, it's my job to make sure that I do it anyway."

"And that never makes you tense at all," I said.

"No," he said.

"All that noise, and all those eyes focused on you."

"No," he said. "It's fun."

It wasn't precisely the word I'd been expecting. But it was probably, once I'd thought about it, the most accurate one.

"Doesn't that sound like fun to you?" he said. "Everyone in the building knowing you have to do something, and everyone on the other team not wanting you to do it? And then you have to do it in spite of all that?"

"It sounds like just about the most fun in the world," I said.

"It is," he said. "Believe me on that."

Love of basketball or not, though, some scenes at the Stadium emphasized the fact that the computer chip–driven pace of modern life had made itself right at home with the men who played the game.

As the Bulls and the Clippers were going through their pregame drills that Friday, Jordan caught my eye and motioned with his head in the direction of the L.A. team. At first I didn't see what he had noticed. Then I looked over toward the out-of-bounds line near the benches.

Some fans had approached one of the Clippers in an attempt to get an autograph. They were having to wait, though. Even as they held their programs in front of the Clipper, hoping he would sign, he was busy. In full uniform, he stood by the edge of the court, deep in earnest conversation on a pocket-sized cellular phone.

There was another side of the coin to the phenomenon of these men, by virtue of their basketball talent, being elevated to big money and a professional lifetime of gameplaying. Horace Grant might be making his million-plus and performing in front of adoring fans instead of marching in the military, but every player in the league understood that one wrong turn of an ankle, one unforeseen banging of a wrist, had the ominous potential of sending them away from this forever. The luck of the draw works in a number of ways.

So as the Bulls cruised to a 128-88 win over the Clippers, a Clipper guard named Ron Harper sat on the bench, watching. Harper was traveling with his team, but he was dressed in a checked business suit over a black turtleneck. A member of the NBA all-rookie team when he was playing with the Cleveland Cavaliers in 1987, Harper had since been traded to the Clippers, had sustained a serious knee injury, and now was waiting to heal before he would be permitted to attempt to play again.

There is inevitably a lot of bravado, a lot of swagger, in professional sports; it apparently comes along with the need to match skills with the best athletes on the planet. It's not difficult to understand, though, that the bravado can evaporate with the sickening sound of something snapping inside a leg or something tearing inside an elbow.

The press tables were directly perpendicular to the visiting bench in the Stadium, so we were just a few feet away from the opposing team every night, and could see their expressions from close range, could hear snatches of their conversations. During the game on this night, Harper rose from his seat at the end of the Clippers' bench, walked slowly over to where we sat, and asked if he could have a program.

There were usually plenty of programs scattered around; one of the sportswriters handed one to Harper. He returned to the bench. The cover of the program featured a highly stylized color photograph of Jordan floating across the blue above the downtown Chicago skyline.

On the court, Jordan drove to the basket. Jordan was in a different universe from Harper even when Harper was well, but tonight the chasm between them was significantly more pronounced. Jordan was a physically sound professional athlete tonight, playing in the game; Harper was an infirm man, watching as any ticket-holder would watch. The only difference this evening between him and the eighteen thousand people in the stands was that he had a better seat.

Jordan took a pass from Pippen and sailed toward the hoop. Harper looked at Jordan on the court, then looked at the flying Jordan on the front of his program.

"Michael," he said to the cover.

If being a player in the NBA offered both the promise of fabulous riches and the fear of instant, involuntary exclusion, being a coach seemed to offer fewer of the lures and more of the indignities. The coaches were generally older than any of their players, generally made considerably lower salaries than most of their players, and had to accept as part of their jobs the implicit acknowledgment that the world at large—and the players in particular—ranked the players as far more important than the men who coached them.

And, accepting that, the coaches had to go out every night

and tell the athletes what to do. A fifty-seven-year-old coach would routinely have to tell a twenty-five-year-old player who was making five times what the coach was making that the player had to sit down on the bench. It was intriguing to watch the interplay every night, and to observe the fragile balance the coaches tried to maintain.

Most of them were fashionable as they strode back and forth along the side of the court—the NBA mandated that the coaches dress dapperly, or at least respectably, to enhance the league's image—but some of them came to the arena in casual clothing, changing into fancy suits in the locker rooms. For them, the Italian-cut suits and hundred-dollar neckties that were seen on TV broadcasts of the games each night were not much different from the uniforms their players wore. The players' uniforms were costumes, and the coaches' elegant suits were costumes—they were what a coach was expected to wear on game nights, a little bit of Halloween in the winter.

The clothes were a superficial part of their jobs, though. Maintaining an air of command over their players was more basic. The coaches all had different mannerisms and techniques. During the game against the Clippers, for example, Los Angeles coach Mike Schuler wanted to take guard Gary Grant out of the game and replace him with Winston Garland. There were all kinds of potential ways for him to summon Garland.

What he did was this: He made the briefest possible eye contact with Garland on the bench, crooked his finger at him, and wagged it exactly once—and that was the signal that Garland was supposed to go in. It was so quick and so offhanded that no one who wasn't paying the closest attention could have been expected to notice it. Schuler looked away from Garland as soon as he had wagged the finger. The message plainly was: I'm the boss here. You may be the NBA athlete, but I will determine whether, and when, you play tonight, and you'd better be watching. Schuler had the power to determine the course of Garland's night, and, eventually, the weight of his wallet—and Schuler clearly knew it.

Later in the game, with 3:54 left in the third quarter, Schuler decided that he wanted to put center Ken Bannister into the contest. The glance again, the crook of the finger, the waggle, the look away. Bannister didn't see this.

His neighbor on the bench did, though. "Kenny!" the

neighbor whispered to him in alarmed tones. They were momentarily like pupils in a junior high school math class, the one friend rousing the other who had been daydreaming when the teacher called on him. Bannister heard the whisper; he leapt to his feet with great apparent purpose and energy, and dramatically ripped his NBA-style snap-away warm-up pants from his legs as a sign of his perpetual vigilance and his ferocious readiness to charge into battle at any time. It didn't seem to fool Schuler, who had been watching all of this from the corner of his eye.

Schuler had maintained his authority, at least for the night. But, as I was learning, there were games within games within games, all of them educational in their own peculiar ways.

Jordan's father was in the crowd a lot of nights. Although James Jordan lived in North Carolina, he frequently flew to Chicago to watch his son play. He looked like Michael probably was going to look by the time Michael reached his fifties; although he was shorter than his son, the physical resemblance of the two in almost every other way was just about complete.

He was easy to spot in the stands, and was a celebrity in his own right at the Stadium. Fans would see him, come up to greet him, pose for pictures with him, ask for his autograph. He didn't seem to mind this at all.

I asked Jordan if he felt differently on nights when his father was present than when he wasn't. For a lot of people—myself included—the presence of a parent or parents at a public event is disconcerting. Not necessarily in a bad way—you want them to be there and to be proud of you. But even in a big crowd, you sense that their eyes are on you, and they become the most important members of the audience. Maybe because they were your first audience.

"I've always had a thing if my dad or mom are coming to a game," he said. "I want to know where they're going to be sitting."

"So you can be aware of them looking at you play?" I said.

"No, that's not it," he said. "It's just that if I know they're coming to a game I feel I have to make sure that they're there safely. I have to check before the game, just so I know."

"You go up there and look?" I said.

"I can't go up there myself to look," he said. "But when I'm dressing in the locker room before the game, I ask someone to go out and check to see that my parents are in their seats, and then come back and tell me. I've been doing that ever since high school. It's a sense of safety, I guess. I just want to make sure they got there."

"So it's not that you feel self-conscious with your father watching you?" I said. "I was thinking that would be a pretty understandable reaction. Even with eighteen thousand people there, I figured maybe having your dad in the crowd made you put even more pressure on yourself to do well."

"No," Jordan said. "When he's there, I know I have at least one fan."

"Come on," I said. " 'At least one fan'?" The smile that crept across his face was an indication that he knew what an absurd statement that was.

"All right," he said. "But the fact is, when he's there it makes the game a little bit more enjoyable for me. Even if I have a bad game, I know I have a little more support. But the main thing is, if I know my parents are coming to a game, it's very important to me that before the game starts I'm sure that they got there."

"Would you know it if they weren't there?" I said.

"Of course," he said. "I know it when they're supposed to be there and they're not there. It makes me nervous. That's why I have to make sure. I can't play the game unless I know that they're in their seats and they got there safely."

It was conversations like that one that made me stop and think, days and weeks later. A man who could draw unruly mobs by the simple act of walking down the street on any continent on the map. A man who looked into the stands to reassure himself that there weren't one or two specific seats whose special owners were unaccounted for. The clock running down at the end of a quarter while he, alone near midcourt, balanced the ball in his hands and decided what to do as thousands of people screamed—that didn't make him edgy. The idea that his parents were supposed to come to a game, and that they might not have arrived for some reason—that had the power to scare him. That, he had to reassure himself about before he could step onto the court.

"I think everyone would be like that," he said.

"Me, too," I said. "I think that's the whole point."

"Can you imagine playing if you had to keep wondering where your parents were?" he said.

"Sometimes I think we never stop being who we were when we were eight years old," I said.

"That's fine with me," he said.

"It's not like we have any choice," I said.

"Probably not," he said. "But I think I'd choose to be that way anyway."

Full winter was upon Chicago by mid-December. I would leave the Stadium after the final buzzer to find snow filling the night and blocking the moon, and drifts piling up outside Gate 3½.

It would take me about half an hour to get home. Some nights my family would be asleep by the time I got there. My evenings at the Stadium were very much a gift from them to me. I had managed to get through a lot of years without going to arenas or ballparks. This was different, and they let me know they understood that, for whatever reason, the Stadium nights were necessary in ways that had nothing to do with sports. Their understanding gave me the chance to have those nights.

So sometimes when I arrived home the lights would be out. I would still be wide awake, and I would fix myself a sandwich and a Coke, and then I would turn on the television set.

On ESPN and CNN, the late-evening sports highlights shows would be going on the air. Less than an hour before, the Bulls had been playing the game at the Stadium. Now the most dramatic of the plays I had been watching an hour ago would be bouncing off some space station somewhere and down into millions of homes across the country, across the world, my home included.

There would be Pippen, there would be Grant. And always, there would be Jordan, in slow motion, drifting toward the rim at quarter-speed, his every gesture and grimace drawn out on the videotape so that people all around the globe could savor each nuance, each movement. Sometimes on the TV screen I could see myself at the press table, my eyes looking up toward the basket. At home my feet would still be numb from where they had rested on the thin wooden surface that covered the hockey rink. On the screen the game was still being played, languorously and in suspended time and in vivid and repeated close-up, like a dream that's supposed to last forever.

9

ONE THING I HAD LONG been curious about was the woman who allegedly had asked Jordan to run her over in his car. But it was a while before I felt comfortable enough to ask him that one.

The rumor was this: A woman—one of many who were attracted to Jordan from afar—had shown up at the Stadium and had tried to meet him. When she failed, she lay down in front of his car until he came out. Then she told him that she'd like him to run her over.

As outlandish as it sounded, it wasn't entirely impossible. Jordan's fame was so powerful, the kind of adulation he inspired so extreme, that the idea of a woman wanting the thrill of being run over by his automobile was not outside the bounds of plausibility.

"It happened," he said after I'd spelled out the details of the rumor to him one day. "It's a true story. Not exactly like you heard, but it's true."

He was shaking his head as he recounted it. Even with all the aspects of his life that verged on the unfathomable, there were some that stretched the barriers of credulity.

"It wasn't at the Stadium," he said. "It was during the summertime. A couple of years ago. I had been doing something somewhere, and when I went to my car she was lying in front of it. She was about eighteen, sort of attractive. And she said, 'I'm not getting up until you give me your autograph.'

"I was in a hurry, and this was very strange. I asked her to move. And she stayed on the ground, and she said, 'If you're going to run me over, I wouldn't mind being run over by Michael Jordan.' "

"Was it some sort of sexual thing or a nuts thing or a combination—what do you think it was?" I said.

"I have no idea," he said. "I said to her, 'Look, I'm not going to run you over.' So I gave her the autograph, because for some reason she had convinced herself that it might be all right if I ran her over in my car."

There are very few men in the world who ever go through an experience like that—most of us were once kids who were nervous about making a phone call to ask a girl to the movies on a Friday night, and it's a fairly considerable leap to becoming a man who gets a request to run over a woman—and I suspected that Jordan had not always been a person who was unfailingly smooth with females.

"When I was young I was playful with girls," he said. "I was never very successful romantically. I was like the guy who carried their books home for them. I was always the guy they wanted to be their friend, not their boyfriend. They always wanted the athletes."

"So obviously it worked out okay," I said.

"Why do you think I started to play sports?" he said. "So girls would like me."

"Not because you wanted to become some sort of champion?" I said. "It was because of girls?"

"Absolutely," he said. "I thought, 'I've got to do this, because the girls like the guys who play all sports.'

"There was this one girl, Angela West, and she was a year older than me, and ever since the fifth or sixth grade I wanted her to like me. And I would get on the school bus every morning, and her stop came after mine, and I would save her a seat next to me. I would make sure that there was no one sitting next to where I was sitting.

"She would get on the bus. And she would share a seat with her friends, even if it meant that three or four of them had to push together in one school bus seat."

"So you were still sitting there saving the empty seat for her?"

"Yep," he said. "I was disappointed, but I knew exactly what the reason was. The reason was that she wanted to go out with the athletes. All during high school, I never did go out with her. I just knew that the Angela Wests of the world weren't interested in you if you weren't an athlete. It didn't matter what else you were."

Jordan was married and a father now; any insecurities he'd

ever had about women—especially young women who might reject a young man because he wasn't an accomplished athlete—must have seemed like something that had happened centuries ago. He didn't talk much about the women who approached him and made themselves available to him, which was understandable.

"The letters I get," he said, "the fantasies women write me about . . ."

He looked at me and shook his head again, smiling a little but not showing any particular mirth.

"Some send me these pictures of themselves," he said. "It's like a three-sixty for me. The way I was when I was a kid, and now . . . I never would have believed it."

"Well, apparently you were right," I said. "Becoming an athlete seemed to do the trick."

"Yeah, but part of me is still on that school bus," he said. "Part of me is still saving a seat for a girl who would rather sit scrunched up with three other girls than sit next to me. And part of me gets these letters in the mail, and has a woman ask me to run her over."

"That one," I said. "Of all the things that have happened to you . . ."

"I know," he said. "Run her over. And she wasn't kidding. She would have let me."

"In your car," I said.

"In my car," he said.

He had so little time to himself, which was partially by his own choosing. Because he realized that he was under ceaseless scrutiny, compounded by his acceptance that his commercial endorsements were based upon his image of being amiable and accessible, he was careful any time he was in public not to appear curt, or short-tempered, or discourteous to strangers. Often this meant that while Pippen or Grant could brush by fans who wanted to stop them, Jordan couldn't—or wouldn't. He seemed to understand that part of the bargain he had made with life was that he would be held to a higher standard of comportment than the rest of the world.

So he knew that his moments of privacy would be few. Some of them, which he valued for both professional and personal reasons, were those moments he reserved for himself in the locked Stadium before the doors opened. Not only could he work on his livelihood without interruption, but he could savor the rare pleasure of thinking his thoughts knowing that no one would approach him. Which is what he was doing before a game against the Cleveland Cavaliers. He was all by himself at the foul line, shooting one free throw after another.

Two children who had performed as halftime entertainers at an earlier game—they were very small and very cute, they had been taught to do tricks with basketballs—had been invited back to do their show at tonight's contest. Along with their father—both the boys and the dad were in fancy warm-up suits—they had been admitted to the Stadium early, and were watching Jordan from the sidelines.

They knew the rules about this; everything had been explained to them. But at 5:55 P.M., the father whispered something to the older boy. The boy, obeying his dad, walked onto the court until he was standing next to Jordan, who had not seen him coming.

Jordan looked down. The boy was holding up a cardboard picture of a basketball, and a pen. Wordlessly, Jordan accepted the picture and signed his name. I could see him looking around for someone to deal with the situation. The father apparently had sent the son up to Jordan as a test; emboldened now, the man himself walked briskly onto the playing surface with a pile of pictures for Jordan to sign.

Down at the other end of the court, Lisa Harris, a Bulls front-office official, caught sight of what was happening. This was the one thing that Jordan had been promised—that when the Stadium was locked and he wanted to work, he wouldn't be put in this position.

Harris hurried down to where Jordan was still signing. She said to the father: "Don't do that." Her voice was not as much angry as it was imploring.

Jordan had not uttered a cross word, had not hesitated an instant before signing. But within thirty seconds after Harris had escorted the man and his son from the court, Jordan, his face showing nothing, dropped the basketball to the floor and walked down the stairs to the basement. Up until tonight the pregame hours had been a guaranteed source of solitude for him, but now he knew that he shouldn't count on even that.

Before each game, the public address announcer, a man named Ray Clay, would summarize the Bulls' most recent road trip. His voice would sound through the arena: "And in Milwaukee, the Bucks held the Bulls under ninety points, defeating Chicago ninety-nine to eighty-seven in the Bradley Center. . . ."

Most of the fans in the Stadium listening to Clay's words likely had watched the game on television, and some of the images from it probably remained real to them. The Bulls, warming up, seemed not to hear Clay, or at least not to be paying attention to him, and, in a peculiar way, to have nothing to do with what he was saying. He announced that Jordan had led the Bulls with thirty-one points, that Grant had grabbed nine rebounds, that Milwaukee's Jay Humphries had led his team in scoring with twenty-one points.

The numbers, and the collective memories of the fans in the Stadium of a televised basketball show the week before, lacked a conspicuous connection with the twelve men talking with each other now as they got ready to play. The Milwaukee game was off in the ozone somewhere, it was something that had ceased to exist, and the twelve men in the white uniforms were here tonight, living in the present, about to create a new box score that some P.A. announcer somewhere could sum up as recent sports history next week.

It would have been easy to make fun of the nightly ritual at the basement press buffet. The obvious jokes would have been about Oscar Madison–types—and many of the basement habitués could, indeed, have played that role in an "Odd Couple" revival—engaging in grandiloquent gourmet repartee.

"The swordfish is better than the chicken tonight."

"Are you sure? That looks like the good wine sauce we had with the chicken last week."

"Trust me—go with the swordfish."

A media critic who happened upon the scene might have pounced on the nightly dinner as a juicy example of press freeloading. And indeed, I was made more than a little uncomfortable by the fact that we were not permitted to pay for our meals; the way I decided to deal with it was to make a contribution to CharitaBulls, the team's community fund that distributed money to various deserving causes around Chicago, in a sum approximating what all of the season's suppers would have cost in a restaurant.

But the story I saw here had nothing to do with freeloading. These sports reporters, who worked the various Chicago teams' beats full-time, had obviously become, over the years, a family of sorts, and this, in a way not too far from truth, was their family dinner table. At least it was an approximation; here they gathered with people who understood them, and talked about the events of their days; here they unleashed their problems and gripes, and as I saw and heard this every evening I wondered how many of them would have agreed with the analogy: a dinner table where, at the end of the day, an eccentric family congregates to break bread with people to whom they are bound. At a time of the evening when real families are gathering at real dinner tables.

"Did you hear how much Dave Stewart signed for today?" one of the sportswriters, speaking about a major-league baseball player, said as he dug a fork into his salad.

"What, was it two-and-a-half million?" the man next to him said.

"Three," a fellow across the table said. "I heard three million."

There was a wide gap between the economies of sports and the economies of sports journalism, yet the men, and a few women, in the basement had the job of stepping into dugouts and locker rooms to interview the Dave Stewarts—and Scottie Pippens and Bill Cartwrights and Michael Jordans—of the world, and to ask the athletes, without flinching, whether the $2.5 million was considered sufficient. How many years can a man with a mortgage be required to ask questions like that without getting at least a little bit of a knot in his stomach?

I, for one, didn't begrudge anyone his swordfish.

"Mike!" Craig Hodges called.

Hodges, a long-range shooter who came off the Bulls' bench when the team needed a chance at some quick points, fired a ball to Jordan during warm-ups. Jordan turned to catch the ball; he was wearing a T-shirt with a drawing on the front.

He'd wear different T-shirts just about every night; tonight the figure on the front was a logo that looked like a cat but was really a stylized dog—symbol, I was told, of the Barcelona Olympic Games. One more alien aspect of Jordan's life was that virtually any company or business concern in the world would do almost anything if Jordan would only wear their logo in public. Which he virtually never did. Here, with his teammates, he could bang around in different T-shirts until the doors opened. In front of crowds of strangers, though, he had to be careful.

Careful because he knew that he had the power to help any

business by the simple act of displaying its name on his body. This was the exact opposite of how things are for other people; other people, at least a lot of them, attempt to enhance their own identities by the cachet of logo-strewn clothing they buy and wear. They hope that by displaying the name of a prestigious fashion designer, or athletic-gear manufacturer, or rock group, or sports team, they will somehow be elevated in the eyes of people who see them.

Not Jordan. He was King Midas of logos; he had the mystical capability to touch them and bequeath upon them pecuniary worth.

"What's that cat?" Hodges called.

"Olympic cat," Jordan said, hitting a jumper.

As much affection as I was feeling for my swordfish-eating friends in the basement, there were times when I wondered whether some of them ever considered the irony of certain things they were saying.

As a player jumped for a rebound in front of us during the Cavaliers game, a writer two seats down from me—like many of us, he was a fellow who looked as if he might become severely winded by climbing a long flight of stairs—gestured with his pen toward the player and said: "Look at his ass. It must be carrying an extra twenty-five pounds."

The observation may or may not have been valid. But the one thing I would have had trouble doing, had I been a sportswriter, was engaging in the constant, almost blithe derisions of the players' athletic failings and physical condition. Granted, that was part of what sportswriters were traditionally expected to do: evaluate how well the athletes played the games, and look at them with an unforgiving eye. And the athletes were being paid a lot of money with the understanding that they were required to perform physical duties well in a public arena, under public scrutiny.

Still, I sometimes wondered whether some of my neighbors under the basket ever stopped to look at the men in front of them—men who might miss a couple of what would be termed, in the next day's paper, "easy" shots—and ever thought: Could I do that? How would I do out there under the same circumstances? What must it be like to try to do that?

Not that asking those internal questions would prevent them from knocking the players in print or on the air. If the

NBA was theater, my colleagues on press row were drama critics with rigid standards. But it always made me pause when a wheezing, two-hundred-pound, tobacco-addicted, vodka-marinated journalist peered up at an athlete battling for the ball above the rim, and the sole observation he chose to make was how fat and tired the athlete looked.

I suspected that, when we weren't around, the players might occasionally indulge in similar physical evaluations of us. I was just as glad that we weren't there to hear it.

"The fewest points ever scored by an opponent in a quarter against the Bulls was six," Tim Hallam said in a hurried monotone. "Los Angeles Lakers, November 20, 1977 . . ."

He was moving down the row, saying this above the head of each reporter, over and over. The Cavaliers were having a terrible first quarter against the Bulls; with forty seconds to go, they had scored only five points. Hallam had checked with the Bulls' statistics crew, and now was letting everyone know, so the information would be available for inclusion in their stories. I sat and watched the game, and his voice was like a train whistle, getting louder as it approached, then fading as he drifted past, continuing to say it as he moved along: "The fewest points ever scored . . ."

The season, too, was moving right along. No one yet knew that it would culminate in a championship, but piece by piece, basket by basket, it was being played and recorded and reported, and meanwhile the final scores and official numbers continued to be the least of it for me. Tonight, every time a player went to the hoop, I heard a click and then a whirring. It took me a few seconds to figure out the sound.

Mounted on the table just a foot to my left was a still camera, bolted in place with its lens prefocused directly on the basket. The photographer, whoever he might have been, was stationed elsewhere in the Stadium; he was activating it via a remote-control device. He would watch the players drive, and he would hit some unseen button, and the shutter would click, followed by the sound of the film advancing. When the shots appeared in a newspaper or magazine, showing furious close-ups of NBA action from a vantage point directly beneath the basket, the readers would have no way of knowing that the person who took the pictures wasn't there. Jordan, driving the lane, his arm extended in front of him, flipped the basketball skyward to the accompaniment of the disembodied click, illusion building illusion.

"I watch some TV and I make some phone calls, but mostly I just think," Jordan said.

I'd been curious about the moments when he was totally alone. There weren't many of them—around the Stadium and in public places in the Chicago area and even at home, there was always someone with him. On the road, though—during the forty-one away games of each regular season—he roomed by himself. I'd asked him what went on when he closed the door and found himself in complete solitude.

"It's not just basketball things I think about," he said. "I'll think about a lot of stuff. I'll have the TV set on just to have it on. I make as few phone calls as I can—I really don't like being on the phone. You can ask my wife—she always wonders why I'm so quick to get off the phone when I call her. I just don't like it."

"Do you ever look around you?" I said.

"Sometimes I'll be in my room on the road and I'll just pull open the curtains and look outside," he said. "I'll just sit there and do that. No TV, no music, no telephone. I'll just sit in a chair and look out the window and try to clear my mind. But it never lasts very long. I find it peaceful, and I wish I could do it more. Just looking outside. But then something always comes up."

Sometimes it seemed as if the game being played by Jordan and his cohorts on the Stadium court was so complex and splendorously tuned that what they were doing had nothing at all in common with what the rest of us used to do on basketball courts when we were children learning the game.

And sometimes—this happened repeatedly, every night, always after a referee had blown a whistle—there was a flash of recognition that, at least in fleeting ways, these men were still children, too.

It happened as usual during the Cleveland game. Craig Hodges had the ball in the backcourt and was about to try for a long jump-shot. Just as he was setting up, one of the officials noticed something going on down in the lane, and sounded his whistle to indicate a foul away from the ball.

So the game halted and all the players stopped in their tracks and relaxed for a moment. And Hodges—I don't think he even realized he was doing this—aimed the ball toward the basket and shot. The clock was stopped, the contest was plainly on hold; Hodges knew that the shot wouldn't count. It was simply that, with a basketball in his hands, he evidently had no choice but to toss it toward the hoop. And he watched it, too; he watched until he knew whether it would go in or not.

This is what I was seeing every night: the shots after the whistle. They all did it, players from the Bulls and from all their opponents. You might think that, playing basketball to make their livings, shooting every day of their working lives, they would no longer necessarily have this instinct. But they did. It was involuntary. If a basket was there, chances were they were going to shoot at it.

None of these shots ever showed up in a box score, but I looked forward to seeing the shots every night, and they invariably made me smile; they made me feel good. This was the link between the players in the NBA and the boys they used to be; this was the link between the players in the NBA and us. When you're a kid starting out on a basketball court, the shooting at the hoop is what you look forward to. If you know you're going to play basketball in gym class, or in someone's driveway after school, you wait all day for it and as you wait you can almost feel the ball on your fingertips, you can almost see it sailing through the air toward the net. You might want to win the game, and you might want to impress your friends, but mostly you want to shoot. You want to stare down the basket and sink your shot. That's what excites you and gets you onto a court in the first place.

These men, too, apparently. Horace Grant took a pass from Jordan and went up for a layup and was fouled hard. The whistle blew, and he headed to the free-throw line, but first he turned and completed his motion; he sneaked in a shot. Brad Daugherty of the Cavaliers, also, and Bill Cartwright of the Bulls—none seemed able to resist. And they were trying with these shots—they weren't just flinging the ball, they were hoping that the ball would go in, even though it would count for nothing, and they were following its path with their eyes. They obviously didn't believe that a man has only a finite number of baskets granted to him in his life, and that he should thus conserve his attempts. They believed, at least on some level, that they could shoot until eternity, that they could shoot until dark, and that every shot held the promise of being a good one.

Other aspects of the game were harder to identify with.

The jarring physical contact under the boards—so artistic looking, almost choreographed, when played back on television highlight reels to the strains of cleverly selected music—was, observed from a few feet away, so potentially damaging to the human body that it was incomprehensible to watch it repeatedly and understand how the players kept going.

This was another case in which it was instructive not to take what we were seeing for granted, but instead to try to imagine how we would react to the same punishment. Scottie Pippen, reaching for a rebound, would be smashed to the floor by the elbows of some six-foot-nine inch, two-hundred-and-forty-pound power forward on the opposing team who came down full-force on his back. Pippen would wince and stay down—and fifteen seconds later he'd be running up the court again. On the TV broadcast of the game the play-by-play man might say, "Scottie really got hammered on that one!" Then the narrative of the night would continue.

Yet it was the kind of brutal blow that would send the rest of us to a doctor, and perhaps keep us home from work for days or even more. Yes, the players were, by definition, in much better condition than the rest of us. That still didn't completely explain how they managed to accept the kinds of things that went on under the basket as a customary component of their workday, to be dealt with stoically and shrugged off, as if all this were part of some purely mental process, able to be willed away.

It wasn't only the pounding. On the morning of a game against the Miami Heat, the newspapers said Jordan had been stricken with a stomach virus so noxious that he hadn't been able to get out of bed the day before. There was a strain of flu going around Chicago that week that was thinning out the ranks of offices and factories; it was an especially vicious one, and apparently Jordan had caught it.

Some of the sportswriters at the Stadium early that night reacted skeptically to the stories; "He's just resting up for Detroit tomorrow night," one of them said, expecting him not to show. Even the ones who believed he was truly ill didn't seem too concerned. Cheryl Raye, a radio reporter who had covered the team for a number of seasons, told me, "Oh, we have six M.J. flus a year. He comes out and scores fifty-seven points."

When he arrived he looked awful. He was sweating and in a lousy mood, and some of the other players said he told them he'd been running to the bathroom throughout the entire night before and most of this day. He spoke to almost no one, then went out and scored fifteen points in the first half. At halftime the team physician, Dr. John Hefferon, went down to see him, and said to me as we waited for the second half to begin, "He's really sick."

Which led to the question: Exactly what does being sick mean in this league? You could say that the strong first-half performance was just a case of Jordan deciding, "I may be sick, but as long as I'm here . . ." But the idea of being sick and scoring fifteen points in a half against professional athletes made no sense, at least in the context most of us place being sick, particularly with stomach flu. When you're sick you're debilitated; when you're sick you feel so bad you can't even think about doing your work.

With thirty-five seconds to go in the game Jordan had scored thirty-six points. Phil Jackson had rested him a little during the second half, and Jordan, a towel covering his head, had seemed to be in distress while sitting on the bench. The Bulls had appeared to be on the verge of winning it easily, but then Miami closed the gap until the Bulls' lead was almost chipped away. So Jordan had been sent back in.

Thirty-six seconds left, then, and he drove to the basket through three defenders and scored, was fouled, and converted the free throw. He looked as if he might faint. The victory was assured and, even though the game was still going on, the fans started leaving the building in herds, clogging the exits. The Bulls had sewed up the win, and it was late and this was the West Side in winter and they wanted to get home, for all of which reasons it was hard to blame them.

Jordan saw them, he saw the place emptying out, and maybe I was reading too much into it, but his eyes seemed to be wondering why they couldn't wait just a little longer. He was still on the court, having scored thirty-nine points, he was feeling low, and by the time the final buzzer sounded the building was less than half full.

Nights like that helped the Jordan-as-Superman image grow even stronger. People truly wanted to believe that there was nothing he couldn't step into and make himself accomplish. Certainly nothing in the realm of athletics.

One afternoon I asked him if there was anything on a field of play that he flat-out couldn't do.

"I can't skate," he said. "I've never had a pair of ice skates on."

"That's the only thing?" I said.

"I can't swim," he said.

I'd known that; Jordan had readily admitted that he simply couldn't do it.

"If you threw me into the water, I'd be able to survive," he said. "But I never learned how. I grew up near the beach, but I was never taught to swim as a child. And I never have been taught. I just don't know how."

"Do you stay away from the water?" I said.

"I won't go out on a boat unless it's a big boat," he said. "I mean a really big boat, one that will hold sixty or seventy people. Otherwise, I'll say no thanks."

"Do the people who ask you to go on the boat know why you're turning them down?" I said.

"I won't volunteer to people why that is, but if they ask me, I'll tell them," he said. "I'm not ashamed of it or embarrassed about it. But I won't go out on a small boat, even with a life jacket on, because I don't know what would happen to me if I fell in."

"What about parties and corporate receptions?" I said. "Aren't a lot of them held next to swimming pools?"

"Yep," he said. "And I have to go to a lot of those parties."

"Don't they get pretty crowded, next to the pools?" I said.

"I'm always aware at a party like that if there's a chance that I might fall in the water," he said. "If there's a big party around a swimming pool, and there are a lot of people and I think I might get pushed in by accident, I'll make sure I stay away from the edge of the pool. I'll look to see where the deep end is, and I won't stand near it, and even when I'm standing near the shallow end I won't stand very close to the edge."

"Do people notice what you're doing?" I said.

"I don't know whether they do or not," he said. "But I'm always looking at the pool to make sure I'm not too close."

"Do you have any intention ever to learn?" I said.

"I don't think I ever will learn how," he said. "But I do want my children to learn, because they should know how."

I said I found it striking: All of the people all over the world who assume that, when it comes to anything physical, Jordan could make them all look silly. Yet most of them can do this one fairly simple athletic task—something they no longer probably even think of as a skill—and Jordan cannot.

"That's right," he said. "Any four-year-old boy or girl who's just learning to swim can do something that I can't."

"The game doesn't start this early, does it?" the cabdriver said from the front seat.

I was making my usual late-afternoon journey to the Stadium.

"No," I said. "Not until seven-thirty."

"Any particular place you want to be dropped off?" the driver said.

"Players' entrance," I said. That I enjoyed saying those words every cab ride was childish in the extreme, but enjoy it I did. It had become a part of the game-day routine.

"You a player?" the driver said.

"I am," I said.

"Which one?" he said, sarcasm in his voice.

"What, you don't know?" I said.

"No, really," he said, laughing. "Who are you?"

"Horace Grant," I said, happy in the wintertime and delighted to see nightfall coming.

10

THE MOMENT WHEN I REALIZED how goofy I had gotten about these Stadium nights came when I found myself calling Steve Schanwald's office just to be put on hold.

Schanwald, as the Bulls' chief marketing executive, was generally on the phone all day long. Every business that wanted to be linked up with the Bulls, every broadcasting entity that wanted a chance to beam its signal out of the Stadium, every merchandiser that had a Bulls-related scheme it thought would make it rich—all of them rang Schanwald's telephone in the Bulls' offices on North Michigan Avenue. And because Schanwald's phone was constantly busy, new callers got put on hold.

Which was what I wanted.

Because what callers on hold heard was a tape of the spotlight introduction.

The spotlight introduction happened in virtually the same manner at every game, yet somehow it had the power to move people in ways that continued to surprise them.

With all the lights in the Stadium still glaring, the opposing team would be introduced first. Then the lights would go out, and amplified, urgent electronic music would come blasting through the Stadium speaker system. Suddenly, there would be the loudest noise you could ever imagine. The noise was of more than eighteen thousand people screaming, and in any other setting it would have been frightening.

Above the throbbing music, Ray Clay, sitting in the dark at his announcer's station in the middle of the scorer's table, would shout the words:

"And *now,* the starting lineup for *your* Chicago Bulls . . ."

What followed was a tribute that few men or women will

ever know in their lives. For a man to hear that roar at the mention of his name must be so unnatural. Inside the uniforms of the Bulls, though, were human beings, and night after night they heard the sounds and thought their private thoughts. I had talked with each of the starters about it.

The same man's name always was first: "From *Clemson,* a six-ten *forward,* Horace *Grant* . . ."

"It's not that I see the spotlight," Grant said. "It's more that I feel it. You really can feel it. It's warm. That's how you know that the man who runs the spotlight has found you in the darkness. You can feel the heat. It's a welcoming feel."

Next: "A six-seven forward, from *Central* Arkansas, Scottie *Pippen* . . ."

"It's so loud every night that you would never believe that it could get louder," Pippen said. "But once the playoffs started last year it really did get louder. I don't understand how."

Then: "The *man* in the *middle,* from San Francisco, Bill *Cartwright* . . ."

"Do you know when it helps you the most?" Cartwright said. "If you ever come to the game lacking energy. The introduction, and the noise, gets it back for you. No question about it."

By now the noise would be approaching the level of pain. The music would still be pounding, and Ray Clay's voice would strain as he would shout: "A six-two guard, from *Notre* Dame, John *Paxson* . . ."

"Amazingly, it never gets old," Paxson said. "I've been seeing it and hearing it every night for years, and the feeling never wears off. It's hard to articulate—the emotional level just rises. I look in the stands to see if my little boy is standing up. He's four-and-a-half years old, and he comes to see us a lot. I know where he sits, and I try to find him. He and I do the introductions at home—we turn the lights off in the living room, and he pretends he's all the players. I bet there's a lot of houses in Chicago where that goes on. So that's who I'm looking for every night—my little boy."

So the noise would be as loud as you would think noise could possibly be—you would think there was no higher volume imaginable. Then, miraculously, in a moment that moved some fans to tears, the volume would seem to triple. There would still be one player to go.

There is no way to describe the sound in the Stadium. You could hear three words: "From North Carolina . . ."

Then you could hear only raw, shuddering noise.

"I've never heard a word after 'Carolina,' " Jordan said. "It gives me chills, every time. You hope people respect you, but for that immediate moment you know that they do.

"I think they stand up when I come out. I can't see very much in the darkness, but I think they're standing up. The sense of respect that I get from the people . . . I get chill bumps. Sometimes I'm misty-eyed, and it doesn't have anything to do with whether it's a big game or not. I've thought about why I get misty-eyed on those nights, and I don't really know. It will just happen.

"And at the same time, it's a little embarrassing—to have the spotlight on you."

Embarrassing—the spotlight is embarrassing for Michael Jordan?

"It would be for anyone," he said. "I'm not talking about what people usually mean when they say 'in the spotlight.' That usually means that you're in the public eye. I'm used to that. But during the introduction, it's a real spotlight. For that moment, it's just the light on you. I think anyone would be a little self-conscious about that.

"When I'm out there and I'm hearing that noise, I look up toward where the noise is coming from, and I always think the same thing. Even though I can't see many of the people, I think that for some of them this may be the only time they're going to be there. They've never had a ticket before, and they may not have one again, and this is the one night for them. I think about that."

And then, every night, the lights would go back on, like a song suddenly ending, and a basketball game would begin.

And on dreary afternoons at work a person, remembering the feel and the sound of the darkened Stadium, could call the headquarters of the Bulls, ask to be connected with Mr. Schanwald's office, and hope that he was busy on his line.

Because of Jordan's omnipresence in commercials, Americans were almost as familiar with the sound of his voice as with his face. In the breakfast cereal commercial he could say "Ah! Better eat my Wheaties," and there was no question in the mind of the public that the voice was his. They'd seen him and they'd heard him so often that he was like a Robert Redford or a Jack Nicholson. He walked, he talked—he entered their worlds in several dimensions.

Most of the other players, though, had only one way to win the hearts of the public—visually. Basketball fans fell in love with certain players from a distance, and the process was strikingly close to the process that made Tom Mix and Charlie Chaplin international idols back in the days when movies were silent. There's a special kind of chemistry at work that makes certain people exceedingly attractive without the need of words. Their personalities must be able to come through without any accompanying soundtrack.

Or at least without a voice track. Silent movies had organ music in the background; NBA basketball has the roar of excited crowds (along with occasional organ music, come to think of it). Even though most players talked to the sportswriters and broadcasters after games, the strength of their public personalities had little to do with either their words or their voices. Like the silent-movie stars, they were embraced for their heroics on the screen—a television screen now—and their fans read volumes into every trace of a smile, every flash of pain.

Dominique Wilkins of the Atlanta Hawks came across the screen like a matinee idol with the power to make hearts flutter; Dennis Rodman of the Detroit Pistons came across like a wicked-witted espionage operative with sly intentions and a short fuse. Karl Malone of the Utah Jazz was full of quiet menace on the screen; Kevin Johnson of the Phoenix Suns was a good-guy little brother. Kevin McHale of the Boston Celtics had an earnest, workmanlike screen presence. Clyde Drexler of the Portland Trail Blazers was an enigmatic cowboy riding into town and leaving before anyone could figure him out. Fred Roberts of the Milwaukee Bucks was a neighborhood handyman-for-hire with a hint of a secret past.

Whether these men were really like this was beside the point. They made their livings in a profession where, most of the time, they were closely seen and were heard not at all. A Greg Anderson scowl or a Buck Williams pout would, in vivid close-up, be delivered to millions of homes, where viewers would interpret the meaning of what wasn't being said.

To watch the game as a silent movie was to receive little lessons in the craft of basketball. Especially from the intimate vantage point of the courtside press table, close observation revealed an intricate game-within-the game. Bill Cartwright, under the basket, would find himself trapped with the twenty-four-second clock ticking down, and would fire a pass to B. J.

Armstrong, free in the corner. But even as the ball was on its way, defenders would be following it, converging; the Cartwright pass to Armstrong would be six or seven inches to the left, and although Armstrong could easily catch it, the frustration on his face would be testament to his knowledge that he must now do two things—first, pull the ball back to where he'd like it; then, shoot—instead of merely shooting. At this level of play, the fraction of a second it would take to grab the ball and make the adjustment was enough to allow the defenders to catch up and force Armstrong to hurry the shot. You could see him rush his arm movements in a too-quickened effort to trap and then get rid of the ball before the defenders arrived.

Jordan, trying to block a Drexler shot, would realize at the last second that Drexler was going to get the shot off safely, and that the best he could do now was escape picking up a foul. So in midair Jordan would recoil, his face for an instant showing an expression like a little girl makes on a playground when she is trying to avoid stepping in a mud puddle, his fingers raised and splayed, his mouth a circle, part of this a show of innocence for the referee, part of it apparently involuntary, all of it almost dainty. This would come and go in a single beat, one frame in the film.

Sometimes when both teams were racing to pick up an errant ball it would bounce off one player, then another, then a third before skittering out of bounds. A voice—a rarity in the silent movie—would be heard: the referee, yelling, "White's got it, let's go, white!"

White. The color of the Bulls' uniforms. The referee would be announcing that the Bulls had the right to inbound the ball. Jordan—number 23 on the white team—would nod in approval. A flashback to the world of kids playing pickup basketball—shirts and skins—before logos and lawyer/agents and licensed team merchandise. The festooned costumes in these silent movies, the uniforms of the Bulls and their opponents, were copyrighted, trademarked properties, with stiff penalties waiting for anyone foolish enough to dare to infringe. "Let's go, white!" the referee would call, still back on the playground by vestige or by choice, his voice audible only to the players and to the spectators in the first row or two. Not Bulls' ball. Not Chicago ball. White ball. Everyone understood.

* * *

"When was the last time you had a fight?" I asked Jordan one afternoon.

"A fight?" he said. "You mean a fistfight?"

"A fight," I said. "A real one."

He thought for a second.

"I guess it had to have been in ninth grade," he said. "I can't remember having a fight in the years since then."

"Was it with another kid in school?" I said.

"It was with a guy who called me a nigger," he said.

The word sounded so strange coming out of his mouth. The accepted lore on Jordan, repeated endlessly, was that he transcended race. You heard that phrase again and again—Jordan's appeal was so broad and so all-inclusive that he had made race irrelevant.

If he was once a young and hopeful child who could have had no idea that one day he would be Michael Jordan, though, the converse was almost surely true, too: that he was probably once a young and hopeful child who to certain white children was just another nigger. And to hear him use that word now was jarring in the extreme.

"We were supposed to have a baseball game after school," he said. "A friend and I were let out of school early so we could put the chalk lines down on the base paths. It was okay with the teachers and everything—we were excused from school.

"So my friend and I were out on the baseball diamond, and we were chalking the lines, thinking about the game we'd be playing soon, and this kid comes by and asks us what we're doing. Why we're out of school. So I look up from chalking the line and I tell him that we're getting ready for a baseball game.

"And the kid says, 'I don't care what you niggers are doing.' Something like that. But he used that word.

"The thing is, I had been watching the *Roots* miniseries that week—it was being broadcast for the first time. It seemed like everyone in the country was watching it. You'd think that, with everyone watching that show and talking about it, people might be careful about the way they talked. But apparently to this kid it didn't matter. Or maybe he was using that word *because* he'd been seeing *Roots*. I don't know. But he called me that word.

"God, it pissed me off. Ninth grade was my rebellious year

anyway, and I went after him, right there on the baseball diamond. We fought right there."

"Did you win?" I said.

"I think I won," he said. "But I don't know. You get in a fight, everybody loses. But on that one day, yeah, I guess I won. I can still hear him saying that to me. I don't think I even knew the kid."

Arena etiquette:

Numerous times each night, one of the statistics-crew assistants would walk briskly behind press row, dropping flimsy yellow or blue sheets of paper in front of every third or fourth sportswriter.

These were not the end-of-the-quarter or end-of-the-half statistics; those numbers were run off in great quantity, and each reporter at the game was given one of those more comprehensive sheets. These flimsy half-sheets were interim reports, scrawled in pen or pencil on carbon books: a running account of field-goal percentages for the past few minutes, free-throw percentages, rebounds, assists, turnovers—up-to-the-second stuff.

And because there weren't enough of these half-sheets to go around, the stats-crew assistants let them flutter onto the press table every five or six feet, with the understanding that one sportswriter would check them out, then pass them on to his neighbors.

Which is where an appealingly odd form of etiquette came in. The only thing I can compare it to is when the waiter brings wine around in a fancy restaurant, and hands you the first splash in a glass to sip or sniff, and then to either approve or disapprove. If you're like most people, you haven't got the slightest clue whether the wine is any good or not. But you sip or you sniff anyway, usually waiting a few seconds before responding with some stilted and silly sounding version of: "Very nice."

It's a comical scene that I'm sure generations of waiters have howled about back in the privacy of the kitchen. Certainly I've always assumed they've been howling at me when I've been the one unlucky enough to be handed the sip 'n' sniff glass. I envision the waiters in the kitchen almost doubling over, gasping to get out the words: "And then the dork . . . holds the glass up . . ." (great bursts of hilarity here as the waiter and his colleagues tumble to the floor in their mocking mirth) "and he about buries his nose in this swill" (sounds of hoots and of thighs being slapped and air being sucked in) "and he looks back up and he says" (sounds of whooping hyperventilation) "he says, 'That will be fine' " (the sound of a chorus of waiters rolling over and over across the floor, tears flowing down their cheeks, wheezing and bellowing in ridicule and disdain).

At least that's what I've always imagined happens back in the kitchens. And on game nights, when the statistics crew dropped those yellow or blue flimsies onto the press table, I always felt the same way. I didn't know what to do with the numbers. Study them? Take notes from them? Nod at them as if they were meaningful? Comment on them to the guy next to me?

The half-sheet would rest on the table in front of me tauntingly, like one of those barely filled snifters of wine that wasn't going to go anywhere until you deal with it as everyone else at dinner stops what they're doing and waits. So several times each night I would pick a half-sheet up, stare at it, sometimes (just in case someone else at the press table, or someone up in the stands, was looking) raise my eyebrows a little bit, as if a particular statistic was especially compelling—and then, with a weary sideways flip of the hand as if I'd had just about all the significant numbers I needed for the rest of this quarter, thank you very much, pass it along to the sportswriter next to me.

Who always seemed much more at ease with the statistics sheet than I did. But then, some people can fake it with the wineglass in restaurants, too. Doesn't mean they really know anything about wine. Or so I would tell myself as a fast break pounded its way down the court toward us.

My neighbors at the table were starting to rag me a little bit because of my evident high regard for Jordan, and because they realized that spending time talking with him and watching him play—as opposed to reporting the nuts and bolts of the basketball games—was the reason for my constant presence.

So I was getting used to the banter aimed in my direction. One of the reasons I was starting to enjoy the company of these guys so much was that they always tended to put themselves down, too. So many journalists—especially the ones who cover national politics and other grand topics—addressed everything they did with such gravity. These sports reporters, on the other hand, were always going out of their way to protest that the things they wrote about didn't matter, that they worked in the toy department. But the fact was, they were doing deadline work late at night under enormous pressure. There was no other part of the newspaper where a larger percentage of urgent copy came in right on the gun every night, and I was gaining a new appreciation and respect for just how difficult their jobs were.

Thus, when they poked fun at my esteem for Jordan, I realized my best course of action was not only to go along with them, but to give them more ammunition. One night I was sitting between Dave Hoekstra of the *Sun-Times* and Paul Sullivan of the *Tribune,* and Jordan came downcourt and dropped a pass. His error led to a turnover.

Sullivan looked up from his notepad and said, "He's human after all."

"No, that's not it," I said, in the best ponderously mystical tones I could muster. "That was a signal."

"What are you talking about?" Sullivan said.

"It was signal to a child in need somewhere," I said. "He has obviously promised to drop a pass as a signal to the child who's watching at home on TV."

"Shut up," Sullivan said. He'd heard enough of my Babe Ruth theories.

Later Jordan missed an easy shot.

"Signal to that poor child," I said.

"Stop it," Sullivan said.

Toward the end of the game Jordan took a long shot that didn't have much of a chance, and missed badly.

"Now why would he take a shot like that?" Sullivan said.

"Signal," I said.

"He takes it because he's Michael Jordan and he doesn't give a shit," Sullivan said.

"You're so wrong," I said. "Signal. Child at home."

"What if the child doesn't have cable?" Sullivan said.

I had always assumed that professional athletes entered the opening seconds of each new game brimming with anger and invidious energy, or at least with their pulses racing and their minds full of unwavering, concentrated resolve.

Jordan acted like the host of a dinner party. Literally. He was always the final man onto the court—he had a brief last-

minute sideline ritual he invariably performed, during which
he filled his palms with resin and then dusted it all over
Johnny "Red" Kerr, the veteran Bulls TV/radio broadcaster
who did the games from a courtside microphone—and when
he finished doing that and strode to the center of the playing
surface he would greet each of the visiting starters as if they
were guests in his home. It was almost as if he was endeavoring to make the others feel comfortable in the Stadium. He
didn't expect them to come to him—he approached each of
them to shake hands or say something.

I was never sure whether this derived from some basketball
sense of noblesse oblige, or whether it was his clever way of
momentarily disarming the opponents, or what. One thing I
figured out early on was that a lot of these players, when they
got back home, were going to be asked by their friends, and
even by their families, about Jordan. It sounded ridiculous—
these men were all NBA pros, after all, they were supposed to
be stars—yet it had to be the case. In the minds of the public
Jordan was something else entirely, and these extraordinary
athletes, regardless of their own talents, almost certainly had
to go home and hear: "I saw you guys play the Bulls on TV.
What's Michael Jordan really like?"

As Jordan did his little greeter's bit each night, he moved in
a circle, making sure he had a word with each of the five
opponents. The referees, one of whom was balancing the ball
in his hands in the hopes of getting the game going, waited.
The paradox was unmistakable; what he was doing had the
effect of sending the message: Welcome, I'm glad you're here,
have a good time in Chicago, and if there's anything you need,
just let me know. While all five of the visiting starters—not to
mention the more than eighteen thousand other people in the
building—were aware that Jordan was about to do everything
in his power to make sure his guests had the most miserable
possible time while they were in town.

Sometimes this attitude reached loony lengths. In the clos-
ing minutes of a game against Miami—the game Jordan
played during his bout with stomach flu—Craig Hodges was
shooting a free throw at the end of the court next to the Bulls'
bench. Most of the players from both teams were in the vicinity of that foul line, but Jordan stayed down at the other end
of the court, where the visitors' bench was located.

And as Hodges was shooting—this was bizarre—Jordan
walked over to the Miami bench and began making light-

hearted conversation with Ron Rothstein, the head coach of the Heat. Jordan had ensured that Rothstein's team would lose; by coming back into the game to score the last of his thirty-nine points, Jordan was responsible for sending the Heat away from Chicago in defeat.

But here he was, hands on his hips, still in the lineup and still on the court of play but just an inch from the sideline, smiling in his uniform and saying something to Rothstein, who stood there in his business suit and smiled and talked right back. It was easygoing and it was casual and as they conversed Jordan wasn't even paying attention to the NBA contest that was in progress.

Rothstein appeared sincerely pleased, even flattered, that Jordan would do this. Jordan had just beaten him, yet in a way Rothstein seemed elevated to be a part of this little chat. Jordan might as well have been saying, "I hope you had a pleasant visit tonight, and please don't hesitate to come see us again on your next trip to Chicago." The two men continued their conversation, all smiles, as at the other end of the court two basketball teams played a game.

The fathers and sons waited outside every night.

They didn't have tickets; they didn't have any way to get tickets. So the fathers—most of them from the crumbling, impoverished neighborhood that surrounded the Stadium— stood on the sidewalk next to the fence where the players drove in before the games. A lot of the fans screamed and made noise when they caught sight of the Bulls, but the fathers and sons didn't say much. Usually the fathers just stood there in the cold, their hands on their sons' shoulders, and together they watched.

The faces were different every night—different fathers, different sons. They wanted to see any player, but more than anyone else, of course, they wanted to see Jordan. I asked one of the security guards one night whether he thought all of the fathers and sons were from the neighborhood. "They come from all over the world to try to get a glimpse of Michael," the guard said. "They come here from fucking Sweden."

But mostly they came from the neighborhood. The only other place where I had seen something like this—people standing in such respectful silence, looking at a secular building with such reverence and hope—was at Graceland. This, though, was infinitely more poignant. It wasn't hard to imagine the talks at home that had led to this. The sons asking if the fathers could take them to a Bulls game. The fathers knowing there was no way to get a ticket, and no chance of affording one even if it should somehow become available; the fathers swallowing hard one night and deciding to take the sons to stand on the sidewalk in the cold instead, to try to see Jordan driving into the parking lot.

I told Jordan how sad the sight of the fathers and the sons made me feel.

"I know," he said. "I can't get that sight out of my mind. But when you think about it, that's not the saddest thing."

"What do you mean?" I said.

"Think about this when you see the fathers and sons," he said. "Think about how many kids there are who don't have dads to take them. That's who you don't see—the kids who don't even have fathers to ask. At least the kids who are standing there with their dads have fathers, and their fathers care enough to bring them."

I asked him what went through his head as he drove down the ravaged streets around the Stadium every night.

"I don't know why this is," he said, "but instead of thinking about the bad things, I'll find myself trying to think about what good things the people inside those houses may have in their lives. You know what I think about sometimes? I'll look at the windows of the homes, and I'll find myself wondering what Christmas is like for the people inside."

"Christmas?" I said.

"I don't know why it's Christmas that always comes to my mind," he said. "The people in those houses, they have so many bad things to put up with. The crime, the lack of money, maybe the gangs. And the kids, on top of all that, having to walk through that neighborhood to school on those cold winter mornings.

"I've never had to live in a situation like that. Growing up in North Carolina, there just wasn't a situation in my life where I had to live all crowded together with other people, and with snow covering everything in such a bitter wintertime. That's what's so impressive about the neighborhood around the Stadium. It's easy to think about the bad things. But think about this:

"Think about what motivates the people in those houses, day in and day out, to get up and to go out into the world and go through their routine. To go to work, or to go to school. It's really something—just the doing it."

"And when you look at the houses, it's really Christmas that you think about?" I said.

"How do they have Christmas?" he said. "I drive to work and I see the houses, and I wonder, is one gift what they want? If they get the one gift, is that going to make them happy for Christmas? In my house there are going to be ten gifts or fifteen gifts or more, and I drive down those blocks toward the Stadium, and I think, are they waiting for one little gift? It's so crowded, so close, no room to get out and move around. Everyone is on top of each other."

I mentioned all the BMWs and Mercedes that the fans with so much money drove to the games. I asked Jordan if he thought that seeing all the obscenely expensive cars made the people in the neighborhood more frustrated than ever—whether he thought that seeing the wealthy fans in their fancy cars overwhelmed the neighborhood people with renewed anger and resentment.

"I'm not sure," Jordan said. "Maybe so. But maybe it's not really a case of the people in the neighborhood resenting it. In a way, it may even be a goal for them to have. It may represent what else is out there."

"Do you really think so?" I said. "Do you think that's right? I don't know."

"I don't know, either," he said. "I don't think anyone really does, unless you live there."

I was going steadily to Juvenile Court, continuing to work on the case of the little girl who had been taken away from the people who had brought her up, the people she had loved.

It didn't take many minutes in that building to yank me back to the reality the Stadium nights were helping to anesthetize. I could kid around by calling that Bulls front-office phone number to listen to the spotlight introduction tape; I could even joke with Paul Sullivan about Jordan missing shots to send Babe Ruth–style signals to some apocryphal child in need. All of that was okay, and all of that made me smile.

At the Juvenile Court building, though, it was hard to find a smile anywhere. The children in need there were real, and often their need was so desperate that your heart began to hurt as you walked the hallways. The child I was writing about was being forbidden to see or talk on the telephone to the foster parents she had cherished, and from whom she had been taken by the judge; astonishingly, there were reports that the former prostitute who had gotten her back and the former prostitute's boyfriend were forbidding the child even to speak about the foster parents in their home. They had won her, and now they possessed her, and they were forcing her not only to give up the parents she loved, but never to talk about them.

I had gone to the governor of Illinois, James Thompson, to help with the case, and he had gotten involved on the child's behalf. Now, though, Thompson was leaving office, and I was in contact with the incoming governor, Jim Edgar, to seek his intervention. He said he was interested in doing something, but he had not yet taken over. While I waited the weeks went by, and the child was kept away from the people she had loved the most, and on the days I went to that Juvenile Court the joyous Stadium nights seemed like a distant mirage. Once in a while in the hallways of the courthouse I would see a boy wearing a Michael Jordan T-shirt, or a pair of Air Jordan shoes he had somehow managed to obtain. In that building of pain and tears I would see Jordan's face smiling back at me from where it had been printed in glad colors on a piece of cloth.

11

"**I**T'S PROBABLY JUST AS WELL that people can't hear," Jordan said, laughing.

I had told him about the silent-movie feel of watching the games; I had told him that even when everyone in the arena saw him and the other players talking on the court, we had no idea in the midst of all the crowd noise what was being said.

"It's like at the end of a talk show," I said. "You'll watch and listen to the whole show, and the conversations may or may not be interesting. But then at the end, after the host has said goodbye and the theme song is playing, you'll see him lean over and whisper something to the guest next to him. You'll see them talking, but you won't hear them. And all of a sudden that becomes more interesting than anything you've heard them say. Because you don't know, and you can only wonder about it."

"So you think people are wondering what we say?" Jordan said.

"Of course," I said. "That surprises you?"

"I guess," he said. "It's usually nothing very important. I'll say to one of my teammates, 'What's the call?' or 'What's the next play?' Pretty basic stuff."

Basic to him, but another facet of the interior world that the players live in and the rest of us don't. He seemed genuinely disbelieving that a lot of people could be trying to figure out what the on-court dialogue might be. "It's just basketball stuff," he said. "It's just a lot of basketball talk."

"Think of what you might have specifically said," I asked him.

He thought for a moment. "Usually it has to do with something that's going on right that second," he said. "I might say to Scottie, 'My man is overguarding me, he's guarding me too close. I'm going to go back-door on him and I'll look for a lob.' Something I'll want to do right then. Just stuff for the next play."

"But there are times when you seem to pull one of your teammates aside and almost lecture him," I said. "Like you're going for a private walk with him because you have to tell him something."

"Give me an example," he said.

"With Horace Grant," I said. "He'll be called for a foul, and he'll disagree with the call, and you'll walk him away and you'll be talking to him a mile a minute."

"On something like that, I'll just be saying, 'Calm down, don't get a tech,' " Jordan said. "I'll be saying, 'You're not going to be able to change this call. Just let it go. The ref's not going to change his mind.' "

"Sometimes when Phil Jackson gets exercised, you seem to be telling him that, too," I said.

"He doesn't like that," Jordan said.

"Even if you're trying to calm him down?" I said.

"Phil feels like he's always in charge," Jordan said. "He hates it if I touch him if I see that he's getting angry. He really doesn't like it. He warns me—he tells me, 'Don't grab me.' "

"You'll talk to the opponents, too," I said. "It looks like you're goading them a little bit at times."

"I am," he said. "Especially if someone is trying to stop me from scoring. I'll come down the court and I'll say, 'You can't guard me.' Or I'll say, 'This could be an all-day job for you.' I like to play with their confidence and piss them off a little bit. I do it for a reason. I do it so that I get into their heads, because as soon as I'm in a guy's head, then I have him beaten."

"Can you tell when it's working?" I said.

"Oh, yeah," Jordan said. "If a guy has four fouls on him, I'll be next to him on the court and I'll say, 'You know, you've only got two fouls left.' Or just as I'm getting ready to drive on someone I'll say, 'You're about to get an education. You're going to flight school.' I'll do more of that stuff when I know it's getting to someone."

"They must do it to you, too," I said.

"Fine," he said. "Good. I like it when they do. It challenges me. If they talk to me, I'm going to get them."

* * *

Magic Johnson met Jordan and Bill Cartwright in the middle
of the floor. Within a year this scene would seem like something out of a time capsule, but on this night Johnson was
captain of the Lakers, and in that role he gathered with Bulls
co-captains Jordan and Cartwright, and with the referees.

This nightly center-court conference was not televised; unlike the coin toss in football, the meeting of the captains in the
NBA was a quick, largely unnoticed and rudimentary piece of
necessary business. Even the setting was devoid of big-league
glamour. Each night the ball boys would roll out a battered
ball cart, painted with the words "Spalding: Official Game
Ball of the NBA," and that's where the captains would con-
gregate. The cheesy-looking cart, with the balls resting on top,
was something you might find in the storeroom of a community recreation center. Tonight, here the pleasingly crummy
cart was again, and, incongruously, two of the people talking
in the airspace above it were two of the most famous men in
the world.

Magic wasn't a smiler; I had noticed that earlier, when he
had come out to warm up. His smile was his calling card, and
he displayed it often and willingly, especially when cameras
were trained on him, but it was not his natural expression. I
had seen him in so many commercials and advertisements, I
had seen that radiant smile beaming off so many magazine
covers, that to look at him in person for the first time was to
take note of the obvious: that as with most of us, a smile was
something he chose to wear when he wanted to.

Talking with Jordan and Cartwright, Johnson seemed to be
a serious and even quiet man. The sight of Johnson and Jordan together was like seeing, say, the logos of General Motors
and Apple Computers; Johnson when he smiled and Jordan
when he soared were two of the most powerful symbols in the
heady universe of global business, and their corporate entities
were themselves.

Johnson did not smile now, and Jordan did not soar; instead they methodically went through this nightly untelevised,
unamplified meeting with the referees, and when it ended
Johnson said, "I'll see you," and Jordan said, "Yeah, see you
later." On the sports pages the win-loss records of the Bulls
and the Los Angeles Lakers were being meticulously recorded, day by day. I had no context of other seasons in which

to place this one, and while for me it was my first as a regular inhabitant of an NBA arena, for most of the fans and players —for Jordan and for Johnson—it was one season among many. Still, the schedule of the games, printed well ahead of opening night and determining months in advance where everyone would be on each evening of winter, was providing a kind of symmetry for me, a symmetry I found agreeable, and I understood how so many people, athletes and spectators, could get used to planning their nights by that schedule. A schedule, unlike the rest of life, is rigid; a schedule contains no surprises. Magic Johnson, in warm-up pants and his game jersey, walked away from the banged-up and chipped old ball cart.

"I just need a minute," Hubie Brown said with some agitation in his voice. "This was supposed to have been arranged."

Brown, a former coach of the New York Knicks, was in town to serve as a color commentator for the TNT national broadcast of the Bulls-Lakers game. He was imploring one of the Bulls' front-office staff to get him together with Jordan— not for an on-camera interview, but just for a few person-to-person words.

To a lot of people, television work seems better than coaching—less pressure, easier hours, higher prestige. It's not hard to understand, though, how former coaches always seem to think that a TV job is somehow inevitably lesser than a coaching job. When you're a coach, you're a boss in the arenas, you set the agenda; when you're a broadcaster, no matter how famous, you're one step removed.

A coach can tell basketball players what to do and when to do it. A broadcaster can only ask for an audience with them. It's important for a broadcaster to be granted that audience, if only so, at some point during the contest, he can say into the microphone: "I was talking with Michael before the game, and he said . . ."

It's not name-dropping; it's not being a blowhard. It's simply one of the things that broadcasters end up doing. They wait around for a few seconds with a player, so they can allude to those few seconds later, when they're on the air. The viewers never see the broadcasters asking and waiting for the few minutes with the player, never see the broadcasters in their roles as supplicants. It's a small indignity, as indignities go, and it's something that coaches never have to put up with. Former coaches do, and Hubie Brown waited for Jordan.

"Let's go, Chicago!" the Luvabulls chanted from their post underneath and behind the basket.

It was a pretty safe bet that the Luvabulls would never produce a Paula Abdul. Nothing at all against the young women who served on the Bulls' dancing/cheering squad; their skills very well may have been just as finely tuned as those of the women who danced with the famous Laker Girls. It was merely a matter of opportunity, or lack of it. Chicago is not Los Angeles, and never will be; the Stadium crowd is sparse on talent agents and movie producers, tending more to podiatrists and commodities traders. In Los Angeles the Laker Girls know that they may be discovered by a show-business heavyweight at any moment during any game; at the Stadium the streets outside are covered with snow and ice, and what waits for the Luvabulls after a game is usually just the forty-minute commute back to Berwyn or Elk Grove Village.

The very word "Lakers" has an L.A. feel to it today; you hear the word and you envision the gold uniforms and the celebrity-heavy crowds and the sense of West Coast cachet. "Lakers" is a word with contemporary Southern California resonance, right up there with "Spago" and "Paramount"; it is a word that seems to be wearing pricey sunglasses. It wasn't a Los Angeles word to start with; until 1960 the Lakers were the Minneapolis Lakers, a team from the vast northern Land of Lakes, with big, bony, poker-faced, bespectacled George Mikan as its no-frills star and symbol, and about as much high-fashion status as a Sunday night fish fry. But American culture is nothing if not malleable, and now "Lakers" is a Hollywood word that has everything and nothing to do with Hollywood, an immensely valuable trademark word that people all over the planet immediately connect to a place quite short on lakes.

If some things change seamlessly, however, some things manage to change not at all. Magic Johnson, fifteen feet to the left of the basket, dribbled high, getting ready to shoot. Jordan, in front of him, jumped up and down, up and down, up and down. On their uniforms the Lakers wore the copyrighted team name that had long since lost any association with its Minnesota birthplace, and Jordan and Johnson were a pair of multinational logos themselves, but once they were children with only one thing to separate them from other children—their fervidly competitive, ambition-fueled talent—and now Jordan was jumping up and down, up and down, maybe not even having time to think about what he was doing, reading a need from somewhere inside himself to get in the way of Johnson's shot. On the Laker bench, James Worthy called loudly to his teammate, "Wait for the shot! Wait for the shot! Wait for the shot!" This had nothing to do with marketing and nothing to do with fame, and Johnson did wait for the shot as Jordan moved ever closer.

If one of my reasons for being at the Stadium was to get away from the more appalling sides of life, I could have done very well without ever having to witness the Diaper Derby.

The Diaper Derby, it turned out, was one more part of the total-entertainment-package concept. At halftime three babies were placed on their hands and knees on one of the foul lines. Then, to the accompaniment of music from the P.A. system and howls from the crowd, they were supposed to race the length of the court. Crawling.

"I can't believe this," I said to the person next to me.

"This is awful," I heard a voice behind me say.

The parents of the babies—promised prizes if their son or daughter came out the winner—faced the children and goaded them on. The parents walked backward down the hardwood, attempting to lure their infants to follow them. The packed Stadium was reverberating with noise; people all the way up to the ceiling were shouting for their favorite baby. Two of the babies froze where they were, not understanding what was going on; one began to cry as his parents motioned impatiently for him to crawl. A father bounced a minibasketball in front of his baby, trying to make the baby lunge forward toward it.

Thankfully, after a few minutes this ended. One baby crawled the length of the court until he reached the other foul line. The crowd erupted in cheers, and the event was over.

Maybe.

Because it wasn't hard to imagine the scene in some psychiatrist's office, thirty or forty years from now. The psychiatrist, a puzzled expression on his face, is saying to his patient: "Now, will you explain this recurring dream to me again?"

And the patient is saying: "I don't understand it. It's the same dream every night. I'm down on my hands and knees in

a huge building, and thousands upon thousands of people are
screaming at me. . . ."

Sometimes the things Jordan did on the court were so beautiful, yet seemed so effortless, that it became possible to take
them for granted.

He would float past a defender, shift the ball from hand to
hand, look off in one direction, and then flip the ball onto the
backboard, where it kissed the glass, turned a quarter-revolu-
tion, then sank through the net without ruffling the strands of
rope. Or he would find himself guarded closely in the
backcourt, would hold the ball with one hand down by his
side, would motion with his knee as if he were going to drive
the lane—then leap backward, in a move that looked like
retreat but was the exact opposite, and startle everyone in the
building by launching the ball skyward on a perfect path to the
hoop, where it would drop neatly in as every eye in the Stadium watched, except for Jordan's eyes; he would already be
turning the other way, getting ready to play defense.

During the Laker game, in the midst of one of those moments, a statistics assistant handed me a scoresheet. The fun-
damental preposterousness of this hit me once again; a few
feet in front of me was Jordan doing these impossible, radiant
things, and in my hands was a piece of paper that reduced it
all to figures. I glanced down to see what percentage of his
shots he was making; when I looked up he had one hand
extended while, with the other, he snaked the ball under a
defender's outreached arm and twisted a soft shot toward the
basket. Cold numerals versus warm and fragile grace.

There was an out-of-town sportswriter sitting next to me,
and later in the game, while Jordan was bringing the ball
downcourt, I took a glimpse at the screen of his portable computer, to see what he was writing. These were the opening
words of his lead paragraph:

"Expansion teams have lost 28 straight road games going
into tonight. . . ."

Maybe it was explainable; maybe he was merely working on
some advance story that had to be filed the next day. But I
wondered how he could possibly look out at the loveliness of
what was going on in front of us, then look down at his keyboard and type those particular words. How can you see glory
and type statistics? Maybe he was right and I was wrong,

though; maybe when you see something like this long enough, you inevitably turn it all into numbers.

I looked out onto the court, and I hoped not.

It would usually be almost ten o'clock when I left the Stadium after a game. Even if I'd been feeling tired at work late in the afternoon, the excitement of the arena would have me full of nervous energy by the time the game ended. I'd asked Bill Cartwright about this feeling; he had said, "Afterwards, I can never get to sleep for hours. It's like anyone who has a night job—they're not going to fall asleep right after their shift ends. If you told me that I had to go to sleep after a game? It would never happen. I'm up for hours, no matter what."

Watching Magic Johnson leave the court after the Bulls had defeated the Lakers 114-103, I wondered whether he felt the same way. Part of me thought that he shouldn't even have to be here. He was a legend and a multimillionaire and an endorsement king; it was basketball that got him here in the first place, but couldn't nights like this one just be ceded to him? We know you have the capacity to be here and play basketball well, so we'll grant it to you on faith, like a tap-in putt?

He headed toward a dank locker room, a shower, and the bus.

Christmas was almost here. Between working on the column all day at the office, and heading to the Stadium at night, I had neglected to do any shopping.

I went to an arena concession stand and stocked up on all-purpose gifts: Bulls boxer shorts, suitable for wear by both men and women. As I walked away with my purchases, I hid them, just in case anyone was looking.

The only time I ever sensed a rolling-of-the-eyes reaction in Jordan was when I made him talk about Elvis. But that was okay; most of my friends rolled their eyes, too, when I brought up Elvis.

I thought it was a good idea to at least tease Jordan into thinking about the parallels in their lives. Not the sad stuff—just the ascension of both of them, at such a young age, to international idolatry. Jordan was handling it much better than Elvis had been able to, but I felt he ought to give some thought to the Life of Elvis, just because he was one of the few people who was going through something close to what

Elvis had gone through. I was kidding and I wasn't kidding; I brought up Elvis partly because I knew it bugged Jordan, but I also believed that some of the similarities of their experiences were real.

For his part, this theory escaped him.

"So what do you know about him?" I said.

Rolling of eyes.

"Really—what do you know about him?"

"I used to watch him in movies and stuff," Jordan said.

"So you were aware of all the excitement around him," I said, a fisherman in a lifeless pond.

"It was before my time," Jordan said. "My impression of him was that when he came along, he was really different, and that he started a lot of fads." I felt appreciative of Jordan's earnestness as he was saying this; he was like a kid trying to please a hopeful teacher by delivering an oral book report about something he hadn't read and had no intention of ever reading.

Still, he had to learn.

"So that's all you know?" I said. "He was different and he started fads?"

"It's hard for me to relate to him, because I wasn't around for that," Jordan said.

True enough. Jordan was born in 1963; by that time, Elvis was already out of the army and in his bad-movie phase. When Elvis died in 1977, Jordan was only fourteen. A more compassionate man than I would have let it go.

"What else?" I said.

"What else what?" Jordan said.

"What else do you know about Elvis? This is important."

"I never had his records in my collection," he said. "He wasn't in my age bracket. It was toward the end of his life that I was aware he was alive."

He was trying so hard.

"So you do remember seeing him," I said.

"I mostly knew him from the movies that were on TV," Jordan said. "I didn't make a point of watching the movies, but when they came on sometimes I saw them. All I remember about the movies is that the women always loved him. Or loved his character. He was very likable in the movies. You wondered whether in real life he was like that person in the movies."

Silence from me.

More silence.

"Was he?" Jordan said.

"Was he what?" I said, sensing a breakthrough.

"Was he like that person in the movies?" Jordan said.

All right. A glimmer of interest at last.

"A little bit," I said. "He kind of was and he kind of wasn't."

Now it was time to hook him and reel him in.

"Do you know where he used to play when he came to Chicago?" I said, feigning casualness.

"Where?" Jordan said.

I paused for dramatic effect.

"The Stadium," I said, playing my trump card. I knew that one would get him.

"Is that right," Jordan said. No interest at all. Such an absence of interest, in fact, I knew I'd been wrong when I'd sensed interest in his question about the movie roles.

"He did," I said, trying to rekindle things. "He played the same place you play. He even came in through Gate 3½."

"Is that right," Jordan said again, with—if this is possible—even less enthusiasm.

Some day he'd understand. He wasn't the first smart person I'd met who was slow to pick up on the Meaning of Elvis.

"Yep," I said. "Same building. Right in the Stadium. Walked through the same gate. I'm not kidding."

"No one ever told me that," Jordan said, fading.

"I'm not boring you with this, am I?" I said.

"No, no," Jordan said, ready to doze.

"Because I don't think Elvis is a boring topic," I said.

"I know you don't," he said.

"I really liked Elvis," I said.

"I know you did," he said.

"I used to take my daughter to Bulls games," the cabdriver said on Christmas. "When she was a little girl."

We were driving past the locked-up corned beef and pickle warehouses on Randolph Street, particularly desolate on the holiday afternoon.

"No one ever used to want to go to the games," he said. "I could drive my cab right up to the Stadium, park it on the street, walk in, and buy my tickets at the box office."

At first I'd figured I wouldn't go to the game on Christmas, but then, at the last minute, my family urged me to go on out for a few hours. A thoughtful and exceedingly generous stocking-stuffer, as it were, from them to me. This was an afternoon game against the Detroit Pistons, broadcast nationally on NBC; I said I'd be back home well before dinner.

"There would be so few people at the games most nights," the cabdriver said, "you could buy the cheapest seats in the house, way up in the balcony, and then move down to the best seats near the court, and no one would stop you. My daughter's grown up now. I'd like to take her again some day."

"Do you think you'll do it?" I said.

"I doubt it," he said. "You can't just buy a ticket anymore. It's changed now."

"What do you think has changed?" I said.

He laughed. "You *know* what's changed," he said. "Michael Jordan came to town."

Jordan's wife had given birth to their second son the day before. Now, on Christmas, Jordan was accepting congratulations at the Stadium. I steered clear of him; it seemed that there were literally hundreds of people—reporters, cops, building workers, everyone—lining up wanting to shake his hand.

"He can't even give out cigars," one of the Bulls' office staff people told me. "He's afraid someone would make a big deal out of him advocating tobacco use if he did."

I'd eaten at home; I went down to the press buffet in the basement to get a paper cup of ice water, but I didn't stay around. It was too depressing—it was one thing to draw the family dinner analogy on most nights, but to see the regulars eating their Christmas dinner here was too much. Chuck Daly, the coach of the Pistons, was hanging around the buffet room, a traveling businessman on the road on Christmas Day. Upstairs, the ball boys had on their customary satin jackets with "Near North Insurance" sewn on the back, but they were wearing red Santa hats today, as were the cocktail waitresses who served the patrons in the expensive seats.

Setting up to work at the *Sun-Times*'s position at the press table, Dave Hoekstra said, "I only bought Christmas gifts for two people—you and Horace." I was strangely yet undeniably touched that he'd think to do that. He'd gotten the same joke gift for Grant and for me—it was a pair of plastic goggles made to look like women's legs, the kind of corny thing your dad might have purchased as a gag for a friend at a big-city novelty shop, circa 1955—and it was a takeoff on the goggles

Grant wore during the games. Still, silly as the goggle-gift was, it was a sign that perhaps some of the good sentiments I was having about coming here were being reciprocated, and it made me feel genuinely gratified that Hoekstra had done it. Grant, on his way to the court for warm-ups, saw me opening the package and said, "You too, huh?"

On the P.A. system, the Beach Boys song "The Man With All the Toys" was playing; I was a senior in high school when that song came out, and it was supposed to be a gimmick record—the twist was that the Beach Boys were winking a little bit, because it was unusual for a rock group to write and sing a Christmas song. By now the Beach Boys were as mainstream as Christmas itself, and on the P.A. "The Man With All the Toys" segued into Gene Autry singing "Rudolph the Red-Nosed Reindeer," and there didn't seem to be all that much of a difference in tone between the two songs.

When the game started Bill Laimbeer of the Pistons was bellowing directions to his teammates on the court, and up on the NBC camera platform I could see that the network crew had erected a little tree, complete with decorations and lights, to brighten their trip to Chicago on a day when no one wanted to be working. There were 18,676 in the Stadium, and for a moment I was puzzled about why all those people would come out on this particular day, when they could have stayed home and watched the game just as easily. But I was present, too, I had made the same decision to be here. Jordan was on his way to scoring thirty-seven points on the day after his son was born, and during a time-out the P.A. system featured another song that the Beach Boys had recorded during that high-school Christmas season past. It was called "Little Saint Nick"; I used to happily cruise the winter streets of central Ohio with my friends as "Little Saint Nick" played on the car radio during our Christmas vacation from school, in that last winter before we all left town and went our separate ways, and when the game resumed in the Stadium a loud chant started coming from up near the rafters. It took me a second to decipher the words, and then I figured out what they were. The words were "Detroit sucks," hollered over and over in unison on Christmas Day. "Detroit sucks," the voices chanted, "Detroit sucks," and for a second I found myself wondering what I was doing here.

* * *

Four nights later, against the Seattle Supersonics, Pippen and Jordan raced downcourt on a fast break, and Jordan darted for the basket and Pippen, appearing not even to look, fired a perfect pass behind his back, catching Jordan at precisely the right instant to make the basket, and the entire building began to shake, so fierce was the devotion and adoration of the fans, who were on their feet and screaming and waving their arms in the air in tribute. Moments like that were bestowed upon Jordan all the time, and Pippen was beginning to receive more of them, too, and the eighteen-thousand-plus voices cried out in praise for the skill of the two men, and as I watched all of it I knew that most people on this earth would trade a great deal and give up a great deal if, in their whole lives, they could have just one moment like that. One.

12

FROM THE CHAIR in front of his dressing cubicle on a frosty January Saturday night, Jordan activated the VCR attached to the locker-room television set, using a remote control wand he held in his hand.

He hit the "Play" button. On the screen, a basketball game appeared. The players in the white uniforms were the same players who, in the locker room tonight, had white uniforms folded neatly on the carpet in front of them as, in their street clothes, they flipped through mail and thought about getting dressed for the game.

Tonight's contest would be against Cleveland; the tape was of the last time the two teams had met, three weeks earlier. The assistant coaches always arranged for tapes of the Bulls' previous games against that day's opponents to be available in the locker room—clearly the videotapes were just as vivid a reminder of a specific team's strengths and weaknesses as any chalkboard scouting report. Jordan, a fresh number 23 jersey at his feet, sat back in his shirt and tie and glanced at the screen.

"Jordan with the steal!" the TV announcer, in a voice filled with excitement, screamed. On the screen Jordan had just grabbed the ball from in front of a Cleveland player and was sprinting down the court toward the basket.

From the TV monitor came the sounds of the crowd roaring. Jordan—the real Jordan, the one who had turned the TV and VCR on—was no longer looking. Resting on top of his right knee was one of the shoes he would wear in tonight's game; he was checking the laces to make sure they were tight enough.

"Michael came to play tonight!" the announcer's voice

boomed, and on the screen Jordan continued to do athleti-
cally heroic things. If any of the players were struck by the
oddity of all this, by the juxtaposition of their electronic images and their human selves, they did not show it. This was
something they were quite accustomed to—living on a TV
screen and living in the real world, all at the same time.

"Michael Jordan!" the TV announcer called out.

Jordan was leaning forward in his chair, rummaging
through the gym bag at his feet, searching for something he
couldn't seem to find.

"Hey, B.J.," Scottie Pippen said in a deep and tired monotone, his voice directed at the open locker-room door. But
B. J. Armstrong was already out the doorway, on his way
upstairs to warm up on the court.

"Close the door," Pippen said to the Armstrong who was no
longer there.

Pippen's cubicle was directly in the line of the draft from
the doorway. Whenever the door opened, a cold breeze came
straight in and hit him. In addition to that, anyone standing
out in the basement hallway could look right in at him.

Pippen resignedly got up, walked to the door, and closed it.
His carriage left little doubt that, over the course of a long
season, a lot of his teammates neglected to remember to close
that door on a lot of chilly nights.

"The Bulls are on a run!" the voice of the TV broadcaster
screamed, accompanied by frenzied cheers.

Not one eye in the locker room was on the screen. Cliff
Levingston stood up from the chair in front of his cubicle,
walked to the door, and departed for warm-ups.

"Hey, Cliff," Pippen said.

Levingston was gone and the door was open.

"Close the door," Pippen said.

Most nights Jordan arrived at the Stadium in a suit and tie.
Part of the reason for this had to be that he knew there were
always going to be television cameras recording his every
move and every word. On the slushy winter streets of Chicago
it might have been more convenient for him to come to work
in boots, a pair of jeans, and a bulky overcoat. Television,
though, is merciless; when you're watching something at home
you make a judgment quickly, and it's a judgment that tends
to last. Whether by design or by instinct, Jordan seemed determined never to let people he couldn't even see sit in their

living rooms or bedrooms and say, "Michael looks like a slob tonight."

So suit and tie it was—and always clothing with a conservative, if elegant, color and cut. In the Jordan era, memories of the mid-1970s days of the NBA—the days when professional basketball seemed almost endangered as a national entertainment—were fading fast. The image of the league then had been closer to *Superfly* than to Disney World; most fans were probably willing to believe that drug deals were not actually being consummated *on* the court, but beyond that the aura of the NBA was more than a little seamy, more than a little redolent of contraband and unsavory back-passageway concealments.

To avid basketball fans of the seventies, none of this was important when placed next to the fact that, as always, the best players in the world were competing in NBA arenas every night. To the rest of the public, though, the NBA in those years was a sports league that was becoming increasingly easy to avoid. People were generally careful not to cast this as a baldly anti-black sentiment; maybe they thought in racial terms or maybe they didn't, but somewhere in the recesses of their minds there was something that bothered them about the NBA. The off-kilter flash of the league in those days was both its identifying characteristic and the feature that seemed destined to forever hold it down.

If this was unfair to the league and to the sport of basketball, it was even more unfair to black athletes—and black fans. The snickering, unspoken professional sports equation back then seemed to be: NBA = black league = jewel-encrusted drug addicts. As if by being a talented black basketball player with money to spend, a man must also inherently be an ostentatious, gaudy dope consumer. A clause was added to the NBA rule book: "The officials shall not permit players to play with any type of hand, arm, face, nose, ear, head or neck jewelry." The stereotype was mean-spirited and harmful, but it was there; for children growing up, the image of the NBA was some impure melding of athletic superiority and tawdry garishness.

"You always have your own perceptions about what success looks like," Jordan told me one night. As usual, he was dressed much better than most downtown bankers; as always, he was dressed much better than I was.

"I was very young when I came into the NBA, and to me

what success meant was a nice car and jewelry and a fur coat," he said. "I was making a good salary that first year, and I was doing well in the NBA, and I really thought that that's what you did when you were doing well. That was the sign that you were a successful person.

"So that first year, I did all of that. I bought myself a fur coat—it was a Russian raccoon coat—and I wore all these necklaces, these chains. And I think even as I was doing that, I realized, 'That's not the person I am.' "

"Then why did you do it?" I said.

"I was a successful rookie in the NBA, and I thought that was what a professional basketball player looked like and dressed like. Like, if you didn't look and dress like that, you weren't successful. I was copying. I didn't know, so I copied.

"I guess I thought that was the only way to show the world I was successful. Like I had to show people. And inside I think I understood that it was giving a bad perception of me as a person, because that's not who I was. It's not that I was trying to be an arrogant person—it's just that I thought that's the way a successful person was supposed to be. I saw the other players, the older guys, and that's how they were dressing and looking, so that's what I did, too. The coats and the rings and the necklaces."

"When did you figure all of this out?" I said.

"When I went to the All-Star Game my rookie season, I started hearing that the older players were saying things behind my back. They were saying, 'Who does he think he is?' They were saying that I was full of myself and that I was cocky and that I had a bad attitude, and the truth of it was, all I was trying to do was to be like them. And they froze me out during the game, they kept the ball away from me, and I kept hearing that they were saying those things about me.

"And I was really shattered. Because I didn't know—I was just following their lead, really. I wasn't so much different from a younger kid in high school who wants to be like the bigger kids. So the combination of that, and the fact that I knew being like that wasn't really me in the first place, made me stop trying to be like them. I didn't want the fur coats or the jewelry anyway, so I just stopped. If they weren't going to accept me, they weren't going to accept me."

There were some people, I told him, who said that his physical appearance was a calculated attempt to soothe and prove palatable to men and women who had been frightened away by the old NBA. That the gentling of the image came from marketing savvy, not human instinct. "Michael Jordan" was a name that had a softer sound to it than "Mike Jordan." The close-cropped haircut was an almost subliminal reassurance to a threatened public after the NBA years of towering Afros.

"My name has always been Michael on the public address system, but Mike to the people who really knew me," he said. "I never had an Afro, even when I was younger. People can think whatever they want to think.

"Basically, with all of this, I just made the decision that I wanted to go back to who I really was, because whoever I was trying to be that first year, it wasn't me. I looked around me and I said, 'This isn't me,' and I stopped trying to fit in with people who obviously didn't want me anyway."

"And now?" I said.

"Now when I look in the mirror, I like the person I see," he said.

Phil Jackson came into the empty arena early one night while Jordan and I were talking. "Evening, Bob," he said, passing me first. "Evening, M.J." He continued downstairs to his office.

I found Jackson to be a pleasingly mysterious figure. The broad outlines of his life—member of the 1973 world champion New York Knicks, iconoclastic maverick in his youth, voracious reader—were staples of the sports pages. Undoubtedly, there was truth in all of that. But what intrigued me the most about Jackson was that he seemed to serve as a kind of walking Rorschach test for everyone who observed him.

That's the case with a lot of people in authority, especially those who are neither loud nor loquacious. If you're the boss, and you don't go around spilling your inner thoughts and fears to anyone who asks, the people around you will start to read qualities into you. If you don't tell them who you are, they'll try to figure it out on their own. Which is where the Rorschach test theory came in. The test, of course, is a staple in psychiatry; it is the much-parodied test in which patients are asked to look at inkblot patterns and to tell the examiner what shapes the patterns form. The key is that there is no right answer; the answers tell much more about the patients than about the inkblots.

So it is with certain people. As Jackson walked past Jordan and me after saying hello, here's what I saw: a man arriving at work who, in a matter of hours, would be in the middle of a boisterous arena, making decisions that would immediately be critiqued not only by the eighteen thousand witnesses present, but by many more watching on TV. What I saw now, in the temporarily quiet building, was a man who by the very nature of his job must always be alone. He had to know his players as well as anyone else in the world knew them, but he could not truly become their friend, because he had to judge them nightly and, ultimately, perhaps hurt them and even deprive them of their livelihoods. He had to court the fans and the press, but keep them at more than arm's length, too, because even if he heeded their constant unsolicited advice, they could turn on him in the end. I saw almost a Gary Cooper figure, *High Noon* on blond hardwood, making himself stay perpetually removed. That was my response to the Phil Jackson Rorschach test.

How would other people do on the test? You can't know for sure—that's the essence of a Rorschach test—but it was possible to guess. At least some of the sportswriters, for example, probably saw him as a man they deemed depressed and anxious because, two nights earlier, his team had been beaten humiliatingly in Houston, losing 114-92 to the Rockets. Those writers worked full-time covering the portion of Jackson's personal universe that was governed by a win-loss record; some of them might look at him walking away and, checking out the Phil Jackson inkblot, see the neatly ledgered Central Division standings of the NBA.

There was a reporter I worked with every day, a fellow with a skeptical-eyed, investigative outlook on the world; I tried to think what he might see in this Rorschach test. Probably he'd look at Jackson and see the coach's license plates; it was well known that some of the players and coaches had special deals with various local auto dealers, and this ever-suspicious colleague of mine always viewed such arrangements as inherently improper. Probably he would look at Jackson and see a mint-fresh pair of dealer plates.

"Phil looks like he's in a big hurry tonight," Jordan said.

"And what do you think that means?" I said, trying to draw him into the psychological twists and turns of the test.

"Ah, he's probably late for his pregame radio show," Jordan said.

Oh, well. Some people are saner than others. And Jordan

couldn't be expected to participate in the test; he went through life as a walking Rorschach test himself.

When you're young and you're going to your first sporting events—when you're a kid who is thrilled to be old enough to go to the local high school football and basketball games—the scores mean everything and they mean nothing. You care deeply about whether your team wins each game, or at least you think you do. But the excitement, as you will realize when you're older, has more to do with seeing the colors. As important as your hometown high school's success on the field of play seems to you when you're eight or nine years old, just being there and seeing the colors of the different uniforms that come to your town every week is what you will recall.

It's the first time you sense that the world is bigger than the block where you're growing up; it's the first time you see with your own eyes that there are other people growing up, too, people you've never met, people who have lives and houses and families you know nothing about. They arrive at your local high school on their team bus, and they jog out onto the football field or the basketball court in their uniforms of red or gold or orange, and the colors are new. The colors aren't the colors of your town's school, and every week the colors make you curious and a little nervous at the same time, the colors make you think about what lies beyond the borders of everything that is familiar to you.

As January moved along the New Jersey Nets came to the Stadium, and the Atlanta Hawks, and the Milwaukee Bucks; the Bulls wore white and the visitors wore blue and they wore red and they wore green. The Bulls were winning more than they lost, and although no one yet knew, of course, that they would finish this season as champions of the world, there was a sense building that the team might be better than anyone had supposed. So all of us watched the wins begin to build, and some people thought it was a presage of more good things to come and some people thought it was simply a false spring, and on the late-evening newscasts the sportscasters not only would announce the scores and show the highlights, they would also talk in hopeful detail about the Bulls' push toward first place.

Which was all very nice, and which added even more commotion and tumult to the Stadium nights. But the colors were still a big part of the draw, at least for me they were. At the end of a hueless day I would arrive at the Stadium and there would be the visitors, bringing their colors to town.

The best things never truly change. One evening Jordan, surrounded by alien royal blue uniforms, scrambled for a loose ball, and it went bouncing off the court of play, bounced once on the press table, bounced again, then rolled onto the floor, settling directly between my chair and the chair of the person next to me. The referees turned toward where we sat, and the players, the home team in white trimmed with red and black, the visitors in royal blue trimmed with orange and white, waited, too. All the colors, brightening the night. Everything was stopped; time itself was stopped, in all kinds of ways, and just for a moment I kept looking at the colors. I reached down then and retrieved the ball. There was Jordan, there was Pippen, there was Grant; there, too, were the visitors from another city. I no longer lived in a world where anything beyond my neighborhood seemed automatically foreign and new, but I could try to remember. The referee was yelling that the visitors had touched the ball last, that it was the Bulls' ball to take out of bounds. The visitors in royal blue were standing there, and I tossed the ball to the familiar figure of Bill Cartwright in white, and the game of the night resumed.

Jordan handled himself with such seeming effortlessness in talking to people—he could converse with a kid outside the Stadium, the CEO of a billion-dollar corporation, or the lead singer of a visiting rock band with equal facility—that, perhaps unfairly, all of his teammates were judged by the standard he set in that department. Every day he demonstrated that not only did he possess basketball skills the likes of which few people had ever seen before, but that he was entirely at ease discussing just about anything that anyone might wish to bring up. It was impossible to rattle him on the court, and it seemed impossible to rattle him in conversation, either.

Pippen was just about the opposite. I was never sure whether he simply didn't like to talk to people other than his teammates, or whether on some level it scared him a little bit. He was very, very good at basketball; he wasn't very good at all at expressing his thoughts. There is no shame in that, and no meanness intended in pointing it out. It is remarkable enough to come out of a tiny town in Arkansas and end up in the NBA. You shouldn't have to explain what you do out loud; simply doing your job well should be sufficient.

In the closely examined world of professional sports, such a luxury is not always allowed. Some sportswriters, and some fans, considered Pippen to be purposely curt and rude when he walked past them without speaking or responding to their words. I thought there might be another factor. The youngest of twelve children growing up in rural Hamburg, Arkansas, Pippen was still a boy when his father suffered a devastating stroke from which he never recovered. Pippen did not become a Chicago Bull because he could talk well; none of the Bulls were hired for their eloquence, including Jordan. All that got all of them here was what the world could see during the forty-eight regulation minutes of a basketball game. If they couldn't do that, all of the talking in the world would neither bring them here nor keep them here.

Yet talking was required. Before and after every game, Pippen was asked questions, and often he seemed to struggle with that. On some occasions when I found myself alone with him, I would make an effort to begin a conversation, and almost immediately I would understand anew that on some level this kind of thing seemed close to painful for him. My guess was that, if he were given a choice, he would seldom talk to any outsiders. He would just play the game.

"Do you think it's kind of surprising that athletes get better when they're in their mid-twenties?" I said to him one night, just killing time and breaking the silence.

"How do you mean?" Pippen said, with that constant flash of an expression that hinted he thought other people might be trying to trick him.

"It's just that most people never feel as physically strong as when they're in high school, or in college," I said. "But professional athletes seem to get stronger in their mid-twenties and even their late-twenties."

Jordan would have taken a comment like that and run with it. I have no idea whether he would have agreed with it or disagreed with it, but he would have been able to construct a little spoken essay around it, an elegant little dance, without breaking a mental sweat. He could do that as easily as making a layup.

"Twenty-five," Pippen said.

I didn't say anything, and he wasn't going to elaborate. He looked down at something he was holding in his hands.

When several seconds had passed, I said, "Twenty-five?"

He didn't continue right away. Several additional seconds later, in the midst of more silence, I repeated: "Twenty-five?"

"I think you're strongest at twenty-five," he said. That was it. For him, it was a gracious gesture; for him, it was an indication that he was trying to be a participant in this conversation.

Sometimes, in the newspapers and sports magazines, I would see long, flowing quotations from Pippen. I could only imagine what the interviews had really been like. Either the interviewers were absolute geniuses at getting him to open up, or they had spent hours and hours piecing together bits of comments into a comprehensible whole. Which was okay, in a way; Pippen was doing something he didn't enjoy doing and wasn't polished at doing in an effort to help them, and they in turn were helping him out, too; they were making him sound smoother than he was capable of sounding unabetted.

I didn't know whether he was, at his core, shy; I didn't know whether he was self-conscious about his lack of verbal finesse, especially because he had to travel the country observing Jordan, who had so little trouble with words. Sometimes I'd see a little thing—Pippen being ministered to on the court by one of the team physicians, who were affiliated with Chicago's most prestigious hospitals—and I'd think: eleven brothers and sisters, a father too ill to work, back-roads Arkansas farm country. Forget the big salary, forget the sumptuous NBA way of luxury living; there was a real possibility that, had Pippen not made it to here, he'd never even have had a chance for this kind of good medical care.

One evening I found myself sitting next to him and I asked him the same thing I'd asked Horace Grant: What did he think would have happened to him had he been just a little less talented in basketball? Just a little short of the level required to earn a job in the NBA?

I didn't think he was going to answer, so long did he sit there in silence.

Then he said:

"You mean a job? A way to make a living?"

"Yes," I said.

I waited. Finally he said:

"I have people I know back home in Arkansas. They would have helped me find something to do."

* * *

The expectations for Jordan were just about absolute; question marks were not included when people summed up their views of what he would accomplish. Thus, just before a short road trip, the Bulls front office issued a news release.

The headline was: JORDAN TO BREAK 15,000 MARK THIS WEEK.

The text of the news release said that Jordan was about to reach another landmark in his career: He was about to score his fifteen thousandth NBA point. The text added, "Jordan should most likely break this mark in Wednesday's game in the Philadelphia Spectrum."

This remark was presented straightforwardly, a dispassionate statement of fact. The assumption, made without irony, was that Jordan would of course score forty-eight points during the next two games, which is what it would take to put him over the fifteen thousand level during the contest against the 76ers. Never mind that scoring a total of forty-eight points in two consecutive professional games was something that even most top-echelon NBA players could not presume to do on demand. Jordan always did that well, and on corporate letterhead the Bulls front office was informing the world that this would be the week when the milestone would be reached, and that Philadelphia would be the city where it would happen.

Joyce Szymanski, a stack of the news releases in her hands, distributed them along press row as, in front of us, the Bulls played the New Jersey Nets. I looked at my copy of the release and wondered whether Jordan felt even remotely pressured by something like this. To be on the verge of the fifteen thousand points was one thing; to know that your employers are informing the public that you will do it during a given week, on a given day, is another.

Out on the floor, there was a tenth of a second remaining in the quarter. Jordan, calmly and without apparent undue concern, lofted a long shot from behind the three-point line. Right through the hoop, as if he'd never had any question in his mind about it, and the players on the New Jersey team, the buzzer ringing in their ears, turned in frustration toward their bench.

If Jordan was accustomed to every eye in every building being trained on him, there were players who went through entire stretches of games with no one at all even realizing they were present.

Jordan was number one not only in the echelon of the Chicago Bulls, but in all of basketball. Yet on every NBA team there were twelve players, and if someone had to be number one, someone had to be number twelve. On the Bulls, it was widely agreed, the number twelve player was a man named Dennis Hopson.

Hopson was a high-scoring All-American in college who had come to the Bulls in a trade before the beginning of this season, after three commendable NBA years with New Jersey. But something wasn't working for him in Chicago; he seemed uncertain and even awkward on the court, he was scoring hardly at all, and game by game he was seeing less and less playing time.

Sometimes when the joyous cries of approval and love came raining down on Jordan from every section of the Stadium, I would look across the court at the Bulls' bench and try to get a read on Hopson, still sitting in his warm-up clothes. The newspapers were full of trade rumors about him; anonymous sources in Bulls management were telling sportswriters that the team would like nothing better than to get rid of him.

Sports-page trade rumors were the stuff of professional athletics—baseball's mythical hot-stove league was built around the existence of trade rumors—and they provided mild entertainment for the fans, they served as convenient fuel for conversations between games.

This season I would look away from Jordan and look at Hopson, sitting there waiting to get in, and I'd find myself wondering what he was thinking at that exact moment. To Hopson, the seriousness of the trade rumors—and there was no doubt that they were serious—meant only one thing: that his bosses didn't like him, that they wished he weren't working for them, that they regretted ever having hired him. Certainly no one could be expected to feel sorry for him—as an NBA player he was making an enormous salary compared to the rest of the working world, and he was being paid even though he wasn't on the court very much.

Still, I have always found that the best way to think about any situation is to put yourself in the place of the person involved. Ask yourself how you'd do. You go to work every day knowing that every one of your colleagues who looks you in the eye is aware that you're not wanted. You report for your shift knowing that none of your superiors wish you to be there. You go home after the workday is done knowing that if you were to announce that you had decided never to come back, your employers would be relieved.

A factory assembly line or a private office at an accounting firm or the bench of a National Basketball Association team; the paychecks may be vastly different, but the emotions can't be. Jordan would make an impossible move and eighteen thousand people would rise to their feet, and I would look down at Hopson, a man alone in a boisterous building jammed to the bursting point.

"Have you ever been in a situation in a game when you thought to yourself, 'I can't do this'?" I said.

"Not yet," Jordan said.

"I'm serious," I said.

"So am I," Jordan said.

The funny thing was, he didn't sound like a braggart when he said it; he didn't sound like a person who was showing off or trying to get a rise out of someone. He wouldn't have addressed the topic if I hadn't asked. I'd asked; he'd answered.

"Never in your life," I said. "You're expected to do something on the court to win the game, and never in your life you've thought: 'I just can't do it tonight. I can't get it done.' "

"No," he said. "I've just never felt that way. If there's something that has to be done to win a game, I truthfully have to say that I've always thought I could do it. Obviously, there have been times when I've failed. But I haven't thought that I was going to fail. I have always thought I could do what was necessary."

The world seems to be divided into people who, in crucial moments, want the ball—want the responsibility—and people who want someone else to take care of it. In basketball and in life, you find out in those moments which people are which. Some people would do anything not to be the one everyone depends on. Other people would feel only shame if they were to turn nervously to someone else for leadership.

On nights of close games, I would see Jordan come alive at the most intense junctures. More than his skill, more than his pure athleticism, this need of his to take charge when a game was on the line was the thing that was beginning to impress me the most. You could look at all ten men on the court at moments like those and see it in their eyes. You could see who wanted the ball, and you could see who preferred to watch.

"What about if there's only a minute left, and your team is down by eight points?" I said.

"I think I can do it," he said.

I started to laugh a little. I had to; I hadn't even told him what the precise hypothetical scenario was.

He laughed too, but he said, "I'm not kidding you, or trying to make a point. In a situation like that, I think I can do it."

"There are some situations where you know you can't do it," I said.

"Like what?" he said.

"If there's a minute left and you're down by *twenty* points," I said.

"Phil will probably have taken me out by then in a situation like that, because he's worried that I might get hurt, and we aren't going to win anyway," he said. "But if we're down by twenty, I feel like I'm partly responsible for having gotten us in that situation. In a situation like that, I feel I should be in all the way to the end, because I want to see it through."

"Even though it's going to be a loss," I said.

"Especially because it's going to be a loss," he said. "We lose a game like that, I think it's my responsibility to be out there playing at the very end."

We all talked about how hard certain shots were to make, and the players made them anyway; we all talked about how hard the teams played on nights when the contests were close.

And what the players did was, indeed, hard. No doubt about it—the eighty-two-game schedule, and the postmidnight arrivals in distant cities after a long game and then a long plane flight, and the playing through acute injuries, all of it was undeniably difficult.

They were all well-compensated, though, not only in cash and in fame, but in ancillary ways. John Paxson arrived at the arena one evening, and we talked for a while, and on his way downstairs a Bulls executive stopped him and said something, and I saw Paxson nod, and the executive said, "Do you want that in your car, or do you want one you can carry with you?" Paxson thought for a moment before he answered: "Carry with me." A cellular phone deal, I presumed; another Bulls merchandising tie-in, with the players getting samples.

So there were all the perquisites like that—Jordan, because of his Nike association alone, probably would never have to buy leisure-time clothing for the rest of his life if he didn't want to—and all of those things were the rewards of working hard. Working hard and working well.

Out in the dingy lobby of the Stadium was a soft drink and hot dog stand; there was a short, lovely, white-haired lady who worked behind the counter, an older lady who reminded me of someone's grandmother. You don't necessarily want to see someone's grandmother working the night shift on the West Side of Chicago, but this lady, every night, had the sweetest, softest smile for everyone, even when they were crowding toward her and barking their orders and cursing because they were getting shoved from behind. She smiled for everyone who pushed a crumpled bill in her direction; she smiled for everyone who grabbed a beer without even looking at her.

The night of the New Jersey game it was lousy outside, and she had a cold. Her nose was red and her lips were raw and she was sniffling, and it wasn't difficult to tell how miserable she must have been feeling. I went out at halftime to get a Coke, and you could almost feel her fever, just by looking at her. Full winter on the night shift, with more labor to go before she headed home, and she handed me my Coke in a paper cup and she smiled as if it was her first day on the job and she was eager to make a good impression. She smiled as if she cared about her work. Now that's hard. That, I thought as I heard the horn sounding back inside the arena, is trying hard.

13

"**S**O IT MUST HAVE BEEN a pretty exciting moment," I said to Tim Hallam.

We were standing under the basket in the minutes before the Atlanta Hawks game; Hallam had just returned from Philadelphia where Jordan had, indeed, scored his fifteen thousandth career point, right on schedule.

"I suppose it was exciting, but I was kind of bummed," Hallam said.

"You were?" I said. "Why?"

"Because it came on a free throw," he said. "Screws up my highlights film for next year."

John Diamond, Hallam's young assistant, said, "Ninety-nine and oh-one were so good."

Meaning: Jordan had made a picturesque shot from the field to score points number 14,998 and 14,999; he had made another gorgeous field goal that resulted in points number 15,001 and 15,002. But point 15,000 had come on a free throw —thus it would look boring on film, and probably wouldn't even be included on the season sum-up highlights reel that the Bulls front office prepared for promotional use.

"Pretty inconsiderate of him," I said.

"I mentioned it to him on the plane," Hallam said, laughing. "He was very apologetic."

There were nights when, just for an instant, you could see a flash of what it was going to be like when all of this started to go away.

Maybe it was just me; maybe there's something about some of us that makes us need to look ahead to uncertain times even while we're in the midst of good times. But Jordan would have the ball stolen from him twice in a row, and I would think: Get ready. This is how it's going to be some day. He would bounce a pass off his own foot, and the thought would be: What if he stays too long? Is this what it's going to look like every night? He would stumble as he lunged for the ball, and an opposing player would fall hard on top of him, and Jordan would hesitate on the floor for protracted seconds before getting up. As he would lay there I would know, and everyone else in the Stadium would know, that they might as well sell the building. All of these glorious nights had become so deceptively commonplace, and we'd see him motionless for a moment on the floor, and they might as well just shut the building down and sell it for salvage.

Those moments of Jordan's weakness were so infrequent that, once they had come and gone, they were easy to ignore. But if we were having these thoughts, he was too; the inevitable decline was very much on his mind, and for him the question was not if, but when.

"It's going to happen," he said. "My thinking is that I want to get out of the business before it happens."

"I know you've said that," I said. "But how will you know when it's time?"

"Right at the peak, or before," he said. "I want to get out and walk away right at the peak of my game."

It wasn't all that unpredictable a wish for him to have. When you're strong and on top, of course you think about getting out at your peak. But what, specifically, bothered him about the concept of growing old on the court? What did he picture about it that he hated?

"I just can't allow myself the frustration of people looking at me and expecting me to be twenty-five or twenty-six, when I'm not twenty-five or twenty-six anymore," he said. "I can imagine what it would be like. I'm losing my skills, and they're sitting there in the stands watching me and trying to figure out what's wrong. They're sitting there waiting for me to take off from the free-throw line, and I can't do it. They come to the games and they wait for me to score sixty-nine or sixty-three points, and I can't do it. It's what they've come to see, and I can't do it."

When Jordan was first breaking into the league, Julius Erving of the Philadelphia 76ers was the dominant star. There were whispers that year among fans all across the country that the new show to see was Jordan; Erving was yesterday, and

Jordan was tomorrow. I asked Jordan what it had been like to be the young hotshot in that pairing.

"People started saying that he was old," Jordan said. "He was a wonderful player, but when I was going around the league as a rookie all these people were saying that he was old. I was the new kid. I had seen old films of him, and I'll tell you, when I was coming in and he was going out, he was still a good player. But I don't want to go through what he went through when I was coming in. To have people saying, 'Is he losing it? Are his skills diminishing? I think he's lost a step.' I don't want to look up into the stands and know they're saying that."

"But how will you be sure the day has come?" I said. "It's easy to talk about it now, when it's still off somewhere in the distance. How will you be sure, though?"

"I think I'll know it before anyone else knows it," he said. "You can see it in the statistics when it starts to happen, but I think I can figure it out before the statistics show it. I want to be able to get out before the statistics begin to go down."

"What exactly would that spare you from?" I said.

"I just don't want to deal with the hurt of people saying, 'You're too old,'" he said. "Even if they're saying it behind my back. Or of people watching me play and wishing the coach would take me out of the game. I don't think I could stand it—knowing that. To know that people no longer respected me."

"But if you quit so early, wouldn't it take you away from something you love?" I said.

"I do love it," he said. "But I couldn't stand to know that people were saying those things, or thinking them. I could stand not playing basketball more than I could stand knowing that they were thinking that about me."

"The Bulls are playing early tonight?"

"No," I said. "Same time as usual."

"Well, you're awfully early, then."

It was a variation of the same conversation I had been having with cabdrivers every night. Tonight the weather was especially sloppy, even for Chicago in January; the floor of the backseat of the cab was wet with melted snow, and I could feel the water seeping into my shoes. There was a discarded newspaper on the seat, and I threw it onto the floor, hoping it would sop up some of the grunge.

"I sent away for some old fight films," the driver said. "A long time ago. Many, many years ago. Now I want to get them transferred to videotape."

The newspapers on the floor weren't working. This was like standing in a cold and dirty pond.

"In one of those films, Jack Dempsey is fighting, and Bat Masterson is the referee," the driver said. "You couldn't really see the fight very clearly. Up until 1940, they filmed the fights from the tenth row of the seats."

"Is that right," I said, trying in vain to find a patch of dryness on the floor.

"I used to order the fight films out of the back of magazines," the driver said. *"Argosy,* magazines like that. One time I sent in my order, and they sent me stag films instead."

I wasn't sure I wanted to hear this. I knew I didn't have a choice.

"Real old stag films," he said. "The interesting thing about those old-time stag films is to watch the apparatus."

That was the word he used. He said something about the women's bras; he said something about the men's socks. About the socks being "folded up on the men's ankles." Even though I didn't especially desire to be learning this, I found myself mentally correcting him: He had to mean that the socks were folded down, not up.

"The people in those early stag films were extremely hairy," he said from the front seat. "The women more so than the men."

Schwartz Pickle Company to the right; five more minutes to the Stadium.

"Once they sent me by mistake a fight between a lion and a tiger," he said. "I wanted boxing, but they sent me the lion and the tiger. The film speed was so fast back then. Even in slow motion, it looks fast. A real tiger and a real lion."

"You mean like from a movie," I said, regretting it as soon as it left my mouth; this was going to prolong the narrative.

"No, *not* from a movie," he said, exasperated with me, as if we'd had this debate dozens of times before. "They really filmed a real fight. The lion had a mane as big as a bear's. The words on the screen said 'King of the Beasts versus King of the Jungle.'"

We were making the left turn onto the little street that would take us to Gate 3½.

"The lion finally won," he said. "By virtue of the mane."

I didn't follow the logic. I knew that when all of these nights were just a memory, the long ritualized rides in the dark would stay with me, too, perhaps not as vivid as the bright hours inside the arena, but always serving as a weird counterpoint.

"How would the mane make the lion win?" I said, paying him.

"It's apparent if you watch the film," he said.

I walked through the players' parking lot, my feet soaked, and instead of thinking about the basketball game to come I involuntarily kept trying to recall from school days: Which is the king of the beasts and which is the king of the jungle?

Maybe it was because the Bulls had moved into first place, or maybe it was just because he was in a happy mood about something else, but when Jordan came upstairs before the game against Milwaukee he was ebullient and full of good cheer. He joked with everyone within earshot; the arena lights were still turned down low, and he dribbled between the Luvabulls, who were rehearsing their dance routines, and one of the women said something to him and he answered her and, while he was still looking at her and without looking toward the basket, he lobbed the ball he'd been carrying high into the air and, improbably yet predictably, it came down right through the hoop, perfect.

This seemed to break him up; this was his idea of something funny—a miraculous shot when no one was in the seats and the building was still locked—and he about doubled over at the humor, or whatever, he found in it. He was wearing the old University of North Carolina gym shorts he liked so much —light blue, with "UNC 11" on one leg—and he shot for a while and we talked a little as he did it, he was having fun tonight, and as he grabbed his own rebound he said, "Look who's here."

I followed the path of his eyes. On one side of the building, behind the rows of courtside chairs, a group of Chicago White Sox players were standing. The Sox were owned by Jerry Reinsdorf, the same man who owned the Bulls, and although the players on the baseball team were big-league professional athletes the same way Jordan was a big-league professional athlete, they, like everyone else in the city, considered it a treat and a privilege to come out and see him work. None of them would even bother to argue that they operated in the

same universe that he did—no one operated in that universe
—and if Jordan hadn't pointed them out, I probably wouldn't
have known who they were. Like so many pro athletes in
street clothes, they blended into their surroundings once they
were away from their field of play. These guys tonight could
have been any young group of Chicago buddies out for an
evening on the town. Out for an evening to watch Michael
Jordan.

Jordan walked across the wooden playing surface to the
courtside chairs, then stepped over them until he was on the
pathway where the White Sox players were standing. For him
to go to them was unnecessary, which was exactly why he did
it. He could have beckoned them to the spot on the court
where he'd been shooting, and they would have been flattered. But something tonight—being in first place, being in a
happy mood—led him to make the gesture, and it was not lost
on the baseball players. He shook hands with each of them—
they might have been eager youngsters waiting for an autograph, to judge from their expressions—and they talked for a
minute or two, and then, just as abruptly as he'd come over,
he said to them with a wave, "I've got to go to work. See you
guys later."

He climbed back over the folding chairs, and he took one
more shot at the basket, missing, and he headed back downstairs to get taped and to put on his game uniform. It's like the
sun coming up, I found myself thinking; you know it's not
going to light up the sky forever, so you savor it while you can
before sundown. The White Sox players were talking among
themselves about him and watching him go down the stairs,
and the Luvabulls were still glancing toward the basket where
he'd made that amazing shot, and soon enough the 18,676
would be in place, waiting for him. Later on, months down the
line, when some voices were starting to denounce him and
find fault with various aspects of his life, when some of the
words spoken about him would suddenly turn harshly con-
temptuous and he'd find himself low and confused, I'd think
about moments like these. What must it be like, to have the
power to make so many people feel so good? What must it be
like, to light up everything and then come back and do it
again, day after day after day?

A team of girl gymnasts from Fargo, North Dakota, had been
invited to the Stadium as halftime entertainers. They ap-

peared to range in age from high school on down, and as they did their acrobatics, leaping and twirling into the air, then alighting on mats that had been positioned on the hardwood, you could tell from their nervous sidelong glances that they sensed the West Side of Chicago was a long way from home.

If they were tense anyway, the feeling had to expand when, before the Fargo girls were finished with their show, the Bulls, in full uniform, emerged from the basement. Usually the half-time show would be over long before the Bulls came back to begin the third quarter; the standard drill was for the team to trot right onto the court to warm up after intermission.

Tonight, we would learn later, Phil Jackson, annoyed by what he perceived to be lackadaisical play in the first half against Milwaukee, had disgustedly told his team to just get out of the locker room and go upstairs. No one knew this at the time, though, and the Fargo girls seemed embarrassed and out of sorts, as if they'd screwed up by still being there.

The show continued. Some sportswriters were wandering around the arena or using the men's room, so many of the seats on press row were empty. The Bulls, not wanting to cross the court while the girls were still on it, helped themselves to the vacant chairs, and sat where the reporters usually worked.

It was intriguing to watch the varying reactions of the players to the gymnasts' performance. There is such a vast chasm these days between the lives of professional athletes and the lives of the rest of the world; someone had told me that John Paxson's father had been an NBA player in the early days of the league, but had quit because he could make more money selling insurance full-time. Selling insurance, especially during the off season, used to be an accepted part of how professional baseball and football and basketball players supplemented their incomes. Little boys worked the idea into their dreams of glory; Eddie Weston, a kid I grew up with, used to say that his goal was to "play pro basketball and sell insurance in the off season."

That had all changed, though. The idea of top-level professional athletes needing to work a second job for a decent income, of them being a part of the everyday world, was gone now, and the sight of these handsomely compensated Bulls sitting patiently as spectators and watching the high school gymnasts was at the same time odd and endearing. Each of the players responded differently to the situation. Jordan, of course, was quite aware of what was going on: The girls from

Fargo were making excuses to take longer run-ups to the mats, so that they could back up to where we were and stand next to him. They didn't speak to him; they merely took those extra steps backward until they were close to him, and they sneaked looks at him out of the corners of their eyes, and their complexions grew flushed as they exchanged glimpses with their friends and made faces, as though they couldn't believe it. They ran onto the court and completed their moves, and they gathered together and looked back toward Jordan, their mouths going, "Oh, my . . ." He knew it, he knew all about it, and he didn't embarrass them. He pretended he didn't know.

Scott Williams, a rookie, sat at the press table in his uniform and imitated the take-off motions the girls made before they aimed themselves at a trampoline; every time one of the girls would propel herself forward, he would mime the motion, having fun and fooling around. Scottie Pippen and Horace Grant, best friends, just sat and talked, barely noticing; for them, this was like waiting in a restaurant for the table they'd reserved to open up. Bill Cartwright was visibly bored, if not actually annoyed; he was the oldest Bull and he had seen just about every halftime NBA show there was to see, and he wasn't amused by this set of events, he just wanted to get on with it and finish the game and go home.

So they all sat on press row while the girls did their acrobatics, and the most heartening reaction was probably the one that came from B. J. Armstrong. I'm not sure he was even aware of what he was doing, because it seemed so unstudied. Armstrong was still very young—when Bill Cartwright had been traveling the NBA circuit as a rookie pro with the New York Knicks, Armstrong was a twelve-year-old seventh grader in Detroit—and he appeared ever open to the sights and sounds of life. As each gymnast completed her move and landed on the mats, Armstrong, his face coming alive with a wonder-filled smile, sat and observed and applauded energetically. His appreciation of the more intricate acrobatic routines seemed genuine; the impressed, startled look on his face after a finely completed double flip was the nonverbal equivalent of "Wow," and he might have been a youth at his first circus instead of an NBA player in uniform as he clapped his hands enthusiastically together, a fan showing his support for each of the halftime athletes, thanking them with his applause for coming.

* * *

It was considered extremely unfashionable to talk much about
the racial aspect of the NBA. Not that anyone was especially
sensitive about it—the players in the league were predominantly black, and predominantly wealthy beyond the dreams
of most people, and the reason that no one mentioned this
much out loud was not because it was a delicate subject, but
because it was just so obvious that it no longer even warranted
discussion. Most of the players were black—so what? Jackie
Robinson was a long time ago.

On certain nights, though, I would look over at the little
tunnels leading from the outer lobby into the arena, and I
would see some of the waiters and bartenders. These were
older black men—some appeared to be in their sixties—and I
didn't know exactly where in the building they worked, but I
had a hunch that it was in the Governors Room, which was a
private white-tablecloth restaurant reserved for the teams'
board of directors, investors, and corporate sponsors.

In the third or fourth quarter, I'd see the waiters and the
bartenders, in tuxedo shirts and bow ties, standing in those
tunnels, watching the game. Their eyes would be on Jordan,
and American history has moved so quickly that it's easy to
forget that when these men were born, when they were little
boys, a sight like the sight they were taking in was simply not
within the realm of possibility. The domination of the NBA by
wonderfully skilled black athletes may be taken for granted
now, but as recently as 1958 the NBA championship team was
entirely white. You look at a team picture of the '58 world
champion St. Louis Hawks, and there is not a black face in the
photograph. Not a player, not a coach, not a trainer—no one.

So on certain nights, when the voice of the public address
announcer would scream "Michael *Jordan!*" and Jordan
would turn back upcourt after having wheeled through the air
to make a stunning dunk shot, I'd look over at the tunnels,
and I'd see those men. They were watching the proceedings
with a perspective the rest of us perhaps were not privy to.

"My own hero?" Jordan said. "I've never really had one."

He was so accustomed to being considered a hero to other
people that I had wondered who played that role for him.
Maybe not now—maybe there comes a time when you're no
longer in the market for heroes. But what about back when he

was looking? What about when he felt the need for someone to look up to?

"My heroes are and were my parents," he said. "I can't see having anyone else as my heroes. Because of the situation I'm in, I've seen a lot of what people expect in heroes. People expect their heroes to be flawless, never to make mistakes, to be happy all the time. And no one can do that. No one never makes mistakes, and no one always does everything right, and I can tell you for sure that no one is happy all the time."

Most people, however, when they think of heroes think of larger-than-life figures. Your parents, no matter how much you respect them, are the people around the house. They don't loom as imposingly to you as does a distant idol on a movie screen or a rock concert stage. Or a basketball court.

"You can't really depend on those other people for guidance, though, or for setting an example you see every day," Jordan said. "I can admire someone's talent and respect that person, but I leave it at that. I don't think I could ever pattern my life after another person. Because each person can only be himself—there's only one of each person. As hard as you try, you're always going to be that one person."

"What was it about your parents that made them heroic to you?" I said.

"It wasn't that the rest of the world would necessarily think that they were heroic," he said. "But they were the adults I saw constantly, and I admired what I saw. I don't know how many children can say that. My father was and is a very smart man. He was homemade smart—he never went to college. So he made himself smart in a sense, he learned about things all by himself, and that taught me something about making yourself better. My mother always had a job when I was growing up, and when I saw her leaving the house to go to work it made me know there was something good about the discipline of accepting what your job is and then fulfilling your responsibilities to that job. My father was very funny around the house, and I liked to watch his mind work; my mother was very focused, and by watching her I learned that you have to be serious about what you want out of life."

"This life you're going through, now," I said. "Has it had the effect of souring you on the whole idea of heroes?"

"I'm not sure whether anyone, if he's telling the truth to himself in the middle of the night, is a hero to himself," Jordan said. "You're not a hero when you look at yourself. You just try to do the best that you can. And you don't learn that from a sports star or a TV star. If you're lucky, you grow up in a house where you can learn what kind of person you should be from your parents. And on that count, I was very lucky. It may have been the luckiest thing that ever happened to me."

I really liked these guys—the twelve players on the Bulls—but sometimes, during the chip race, I wished I could walk over to their bench and snap some of them out of their trances.

The chip race was a nightly promotion at the Stadium. Sponsored by a corn-chip manufacturer, it was a "race" on the scoreboard between three electronic dots (each representing a different flavor corn chip), held while time was out on the court. Fans had been handed little cards on the way into the arena, each card designating its owner as having bet on one of the chips.

On the scoreboard, the dots skittered three complete rotations around a track. This, of course, was all preprogrammed; the tape-recorded voice of longtime Chicago horse racing announcer Phil Georgeff described the action. "Here they come, spinning out of the turn" Georgeff's disembodied voice would boom out of the Stadium public address system, and the fans would be on their feet and cheering.

It was goofy enough to see the fans rooting for dots whose precise paths had been preloaded into a computer some time well before the doors of the arena had opened for the night. At least the fans had a minor stake in the outcome—the patrons whose cards contained the number of the winning chip would be able to turn those cards in for real corn chips at a local grocery store chain.

But why were the Bulls so interested?

Every night, while Phil Jackson would be talking to them in a huddle by the bench during the time-out, some of the Bulls would turn away from him and look up at the scoreboard to watch the chip race. Stacey King, a big reserve center, could not take his eyes away from the race; Scott Williams seemed addicted to it also, as did Cliff Levingston. Scottie Pippen and Horace Grant pretended not to know the chip race was going on during the first two laps, but almost invariably angled their necks upward during the final sprint; Will Perdue appeared sometimes to be talking to the dots.

This happened even on nights of the most tightly contested games. This happened even when the real-life drama on the basketball court, where the ending had not been decided, was a hundred times more compelling than the stupid chip race. I tried to find logical excuses for why the players should have any interest at all in the scurrying dots; the closest I could come was that they were so attuned to competition, they would reflexively turn to any contest, including a contest between bits of colored light masquerading feebly as corn chips.

Even that excuse wasn't good enough, though. The top part of the scoreboard would show that the Bulls and their opponents were tied. The center part of the scoreboard would show the dots flitting about. And the Bulls—the men who had the power to break the real-world tie—would be staring at the dots, as if the dots were playing in the Super Bowl or the World Series or the NBA Finals.

I thought about finding out the winner of the chip race in advance from the scoreboard operator, and just telling the results to the Bulls before the basketball game even started. But that didn't seem quite fair to them; to be honest, there was no evidence that the chip race was affecting their level of play, and why presume to deprive them of their fun?

Jordan's wandering enthusiasms arrived and departed rapidly, but when he got interested in something he tended to do it all the time for a while. That was the case with the locker room VCR and the remote control wand; for a few weeks, Jordan in front of that VCR was like a suburban dad who had absolutely no inclination to get off the couch in the den.

The part of the season had arrived during which the Bulls were playing teams they'd already met two or three times since opening night. In the locker room on a Friday evening, when the Miami Heat were making a return trip to Chicago, Jordan had pulled a swivel chair right in front of the TV set. He was leaning back; the visual stereotype of the zapper-wielding TV glutton is of a fat, tired guy with a stubble of beard on his face and a beer can at his feet, but if Jordan was affecting the posture, he was completely different in all other pertinent physical respects.

The Bulls' most recent Miami game was on the videotape. Jordan watched himself do something, hit the "Rewind/Search" button, and watched himself do it again in reverse. Once more on the tape he completed the shot; once more he zipped the tape backward, and the Jordan on the screen dropped from the hoop to the floor, then dashed rearward, like in an old-time comedy.

His legs were stretched out in front of him. If he was like the dad in the den, B. J. Armstrong and Scott Williams, standing behind him, were like duteous sons who had sneaked downstairs from doing their homework to watch TV with their old man. On one play, Jordan drove through the lane and delivered a powerful dunk. Armstrong and Williams literally let their mouths drop open as they watched.

Jordan hit the "Pause" button. He turned around to Williams, the rookie, and said, "You'll learn that."

Williams shook his head. "I don't know," he said.

"Sure you will," Jordan said. "Look at it again."

He reversed it, stopped it at the beginning of the sequence, hit "Play," and the unbelievable move unfolded on the TV screen anew.

"Okay, now look at this," Jordan said. He rewound the tape.

Armstrong and Williams watched the screen. Jordan hit "Play"; on the screen, he seemed to push the defender as he sailed toward the hoop.

"I just moved his arm," Jordan said to Williams. "They can't call offensive on that."

"Do it again," Williams said.

So Jordan, showing the excited kids the home movies from the trip to the beach last summer, ran through it one more time, letting Williams study how best to go to the basket against a stubborn defender to jam home a shot.

And later that night, when Phil Jackson put Williams into the game as the first half wound down, Jordan found him under the basket and hit him with a pass. But Williams, hesitating for just a second, didn't go for the ferocious drive and the dunk; the situation was a mirror of what had been on the videotape, but this wasn't Michael Jordan on tape, this was Scott Williams in real life, in his first NBA season, and he safely went with a modest layup instead. He got the same two points as if he'd tried to match the spectacular maneuver on the video, but the arena was relatively quiet, and Jordan made sure he caught Williams' eye and then raised his own eyebrows, imparting to him a whimsical and unspoken evaluation.

14

THE 1991 NBA ALL-STAR GAME in Jordan's native North Carolina received national coverage on network news broadcasts as well as on sports segments, and one bit of news footage in particular pointed out the oddness, melding into awkwardness, of what was happening to him.

The videotape showed the Eastern All-Star team getting into their team bus to go to practice. Within range of the camera was a white stretch limousine, which had been hired to take Jordan somewhere else in Charlotte, presumably a public appearance separate from the team.

Jordan, trying to make light of a clumsy situation and ease the discomfiture, pointed to Patrick Ewing of the Knicks, his All-Star teammate, who was walking toward the bus, and said: "This is what happens to you when you're in last place."

But the visual image—Jordan alone in his limo, the other athletes together on their bus—was lost on no one. As the game itself was ending on All-Star Sunday, NBC broke for a final commercial. It was for *Michael Jordan's Playground,* a new video of Jordan highlights, aimed at the home market. The point of scheduling the commercial late in the game was to remind people that, no matter what the score of the contest might turn out to be, Jordan would be for sale in stores nationwide the next morning.

The All-Star Game had fallen at the end of a two-week Bulls road trip. When I next saw Jordan it was the second week of February. Nothing at all at the Stadium had seemed to change, which was undoubtedly by design; this was supposed to feel like home to the players, and when they returned everything was precisely as they had left it.

So as Jordan, in a dark suit, walked across the court two hours before game time while the Luvabulls rehearsed a number to the old rock song "The Boys Are Back in Town," his game uniform was already laid out and waiting for him on the floor in front of his locker in the basement, the jersey folded so that only the letters "RDAN" on the back were facing up and visible. Each player's chair was positioned exactly where it had been in front of each cubicle; the trainer, Chip Schaefer, and the equipment manager, John Ligmanowski, were on hand to make sure that every roll of tape, every basketball shoe, every bottle of fruit juice were in their customary locations. The team had played five road games (not including Jordan's appearance in the All-Star contest) since they had last been here.

I'd been doing my usual newspaper work while they were gone; the columns I wrote did not concern themselves with basketball. I had been out to Juvenile Court again, and I had written about a variety of other topics: a column about military weapons, a column about a death at a rock concert, a column about a public library fire in Ohio. It had been a strange feeling for me to read the reports from the road by the men who, during the course of the season, I had come to know as my neighbors on press row. The matters I was covering might have varied daily, but the beat writers who covered the Bulls for the sports pages—Sam Smith of the *Tribune,* Dave Hoekstra and Lacy Banks of the *Sun-Times,* Kent McDill of the suburb-based *Daily Herald*—were chronicling the basketball intricacies of the team, every day in every edition.

Reading their accounts from the cities around the league, I was even more impressed by the logistical difficulties of what they were doing on deadline. There was one very late West Coast game, in Sacramento; it didn't end until almost midnight Chicago time. The *Tribune* that is delivered to my home arrives in the middle of the night, just after four A.M. So barely four hours after the final buzzer of the Bulls-Kings game, I found myself awake, looked outside the door to find the paper there, brought it inside to read—and there was the game story, not only with the details of the contest and the box score, but with quotes from Phil Jackson and the players.

The locker rooms didn't open to the press until at least ten minutes after each game concluded. Thus, the beat reporters from Chicago would have had to leave press row in Sacramento, wait outside the locker room, go inside to get their quotes, return to their laptop computers, and do their best to make their stories sound as if they had been written with the benefit of leisurely reflection. Not a bad bargain for thirty-five cents, I thought, as I read the report of the game less than five hours after I had seen it end on television. For thirty-five cents they'll run down to the locker rooms for you, ask the coaches and the athletes to explain what they'd done—and all of this will somehow be transmitted across the country, printed up, and hand-delivered to your house while you're sleeping. Sometimes I love newspapers as much as I did on the first day I walked into a city room.

On this first night back in Chicago for the Bulls, Jordan and I talked quietly at his locker. "The trip was fine, but I really missed seeing my new baby," he said. "When all of this is over, there are a lot of things about playing basketball that I'll feel the absence of, but at least I won't have to go away so much and be so completely disconnected. These long trips can make you feel very lonely."

Bulls fans, of course, had felt no such loneliness; every road game was televised, so Jordan and his teammates had been present in most Chicago area homes the same way they always had—as welcome fixtures on a color television screen. One of the Bulls, Craig Hodges, had won the three-point shooting contest during All-Star weekend. Hodges wasn't a member of the All-Star team itself, but during a special nationally televised individual competition on the Saturday night before the Sunday game, he had made nineteen shots in a row from behind the three-point barrier on his way to winning the prize.

On the Bulls' first night back, Hodges went upstairs to warm up for the game. Two early-arriving Andy Frain ushers in yellow sweaters applauded when they caught sight of him, but that was the only sound of greeting. The arena was empty, the All-Star break was history, and three-point title or not, reality was what waited for Hodges. He was a reserve on the Bulls; it was nice that he was three-point champ, but the only question that mattered now was whether he'd get into the game or not.

At the press table in the moments before tipoff, Joyce Szymanski made the rounds informing the sportswriters, "Dennis Hopson isn't going to play tonight because he has turf toe." Again and again, the length of the row: "Dennis Hopson isn't going to play tonight because he has turf toe." After the third or fourth repetition I heard her say to herself: "Whatever that is."

This universe in miniature was starting up again. By now the Stadium nights were something I not only looked forward to, but counted on. That first night back, as the teams took the court and the game was ready to begin, I looked up at the big four-sided scoreboard.

There, as they had been on the day the Bulls left town, were the electric-light uniform numbers of the Bulls' starters: 54 for Grant, 33 for Pippen, 24 for Cartwright, 5 for Paxson, 23 for Jordan. The names weren't up there, just the numbers, in a severe vertical line, with blank spaces following them. Once the scoring began, the blank spaces would fill; every time a player made a basket or a free throw, his cumulative points would appear in the space directly to the right of his number. As happy as the players were to be back, I was happy, too; I was happy to be back in this place where, unlike in so much of the rest of the world, the rules were clear and incontrovertible and always understood by everyone, and someone was keeping score at every moment, and when the day was done you knew who had won and who had lost. The losers would get another chance to win tomorrow, and the winners would get another chance to lose, but for all the lyric fluidity and seeming extemporization of the players as they made their moves on the court, this was a place of absolutes, in a world where absolutes were becoming something of a rarity.

There was constant talk about the pressure Jordan was under on the court. The pressure of trying to lead his team to a championship, combined with the pressure of defending his NBA scoring title, combined with the pressure of knowing every fan expected him to play like Michael Jordan every night—all of that conspired to make his time on the court during each game a period of incredible strain.

Or so the theory went. I wasn't so sure; the more time I spent with him, the more games I watched him as he worked, the more convinced I became that maybe the basketball court wasn't a place of very much pressure for him at all. For most people, of course, it would be; for most people the demand of being close to flawless in front of eighteen thousand people a night would be crushing.

But for Jordan—or so I was beginning to believe—the banging under the backboards, the shoving and the contact, the ticking down of the shot clock, were nothing compared to the demands on him out in the real world. The parameters of the public's expectations of him were becoming so unprecedented, the stir he was causing whenever he ventured outside was becoming so uncontrollable—people had been known to burst into tears at the mere sight of him, he had that kind of power now, the power to make strangers cry without saying a word—that I was beginning to believe that next to life out in the world, the court might seem like a place not of tension, but of sanctuary.

"The basketball court for me, during a game, is the most peaceful place I can imagine," he said as we talked about that one night. "I truly feel less pressure there than anyplace I go. On the basketball court, I worry about nothing. When I'm out there, no one can bother me. Being out there is one of the most private parts of my life."

His choice of that word—"private"—was a telling one. On the surface, there is nothing at all private about doing something while eighteen thousand pairs of eyes and a battery of television cameras are trained on you.

"That may be, but I'm really by myself out there," he said. "No one bothers me at all, even the other players on the court, except when I get fouled. Being on the court is very much like meditation for me. If something is on my mind, I can think about it on the court. If my wife and I have had a disagreement at home, I know that if we have a game that night, I'll be out there on the court by myself for a few hours, and by the time I get home again at the end of the evening, all of that will have passed."

"Do you ever think about why you feel so protected in such a public place?" I said.

"The basketball court is the one place where the rules say that no one can talk to me or walk up to me when I'm playing," he said. "During the game, for one of the few times in my life, I feel like I'm untouchable. I'm not untouchable anywhere else. I meant that about a game being like a meditation period for me. Any time I'm playing serious basketball, it's like meditation."

"I guess the out-of-bounds lines must be sort of like walls," I said. "The only people allowed inside the lines are you, the other nine players, and the referees."

"That's why it's so peaceful," he said. "In an airport or an office building or somewhere, you're always looking around, wondering who's going to come up to you and start talking. Who's going to start the parade by asking for the first autograph. There may be eighteen thousand people in the stands, but the painted lines surrounding the court keep them away."

"Do the games go by in a blur?" I said.

"Not really," he said. "Sometimes even in the middle of a game, I'm able to think about things. As loud as it is, it's almost a quiet time for me. I know that basketball games can be very exciting, but for me the game is one of the calmest parts of my life. No one can come onto the court. No one can cross those lines. It's a very calm place, and I look forward to being there."

In the years just before Jordan came to Chicago, Reggie Theus was probably the town's most popular basketball player. Not that this meant very much; professional basketball had gone into the dumps in Chicago right before Jordan arrived. But the Bulls were, at least, still an NBA team then, and Theus was the team's star.

Now Theus was on the New Jersey Nets. They returned to town in February to play the Bulls for the second time in a month; Theus, a shirt-advertisement-handsome guard in a crazy-quilt light-blue Nets uniform, was back on the Stadium floor. A rookie referee named Mike Callahan called a foul on him under the basket.

"Don't guess at me," Theus said angrily to Callahan. "Don't guess at me. Do not guess at me."

He wasn't yelling; as incensed as Theus was, this was not an outburst designed to be heard by the spectators. Theus was a thirteen-year veteran of the NBA, and this was Callahan's first tour around the league, and Theus was exercising his seniority; he may have been a mere player and Callahan may have been an official, but Theus was lecturing him, because he thought Callahan had made a call he was unsure of.

Callahan, young looking in his regulation referee's shirt and beltless slacks, must have realized that there was some merit in what Theus was saying, because he listened to Theus and didn't react. He wasn't going to rescind the foul call, but neither was he going to call a technical on Theus for berating him. "Don't guess at me." Meaning: Unless you're sure of what you've seen, resist blowing your whistle. Do not guess at me. Another bit of lexicon from the interior life of the NBA, where too many wrong guesses can decide the outcomes of games.

The most interesting matchup on the night of the New Jersey game, however, was not between Jordan and former Stadium star Theus, but between Jordan and a member of the Nets who spent much of his evening on the bench.

The player was Sam Bowie, a seven-foot-one-inch center with a pleasant, melancholy, often puzzled countenance. Bowie was not much of a factor in the evening's contest, which the Bulls won easily. In a way, though, he may have been the biggest factor of all.

On June 20, 1984, the National Basketball Association held its annual draft of college players. Pro scouts are never completely sure about which college stars will effect a successful transition to the NBA, but they make their best assessments and hope they are correct. The Houston Rockets had first pick that year; they needed a powerful center, and they went with Akeem Olajuwon of the hometown University of Houston. Next was the Portland Trail Blazers. They looked around at all of the university talent that was available. They decided on Bowie, of the University of Kentucky. The team with the third pick in the draft rotation was the Chicago Bulls. They saw that Olajuwon and Bowie had been selected number one and number two, and they made their choice from the players who were remaining. They selected Michael Jordan of the University of North Carolina.

Now, on this February night in the Stadium, Jordan, a multimillionaire, an icon to people around the world including many who did not even speak the English language, a man whose face was as recognized internationally as any movie star's or any government leader's, captivated the crowd as Bowie spent long minutes observing from the New Jersey bench. The NBA eminence that had been expected of Bowie had never quite happened. He had missed more than three hundred games in his career because of various injuries. While he was still with Portland he had undergone surgery to correct a defect in his left tibia, and to remove bone spurs from the base of his big toe. The next year, his right tibia shattered. The year after that, attempting to return, he rebroke that tibia before a preseason game. He was traded from Portland to the Nets prior to the 1989–90 season. Tonight, with the other reserves on the bench, Bowie, the man who was chosen ahead of Michael Jordan, watched the game.

If Portland had selected Jordan when they had the chance in 1984, the Stadium would undoubtedly have felt very different on this night. I looked at Jordan, grinning after driving for a layup; I looked at Bowie, who was looking at Jordan; I looked around at the 18,676 in the stands. How many of them would be here tonight had Portland decided that an untested college player named Jordan might have more potential than an untested college player named Bowie? With 4:36 remaining in the third quarter Bowie glanced up at the scoreboard, looked back at the game, and rested his chin on his hands. How many lives would have been altered had the Portland front office, on that day in 1984, concluded that Jordan might not be all that bad a basketball selection for the Trail Blazers' franchise?

But you can't know anything for sure in advance. All you can do is make your best assessment, and hope you're right. Don't guess at me. Do not guess.

Jordan as a marketing force was growing to such vast dimensions that other basketball stars were being used in ad campaigns that did not even attempt to disguise their references to him. Nowhere was this more evident than in sneaker commercials.

The shoes weren't called sneakers, of course, but that is what they were. Air Jordans by Nike had become such a phenomenon that Nike's competitors seemed to have given up trying to pretend they could ignore them. Karl Malone for L.A. Gear: "Everything else is just hot air." Dominique Wilkins for Reebok: "Air out." Some consumers might have considered the wordplay to be clever and some might have thought it to be overly obvious, but the message was not arguable: The other shoe manufacturers had to address the power of Air Jordans head on, because there wasn't a kid in the country who was unaware of their mystique.

Never mind that a specific pair of sneakers would never make the difference between a bad basketball player and a good one, or between a good basketball player and a great one; never mind that Jordan, Malone, or Wilkins in cordovan wing tips, bedroom slippers, or barefoot would still be superior at their sport to a well-shod player one skill level lower. "Is it the shoes?" a Nike ad asked, apparently rhetorically, but of course it wasn't; it was never the shoes. The shoes were fundamentally all the same, no matter who manufactured them. I read that the sneaker business had become a $5.5 billion-a-year industry. And at the center of the industry was Jordan.

One night I noticed that some of the Bulls, and many of the players on the opposing team, were wearing Nike Air shoes. This seemed to be the ultimate indignity—not only did Jordan's fellow NBA players have to work constantly in his shadow, but they had to wear his shoes, too.

"How do they deal with that?" I said to John Diamond, the Bulls' media-office assistant, who was sitting next to me at the press table.

"It's not actually Air Jordans they're wearing," he said. "Nike Air shoes are technically different from Air Jordans."

"Still," I said. "The thought must occur to the other players when they get dressed before the games."

"No, there really is a difference," Diamond said. "Air Jordans have the little Michael Jordan figures on them."

"What figures?" I said.

"You'd know them if you saw them," he said. "You've seen them a million times. The silhouette of Michael flying through the air with his arms and legs extended."

I thought I knew what he was talking about, but I wasn't absolutely certain.

"Here," he said, opening a game program. "There must be an ad in here with the Michael figure in it."

He flipped through the pages. "I know it's in here somewhere," he said.

A few seconds passed, and out in front of us a basketball game was underway.

"Why don't we just look on his shoes?" I said. "You don't have to look it up in the program. I assume he has the figure on his shoes."

"Okay," Diamond said. "I'll show you."

But Jordan was cutting and veering so rapidly, his shoes were a blur. We could see them, all right, but even when he was just a few feet in front of us he wasn't stopping long enough for Diamond to demonstrate his point.

This was absurd. As the crowd bellowed at the action on the court, we were sitting there staring purposefully at Jordan's feet.

"Slow down, Michael," Diamond said. "We're trying to look at your shoes."

"I can't justify it," he said.

We'd been talking about the enormous reach of his commercial endeavors. Every spring a new group of excellent basketball players comes out of the nation's colleges; the following fall some of them are added to NBA rosters, and of those rookies a certain number manage to hang around and make a lucrative career for themselves. But what had happened with Jordan—this surpassing of every previous plateau of business success for an athlete—was so different, there was no logical explanation. Unless he had one.

"If I ask myself 'Why me and not other people?' I'll never come up with an answer," he said. "And believe me, I've tried to understand the answer. But I really can't justify it, and I don't think I ever will."

When Jordan had been a college student, I supposed maybe I'd been aware of him by seeing him on some sportscast or reading an account while browsing through a sports section. Because I wasn't a devoted sports fan, though, he really hadn't been someone whose presence in the pantheon of new heroes was obvious to me. Had I been missing something conspicuous there? Was it clear from the start that he was going to be the one to redefine everything in the business of sports?

"I wanted to be a success in my life, but no one can ever dream of anything like this," he said. "When I came out of college, I wanted to do well, as everyone does. Everyone in my business and, I suppose, in every business. But I couldn't get ready for this. You don't prepare for or get ready for something like this."

Had there been a specific marketing plan that had been devised by people who were eager to mold an athlete to a predetermined, sellable image? I'd heard people say that— that maybe it wasn't so much that Jordan himself was special, but that he was part of a master plan to provide the American public with what it wasn't even yet aware that it wanted.

"No," he said. "It's there. I have never understood exactly how it happened. It just happened. No one can explain it, and if they say they can explain it, they're wrong. Because I can't explain it, even to myself, and I'm the only one who really knows."

"Some people say that David Falk had this in mind all

along," I said. Falk was Jordan's agent. I had never met him, but I had heard that he was so adept at what he did, that if anyone could be prepared for the emergence of a Michael Jordan, Falk was the one.

"He's very good at his job," Jordan said. "But he wasn't ready for this, either. You can plan for things, but you can't plan for something like this. He was learning as it happened, too."

I asked him to take me through the exact chronology of his ascension, in an effort to figure out how everything had fallen into place. He started to: He talked about the 1984 Olympic Games, during which he became the star of the United States basketball team before a worldwide TV audience; he talked about Magic Johnson and Larry Bird, and about how they had come to the NBA before he had and about questions concerning whether they had "maximized their marketing potential." When Jordan started to talk in terms like that, he never seemed completely comfortable; he was speaking the language, but he wasn't feeling it.

We went through things of that nature for a while, and then he interrupted himself.

"I suppose you can ask yourself questions and come up with possible answers," he said. "But your answers will be wrong, because whatever happened with me, I didn't know it was out there. I stumbled upon it, and it happened, and to this day I don't know why."

On the 1000 block of West Madison Street one night, eight blocks east of the Stadium, I saw an old man limping in the street.

It was snowing heavily, and the wind was up. The man appeared to be at least seventy years old. It didn't take more than a second to figure out the probable reason that he was walking in the street rather than on the sidewalk.

In that neighborhood the sidewalks can be mean and perilous after dark. An older person who has difficulty walking makes an inviting target. If he's carrying money or groceries, he can be seen as a pushover. By the time the crime is done and the thieves have run off, police response is irrelevant. A man like that can have his money taken and know that he'll never see it again.

So while it might seem dangerous to be walking in the street, amidst the traffic, some people find it safer than the alternative. The sidewalks and empty doorways are in shadows; the street, at least, is full of headlights. The man walked slowly among the cars, en route to wherever he was going.

There had been a ray of hope in the case of the foster child I was writing about. The Illinois Appellate Court had agreed to hold an emergency hearing on her situation. I'd been to the hearing, conducted in the chambers where the Illinois Supreme Court usually met. The three appellate justices, reviewing the facts and questioning the lawyers, seemed appalled by what they were being told. Justice Dom J. Rizzi, during his interrogation of the attorneys, said: "It just seems like there's something wrong. . . . Something just seems inherently wrong." He asked: "Did the judge ever see or speak to this child?"

At the end of the hearing the justices had taken the case under advisement. They would deliberate and go over the court records and then rule; this process could take up to several months.

At the Stadium this night there was one of those halftime contests where boys and girls shoot free throws in competition for prizes. Several hundred of them lined up in front of the baskets. In the end, only one child was left—a boy of perhaps two.

The others had been much older. This boy could not even lift the ball. Someone lifted him up and held him so that he was closer to the basket. It didn't work. Two, three, four times the ball rolled off his hands. The other children had all gone back to their seats, so he was the last one remaining. The entire crowd was watching him.

The man who was holding him lifted him even higher. It still didn't help; he was too small to shoot the ball more than an inch or two. It just kept falling to the floor. Finally a much taller man trotted onto the court. He held the boy so high and so close to the hoop that the boy couldn't miss. The boy rolled the ball into the basket.

The crowd erupted, as if Jordan had hit a three-pointer at the buzzer. The feeling inside the building was warm and happy—it was as if the adult world had arrived just in time to make the boy's life better. By cheering we were congratulating ourselves; by cheering we were embracing the illusion that this is how the world really works. You try your best and in the end someone will come to your side; someone will come to save you.

Maybe it was because this was happening on the same night I saw the man limping in the street; maybe it was the cumulative impact of all those days at Juvenile Court. But even as the child dropped the basketball through the net and I cheered with the rest of the Stadium crowd, part me was thinking: Little boy, enjoy it now. Take in the cheers. You'll find out soon enough that the world will not always come to your kind rescue. You'll find out that the world will usually turn away.

Nights like that, even going to the basketball game didn't offer much solace. Nights like that, I knew the only solution for what I was feeling would be sleep. It was a temporary solution at best, but sometimes it helped.

A nice basketball moment:

In that February game against the New Jersey Nets, halfway through the third quarter with time on the shot clock running out, the Nets were down at the end of the court where the Bulls' bench was.

Back at the other end—our end, next to the press tables, the end where the visiting team sat on its bench—a Nets assistant coach named Tom Newell was up and screaming.

He was counting down the seconds, right along with the shot clock. There was no way the New Jersey players could hear him; the Stadium crowd was roaring at full volume, and Newell's voice had absolutely zero chance of carrying more than a few feet.

But there he was, loud as he could make himself, accompanying the shot clock: "THREE . . . TWO . . . ONE . . ."

That's what coaches do, I supposed, whether at the junior high school level or in the NBA. Take away the chartered jets and the million-dollar paychecks and the jam-packed arenas, and what you have is ten players and an orange ball and a clock ticking down. And a man on the sidelines, part of every tick.

In case anyone really needed an explanation of the difference between Michael Jordan and Reggie Theus, an apt illustration occurred later on in the New Jersey game.

Jordan was the victim of a bad foul call. It was precisely the kind of call that had prompted Theus to erupt: "Don't guess at me." The kind of call that had resulted in him heatedly lecturing the young referee.

Jordan reacted differently. He merely turned to the same

official and, with a look almost of amusement, gave him a little widening of the eyes. Just a little expression of surprise, as in: Boy, you really blew that call. No words at all. Then he turned away from the ref.

My hunch was that the referee would remember Jordan's silent chastisement longer than he would remember Theus's enraged and imploring words. Jordan's implicit message was that he knew he was right, and that he didn't even need to make his case. He wasn't angry at the referee; he was merely showing him the error of his ways. He was like a trial lawyer who wasn't going to waste his fireworks on preliminary skirmishes. That look from Jordan to the referee—there was no question about who was the authority figure here. The authority figure was wearing shorts.

15

SOMETIMES WHEN JORDAN WOULD ARRIVE at the Stadium later than usual there would be other people lined up outside to enter through Gate 3½, and he would have to pause and wait right along with them. It was never a long line; when it happened there would be maybe two or three other players, or some TV technicians, or members of the Bulls' front office staff.

But the doorway into the building was narrow, and only one person could fit through at a time. So there would be that most unlikely of scenes: Jordan briefly waiting in the parking lot for the line to move, for a few moments being just like anyone else who wants to get into the arena.

On a late February afternoon around five-twenty, I arrived at the Stadium just as he did, and it was one of those days when there was a short line. We stood together talking in the mush-filled players' parking lot, and after a few seconds it was our turn to go inside. The young usher assigned to the door said hello to Jordan, and as soon as we were out of the cold, people in the building began to approach. Some clearly had been waiting just inside the doorway in hopes of seeing him.

As they spoke, I noticed the same thing that happened any time people initiated conversations with Jordan: They rushed. It never varied. It was as if they had rehearsed exactly what they were going to say to him, and now they felt compelled to speak the words as rapidly as they could. As we walked along the corridor, the voices sounded like 45-rpm records being played at 78. Requests for autographs, hints of business propositions, questions about public appearances—the specific subjects didn't matter: The voices were always so speeded-up that occasionally it was impossible to decipher what the speaker was saying.

And it wasn't something that happened only as he moved through the hallway. Time and again I'd see people, including out-of-town reporters, come into the locker room for prearranged meetings with Jordan, and it was as if they had to say everything that was on their minds in one uninterrupted breath. Totally understandable from their perspective—the classic "I know you must be a busy man" syndrome—yet, from Jordan's point of view, one more thing he had to accept as an aspect of how his life was different from everyone else's. Virtually no one spoke to him at regular speed.

"It's nervousness more than anything, I think," he said. "People just seem to talk a little faster when they talk to me. They'll stutter a little bit, and they'll be hurrying up what they say, like they have to say it very quickly, without pausing."

"So you're always conscious of it?" I said.

"Of course," he said. "And it's getting worse instead of getting better. It used to happen most of the time, but now it's happening all of the time."

"It's funny," I said. "I thought that maybe it was just so ingrained in what you go through that you might not even be aware of it anymore."

"How could you not be?" he said. "But it's not like you can say anything about it."

"Well, you could," I said.

"No, I've tried," he said. "Sometimes I've told people that there's no reason to be nervous, there's no reason to hurry everything up. I want to joke with them and tell them that I go to the bathroom, I eat, I'm just like they are—but if I were to say that, it would probably just make them more self-conscious, because then they'd know that I'd noticed how they were talking."

"So you don't let on that you notice," I said.

"I just try to listen the best I can," he said. "Their tone of voice—it's almost as if they're a little embarrassed about something. I can't really help, except to listen and not rush them."

"What do you think the instinct is that causes people to get that way when they're around you?" I said.

"If it's that they're afraid that if they don't get everything out real quickly I won't listen to them, then I don't understand that," he said. "I really don't know why they'd think I wouldn't answer them. But it's happening more and more, and I can tell it's happening as soon as a person starts his first sentence."

"Do you think it's a balance-of-power thing?" I said. "Like they're automatically conceding that you're in a more powerful position than they are, so they have to get in and out of your world in a big hurry?"

"I don't consider it as any kind of power on my part," he said. "I really don't. It's them assuming something about me. I think maybe they're assuming that I'll embarrass them in some way—that I'll make fun of them or not want to talk to them or judge them or something. With some people, maybe it's that they don't have a very outgoing personality anyway, and for some reason they're afraid that before they're even finished with their sentence I'll cut them off or walk away. For me to say something about it would just make it worse."

"Do you think many people are aware that you're noticing this?" I said.

"I don't speed up my talk, no matter how fast they're talking, so I hope they'll take a cue from me and just relax," he said. "You hope they'll calm down a little, but the only thing to do, really, is just talk at a regular pace and hope that they'll follow."

Not exactly a dilemma that the rest of us have to think about—how to calm people down when they talk to us.

"It's just one more part of this thing, I suppose," Jordan said.

For all the complaining that sports fans do about how much star athletes get paid, the fans, in the end, seem not to resent the salaries very much at all.

Scottie Pippen had gone to the newspapers in an effort to get more money out of the Bulls. Pippen was said to be earning something in excess of seven hundred thousand dollars a year; he felt this was insufficient. So as the Charlotte Hornets came into town for a game, the sports-page–reading public of Chicago was learning that Pippen would prefer the prospect of being traded to being required to work for his current salary.

It was a pretty transparent move; athletes and their agents have been negotiating through the sports pages for decades. And I had no idea whether, in comparison to other NBA players, Pippen was getting a raw deal or not. Conceivably, in his line of work, seven hundred thousand dollars was low-end.

The interesting thing was not that Pippen wanted the money. The interesting thing was that, as the Bulls played the Hornets, there were actually fans in the stands holding up hand-lettered signs that said "Pay Scottie More."

If you assumed that the fans with the signs weren't plants—and there was no reason to believe they were—then something truly astonishing was taking place. In a dismal national economy, with men and women being laid off all over the country, people in the balcony of the Stadium were fervently demonstrating—protesting, if you will—on behalf of a man they'd never met, indignant that the man was being forced to play basketball for a mere seven hundred thousand dollars a year. With all the wrenching crises that faced the country, they had taken the time and effort to make those signs and display them, ardent in their cause. Pay Scottie More.

Those late days of February were brutal in Chicago. It was an easy time of the year for regular denizens of the Stadium to stay home and out of the weather. The euphoria of the beginning days of the season was over, the playoffs were still two months away, and suddenly many of the familiar faces in the stands were missing, replaced by newcomers. Paul Sullivan of the *Tribune*, looking around the arena during a game against the Sacramento Kings, noticed this; in the lead of his report on the game he referred to the "brothers-in-law, favorite bartenders, and friends of friends of season ticketholders" who made up much of the crowd.

They were present to see Jordan play. The people who had given them tickets for the night might have begun taking for granted their dozens of evenings under the same roof with Jordan each year, and might have been willing to skip a game on a dismal Friday deep in winter, but the brothers-in-law and bartenders and friends of friends seemed more than grateful for their one-time-only opportunity.

Dog days or not, in the middle of the season in the middle of the winter it was business as usual for the men on the court. The games themselves might blend into one another, but at any moment something could happen that had the potential to change a life. Horace Grant crumpled to the floor one night, stayed down, and was eventually led off toward the stairs descending to the locker room. This huge, affable man bore a look of raw hurt on his face as he limped slowly; within minutes Tim Hallam was moving along press row, spreading the word: "Twisted left ankle, probably won't be back tonight, he's in a lot of pain."

Someone looked up and said, "Will he be sent for X-rays?"

"No, no, he could be back," Hallam said. "But you know . . ."

That was Grant's life, summed up in a phrase or two. Such a fine and fragile line between a millionaire's existence in the NBA and a reminder of a Marine recruiting commercial coming out of a Georgia television set, promising a young boy a slender hope of a way out. Hallam moved on down the row: "Twisted left ankle, probably won't be back tonight . . ."

Cliff Levingston, doing everything he could to persuade the coaches that he deserved to play more, was put into the lineup late in an easy Bulls victory. What would happen during the final minutes of the lopsided contest didn't matter much to anyone, including the fans who were leaving early to beat the traffic and battle the weather. But it mattered to Levingston, a nine-year veteran of the league trying his hardest to prolong his career. He lost the ball during a clumsy moment that he knew his coaches had seen, and the referee's whistle blew.

So many nights on so many courts for a man like Levingston. Good enough to make it this far, but not considered good enough to be a starter on this team, knowing that now, just as in junior high school, a coach on the bench was judging him and storing mental notes. With 4:58 left in the contest he retrieved the errant basketball that had betrayed him, held it in both hands, put it down hard on the wooden floor, and during the dwindling minutes of a game that was without consequence to just about everyone else showed a visible flash of something close to personal anguish and said out loud, as if he couldn't help it: "Damn!"

Jordan had turned twenty-eight February 17.

Age is a confusing thing in the context of any professional athlete's life; men who would be considered youngsters at a law firm or in an accounting office are weary veterans in pro sports, men who would be drawing beginner's wages anywhere else are in their peak earning years in the big leagues. But in Jordan's case, age seemed something beyond confusing. You could pick any age for Jordan, and that age would seem wrong.

As twenty-eight did. "Do you feel like you're twenty-eight?" I asked.

"I really don't," he said. "I feel much older—somewhere in my thirties, at least. Sometimes considerably older than that."

This wasn't just the usual small talk of a person who's feeling tired. Jordan had very little in common with other men born at the same time he was.

"I really am a little bit older," he said. "I've been promoted as something, and presented to the world in all these commercial-spokesman situations. People think of me as being a lot older than what I really am. When I ask people how old they think I am, they usually say in my thirties. And that's been going on for several years."

"I guess you can analyze it too much," I said. "The age you are is the age the calendar says you are."

"I am my age, but a lot has happened," he said. "I'm older than I actually am, and I've felt that way for some time now."

"I suppose there could be times when you feel younger than you actually are, too," I said.

"I never feel younger than I am," he said.

"I think there's a part inside of everyone that always feels like it's still seventeen," I said.

"There's no part of me that's still seventeen," he said.

"Never?" I said.

"There just isn't anymore," he said. "That part is gone."

Carmen Villafane was an easy person for people to walk right past. Her disabilities were so severe, her physical limitations so pronounced, that strangers tended to avert their eyes. Seeing her was a reminder of just how terribly wrong things could go.

If people did stop to glance at her, it was probably only to wonder how she managed to get such marvelous seats each night, how she was able to have her wheelchair positioned on the floor directly behind and to the left of the Bulls' bench at every game. She must come from a wealthy or influential family, Stadium patrons might guess; regardless of the awful luck life had dealt her, she must come from a family with a lot of pull.

Not exactly, it turned out.

For a number of games, as I headed toward my seat I was one of the people who walked by Carmen. She was strapped into her wheelchair; her arms and legs were subject to violent spasms, so they had to be tied down. She was nineteen, but had the body of a child, weighing less than ninety pounds. Her face often twitched in a manner she was unable to control. If, for many people, nights at the Stadium were a way to put the troubles of the world aside for a few hours, and to celebrate physical and athletic excellence, for Carmen the simple act of getting ready for the games and coming to the arena had to be an exhausting struggle. But she never missed a night.

We started saying hello to each other; Carmen couldn't speak facilely, but she would gesture a greeting with her head, and I began stopping to talk. Born with cerebral palsy, she had been a quadriplegic since she was a baby. In her short life she had endured twenty-four operations. Because she had so little control of her limbs, she directed her motor-driven wheelchair by pressing a special device with her chin.

She told me that her father drove her to the games each evening. Carmen spoke in uneven gasps; sometimes the words would not come out at all, and sometimes they came in a rush, all jumbled together. She couldn't regulate this very well. But if you stopped to listen to her, she was as good at expressing her thoughts as any other person you might happen to meet. It just took her a lot of time to get through it.

"Is your dad a member of the Bulls staff or something?" I said.

"No," she said, her face suddenly shaking as she struggled to converse. She was such a nice person and this was so hard for her.

"Well, you sure have great seats," I said.

She broke into a big grin. "I know," she said.

And then she told me the story. Later it was something I would think about quite a bit, deep in the night.

The year before, her parents had somehow managed to get tickets to bring her to a game, she said. Her wheelchair had been placed on the main floor. When the teams came out before the introductions, she tried to steer herself close to the Bulls' bench.

She had had a reason for this. It was the week of Valentine's Day. She had brought a card for someone.

"I wanted to give a Valentine's card to Michael Jordan," she said.

She had gotten near the bench, and the security guards had stood in front of her, but then had realized what she was doing. So they had allowed her to move her wheelchair up to the bench.

"I gave the card to Michael," she said, her eyes tearing up even now as she recalled the moment. "He said, 'Is this card for me?' I was too excited to say anything. I nodded my head. He opened it and read it right in front of me, right there, and he thanked me."

This was a young woman whose own mailbox had not necessarily overflowed with cards each Valentine's Day of her life. But she had wanted to give the card to Jordan, and she had managed to do it, and she had actually seen him read it. She just about floated through that night at the game, she said.

Not long afterward, she said, her father had taken her to a big Chicago-area auto show, to let her look at the new cars. She hadn't realized it, but Jordan was at the show, making a promotional appearance. When she learned this, she asked her dad if they could go to the part of the convention hall where Jordan was supposed to be.

"He was right there, and he looked at me," she said. "I said to him, 'Do you remember me?' And he said, 'Aren't you the girl who gave me the Valentine card?'

"He told me he'd been looking for me at the Stadium after that night, but that he hadn't seen me. He said, 'Where have you been?' I thought to myself, 'Oh, my God, he actually remembers who I am.' I told him that we were only able to get tickets that one time. And he said, 'I'll tell you what. I'm going to give you my office phone number. Whenever you want tickets, call this number, and we'll arrange for you to get tickets.' "

Carmen had thought it was a lovely, polite gesture on Jordan's part, although she didn't hold out any strong hope that tickets would really be available. But a couple of times that year her parents did call the number Jordan had given her, she said; the woman who answered said, "Oh, yes, Michael told us you might be calling," and against all expectations, the tickets were provided.

So, Carmen said, she had gone to several more games that year. It had been like a miracle for her, and when the season concluded and the summer began she was a little sad. She had somehow been allowed inside Jordan's world for a couple of days, and she felt the way a person always feels when something wonderful and unexpected comes and then ends. She was grateful and happy beyond words that it had happened, but she was feeling kind of empty that now it was gone.

The summer passed, and more than once she would stop and ask herself if all that had really occurred. It was something, she told herself, that would stay with her for the rest of her days, and even though it was over now, it had been the thrill of her life.

And then, one afternoon as summer was turning into fall, her mother told her that a letter had come in the mail for her.

They opened it together. Inside the envelope was a thick set of cardboard tickets. There was a letter, too.

The letter said, "I hope you enjoy the season ahead." It said, "I'm looking forward to seeing you at every game."

And it was signed: "Michael."

I stood behind the Bulls' bench listening to her tell me about all this. She was so easy to walk right past. She was so easy to hurry away from. As the team came onto the floor from the locker room and the P.A. system blasted loud, big-beat music, I looked over at Jordan in his white warm-up suit. For all the times we'd talked, he had never mentioned this to me. He'd never said a word. I looked at him out on the court, and then I looked down at Carmen, and she was looking at him, too.

The Boston Celtics returned to the Stadium on the last Tuesday night of February. Sitting on the Celtics' bench waiting to be called into the game was a rookie guard by the name of Dee Brown. A month ago I wouldn't have recognized his face, but tonight I knew exactly who he was, and the reason for this was hardly a mystery.

Brown had been a participant in the slam-dunk contest at the All-Star Game, a sideshow competition like the three-point shoot-out Craig Hodges had won. He'd been wearing a pair of those gym shoes that you can pump up by pressing a basketball-shaped rubberized mechanism on the front of each shoe. There'd been no missing this; just before attempting each slam dunk, Brown had leaned over and, with great fanfare, pumped up one shoe, then, with a dramatic flourish, the other.

It was about as blatant an on-court commercial ploy as you could ever devise; repeatedly pumping up the shoes during the contest was analogous to taking a swig of Coke from a well-marked can before each shot, or munching on a Snickers bar while the cameras focused on you at the free-throw line. Not that anyone was blaming Brown for doing it; unlike the Jordans and Birds of the NBA, he had entered this season as a virtual unknown, and he was merely showing economic creativity by being so brazen with his pumping. He could have worked hard for five or six years and hoped against hope to become one of the league's handful of brand-name stars; instead he got it done in one night. He won the slam-dunk contest, and no one who saw him do it was unaware of what shoe he was wearing.

As crass as it was, it served his purpose: It instantly set him apart. Jordan and Bird had millions of dollars worth of commercial commitments, but Dee Brown didn't, or at least he hadn't going into the All-Star weekend; the TV announcers weren't even certain whether he yet represented the pump-on-the-front brand of shoes. But if he didn't then, he would now; in the days after his stunt I read that it was going to be worth at least one million dollars in endorsements to him. If you don't separate yourself from the pack, you're just one more man in a green uniform sitting on the bench on a February night, waiting to get in. Which was what Brown was doing —but unlike the other bench-sitters on this night, now he had a semi-famous face.

Late in the game, Larry Bird spent some time on the bench, also. He was well beyond having to think up ways to promote himself to gain attention, but this was another in a long succession of NBA nights in winter for him, too, and at one point I looked over at him and saw that he was holding a towel against his ear, which seemed to be bleeding. Whatever cosmic game Dee Brown was just entering, Bird had already won, but as he pressed the towel to his ear, inspected it to see if the bleeding was slowing, then pressed the towel again, the expression on his haggard face was: What in the world am I doing here tonight?

If my reading of the newspapers was correct, Pippen was well on his way to victory in his skirmish with the Bulls over getting more money. He was clearly ahead in the publicity battle, and my guess was that it was going to be very difficult for the Bulls' front office to deny him the cash.

I understood that covering the world of sports now meant covering the world of big business, also, and that the days when sportswriters could confine themselves to penning vivid descriptions of towering home runs and broken-field touch-downs and buzzer-beating hook shots were long gone. But if there were moments when I envied my press-row colleagues for the fun of getting to live in the sports universe full-time, as I followed the somber, ledger-languaged newspaper coverage of the twisting-plotted contract intrigue, I did not envy them having to type the words: "Sources close to Scottie Pippen said yesterday."

"There's no one at all?" I asked Jordan. "Not one person?"

"Not really," he said. "No one I can think of."

We'd been talking about envy. I had asked him to think of a person toward whom he felt envious.

"There has to be someone," I said.

"If you envy someone, you have to envy both their good and their bad points," he said. "And I've learned that what-ever there is that's important about a person's life, that can't be seen from the outside of the person—or by people outside. I know that a lot of people may envy me. That's because all they see is the good things. They don't know the rest."

"But it's just not conceivable that you never feel any envy at all for anyone," I said.

"The envy I do feel, I may feel for a regular guy for just that one specific moment," he said.

"A specific person?" I said.

"No one whose name I know," he said. "But I may be being hurried somewhere, people will be telling me that I'm behind schedule and I'm due at the next place, and as I'm being hurried through a crowd I'll see a person in the crowd, maybe just standing there with his son or daughter, and he won't think I've even noticed him. But that's when I'll feel that mo-ment of envy. Just to be that man, for that moment, in the crowd."

"And the reason he's standing there is probably because he envies you," I said.

"There has been so much good in my life," Jordan said, "and I know that when I look back on it some day, I'll recog-nize that even more than I do now. If you envy someone, though, you should envy everything in that person's life. Maybe that's the reason why I don't find myself envying peo-ple—I know for a fact that there's not a person in the world in whose life everything is right.

"The man in the crowd, standing there with his son looking,

may be wishing he was me. But there are a lot of moments when I would like to be that man."

In many cities March marks the beginning of pleasing weather, but in Chicago you'd be foolish to count on it. When the Minnesota Timberwolves came to town for a game during the second week of March, the city was fighting its way through one of the meanest and most sustained attacks of snow and ice of the winter. When I arrived at the Stadium I was surprised to find Jordan on the court.

This was well before five o'clock; this was early even for Jordan. Sensing the treacherous weather, he had gotten a head start from home, and had made quick time on the expressway. Now here he was, on the playing surface of the Stadium with hours to go before game time.

He grabbed a basketball and motioned two of the teenage ball boys to guard him. They glanced at each other; this was new. They were accustomed to shagging balls for him, but tonight he was inviting them to play.

So they, in their fraying-at-the-knees slacks and Near North Insurance windbreakers, and he, in his University of North Carolina gym shorts and a fresh T-shirt, faced off. Jordan drove on them. What a sight—the two kids endeavoring to keep Michael Jordan from getting to the basket.

He made his shot, then tossed the ball to one of them and told them to try to stop him from taking it back. The two ball boys dribbled and passed; Jordan chased them into a corner of the court, laughing with them, reaching for the ball, slapping it out of their hands. The unspoken, priceless message he was sending to them was that they were good enough for this —they were good enough to play around with him. Silently, coolly, they loved it.

This went on for a while, and then Jordan spotted Joe O'Neil, the Bulls' director of ticket-and-stadium operations. Jordan called out O'Neil's name; O'Neil, a no-nonsense looking man in a business suit, looked over to see what Jordan wanted.

"You against me," Jordan called. "We shoot from half court."

O'Neil seemed to think Jordan was teasing him.

"Right now," Jordan said. "One shot each."

So O'Neil in his suit met Jordan in his shorts at center court, and together they stood atop the big red Bulls logo.

"You first," Jordan said.

O'Neil held the ball in both hands. He unbuttoned his suit jacket. He positioned his shiny shoes just right, bent at the knees, then sent the ball soaring toward the hoop.

It fell short, almost coming down atop the head of John Paxson, who had arrived from the locker room to warm up. Paxson, surprised by the ball dropping out of the sky, wheeled around to see the unlikely duo of O'Neil and Jordan in the tip-off circle.

"All right," Jordan said. He balanced a ball on the palm of his left hand. He set his sights on the basket. He lofted it. It banged off the rim.

O'Neil, figuring that Jordan was through with this—and a little self-conscious, as anyone would be, to find himself engaged in competition with Michael Jordan on a basketball court while other people watched—buttoned his coat again and headed toward the sidelines.

"Hey!" Jordan called.

O'Neil turned back toward him.

"No one won yet," Jordan said.

So O'Neil unbuttoned the coat once more and returned to center court.

"We shoot till there's a winner," Jordan said.

And the two of them stood side by side, flinging one shot after another half the length of the court, neither of them making any shots, until O'Neil, wanting to give Jordan an out, said with a false and urgent brusqueness, "I've got to go back to work."

Jordan, left alone out there, scooped up the ball and drove on the ball boys again, spinning past them, tricking them with a between-the-legs dribble, challenging them to come after him. He was laughing and they were laughing and he was as happy as I'd ever seen him on this court. "There's no part of me that's still seventeen," he had told me. "That part is all gone," he had said. But you could have fooled me tonight.

16

I TOOK MY FAMILY to Florida the last two weeks of March. It was good to get away from the daily newspaper deadlines and from the winter-long arctic blasts of Chicago's streets. The sun beat down on the sand just about every day of our vacation trip, and glistened brightly off the water; it was a lovely feeling to wake up not to an insistent, buzzing bedside alarm, but to the sounds of seabirds soaring outside the window.

Leaving the real world behind for a couple of weeks was a pleasure; leaving the Bulls behind was something I was not quite as willing to do. Each morning I'd walk to a vending machine to pick up a paper. I'd toss the news sections to the side temporarily while I looked in the sports pages for a report on the game from the night before. For the first time in my life I found myself reading the box scores as if they were elaborately crafted works of classic literature, full of momentous revelations. I would see agate-type accountings of things that were arguably inconsequential and I would get genuinely excited—the box score would inform me that Cliff Levingston had gone 5 for 6, and it would matter to me. My goodness, I'd think to myself as the sun began to burn through the cloud cover, Levingston's hot all of a sudden.

And the newspapers weren't my only, or best, connection with the Bulls. Games that were telecast on Chicago's local cable SportsChannel I was unable to receive in Florida, but the contests that were carried on WGN television came in just fine. WGN was one of the so-called superstations, and its signal was delivered via satellite with all the clarity of CBS or NBC or ABC. The voices of Jim Durham and Red Kerr would describe the action, and it was like listening to old friends calling on the telephone; Jordan would be shooting a free throw, and the camera angle would show the press table under the basket in the Stadium, and there would be Dave Hoekstra, there would be Sam Smith, there would be Tim Hallam and John Diamond and Paul Sullivan, and I almost felt like waving hello. I almost felt homesick.

From this distance, the ascension of Jordan into something much bigger than a basketball star was more apparent than ever. At the Stadium we'd talk early in the evenings and then I'd sit under the basket and watch the games, and, if it never felt common or conventional, it did take on the feel of something regular. There he was a person. On the television screen in Florida, though, he would make a layup between three defenders to solidify the Bulls' lead, and the opposing coach would, in frustration, call a time-out, and WGN would break for commercials and suddenly there would be Jordan eating a bowl of Wheaties, there would be Jordan chomping down on a burger at McDonald's, there would be Jordan sailing in slow motion past the moon on behalf of the Coca-Cola company. It was all so heroically lighted and stirringly photographed and artfully produced—by the time the commercial interruption was over and WGN was showing a shot of Jordan on the basketball court again, he might as well have been Clark Gable or John Wayne among a group of mere game-players.

One night after my family had gone to sleep I was restless and went out for a walk along the sand. The Gulf of Mexico was gorgeous, and the sound of the waves was soothing, and after I'd looked at the water for a while I passed an outdoor bar just a few dozen feet away from the beach. A basketball game was on a television set above the bartender's head.

The Bulls were playing the Indiana Pacers. I pulled up a stool to watch. Next to me were two Bulls fans—a man named Robert Musgjerd, who was in his sixties, and his son-in-law, Jim Mitchel, who was in his thirties. From the TV set I could hear Durham and Kerr talking into their courtside microphones, saying something about "wherever in the world people are watching us." Durham and Kerr and the sounds of the eighteen thousand in the Stadium in front of us; the lapping, constant waves to our right. This was just about perfect.

Two men standing to our left said they wanted to change the channel.

Musgjerd turned to them and said, "You must be kidding. The Bulls are playing."

One of the men—they were both wearing shirts bearing the logo of a local golf course—said something about the University of Nevada–Las Vegas and the NCAA tournament.

"We've got to watch the Bulls," Mitchel said.

One of the other men asked why a regular-season NBA game should be a reason to avoid checking up on the NCAA championship tournament. "The Bulls game doesn't even mean anything," he said. "Come on. Just for a couple of minutes."

Musgjerd or Mitchel—I'm not sure which—said to the other men: "It's three against two. We're staying with the Bulls."

We did, indeed, outnumber them by one. The first fellow in the golf shirt got flushed in the face; this was making him angry. For a moment I had the absurd feeling that I was about to get into my first fight since high school.

Luckily, all of us seemed to realize how ridiculous this was at the same instant. We reached an uneasy truce; the bartender switched back and forth, and the golfers were able to find the score they were looking for and we were able to see most of the Bulls-Pacers game. "Book it!" Jim Durham's voice, coming off the satellite, shouted as Jordan hit a long jump shot, and I looked toward the Florida moon, trying to see if it could possibly be as glamorous in person as in the soft drink commercial.

At five o'clock on an April afternoon, home from our vacation trip, I rode in the back seat of a cab toward the Stadium, and the look of the drive was different. For the first time since the beginning days of the season, it was wholly light outside on the way west to an evening game. The familiar buildings weren't in darkness or even in shadow, and somehow the route seemed to bear less intrigue. The cabdriver cut over to Madison Street; behind a chain-link fence on the north side of the street was a modern, red-brick Federal Express warehouse with the trademarked orange-and-purple logo on the wall. I had passed the building dozens of times, but in the darkness had never noticed what it was. Now everything was literal and fully visible. Spring was on its way, and with it the end of the regular season and the beginning of the playoffs.

In the locker room before the night's game against Orlando, Jordan flipped through a magazine in front of his cubicle and answered a group of reporters' questions about a double overtime loss in Boston over the weekend. Although eleven games remained on the schedule before the first round of the playoffs, there was a sense in the room of something ending. It's a sensation that professional athletes probably go through in the dwindling days of every season—this realization that something that started out fresh so seemingly long ago is now nearing conclusion—yet I could see how it could be an uneasy thought to deal with. On the backs of trading cards for years to come, each player's statistical output for this season would be summed up in a neat line of small numbers; to the men whose faces were on the fronts of the trading cards, though, the season was something quite different, something immeasurably more complex.

Kent McDill of the *Daily Herald* was talking to another sportswriter about a stage play he had seen the other night, and Horace Grant said to him, "Where is that play showing?"

"Up at the Wisdom Bridge Theater," McDill said. "Up on Howard Street."

Will Perdue, getting dressed in his game uniform at his own cubicle, turned to Grant and said, "We'll have to get together and go see it after the season."

"Yeah," Grant said. "That would be good. Let's do that."

It was sort of a sweet moment. Grant and Perdue were not two men who hung out much together, and by the time the season was over, the play in question would most likely have ended its run at Wisdom Bridge—the seasons of the theater have a finite duration, too. But Perdue's seemingly offhanded invitation to Grant—"We'll have to get together and go see it after the season"—had a meaning beyond the reality of whether they'd ever actually do it. After the season. The idea of wanting to maintain part of these nights. And Grant: "That would be good." It was about as close as these men ever came to talking out loud about what all of this signified to them.

And meanwhile, almost suddenly, the Bulls on the basketball court were giving off to the rest of the world a feeling dramatically different from the feeling they had evinced back in November. Then they were an erratic, uneven team, often conspicuously unsure of themselves, perennial challengers once removed. Gradually, over the course of the months, they had become confident of each other; now, going into the Orlando game, they were 53-18, owners of one of the best records in the league. For a long time any Bulls team out on the court at any given instant was automatically considered to be four guys and Michael Jordan. That was on the verge of changing for good. Jordan would always be Jordan—in tonight's game against Orlando he would lead the team with forty-four points. But the Bulls as a unit had turned into something special. The rest of the team was no longer invisible; these same Bulls in the same white and red and black uniforms they'd worn back in November all of a sudden looked powerful and intimidating when they took the court. Same guys, different message. You could look and you could tell. Other teams were afraid of them.

"Hey, Doc," Jordan called out.

Daniel Spikes, newly arrived at the Stadium for the evening, sitting now in his own motorized wheelchair next to Carmen Villafane in hers, turned his head in the direction of Jordan's voice.

"You on time, Doc?" Jordan said, pointing up in the direction of a clock high on the Stadium wall. This was still well before the doors would open to the general public.

"I'm on time," the young man said.

"You are?" Jordan said. "I don't know."

"We had some traffic in front of us," the young man said.

"I give that excuse, I get fined," Jordan said.

"Well, I'm here," the young man said.

Daniel Spikes—"Doc," incongruously—was around Carmen's age, and was beset by a sorrowful combination of grievous medical disorders. He was usually severely bloated from his medication; he wore a baseball cap in an effort to appear somehow jaunty. His wheelchair was positioned close to Carmen's behind the Bulls' bench at each game; I had asked around and had found out that his nightly place of honor had come to him the same way Carmen's had come to her. Jordan had met him by chance, and had taken it upon himself to make sure Doc became a sustaining member of the Stadium family.

Jordan and I still hadn't spoken about this; I had not brought up the subject of either Carmen or Doc, and neither had he. But now Carmen and I had started to spend time talking with each other every night, and I was noticing something. If either she or Doc was late arriving at the Stadium—if either of them was more than a few minutes tardy beyond the time they usually got there—Jordan would check it out.

He didn't make his concern obvious. I'd see him sneaking

glances around the parts of the Stadium where Carmen and Doc were most often seen; he would seem preoccupied, interrupting conversations with his teammates, interrupting warm-up exercises, to look for them every few minutes. He'd do it until Carmen or Doc—whoever was late—finally did show up. And then he'd mask his concern with banter.

Like on this night. He'd be mock angry, demanding that Doc provide an excuse for being late. He'd act as if, when he saw Carmen or Doc at last, it was the first he'd thought of them all day. As if he'd seen them on the main floor of the Stadium and had just happened to notice what time it was.

Even the people who, later on, were Jordan's harshest censurers gave him one thing: yeah, yeah, he was nice to kids with disabilities. In the midst of all the criticism that was to come, that concession was made almost as boilerplate: "OK, give him that, he cares about crippled kids."

As if that was just some inconsequential afterthought, old news, almost boring, an aspect of him that really didn't speak to who he was, a trivial point to be granted en route to more vital stuff. And maybe, to some people, it was.

But every time I'd hear that, I would wonder whether the people who were saying it had ever noticed his eyes on the nights when Carmen and Doc were late. If they'd ever noticed the most famous athlete in the world, unable to concentrate on what he was doing as he peered toward the tunnel leading into the arena to see who would be coming in next. Saying nothing, looking every few seconds. And then hiding it all with a joke. Hey, Doc, you on time?

In the basement press buffet a longtime sports reporter for Chicago radio stations sat by himself, reading the mimeographed game notes for the evening as he ate his dinner. He'd been around town for close to thirty years; he had known and interviewed every great athlete, every colorful coach who ever passed through the city. Ernie Banks, Dick Butkus, Gale Sayers, Walter Payton, Bobby Hull, Stan Mikita, George Halas, Mike Ditka—he'd covered their contests, talked to them in locker rooms, put their voices on the air.

This year I'd seen him at Phil Jackson's postgame press conferences, and in front of Jordan's locker during the group interviews when Jordan would analyze an evening's performance. This morning the local newspapers had reported that the radio station that currently employed this man had decided to switch formats. The station was going to an all–heavy metal rock rotation. His sports reports would not be required; he would not be required.

No one in the basement said much to him, and he didn't volunteer anything. But then, he never did; for a man who had made his living for decades by projecting his booming, authoritative voice into a handheld microphone, he was generally pretty quiet around the Stadium. He still had his seat on press row tonight; Tim Hallam wasn't going to take away his place at the table under the basket just because some radio station program director had decided that Michael Jordan and Scottie Pippen didn't meld well with Guns N' Roses and Motley Crüe. And tonight he was still here as a regular at the sportswriters' basement dinner hour.

But his presence was a reminder that, like the basketball players whose uniforms apprised the world of their identities, we are all defined by our jobs. Take away a Bulls jersey from a Craig Hodges or a Scott Williams, and they would still in many other aspects be the men they were, but something important would change. They would not be Chicago Bulls; they could still walk into the Stadium, if they had a ticket, or if they had a friend to wave them past the ushers, but something essential would be gone for good, and everyone who looked at them would know it.

Same with this man tonight. Same with all of us. Last week he had a radio station. Tonight he didn't. He flipped through the game notes, looking at the statistics of the season, as if getting ready to go to work.

"I've heard them say it, too," Jordan said. "I don't hear it all that often, because it's not something they'll generally say once they see that I'm around. But I've come walking up to a playground or an outdoor court, and I've heard it."

It was something I'd been hearing just about every time I'd passed by a schoolyard court recently. I'd be walking along the street somewhere, and the kids would be shooting hoops, and one of them would hold the ball for a second as he got ready to drive toward the net, and he would say it: "I'm Michael Jordan."

Not "My turn to be Jordan." Not "I'm going to make this shot like Jordan." Just the simple, shorthand phrase. The kind of grand and giddy playground statement that children have been making ever since children had heroes. "I'm Red

Grange." "I'm Mickey Mantle." "I'm Johnny Unitas." "I'm Michael Jordan."

"When you hear a kid say that, is there a moment when it doesn't register?" I said. "Do you ever hear a kid say that and find yourself thinking for a moment that *you're* not Michael Jordan?"

"It's a little crazy, hearing that, but it's not crazy enough for me to wonder whether I'm Michael Jordan," he said. "The Michael Jordan they're talking about is the thing they see on TV, in the games or in the commercials. The only place I don't have to worry about someone saying they're Michael Jordan is at home. Nobody's going to say it there."

"Even your older son?" I said.

"Well, actually, he does watch TV, and he's starting to realize who that is in the games and in the commercials, so now I guess I run the risk of him saying he's Michael Jordan, which I hope he doesn't do. Because he's not Michael Jordan, he's my son."

"Did you ever do it?" I said.

"Stand on a court and say I was someone?" he said. "Sure. I think everyone, when they're kids, tries to pretend that they're someone. I'd be playing basketball with my friends, or with my older brother, and I'd get the ball and I'd say, 'I'm David Thompson,' or 'I'm Walter Davis.' Because they were older people who were playing college basketball in North Carolina. When you're a kid, you don't just want to emulate someone—you want to actually be that person. You don't think of it in a complicated way—you don't think of it in terms of wanting to grow up and be the same kind of person he is. It's a lot simpler feeling than that. You just want to be him, that's all. I hadn't met David Thompson or Walter Davis, but I'd be standing there pretending I was taking a last-second shot, and the words would just come out: 'I'm David Thompson.' "

There had been a halftime ceremony one night; the Luvabulls had come out first to entertain the fans with a fifties-style dance routine, and then the Chicago *Sun-Times* all-area high school basketball team had been introduced to the crowd, and had been presented with their plaques. The players being honored wore their high school warm-up suits, which must have been hotly prestigious items in their own gyms, but in the Stadium didn't turn many heads. One of the All-Stars, having been handed his award, had crossed paths with Jordan. Literally—he accepted his plaque and the accompanying handshake from the presenting official, and he turned to leave the court and walked right past Jordan, who was coming up from the basement to prepare for the beginning of the second half.

It wasn't difficult to guess what the high school All-Star would remember more vividly twenty or thirty years down the line—the plaque he had been given that night, or the split second during which, for a moment in his life, his universe intersected with Jordan's. From looking at him and his startled reaction as he stopped in his tracks and waited for Jordan to pass him, I didn't have to guess very hard about what he would be telling his friends the next morning. He was in that certain age group, the age group than contained young basketball players who learned the game during the years Jordan was first realizing international stardom in the NBA; it was far from inconceivable that this kid, now a high school All-Star, might very well have stood on a court in his neighborhood with a ball in his hands and said the words: "I'm Michael Jordan." In the Stadium Jordan had nodded at him, and had joined Paxson and Pippen and Cartwright and the other Bulls beneath the glass backboard, and the All-Star had looked at one of his fellow honorees as if to say: "Did you see that?"

I told Jordan that story. "What do you think," I said. "Is it more fun being a kid who still wants to be someone else, or is it more fun being the someone else and having no one left to imitate?"

"It's more fun being me," he said. "I've been on both sides, and this is better. But the irony is crazy, isn't it? All those kids saying 'I'm Michael Jordan,' and I was once them, saying I was someone else. It all kind of goes around in a circle. I know exactly what those kids are feeling, because I was them."

The first week of April, there was a Thursday night game against the Knicks in New York, which was to be followed by a Friday night game against the San Antonio Spurs in Chicago. The fatigue factor of the back-to-back games was going to be bad enough anyway, and it was exacerbated by the fact that the New York game had an uncommonly late scheduled starting time—8:30 P.M.—and the game in Chicago the next night had an uncommonly early starting time—7 P.M.

So as I watched the New York game on television Thursday

night, it struck me that the Bulls could be excused if they were infuriated at what happened. They were all set to go onto the court for the tipoff, and then there was a long delay. The circus, it seemed, was at Madison Square Garden, and had held an afternoon performance. The basketball court—I think this had something to do with the scoreboard, or the clocks—wasn't quite ready. Thus the Bulls had to stand around waiting, which ensured that the night in New York would be an even longer one than they had anticipated.

So less than twenty-four hours later, when I saw them in the Stadium locker room (they had defeated the Knicks and flown directly home after the game), I talked with John Paxson and B. J. Armstrong about the delay. On the TV screen the night before, I'd seen them both pacing as they passed the time waiting for the opening tipoff; I asked if it had made them nuts.

"Not really," Armstrong said. "We knew we were going to play it eventually."

"But every minute they wasted was a minute of sleep you were going to miss that you didn't need to miss," I said.

"They finally got the game started," Armstrong said.

"I just figured it had to be frustrating," I said. "With the late-night plane ride home and a game coming up tonight, you guys had to be anxious to get to bed."

"Didn't matter," Paxson said. "We didn't exactly get to sleep in this morning."

"You didn't?" I said.

"Phil had practice for us at eleven o'clock this morning," he said.

"We got in from New York at two o'clock this morning, and we had to be at practice at eleven," Armstrong said.

"With a game tonight?" I said. "Why?"

"Because he said we had practice," Paxson said.

"What do you need to practice?" I said. "At this point in your lives, couldn't you use the sleep more?"

"It's not up to us," Armstrong said. "We don't vote on whether we want to practice. I got a few hours sleep and then drove to practice."

There were some moments, like that one, when the difference between the lives the Bulls led and the lives the rest of us led was readily apparent. Then would come moments when their lives seemed not so different from ours at all. World-renowned professional athletes, yes—but when I asked Pax-

son whether he'd had a good time in New York after the Bulls
had arrived in that city the day before the game, he said,
"New York, I don't know. My first six years in the league,
whenever I went there I'd just go to my room and lock the
door." I would hear something like that and I'd think: the
classic combination—room service, peepholes, and a wary
traveler from Dayton, Ohio. I'd always felt pretty much the
same way about trips to New York; maybe, I'd think, it was
because Paxson and I grew up just down Route 40 from each
other.

But to think that—to think that the rest of us truly had very
much in common with these men—was to fool ourselves.
When I returned from Florida, Paxson and Grant had asked
me how the trip was, and I'd recounted the story of sitting
with the two other Bulls partisans at the outdoor bar, and of
being on the verge of a ridiculous fight with the two golfers
who'd wanted to change the channel.

I wanted them to understand how weird I thought the
whole thing was—how weird that I'd been down there by the
Gulf of Mexico watching them play basketball on that over-
the-bar TV set, and that now I was sitting here telling them
about the argument. The continuing oddity of the two parallel
worlds in which they lived—the world of a TV screen, and the
world everyone else inhabits. Didn't they think that was bizarre? I told Paxson about how, with a group of other travelers in the Tampa airport on the day I returned to Chicago, I
had looked at a TV console and seen him hit a dramatic
three-point shot against the Celtics. Wasn't that an unusual
feeling for him? To toss the basketball skyward in Boston, and
to know that in Tampa (and in cities all over the country)
people were agitatedly watching that ball, even as it floated
through the air, to see whether it would enter the hoop? And
that we in the Tampa airport would know whether the shot
was good at the same instant he would know it on the court in
Boston?

"I guess that is unusual," Paxson said. But he didn't mean
it. He couldn't. It was not, in fact, an unusual thing for him, or
for Grant, or, most especially, for Jordan; their every professional moment was televised, they were people but they were
software, too, delivered out of the ether to an ever-impatient
and ravenous populace. To expect them to understand the
oddness of this was unreasonable. It wasn't odd at all to them.

"The people in the Tampa airport were cheering," I said.

"I guess we've got fans all over the place," Grant said.

By the time of the Philadelphia game on April 7, Ray Clay was able to add a phrase to his public address announcement as the Bulls ran up the stairs from the locker room and took to the court: "Welcome your *Central Division champion* Chicago Bulls. . . ."

It was an undeniably exciting moment for fans—at last the team had won a championship of some sort. Granted, it was a divisional championship—the vastly more significant conference and NBA championships lay ahead, at the end of the playoffs, which hadn't even begun. But Chicago was a city starved for sports champions, and within hours of the Bulls mathematically clinching their division, vendors on the streets outside the Stadium were selling hurriedly produced T-shirts emblazoned with those exotic-sounding words: "Central Division Champions."

Many fans in the seats were proudly wearing the newly minted T-shirts. So, during early warm-ups, were some of the Bulls.

Not Jordan, of course. For him, it hadn't happened. This was too early to celebrate. He didn't consider himself to be the champion of anything yet.

Jordan had never been shy about saying how much winning a world championship would mean to him; still, an awfully good argument could be made that even if he never won a championship, his position in athletic history was assured. What was amazing to me was not that he, who already possessed so many earthly treasures, wanted a championship ring so badly, but rather that it seemed to matter so much to so many others that he get it.

Yet people truly wanted it for him. Strangers wanted it for him—strangers who had very little themselves. I was riding home from the Stadium after one game, and on the radio there were reports of a controversy involving Stacey King. King, who made approximately a million dollars a year to spend most of his time sitting on the Bulls' bench, was dissatisfied with how he was being treated by the coaching staff and front office, and he was making disruptive noises.

"Can you believe that?" the driver said. He was a skinny old guy in weather-worn clothing. "King shouldn't pull that at this time," he said. "Everyone has to pull together now. They have to win a championship for Michael."

So the fierce desire was there, within Jordan and within people who would never get the opportunity to say hello to him or to shake his hand. Championship or not, though, it was hard to imagine what he had left to prove to people. Even to the other top-level stars of the NBA.

"I don't think I have to prove anything to them," he said. "But there was a time when I did. It was when I was first in the league, and everyone was talking about Bird and Magic. My main drive then was that I was afraid."

"Afraid of them?" I said.

"Afraid I was going to be overlooked," he said. "And everything I did was toward that end: 'Please don't look over me. Don't overlook me. I'd like a chance.' I was young, and I was new, and I would hear about how great Bird and Magic were, and the voice inside of me was saying, 'What makes them great and not me?' By now, though, I think I've earned the right not to have to hear that voice anymore."

"Did that teach you anything?" I said.

"Well, I hope that when the time comes that younger players are hearing all these good things about me and are secretly thinking, 'What makes Jordan so great and not me?', I'll remember how I felt and I won't hold it against them or treat them coldly. Because you work very hard to get to this level, and when you get here you realize that there are players who are coming along who want to get here, too. And you can't help thinking: 'Not through me.'

"But whatever hunger you feel wanting to get to this level, the hunger you feel trying to stay here and protect it has inevitably got to be less severe. It can't possibly be the same kind of hunger, can it? When you're new you want to have the best players think, 'Hey, this guy is good.' I had such a hunger to be on the same level as Magic, and as Bird. And they didn't want to give it up so easily.

"And I hope I will remember that, because with Magic I felt a coldness from him, off the court and even when we were playing basketball. And I hope I never let that happen when younger players start moving on me. I hope I will not be cold. And if a younger player beats me, I hope I'll pat him on the butt, and I hope I won't talk behind his back. I hope that what I'll say behind his back is that he's a good player."

"Does that mean a person who reaches the top is obliged to

make himself a little softer than he was on the way up?" I asked.

"Not exactly," Jordan said. "I'll never give any of this away to anyone. I'll make the younger players earn everything. But once they do it, I hope I'm not afraid to say: 'That guy is good.'"

"Bill!" I heard a high-pitched voice cry.

The voice belonged to B. J. Armstrong. Fourth quarter of a losing effort against Philadelphia, and Bill Cartwright was about to take a shot that had little chance of going in, and Armstrong was trying to warn him away from it. Armstrong knew he was in better position to make the basket.

It wasn't all that often that, from the press-row seats, we could make out individual voices on the court. It happened from time to time, but usually the crowd noise was so great that the silent movie remained silent to us, too, even from the close vantage point.

So Armstrong's voice provided a pleasing little moment. Not because what he was doing would influence the outcome of the contest; it wouldn't. And not because it revealed something especially riveting about him or about Cartwright; it didn't. It was just one more sliver of the game, one more connection between what we all used to play as kids and this, the highest echelon of basketball.

"Bill!" Sort of human—urgent and almost worried. I was still hearing it as I left the arena.

My brother, who's six years younger than I am and lives in Ohio, came into town for a few days in April. There were two Bulls games scheduled while he was in Chicago, and I took him along with me to the Stadium.

The first game was on a Friday night, and I could tell that whatever the powerful draw is, whatever the amazing allure that the Stadium on game night gives off, it was affecting him right away; during the spotlight introductions I could see him shaking his head in wonder at the indescribable noise. After the game we went out for a sandwich and we replayed the night's contest, talking about some of the most exciting moments and imagination-defying shots; he spent the day at my house on Saturday, and he went out to dinner with my family and me on Saturday night, and on Sunday there was an afternoon game.

So we rode out to the Stadium—he was already into the Randolph Street food-warehouse pattern of getting there— and I had an envelope with me. The week before, Jordan and I had talked about a story I had written years ago, a story about how early disappointments in children's lives can affect them later on, when they're adults; Jordan had expressed some interest in the topic, and I'd told him I would bring him a copy. I'd found the story and photocopied it and put it in my pocket, and I went down to the locker room before the game to give it to him and brought my brother with me.

The team was just beginning to come in. John Paxson was there. My brother had known some people who'd gone to Paxson's high school, and the two of them talked about that; B. J. Armstrong said hello, and I could tell my brother was having a pretty nice time, this was, after all, the NBA, these were men he'd watched play, and he seemed to be enjoying himself and then Jordan entered the room.

And it was like my brother had been pierced by lightning. I'd gotten so used to seeing this—there was no getting around it or escaping it, it didn't matter who you were, there was no preparing for those first few moments with Jordan. Those first few moments were an almost otherworldly experience; regular people or celebrities could meet him, and it didn't matter, there was no difference between the reactions of the famous and the unknown, when Jordan walked in things speeded up and slowed down at the same time, everything stopped cold yet flashed by. My Elvis whimsy aside and notwithstanding, that's what this was—this was what Elvis must have dealt with every time he met a new person. You could meet Paul Newman or Burt Reynolds or Frank Sinatra or any of a hundred show business stars and it would be great, it would be thrilling and memorable, but when Elvis walked into a room and said hello it was different. It caused temporary chemical changes in people. This just wasn't supposed to happen, there was no way to get ready for it, you were not supposed to meet Elvis Presley.

Jordan knew the feeling that Presley knew, and although I'd witnessed this happen so many times during the season, this was my brother, who had grown up in the same house with me, and to see his face and hear his voice when Jordan showed up was a new lesson in just how potent the phenomenon was.

Jordan, who always knew that he would probably have to

initiate and lead any conversation, offered his hand to my brother and spoke briefly with him and said some friendly, welcoming things. I gave Jordan the years-old clipping; he said thanks and unzipped his gym bag and put it inside, and we talked a little bit more, and then my brother and I went upstairs to watch the game. We hurried out after the final buzzer; he had an early-evening plane to catch back home.

Lacy Banks, a basketball columnist for the *Sun-Times*, offered us a ride downtown. When we got there my brother grabbed a cab for O'Hare. He had fallen silent and he seemed more than a little low, and I thought I knew why.

When you're a kid, and you have a great time sleeping over at a friend's house, no matter how terrific the sleep-over has been, you feel down and sort of lonely the next day when it's time to go home. It's not that the sleep-over was bad; it's the opposite. The sleep-over has been so good that you don't want it to end, you don't want to go back to your world of school and dull family dinners and homework. It's not that you regret having gone to the sleep-over, but it's close enough —you feel so bad that it's over, you almost wish you hadn't let yourself see how good it was.

My brother had been intoxicated by the sound and the feel and the unrestrained joy of the Stadium; he had tasted it twice, and now, abruptly, it was time to go back to the real world. He'd be at work in the morning, and the Bulls would still be playing their season. You never want the sleep-over to end. I knew the feeling so well. I was still here, wasn't I? It was something that could have ended a long time ago for me, there were many occasions when I could have made any excuse to end the Stadium days and nights, but I was still here, unwilling to let it end, wanting it to go on and on.

17

ALL SEASON LONG my companions at the press table had been telling me that when the playoffs started, it would feel as if something brand-new was beginning, as if the eighty-two previous games had been mere prelude. "You'll feel it as soon as you walk into the building," they'd say.

Maybe so, but it wasn't quite time for that yet. As the last games of the regular season unfolded, the feeling I had sensed in the locker room—the feeling of something ending, not of something getting ready to start—grew even stronger, and it was palpable all over the Stadium. The players, for their part, were quieter than usual before and after the games and seemed fatigued; at the basement dinner table the reporters were making the same kinds of tentative strivings to preserve this that I had seen Will Perdue and Horace Grant delicately stabbing at that one night in front of their cubicles. The last road trip of the regular season was coming up, an all-but-meaningless journey to Miami and then to Charlotte. "Are you going to stay in Miami?" Dave Hoekstra asked a colleague, who responded: "Three days in Miami!" The implicit message was that the idea of a three-day layover—on a trip to cover the team, but away from the team itself except for the basketball game—was enticing and a little exotic. Like the sports reporters welcomed the chance to break away from writing about the Bulls, the chance to have fun on their own.

But the way it sounded, escape was not what they were thinking about at all. The way it sounded, they could have been boys at a great summer camp, in the final days of sunshine together before they had to go their disparate ways, trying to hang on, trying to assure themselves that all of this was not necessarily temporary.

* * *

The Illinois Appellate Court handed down its decision on the child I had been writing about for the last year.

I received word the night before that the opinion would be issued in the morning. It would be delivered in written form; the decision would be available in the clerk's office at 10 A.M.

All the days in Juvenile Court, all the hearings and continuances and legal maneuverings, and it came down to this. The three-judge panel had deliberated and had committed its findings to paper. Here was the child's future.

I slept not at all, knowing that whatever chance that little girl had to reclaim her life lay in what the three judges had made of the case. She had been five when she had been forced to leave the foster parents she loved; until the Appellate Court agreed to review the evidence, no one would even listen to her story.

I got to the clerk's office early. Cathy Pilkington, a lawyer for the state who had argued on behalf of the child, was there, too. The clerk handed out the thick sheafs containing the justices' ruling. Pilkington read through the decision quickly, knowing how to decipher these things better than I did, and I could see that she was crying.

Her tears were tears of joy. The appellate justices had overturned virtually everything the original judge had decreed. They had ruled totally in favor of the little girl, and against what had been done to her in a Juvenile Court where she had not been permitted even to appear before the judge or to speak to him about her life.

The Appellate Court ruled that when the original judge had turned the child over to the woman who had given birth to her and to that woman's boyfriend, it was the judge himself who had been in violation of federal law.

The justices wrote:

"What happened to [the child] as a result of [the Juvenile Court judge's] total ignorance or total disregard of the federal law is shocking. [The] story is the account of a helpless child caught in the quagmire of the bureaucratic maze which we mistakenly call our child welfare system. Unfortunately, the judicial system did not respond to her plight. Instead, it became part of the quagmire, adding to [her] misfortune. . . . Every effort must be made . . . to see that what happened to [this child] never happens to another child in Illinois."

The appellate justices, in a seventy-five-page ruling containing language that bordered on cold fury, said that when the child was taken from the home she loved and was given to the birth mother and the boyfriend, with whom she had never spent a night, she was being handed by the state to people who had "a ten-year history of drug abuse, repeated prostitution, child neglect, child abandonment, forgery convictions, adjudications of being unfit parents and other anti-social behavior. . . . [The people to whom the child was given] had literally never nurtured, trained, or had anything whatsoever to do with [the child's] education or upbringing for the first five years of [her] life."

The justices ordered that the child must immediately be permitted to begin visits with the foster parents who had brought her up, the people from whom she had pleaded not to be taken; they ordered that the best interests for her long-term future be reviewed in a fresh set of Juvenile Court hearings.

Her victory was stunning. The phrase in the appellate opinion that stood out was the one in which the justices characterized the Juvenile Court judge who had so harmed her and who had declined to consider that he might be wrong. "Total ignorance or total disregard" of the law—that is what the judge himself had now been found guilty of.

There were many procedural steps that would need to be taken before her life could begin to be made whole again, if, indeed, it ever could be. But she was going to get her chance; at last, the law had listened.

I stood in the clerk's office and read the decision. That child had been five when she had been taken, shaking with sobs, from the only place she knew as her home, from the only people she knew as her parents. At the Stadium we often talked blithely in terms of the long season. She had been five when she had been taken, and in all the time since, in the house of the birth mother and the boyfriend, she had not been permitted to see, speak to, receive letters from, or even utter the names of the foster parents she had loved. Long season. She had been five when she was taken away, and now, in a week, she would turn seven.

If throughout the season the Stadium had been a source of solace from the sadness of so much of the world outside its walls, I knew that, as soon as the games ended and I walked out Gate 3½ toward home, that sad old world was still waiting. Sometimes this fact presented itself in especially stark terms.

There had been a killing in the news; a boy had been murdered for his satin Chicago Bulls jacket. This kind of crime was becoming more and more prevalent. Clothing modeled after that worn by athletic teams was deemed so valuable in the poorer neighborhoods of America's cities that young men were willing to kill for it. A youngster would leave his house proudly wearing a team jacket; he would die because of it. Clothing with the Bulls' logo on it—and especially clothing with a Jordan connection—was among the most popular in this deadly new turn of events.

"I know it, and it's terrible," Jordan said. "And I do not know what the answer is."

He was peremptorily confident on most subjects; he was persuasive in publicly explaining and defending his positions on topics pertaining to basketball and to the rest of life. But this one distressed him; this one, I sensed, made him worry. There was no person in the world whose name was a greater guarantee of selling a garment or a pair of shoes. And children were dying for wearing that clothing.

"It's very evident that the values people live by have started to change," he said. "When you start taking the lives of people for jackets and shoes—jackets and shoes! You wonder to yourself, what can you do? People ask you to be a positive influence, in a respectable way. You try to make a living—but at the expense of lives? I don't have the answer."

"But your name's on so much of that stuff," I said. "If a parent in a high-crime neighborhood sees his son or daughter going out the door with your brand of shoes on, and the parent is scared . . . what can you possibly say, knowing that?"

"I would tell parents to tell their kids: 'Please, give it up,' " he said.

"Give up the clothing?" I said. "If the child is being robbed?"

"Yes, give it up," he said. "The jacket, the shoes—give it up. Why would you want to hang onto it when you're in a life-threatening situation?"

"Because the clothes mean so much to those kids, I guess," I said. "So many of them don't have anything else. It has to be so hard to have their clothing taken from them."

"But the parents have to tell the kids to give up the clothing," he said. "They should tell the kids, I will buy them a replacement."

"The parents can't say that," I said. "A lot of the parents can't afford to buy a replacement. They can't say that they will."

"Not the parents," Jordan said. "Me."

"You?" I said.

"They should say that I'll buy a replacement."

Even as he was saying it, I could tell it wasn't something he'd really thought out. What he was talking about was an implicit robbery insurance policy with every item purchased that had his name or likeness on it.

"Do you mean Nike should offer to buy replacements?" I said.

"Not Nike," he said. "Me personally."

I knew he understood that there was no way this could ever happen. A kid in Los Angeles or Newark or Little Rock walks down the street, knowing that if someone tries to take his Air Jordans he can freely give them up because somewhere, somehow, Michael Jordan is going to hear about it and make sure that he gets a new pair? He was talking, but this was not reality.

"Why place your life in danger, for a piece of cloth?" he said. "The piece of cloth can be replaced. The child can't. I know that's not a message parents this has happened to are going to be helped by hearing. But parents have got to make their children understand that the clothing is just not that important."

We talked about what would happen if he just stopped putting his face and his name on clothing. Probably nothing, in terms of the robberies and killings. Probably another athlete's or music star's model of clothes would replace his as the brand prestigious enough to kill for. It wasn't Jordan himself that urban teenagers were so willing to murder for. The basis of this was something else, something awful and elemental, and trying to make sense of it seemed almost futile, because the horror was too great.

"If Nike believed that by taking my name off shoes it would stop people being killed, I'd do it," he said. "I don't know. This is one of the ways I make my living. When I was growing up, where I was growing up . . . this would just be unthinkable. I don't know. . . ."

I tried, just for a moment, to put myself in his place. You

reach this position, this unbelievable level, where companies actually pay you to put your picture or your name on clothing they manufacture. You start out like everyone else starts out, as a kid no one knows, and then suddenly corporations are writing you enormous checks just for the privilege of borrowing your name. It sounds too good to be true. And then you begin to hear that children are dying because they went outside wearing the clothes. The police are certain of it: Had they not left the house in those clothes, they would be alive.

"It just makes me so sad," he said. "The whole thing. Everything is changing."

Steve Schanwald slipped into an empty seat next to mine during the New York Knicks' last visit of the regular season. On the court Cliff Levingston, put into the game by Phil Jackson in the fourth quarter, scrambled for a ball on the floor, picked it up under the basket, insistently fought off the Knick defenders around him, and twisted the ball into the hoop for two points. This was the skill that had brought him from the playgrounds and high-school courts of San Diego to the NBA; this was the key to his handsome livelihood.

This was also what Schanwald sold to the public. He and the players may have had very little in common, but as the Bulls' chief marketing executive he was responsible for somehow taking the athletic skills that we saw demonstrated on the court each night, wrapping those skills up in a glitzy and palatable package, and making sure there was never an empty seat in the Stadium. Tonight I observed that he was marking on a sheet of paper in front of him.

"I'm Walking On Sunshine" blasted out of the Stadium P.A. system. I could see Schanwald, unsmiling, make a notation next to the song's title on the preprinted sheet.

"What are you doing?" I said.

"I keep track," he said. The fans were cheering the Bulls on; Schanwald was listening intently to hear what the next song would be. "I like to evaluate the pace."

The dry and meticulous mechanics behind the roar of the crowd. "The fans respond to the mix of the music even if they're not aware of it," Schanwald said. "I like to know how often we're playing each song available on our music list, and in what order. It has an effect on how good a time the people have."

"You think they judge their enjoyment here by the music?" I said. "With Jordan on the court?"

"This used to be a .500 team," Schanwald said. "We have to get ready for when this is a mediocre team again."

He said the law of averages dictates that no professional sports team will always be riding high in the standings. Every team will go through periods of being run-of-the-mill. His job, as he saw it, was to prepare for the day the cycle turned downward again for the Bulls.

With 1:29 remaining in the game and the Bulls ahead 108-100, the Knicks took a time-out. Gary Glitter's "Rock and Roll, Part Two," a modern staple at basketball arenas, boomed out of the speakers at painful-to-the-ear volume. At each appropriate pause in the song, the fans waved their fists and chanted as if on cue: *"Hey!"*

"The players hate this," Schanwald said, no particular emotion in his voice.

"They do?" I said. I was surprised; this was a clamorous part of the Stadium atmosphere every night.

"I think the coaches tell them to hate it," he said.

"Why?" I said.

"They say it disrupts them," Schanwald said.

The implication in his deadpan tone was that few people understood what might happen when Jordan was gone, and when the Bulls were once more just another basketball team. The coaches and players might look around the arena tonight and see bodies in every seat; Schanwald could look around and, even in the middle of a boisterous victory before a full house, envision what the place would look and feel like half-empty. He was being paid to hook the fans on the Stadium experience so that wouldn't happen, so they'd be tempted to come back anyway, regardless of the success of the team, even when Jordan was just a memory.

He wanted to add indoor fireworks to the spotlight introductions, he said; he'd tried it once at the beginning of the year, and Phil Jackson had complained vociferously because, in Jackson's opinion, the residual smoke made it difficult for his players to breathe. "But it can be fixed," Schanwald said. "The smoke can be controlled. The last thing we want people to do is get bored with the introductions. They're great, but they can be better. I'm going to come back with a revised proposal. This can be good."

Twenty-two seconds left in the game. "I Just Want to Bang

on the Drum All Day" screamed out of the speakers. Schanwald found the title on his list, made a mark in the margin next to it. There was a break in the action, and one of the referees laid the ball on the court until play was ready to resume.

Benny the Bull, the team mascot (the man inside the Benny costume was on Schanwald's payroll), pranced and preened for the fans. I looked down at the scuffed, dull-orange Spalding basketball on the wooden floor. A man invented a game a hundred years ago: You take a ball and you try to throw it into a hoop. Schanwald worked on his sheet. Jordan and the Bulls were in the midst of a race for the championship. But Jordan would not always be in residence at the Stadium, and Schanwald was thinking in terms of a much longer race.

In anticipation of the playoffs, the Bulls installed a series of video monitors atop the rickety tables of press row. The monitors looked like television screens, but were actually outlets of a computer device known as Statman—a means of having the game statistics available instantly, as they happened. No more waiting for the mimeographed summaries to come around; the Statman screens showed running box scores for both teams, the data changing with every shot taken, every rebound grabbed.

Just what was needed in this numbers-addicted world: a way to sit in the Stadium and watch the numbers instead of the players. The Statman monitors were placed in front of us, a low barrier between our eyes and the court. They were the ultimate triumph of statistics—TV sports without the athletes. It was possible to sit in front of your Statman monitor and not pay attention to the game at all, only to the ever-shifting, constantly blinking numerals on the screen.

The Statmans were waiting for us before the next-to-last game of the regular season, against Milwaukee. I tried not to look at mine, but it had the magnetic power that all video screens have, and I kept finding myself glancing at it. Dennis Hopson, still struggling, missed two free throws in a row, and I could see my Statman flash a "0" by his name under the column for free throws made, and a "2" under the column for free throws attempted. According to the Statman screen, all of this electronic summarizing was orchestrated by someone known as the "Transaction Editor."

I left after the second quarter, feeling sort of down. This

was the first time of the season I'd departed so early. I half-blamed Statman; Statman was a disagreeable intrusion, Statman was a reminder of our new digital, wired universe, Statman was a long way from the romantic old sports-world concept of "mailing the box scores to the league office." At halftime I walked away from the clunky plastic-and-glass machines.

It was empty on Madison Street. The massive postgame traffic jam would not be forming for another hour or so, and when I left the Stadium there was just one cop and me on the sidewalk. It was warm at last in Chicago. I hailed a cab. The driver was listening to a Cubs baseball game, the team's home nighttime opener at Wrigley Field, across town to the north.

The basketball season was nearing an end for the year; the baseball season was just beginning. The Bulls weren't the only game in town. On the cab's radio, Harry Caray, broadcasting from the Wrigley Field press box, was saying in that unmistakable quavering wail of his, coming from somewhere deep in the bottom of his larynx: "He's hit the ball hard three times. . . ."

I envisioned the green field and the outdoor darkness of Wrigley, the night cut by bright streams of illumination from the towering banks of high-wattage lamps. A much different feeling from the basketball game that was still going on inside the Stadium. Harry Caray, filling time between pitches, said, "Vince Ippolito Jr., fourteen, is celebrating his birthday. He's the son of Vince Ippolito Sr."

I had known a Vince Ippolito back when I had first started writing a newspaper column in Chicago. He had been a nice young guy, a musician and songwriter; I hadn't realized he had a son. But that was well over fourteen years ago; if I had the right fellow, he had become Vince Jr.'s father some time after the day I last ran into him. Now, or so it seemed, Vince was a dad, he was Vince Sr. now, and he was taking his boy to a game this evening. The cabdriver and I rode through the night, listening to baseball.

One of the best movies of recent years, I thought, was *Hoosiers,* a modestly budgeted and wonderfully written and directed film about a high school basketball team in a small Indiana town that wins the state championship, defeating schools with much bigger enrollments. Set in the American era just before the advent of television, the movie resonated with a sure sense of time and place; the basketball scenes were gorgeous and filled with exquisite tension.

I assumed that Jordan must have thought just as highly of the movie as I did. A stirring movie about small-town basketball players—*Hoosiers* was made for him.

"I hated it," he said.

"You what?" I said.

"Hated it," he said. "Didn't enjoy it at all."

"How could you hate it?" I said. "It was a great basketball movie. Not just a great basketball movie—it was a great movie, period."

"Not for me," he said.

"Could you tell me why?" I said.

"I see basketball in a different light," he said.

"But the movie made basketball feel beautiful," I said. "It made you want to cheer. To cheer and cry."

"I thought the movie made the coach be the star," Jordan said.

Gene Hackman, as the stubborn, complicated coach with a clouded past, was, indeed, the focus of the movie. The film was the story of how he led the little school to the state championship.

"That's not the way I was brought up in basketball," Jordan said. "The coach shouldn't be the star. The players are the stars and the entertainers. When I was playing for Coach Smith"—Dean Smith—"at North Carolina, he always put his players before him. Every time."

"So you really didn't like Hackman?" I said.

"The funny thing is, he's one of my favorite actors," Jordan said. "But not in this movie. The coach was arrogant. The coach was obnoxious."

"How can you say that?" I said. "The coach was the person who turned that team into champions."

"The coach in that movie was always trying to control everything," Jordan said. "He had to dictate what happened every second of the games. He had to signal to the players when he thought it was the right time for them to take a shot. Let the players play! It's a game! Don't tell them what to do!"

"They were just a bunch of kids, and he made them the best team in the state," I said.

"If I had been one of his players, he would have taken all the fun out of it for me," Jordan said. "I would have lost every bit of the fun."

"What about that climactic scene?" I said. "When the star player volunteers to take the shot that will win the championship or lose it?"

I had loved that scene. The player, in the huddle with just seconds remaining in the championship game, looks at the coach and, in a pure, even, youthful Midwestern voice that sounded like music to me, says: "I'll make it." Hardly any inflection at all. Not cocky, not nervous, not plaintive—just the voice of a kid at the moment of his life when, for the first time, he reaches full confidence. So simple: "I'll make it."

"Didn't you think that was moving?" I said to Jordan. "Didn't the way the kid said those words get to you?"

"I guess," Jordan said, clearly not overwhelmed by the cinematic basketball heroism.

Sometimes I forgot who I was talking to.

I had to go away for a couple of weeks. A book of my columns had been published, and I was obligated to go out on tour to promote it. I went to the last game of the season—an afternoon contest against the Detroit Pistons—with my suitcase packed. I would be leaving for the airport right after the final buzzer.

At the Stadium an hour and a half before game time, the parking lot guys, who were seldom seen inside the building, and the security men, in their yellow slickers, gathered atop the Bulls logo at center court to have a team picture of their own taken. NBC would be televising the game nationally; Elliott Kalb, the network's statistics man, touched the shoulder of a league official in town from the NBA offices in New York and said, "Jim? Atlanta-Milwaukee starts Saturday?"

"Um, I don't know," the man from the league said. "Let me check."

The rest of the country would be looking on the sports pages and in *TV Guide* for this kind of playoff information; the difference between the public and these two men was that these guys weren't consulting the TV listings to determine which games would be played when, they were scheduling the playoffs like personal airplane flights.

The afternoon's contest began. Marv Albert and Mike Fratello, calling the action for NBC, watched a monitor on their table as they spoke into the microphones attached to their headsets. NBC had paid a huge fee to the league for the broadcast rights to NBA games—the NBC money was a major reason that the players' salaries were as high as they were. But when one of the network's cameramen, during a time-out, knelt by the Pistons' bench to steady himself while providing the director with a live shot of courtside correspondent Ahmad Rashad giving a report, Bill Laimbeer of the Pistons said without a trace of levity to the cameraman: "You have ten seconds to get away from my seat."

The beat reporters on press row filled out forms to record their votes for the league's Most Valuable Player. The chip race was held on the scoreboard with 9:56 remaining in the fourth quarter of this last regular-season contest, and by the Bulls' bench Cliff Levingston, Scott Williams, and Horace Grant looked up and watched. After the game, which the Bulls won, I went downstairs for a few minutes. Jordan's father was waiting for his son. Approximately twenty reporters and TV crews had set up around Jordan's locker, aiming their camera lenses and microphones directly at his chair. But the chair was empty. He had not come out of the trainer's room yet, so while from a distance it may have looked as if a press conference was in progress, from closer range it was apparent that all the reporters and broadcast technicians were focusing their equipment and their attention on a man who wasn't there. I left the Stadium and set off for my trip across the country.

I was in eight cities. Throughout the NBA the first round of the playoffs was beginning, and in every town I would try to find a television set or a radio between appointments. While I was in Washington the coverage of the Bulls was interrupted by a news bulletin from the White House, and when the game resumed I was relieved that the station had gotten back to the important stuff. At Los Angeles International Airport I walked off the plane after a transcontinental flight, and in a terminal restaurant two airline maintenance men were staring up at a TV screen, watching the Bulls, and within moments we were standing together talking, analyzing a slow-motion replay of a Bill Cartwright foul, and I was supposed to be somewhere in L.A. but, my bag at my feet, I stood with them and watched until the end of the quarter. In Ohio I went to a minor league baseball game one night, and there were the expected hundreds of kids wearing Air Jordan shoes and Jordan T-shirts, but in the seat directly in front of me I saw something I wouldn't have anticipated here—a boy wearing a

Bulls jacket with a large drawing of Scottie Pippen on the back. A lovely late spring Midwestern night, and as I watched the game Pippen's face grinned back at me the whole time.

On one of my evenings in Ohio I ended up near my brother's house. I'd had some business late in the afternoon, and in a few hours I was supposed to be at a radio station on the other side of town. The sun had not yet gone down; I went to see my brother and his family, and he had a backboard in his driveway, like every driveway in every suburb you've ever visited, like the backboard in the driveway of the house where he and I grew up. I searched around his garage and found a basketball.

It had been years since I'd taken a shot. At the Stadium some nights, well before the games began, some sportswriters and broadcasters would grab a stray ball and shoot some lay-ups or foul shots. I'd never done that; it would have made me feel more than a little self-conscious and more than a little presumptuous, pretending to play basketball on the court where the NBA players competed. It would have been like walking onto the stage of Carnegie Hall and singing—the Mitty-like kick would be outweighed by the fear that a real singer might appear in the wings to scoff at the sight of the amateur trying to make believe.

At my brother's house, though, it was different. I stood in his driveway at twilight and started shooting. Some of the attempts bounced off the rim; some fell short; after a minute or so the balls began to drop in as often as they missed. All around the neighborhood were trees and telephone poles and the sounds of lawn mowers. Same size metal rim on the basket as in the Chicago Stadium; same size basketball; same ten feet from the ground to the hoop. I shot the ball and thought of Grant and Pippen and Cartwright and Paxson and Jordan, and of the incomprehensibly beautiful things they had somehow taught themselves to do with the ball and the rim and the same ten feet.

I was eager to get back. In hotel rooms all around the country I would watch the early playoff games on TV, and one of the Bulls would do something extraordinary and I would hear my voice shouting in approval. It was unintentional and automatic; it would have provided a stupid and silly sight for someone who happened to walk in unexpectedly—the sight of some guy by himself in a hotel room, shouting happily at a television screen—but there are probably certain advantages to being stupid and silly, in a world that is often miserable and flat. The Bulls, in the Stadium, scored on a fast break, and in delight I laughed aloud in the hotel room. You never know what will appear out of nowhere to change your life and make it a little better.

18

"**Y**OU MEAN FOR A REGULAR appointment?" Jordan said.

"Or for a toothache," I said. "I was just wondering how you went about doing it."

The little things that the rest of us don't even think twice about fitting into our daily routines—things like going to the dentist—each represented a decision for Jordan to make. Or so I had assumed; we were talking about how he handled tasks that to most people would be mundane, but to him meant venturing by himself into public, with all the concomitant difficulties that presented. He'd asked me to give him examples; I had started with a trip to the dentist's office.

"My dentist will agree to see me on one of his off days," Jordan said. "When there won't be any patients in his office. So he'll set a time to come in, and I'll meet him there at exactly that time and he'll unlock the office and let me in and work on me. It just saves a lot of things I'd otherwise have to deal with."

"What about Christmas shopping?" I said.

"That's a tough one," he said. "I really want to do the shopping myself—selecting all the gifts and everything. But when I go to the stores I get killed. It's the most crowded shopping time of the year, and there's no good time to just show up and hope that I'll be able to do my shopping in peace. I mostly call the specialty shops and explain what my situation is and ask if they'd mind staying open a little later. Sometimes, though, I have to just select gifts without seeing them myself, which isn't a very personal way to shop for people you care about."

"The movies," I said.

"The movies are pretty public," he said. "I don't go very often. When I do, I try to be the last person in the theater, after the lights go down, so the other people in the audience don't see that I'm there. If the movie theater is part of a mall, sometimes the security guys will ask if I need help, and I'll say maybe just getting to the car after the show is over. So they'll sit behind me during the movie, just in case, and after it's finished they'll walk with me back to the car."

"Restaurants?" I said.

"I'll phone ahead and explain," he said. "Usually they can put me at a place in the restaurant where my family or my friends and I can get through the meal without too many interruptions. Coming into the restaurant is harder than leaving, because usually when I go out to dinner it's after a game, and it's already late. So as often as not, when I go to a restaurant for dinner I'm the last person to leave."

"What about if you're at home, and you have a headache, and you look in the medicine cabinet and find that you're out of aspirin?" I said. "Do you just run to the drugstore?"

"The headache would have to be pretty bad for me to do that," he said. "Going into a drugstore attracts a lot of attention. On something like that I just wait until someone can pick up a bottle of aspirin for me later. I can't remember doing something like that any time recently."

"The gas station?" I said.

"Full service," he said. "I make sure I go to a place where I won't have to get out of the car."

"The bank?"

"I never go to the bank," he said. "I can't go in a bank."

"What about getting a haircut?" I said.

He smiled. "When I first came to Chicago, I would go to the barbershops on the West Side, because I didn't know anyone and that was the easiest way for me to meet people," he said. "And then when that became something that I couldn't easily do, I started asking some barbers to open up specially for me during off-hours, like my dentist does. But people found out about that, too, and after a while it didn't work. People always showed up outside the barbershop."

"So what do you do now?" I said. "Have someone come to you?"

"No," he said. "I cut my own. For the last couple of years, I have. I bought some professional clippers, the kind that real barbers use, and I taught myself how. It's not very hard at all.

I just stand in front of the mirror in my bathroom, and I do it. I have to do it every eight or nine days. It's just me by myself. It's a lot easier that way."

It was apparent that the playoffs had their own atmosphere even before you entered the Stadium. A trailer had been set up in the parking lot as an intermediate stopping-off point just before Gate 3½; reporters now had to go through a two-step process to get into the building, as a safeguard on the part of the Bulls and the NBA to make sure no one without a ticket or a playoff credential slipped by. The local news anchors were on the scene doing live pregame reports—not the sports anchors, but the main news anchormen and anchorwomen. Press row had expanded; there were now multiple rows of tables extending back from the basket, and more than twice as many reporters, many of them from national publications and broadcast outlets, were on hand as had been present during regular season games. The twelve Bulls, for their part, were wearing black basketball shoes rather than their standard white ones. This was a playoff tradition that had begun several years before, as a sign of team unity. "We didn't vote on it or anything this year," John Paxson said. "It's the playoffs, so we wear the black shoes."

I got back into town early in May, after the Bulls had swept the New York Knicks, and just as they were getting ready to put the Philadelphia 76ers away for good. The place was louder than I'd ever heard it, and suddenly each play seemed to be meaningful, a little self-contained drama of its own. You could see the level of concentration in the eyes of the players each time they came down the court.

For all the significance of the playoffs, though, some essential facts about what these men were doing had changed not at all. Right in front of us, Bill Cartwright jumped to reach for a rebound, found the ball eluding him, then jumped again as it was tipped from hand to hand until he finally snared it. He was about to turn thirty-four, he had been doing this since he was a child, and once you put aside all the NBA highlights films and all the fancy promotional videos about the resplendent intricacies of the game, this was what Cartwright got paid to do: jump in the air. Dress it up any way you like, set it to music, but this was what he did for a living. He jumped. And if he was not able to jump quite as high next year as he was able to jump this year, that was a fact that would affect his life at

the most basic level. His knees might hurt and he might be
worn out after the long season, but all the human-interest
interviews and all the team pictures and all the words of
sports-page praise and sports-page criticism would mean
nothing and matter for naught if one day it was determined by
his employers that he no longer could jump as high as they
wished him to. As he rebounded in the playoffs to the sound
of the crowd screaming, there was a look of ferocious longing
in his sad-eyed face.

Isiah Thomas, the Detroit Pistons guard whom Bulls fans de-
spised more than almost anyone else in the league—with the
possible exception of his teammates Bill Laimbeer and Dennis Rodman—warmed up on the Stadium court several hours
before Game 1 of the Bulls-Pistons Eastern Conference
championship series. He wore a gray property-of-the-Pistons
gym shirt of the type offered for sale in just about any mall in
America, the kind of certified-authentic shirt that mothers
bought for their sons for birthdays and Christmas, except that
of course Thomas' shirt really was the property of the Pistons,
it was a workplace-issued piece of functional equipment for
him.

As he walked off the court to go downstairs to the visiting
locker room, to dress in his blue uniform and wait for the
game to begin, Carmen Villafane and Daniel Spikes tried to
head toward him in their motorized wheelchairs. It was slow
going for them, but Thomas saw them coming and he waited.

"Could I please have your autograph, Mr. Thomas?" Daniel Spikes said.

"Sure," Thomas said, leaning down. "Do you have a pen?"

Daniel didn't; neither did Carmen. I was watching all of
this, and Thomas turned to me and said, "May I borrow
yours?"

"Of course," I said, and handed him the one I was carrying
in my pocket. Daniel and Carmen didn't have pieces of paper
ready, either; Carmen struggled to retrieve one from a knap-
sack that was attached to her wheelchair, and Thomas looked
over at me again and I gave him a couple of pieces of my
notepaper to save her the effort. He signed for both of them,
then continued toward the Pistons' locker room.

I thought this was lovely. Here they were, Carmen and Doc,
Michael's pals, and the hated Isiah Thomas had stopped to do

this for them. This was great; this was touching. I said so to
Carmen and Doc.

"I didn't want his autograph," Doc said.

"Of course you did," I said. "I saw you ask him for it."

"That was just an excuse to get close enough to him," Doc
said.

"Close enough?" I said. "Close enough for what?"

"To put the hoodoo on him," Doc said.

I had to stop myself from bursting into laughter. "To put
the *what*?" I said.

"I put the hoodoo on him," Doc said.

The hoodoo, apparently, was a mystical bad-luck spell of
Doc's devising.

"That's terrible," I said to Doc. "He was trying to be nice to
you."

"I had to put the hoodoo on him," Doc said. "The hoodoo
will make the Pistons lose."

And with that, the mission accomplished, the hoodoo having been applied, Doc and Carmen rolled away in their wheelchairs.

Years later basketball fans would take it on faith that the first
Detroit playoff game was the beginning of the Bulls' final
ascension to NBA dominance. The Bulls were rising to the
heights, the Pistons were no longer to be seriously feared, and
this would turn out to be the initial exhibit of evidence. No
one was yet aware of that as the first game started, though, or
at least no one was willing to say it out loud.

Jordan and the Bulls showed early that they were not
afraid. Things in the league were changing, and the five Bulls
starters on the court knew it before anyone else. "Start Me
Up," the Rolling Stones song that was popular in game-day
arenas around the NBA, boomed out of the Stadium speakers. The idea of having rock music at professional sports
events was to provide a young sound, as if the sports themselves were too old and too traditional, and needed some
goosing. But of course no player on the court was anywhere
near as old as Mick Jagger; the lead singer of the Rolling
Stones was an elder statesman of the music business who had
come along way before the players' time; he would be "Mr.
Jagger" to them. New world, and the Bulls raced up and down
the court as if the thought of becoming tired or worn out was
a totally alien concept. Final score: Chicago 94, Detroit 83.

On my way out of the arena I passed Daniel Spikes. "Is the hoodoo only good for one game?" I said to him. "Entire series," he said, and from his wheelchair he beamed a big smile up at me.

The most striking difference about the playoffs was not the excitement of the games, but the fact that for the first time since November, the faces of the opponents were the same night after night. For whatever reason that the NBA had historically scheduled one-night stands during the regular season —forcing teams to sometimes fly a thousand miles or more for a single game and then to immediately move on—the result of that policy was that you never got used to a team before it was gone. In the playoffs that changed; in the playoffs, as bitterly contested as they were, you got the feeling that you were beginning to know the visitors.

So Thomas, Laimbeer, Rodman, and the rest were back in the Stadium barely forty-eight hours after the end of Game 1. Jordan had been elected the league's Most Valuable Player, and he brought his teammates to center court to accept the award with him. The arena was packed and frenzied—it seemed even more crowded than it had been for Game 1, it was almost claustrophobic. If anything, the playoff drill of seeing the same team again every game made the Bulls appear less intimidated by the Pistons than in the first game. The Detroit team may have gone into Game 1 as the defending two-time world champions; now, though, they had become the guys the Bulls disposed of with so little trouble two days earlier.

Another Bulls victory, with Jordan seeming almost as free of tension as if he were at a scrimmage. Behind me a fan in a suit, tie, and glasses—someone told me he was a lawyer— screamed vulgar insults at the referees and the Pistons all night. If it wasn't "Garretson sucks!" bellowed at referee Darell Garretson, it was "Laimbeer sucks!" hollered at the Detroit center.

In the fourth quarter, when a call went against the Bulls, the man stood up in front of his seat—he was in the first row —and pointed his finger challengingly at Garretson. "Up your ass, Darell!" he shouted. A man sitting next to him, who had his own young son with him, appeared confused; perhaps he didn't know how to explain this kind of thing to his boy. "Up your ass!" the man kept yelling, in a rage.

I thought about what might happen if the man were some-how to charge onto the court. He apparently felt he was standing up for the team he supported, the Bulls, by what he was screaming. The Bulls and the Pistons were opponents—enemies, really—and the referees were allies of neither. But if this guy had taken his bellicosity one step further, and had run onto the court at Garretson, I knew for a fact that both the Bulls and the Pistons would have closed ranks to protect the referee, and maybe one of the players might even have leveled the fan. Every person on the court—every Bull, every Piston, every referee—had so much more in common with one an-other than with the loudmouthed fan. You can buy a ticket and you can buy a cap with the logo of your favorite team, but never fool yourself into thinking that you're one of them. You aren't. It's their special club out there, and none of us could ever hope to be a member of it.

The Bulls were two victories away from making it to the first NBA Finals in the history of the Chicago franchise. In the cab that took me home, the driver said he hoped the Bulls won it all this time around, because "Michael's getting a little long in the tooth." I thought he was joking, but then I remem-bered that twenty-eight, in this particular world, was not espe-cially young.

NBC seemed thrilled that the Bulls were doing so well in the playoffs; the NBA was a good draw generally for the network, but every game in which Jordan played caused a bump in the ratings. However many millions of people there were who were interested in watching a pro basketball game, there were at least several million more on top of that who would watch the game if Jordan were in it.

So you could not watch the network at any time of the day or night during the playoffs without seeing a promo featuring footage of Jordan, and a close-up shot of his smiling face. It was never just "the Chicago Bulls versus the Detroit Pistons"; the accepted promo language was "Michael Jordan and the Chicago Bulls take on the Pistons."

This was not something that was lost on the other players in the league. I asked Jordan how much resentment he sensed from his fellow professional athletes in the NBA.

"I know that there are a lot of players who pay very close attention to what I'm doing," he said. "I try not to force it with them. At the All-Star Game, for example, I make it a point not to try to overshadow anyone else. At that game, I don't want anyone to try to put me ahead of anyone else. If the league or the press tries to push me up, I try to push myself back down. If I sense I'm being made a special attraction, I step back. My attitude is, if you want the attention, be my guest."

"I have to assume that the special way you get treated can be a sore point with the people you play against," I said.

"Not just the people I play against," he said. "It's something I have to deal with even with my friends who are professional athletes in different sports. We'll be out to dinner, and someone will come up and hand me a piece of paper to autograph. I'll sign it, and then I'll pass the piece of paper around the table. Because I can always tell when the person who has come to the table is going to take my autograph and leave. So I hand it to my friends, and I tell my friends that the guy wants their autograph."

"Do your friends buy it?" I said.

"I think I get away with it," he said. "I hope I do. I hope they can't tell what I'm doing. Because I'm afraid that they may say to each other that they don't want to go out to dinner with me, because I get all the attention."

"Do you figure there's an inevitable feeling among other athletes that you're good, but you're not all that good?" I said. "That it could just as well be them getting all the acclaim?"

"If they do think that, or say it to each other, it's because they're going to want that success, and they're wondering if it's going to happen to them," he said. "But so much of it was timing, so much of it was just good luck."

"Yeah," I said, "I know, I've heard you say that before. . . ."

"I'm serious," he said. "Everyone tries to figure out why all of this has happened to me, and there are all these theories, and no one is willing to consider how much of it was just luck. But I'm the one who's going through it, and I think I know how it happened better than anyone else, and I'm telling you, luck has played more of a role than anyone understands."

I flew to Detroit. Jordan had said, "Are you coming with us?" It had never occurred to me to travel for games; I thought that was the province of the beat writers—going on the road with the team was, to me, akin to what going to press row at the Stadium had been at the beginning of the year: I wasn't sure how you did it, I didn't know the logistics or the rules, so it just wasn't something I'd considered. But that same day Tim Hallam said, "If you want to come, just let me know. It would be something different for you to see."

Thus I arrived at the Marriott Hotel in the Detroit suburb of Troy. Red Kerr was in the lobby with some of his broadcasting colleagues, and Will Perdue was in the gift shop; Bill Cartwright came off the elevator, looked around for a few moments, then headed out the front door by himself. This was the Bulls out of context; this was the Bulls as business travelers on the road, biding time before their next sales call.

Which wouldn't come until the following afternoon, at the Pistons' arena, the Palace of Auburn Hills. I took my bag up to my room. Kent McDill waved a greeting as he carried a plastic ice bucket to the machine near the elevator; Dave Hoekstra was letting himself into his room, directly across the hall from mine. The sportswriters were not permitted to fly on the Bulls' chartered jet—that was for the team and its staff only. So the writers took commercial flights, but were booked into the same hotels as the team. Today they were busy doing their advance stories which would appear in tomorrow morning's papers, previewing Game 3. It was a curious little tableau—here on the tenth floor were men in their rooms hunched over laptop computers; five floors up, on fifteen, were the twelve basketball players who were the subjects of the words that were going into the computers, the twelve basketball players the reporters had followed around the country and written about for the last six months. The worlds of the two groups of men—the men on the tenth floor and the men on the fifteenth floor—were eternally separated yet inextricably connected, today just like always.

I put my stuff away and ordered room-service dinner; before I left Chicago I had written some columns that, as usual, had nothing to do with basketball, and I had to call my editors and spend time on the phone going over the stories, which I did while I ate. Later I returned to the lobby. Some reporters and broadcasters were at the bar, and I joined them. "Full House" was on the television set; the network wasn't NBC, so during commercial breaks there was nary a mention of tomorrow's game.

The elevators were just to our right. In the middle of the evening the doors opened, and Horace Grant came walking out. Apparently he'd had enough of gazing at the walls in his room. He stood in his street clothes, carrying a board game called "Balderdash" under his right arm.

He was joined by Scott Williams. Both men stood six foot ten; it was impossible for them to hang out in a hotel lobby with any hopes of being inconspicuous. One guest of the Marriott—he appeared to have had a few drinks—approached them.

The man was a stranger to them; none of us knew him, apparently he just happened to be staying here. He simply stood in front of Grant and Williams and motioned as if sweeping the floor with a broom. His message was that the Bulls were about to sweep Detroit—that they were about to win the next two games and win the series 4-0. He kept making the sweeping motion, and waited for Grant and Williams to respond.

The two players only smiled. Grant nodded hello to the man, but he didn't want to jinx himself or the team by talking about victories that hadn't occurred yet. The man said: "So what finger are you going to wear your championship ring on?"

Again, Grant and Williams smiled politely and kept talking quietly to each other.

The man said that there was a big party going on down the hallway. "You ought to come down," the man said. "There's a band and drinks and lots of beautiful women."

Grant and Williams said no thanks; they wouldn't be going to the party.

"I'm serious," the man said. "The women would love to meet you."

Again Grant and Williams said no thanks.

And then the man said:

"If you brought Michael with you, you'd be sure to get lucky."

There it was. The words hung in the air as if italicized:

If you brought Michael with you, you'd be sure to get lucky.

Grant and Williams exchanged quick looks of resigned exasperation. It wasn't enough that they were superb athletes; it wasn't enough that if they won the series against Detroit they would soon be playing in the NBA Finals, for the championship of basketball. Jordan—who at the moment was upstairs in his own room—was a presence they knew they could never escape, even had they wanted to. Even when he wasn't there.

That first evening the Portland Trail Blazers were involved in a playoff game of their own in the Western Conference, and the TV sets in the Marriott were not equipped to pick up any cable station that was carrying it. So several of the players went out to watch it at a sports bar that had a satellite dish, and by the time they returned the night was getting late.

There was a nightclub/disco called Kicks off a side hallway of the Marriott; as the players came into the hotel Tim Hallam and Joyce Szymanski asked them if they wanted to check out the club for a while. Most said they were just going to go upstairs; Will Perdue paused, shrugged, and said why not.

As soon as we walked in, the crowd started to gravitate toward Perdue. He was in no way one of the Bulls' marquee players; I kept hearing "Which one is he?" from the people around us. Perdue was seven feet tall, and the patrons of Kicks were well aware that the Bulls were staying in the hotel, and that was enough. The scene was astonishing; women were rubbing up against him, they were throwing themselves at him in the most literal sense, and they didn't seem absolutely clear in their own heads as to why they were doing it. The nightclub was full and extremely loud, and it was obvious that many of the customers had been drinking heavily. One woman pulled a chair up next to Perdue, then climbed on it until she was face-to-face with him. He seemed neither shocked nor particularly amused by any of this; he seemed like a twenty-five-year-old guy who, by virtue of his physical stature, was accustomed to dealing with absurdity every day of his life.

The woman who was standing on the chair shouted to Perdue above the pulsating music: "What's your name?" Another shouted to him: "Bring Michael down! Bring Michael down!" And at that moment it was abundantly clear that Jordan could never allow himself to do something as simple as this—never allow himself to wander into a full-to-capacity bar to sip a couple of beers and listen to some dance songs.

This would make itself manifest the entire time we were in Detroit. In another part of the hotel that first night, a local video-marketing organization was having a dinner dance. Hallam and Scott Williams and I walked past the doorway leading into it; the people at the door, looking at Williams and realizing he must be one of the Bulls, motioned for us to come in. We were there for about half an hour, and it was sort of fun.

We talked to people, and Hallam and I had a drink, and Williams, luxuriating in being an NBA rookie center, a Chicago Bull, on the road for the playoffs, signed some autographs and answered some questions and, while indisputably the focus of attention, did not seem all that out of place at the party, at least in anything but a low-key way. Had Jordan inexplicably decided that, for some reason, he wanted to come down here, it wouldn't have looked right. The chasm between him and the rest of the world had become so great, for him to walk in here just to pass some time around midnight would likely strike people as eccentric and somehow off kilter. They'd be talking about it for years—the night Michael Jordan crashed their party. More judicious for him to remain behind that closed door upstairs.

After awhile Hallam and Williams and I left for our rooms. In the morning, in the hotel restaurant on the first floor, I saw Jordan's father eating breakfast. This was Memorial Day weekend; I could only imagine the possible scenario on the plane as Mr. Jordan and the passenger in the next seat flew up to Detroit from North Carolina.

SEATMATE: "So what takes you to Michigan, sir?"

MR. JORDAN: "I'm going there to see my son."

SEATMATE: "Oh, isn't that nice. Does your son live in Detroit?"

MR. JORDAN: "No, he's working there this weekend."

SEATMATE: "He has to work on a holiday weekend? That's a shame. What kind of work is your son in?"

MR. JORDAN: "Well . . ."

Dave Hoekstra had rented a car, and he offered to give me a ride to the Palace of Auburn Hills for Game 3. We drove through Michigan farmland; this was like an outing in the country—whatever this was, it wasn't Detroit. Had I not known that we were on our way to the arena where the Detroit Pistons played—had I mystically been dropped down here from space and told to guess where I was—I probably would have come up with Kansas, or Nebraska.

We had the radio on, and we talked as we drove, and this was more than all right on a warm Saturday in May, this wasn't a bad way at all to be spending a late-spring afternoon. We cruised down the highway through rural Michigan, and the subjects of our conversation ranged from Scottie Pippen to Bob Seger to Woody Hayes, and we were really in the country now, I believe I saw some cows in a field, and then, out of nowhere, the Palace loomed ahead.

If it was possible to come up with a polar opposite of the Chicago Stadium, the Palace of Auburn Hills was it. Gleaming and burnished and modern, set down on expansive, otherwise empty acres, the Palace was like a laugh in the face of the grim old Stadium, hunkered in its cloistered and crumbling Chicago interior-city neighborhood. Hoekstra parked the car, and we entered the Palace through the press gate. We walked up corridors and around corners unfamiliar to me, with that feeling of exploration that always comes your first time somewhere you've never been. In a covered area of the main level the Bulls were just arriving on their bus from the hotel.

As Jordan made the walk from the bus to the locker room, he wore a lightweight stereo headset clamped down over his ears. Later, when I was traveling to different cities in his company regularly, I would see that he wore the earphones virtually every time he was out in public on the road, and I would ask him about it.

"Is there even any music on there?" I would ask.

"I do listen to music when I have the headphones on," he'd say. "But that's not why I wear them. I wear them when I don't want to deal with people, and I want to think about the game."

"Like an invisible shield or something?"

"That's what it does for me, actually. Obviously it isn't a real shield—when I walk through a crowd of people, the headphones won't keep them from seeing me or talking to me or touching me. Even when I walk through a crowd with the headphones on, I know what people are saying. I can see their lips asking for things—I can see their lips forming my name, and I can see them showing things at me to autograph."

"But with the headphones you don't have to respond?"

"They offer me an excuse, really. It wouldn't even matter if there was no music playing. The people see me wearing the headphones, and it makes them realize I'm off somewhere else. Even though I'm not. I still see the people and I can tell what they're saying to me. I just keep walking until I'm by myself."

This afternoon in Auburn Hills he strode quickly into the locker room. For me it was new to hear the Bulls being booed as they came onto the court for warm-ups; it was new to see them in their red road uniforms. My seat was at a table directly behind the Bulls' bench; right behind me were several of the so-called "superfans" I'd read about in sports-page stories: unpleasantly loud, vulgarly abusive ticket-holders in arenas around the country whose pleasure at a game derived from ceaselessly taunting and insulting the visiting team from close range. These men today reminded me of the lawyer in the first row back in Chicago, but they were worse, their language and their message was even more repugnant: "You die, Pippen," one of them screeched maniacally and frantically, over and over, while another screamed in trembling fury at Jordan and repeatedly called him a "bald-headed nigger," which in the eyes of the ushers and security guards who stood by and did nothing presumably was an acceptable thing to say on the grounds that the name-caller was black, too.

This continued for the entire game. It was neither colorful nor excusable. Maybe around the league the home teams had persuaded themselves that this was just another exciting new part of big-time sports, but it didn't require much discernment or compassion to sense that any person who would behave this way game after game was sadly troubled in ways the rest of us might not even come close to understanding. As infuriating and offensive as these nonstop verbal attacks were, it wasn't as much the fault of these unfortunate souls who were doing it as it was the fault of the team's management for allowing it to go on in their building. "You bald-headed damn nigger," the one man yelled again, and another customer—this man black, also—reached over and covered the ears of his young daughter, who was with him. Bulls 113, Pistons 107, one game away from a sweep.

"I can't just sit in my room tonight," John Paxson said. "I was going stir crazy up there."

We were in the lobby bar of the Marriott on the night before Game 4. A lot of people from the team and its staff were hanging around; Bill Cartwright stopped by the piano to listen to someone play a song, Scottie Pippen ducked his head in to check out what was going on, Jerry Krause, the vice president of basketball operations, told some stories about his days as a baseball scout. If you didn't think too hard about it, it was easy to forget that tomorrow some of these men would be national sports heroes, observed by millions all around the country.

Not now. Paxson, in a pair of jeans and an open-necked shirt, stood by the bar and shifted from one foot to the other. If you can pace without going anywhere, that's what he was doing. I said that I'd seen a little plastic doll in the shape of him on the shelf of a toy store; that store stocked dolls— "action figures"—modeled after a number of professional athletes, and his doll had a moustache.

"I know," he said. "My kids have that doll. I used to have a moustache, and I guess they haven't made a new doll since then. I think my kids think the doll looks kind of funny that way."

A doll in his image. Such a hard part of his occupation to identify with. But the next second he was talking in terms that anyone who has ever wondered about job security at the office could understand. He said he had put his house up for sale, and I asked why.

"Oh, Phil took me out with seven minutes left in the third quarter one night, and he didn't put me back in," Paxson said. "I drove home that night and I was telling my wife how I felt about it, and she said, 'Maybe we ought to put the house on the market.'"

He knew there was no guarantee he would forever be a Chicago Bull; his contract was up soon, and he knew there was a chance that he'd be moving on. Might as well see what the house would bring, just in case. He didn't want to leave Chicago, but B. J. Armstrong, the man Jackson usually put into the game to spell Paxson, was twenty-three, and Paxson was thirty. In another kind of work, the signal a man would be attuned to and sensitive about might be when his boss gave a bigger sales territory to the young fellow at the next desk. With Paxson, it was a case of being taken out of the game in the third quarter and never getting back on the court that night. A concern that any human being might feel, even a human being who was on shelf display in toy stores nation-wide as a plastic doll.

Behind the hotel were four massive trailer trucks, each equipped with portable satellite dishes to beam live reports back to Chicago's major television stations. At eleven-thirty Sunday night Horace Grant was due to make an appearance with sportscaster Tom Shaer on WMAQ, the NBC-TV station in Chicago. Grant was wearing a red T-shirt with the slogan "Real Men Wear Red"—I never could figure out exactly what that meant, but Grant was involved with promoting it—and he and Shaer invited me to come along with them to the hotel anteroom where the cameras were set up. The room was warm and stifling, and Shaer spoke toward the lens and analyzed the playoff series, and Grant motioned to his shirt and urged people to buy their own, and seconds after the segment was completed the technicians switched off the harsh lights and Grant headed back in the direction of the elevators that would take him to his room.

Was it possible for any of them to fully comprehend, while it was going on, just how special and evanescent all of this was? When Paxson had been in the lobby he had been stopped by a kid with an autograph book. Paxson had signed his name, and so had Will Perdue, who had been wandering by. Both men put their uniform numbers next to their names, as if the numbers were part of their signatures—number 5 for Paxson, number 32 for Perdue. I wondered when they had started to do this automatically, when the numerals had become immutably melded to their identities, and I wondered how long it would take them to stop once this was over. The boy looked at the autographs and said, without any self-consciousness, to Paxson: "I just need Jordan now. Could you get it for me?" And Paxson, wanting to be helpful, said: "Your best bet is to stand here tomorrow morning when we leave for the game, and try to catch him on the way to the bus."

Before Grant went back upstairs I mentioned to him that, even with Game 4 coming up the next afternoon, he did not appear nervous at all.

"At two o'clock in the morning I'll be in bed," he said. "And my eyes will pop open and I'll just lie there staring at the ceiling."

Jordan led the team at both ends of the court the next day, driving relentlessly for the basket, sprinting down to lead the defense, making sure that Detroit's long domination of the Bulls would end by sundown. This was one of those games when it was better to watch him while pretending you'd never seen him play before. Those of us who were permitted to observe him at his craft every night sometimes fleetingly lost sight of just how exceptional the specifics of it were. So on days like this one—Jordan streaking past Detroit defenders, Jordan leaping to grab the ball before a Piston could retrieve it, Jordan so sure of a distant-range jump shot that he turns his back on it before it even reaches the rim—the ideal way to

comprehend what was going on in front of you was to create
the illusion that you didn't know a man could do this, and
then try to understand how a man could. It was impossible to
watch the day's performance and not see how meaningful this
climactic game against the Pistons was to him.

With four minutes gone in the fourth quarter, and the Bulls
in command, Scott Williams was in the lineup. I thought of
him as I'd seen him at the hotel over the weekend, wandering
through that dinner-dance, enthralled to be an NBA rookie in
public demand; I thought of him as I'd seen him earlier in the
year, Williams watching Jordan run the VCR in the Stadium
locker room forward and back, forward and back, Jordan trying to tell him how to move toward the basket for a dunk with
unstoppable confidence. Now, on the court in Auburn Hills,
Williams took a long pass and barreled toward the hoop and
slammed the ball in with as much confidence as you'd ever
want to be close to, and his teammates on the bench erupted
with loud cheers of delight. This was it; he and they were on
their way. He was about to be a rookie no more, and the Bulls
were en route to the NBA Finals.

But regardless of what was to happen in the final round,
there are things more important than trophies or titles. Every
year there is a reigning champion in every sport. People—
even the most earnest fans—quickly forget what team won
what title in what year. That kind of success is temporary.
Other things, though, are destined to endure.

During that final game in Detroit my seat was directly behind the Bulls' bench again. Seated next to me was the woman
who had sung "The Star-Spangled Banner" before the game.
Her name was Consuelo Hill; she told me that she had driven
twelve hours from Newburgh, New York, for the honor of
singing the national anthem.

I asked her how she had happened to be selected to be the
singer at today's game.

She was an ample woman with a broad, friendly, open face;
her musical training had been in opera, she said, and she had
been in Detroit for a performance back in January and had
sung the national anthem at a regular-season Pistons game
then. She had been invited to come back for this game.

We watched Jordan and the Bulls on the court, doing
away with the Pistons. I said that this whole thing must be
quite a thrill for her. She nodded her head, but seemed a little
hesitant.

"What's wrong?" I said.

"After the game in January," she said, "I went up to Bill Laimbeer to ask for his autograph." Apparently she hadn't been fully aware of Laimbeer's carefully cultivated hard-guy image.

"I smiled at him," she said, "and I said, 'I sang the national anthem for you.' And he just looked at me and said, 'I don't care if you sang a whole concert.'

"It just made me feel so small. I didn't know how to behave; I thought that maybe I'd made a mistake by speaking to him. It just made me feel low."

We watched the rest of the game together, and near the end, when it was clear beyond dispute that the Bulls would win, Phil Jackson removed the starters from the court and put in the substitutes. As the final minutes ticked off the clock, Jordan and Grant and Pippen and Paxson and Cartwright sat together on the bench, ecstatic in their triumph. If ever they had an excuse to shut the rest of the world out and luxuriate in their own accomplishment, it was now.

But out of nowhere, Jordan turned around. He looked back in our direction, until he caught Consuelo Hill's eye. She seemed to think he was looking at someone else. But he was looking at her.

He said: "I just wanted to tell you that I thought you did a very good job on the anthem."

Scott Williams, hearing Jordan and taking his cue, turned around, too, and said: "You really did."

Whatever would happen in the NBA Finals would happen. The real championships in life are not won on a basketball court.

In the last minute of play, their sweep of the Pistons certain, some of the Bulls stood up in front of their bench. I could see Jordan moving down the row, having a quiet word with each of his teammates. Scott Williams, right in front of me, appeared ready to run onto the court as soon as the buzzer sounded. I could already envision him leaping about and waving his index finger and screaming some version of "We're number one!" It would have been an understandable reaction on his part; he was twenty-two years old and he was on his way to the Finals.

Jordan reached him and put both hands on Williams' shoulders and stared into his face, and I could read Jordan's lips and decipher what he was saying to the young center. "Do this with class," Jordan said.

That's all it took. Williams ratcheted down his exuberance a few notches, and waited with the other Bulls for the clock to reach zero. But it didn't, at least not before the Pistons left the court.

In a moment that instantaneously gained assurance of inclusion on basketball highlights films forever, the Detroit team, petulant and livid about being humiliated in four straight by the Bulls, walked out of the arena before the game was over. It was difficult to believe it even as we were seeing it; the game was still being played, five Pistons reserves were still out on the court competing against five Bulls reserves, and the Detroit starters, with Isiah Thomas at the head of the procession, simply left. Walked into the tunnel leading to their locker room.

If they meant the action to be a show of contempt for the Bulls, it had exactly the opposite effect. It made the Pistons look to all the world like losers; it made them seem vanquished and insignificant and yesterday's news. They had been two-time world champions, and in this one moment, on national television, they were throwing away any respect that had accrued to them. Now the Bulls' victory was total.

All around me sportswriters were looking at this and trying to comprehend what they were seeing.

"What could they possibly have in mind?" one man said.

"What the hell has gotten into them?" another said.

But the answer to the Pistons' complete and absolute collapse was easy, and I smiled as I thought about it:

The hoodoo got 'em.

Phil Jackson held a short press conference, and so did Jordan, giving the broadcasters and sportswriters from across the country snippets of words to plug into their stories. Then Jordan, that stereo headset in place to keep the world at bay, got onto the team bus for the ride to the airport. In a few days the NBA Finals would commence.

There would be financial rewards for the two teams in the Finals, and an NBA championship trophy for one squad. But as Jordan and his teammates climbed onto the bus, it seemed that making it to the Finals might not be only about money or plaudits. Jordan at this moment was like a kid in a schoolyard late on an afternoon. When you're a kid on the playground, the best thing about winning a game is not the winning; the best thing is that you get to keep playing. As long as you continue to win, you're allowed to stay on the court. The losers have to sit down and wait.

The playground was a global one now, but it remained a playground. Twenty-seven NBA teams had begun the season. Now all but two had to sit by the side of the court and watch. Jordan and the Bulls still had the basketball.

19

M ARV ALBERT AND TOMMY ROY sat elbow-to-elbow in the third row of the American Airlines jet headed from Detroit to Chicago.

Albert had just finished broadcasting the Bulls-Pistons game; Roy had been the producer of the NBC broadcast. On Albert's tray table they had propped a battery-powered miniature television set with a VCR built in. The TV set was equipped with two jacks for earplugs.

One wire snaked out of the TV set and into Albert's ear; one wire snaked into Roy's. Millions of Americans had just seen and heard their telecast, but they hadn't. At least they hadn't been able to pay much attention to what was going out over the air. They'd been too busy creating it.

As they had hurried out of the Palace of Auburn Hills, an NBC technician had given them a tape of the game. Now, together, they were watching what they had done less than two hours before, evaluating and criticizing it. They were sort of like painters getting a good look at their latest canvas for the first time. By midnight tonight they would have switched planes at O'Hare and would be on the West Coast preparing to broadcast a Portland–Los Angeles game. The winner of that series would play the Bulls in the Finals. I glanced at the screen between them and saw Scottie Pippen driving on Dennis Rodman, and it already seemed like something that happened a long time ago.

The best-of-seven Finals would begin in Chicago with two games against the Lakers, then move to Los Angeles. In the twenty-five-year history of the Bulls' franchise the team had never been to the NBA Finals; suddenly the Stadium was about to become the epicenter of the international sports world, and those 18,676 seats and standing-room-only spots were going to be precious beyond monetary value.

There were all kinds of rumors:

Jack Nicholson wanted front-row tickets, and would pay any price asked. Elizabeth Taylor wanted to come to Chicago. Princess Diana had expressed an interest in the Bulls. President Bush might come for one game. No one knew which of those stories were true and which were fanciful, but none were beyond belief, because the draw of Jordan—especially Jordan playing for the championship against Magic Johnson —was stronger than anything sports-and-entertainment marketeers would have dared to dream up.

Along with the demand for tickets came the accompanying desire, on the part of celebrities, to meet Jordan. A game of status one-upmanship was beginning; if tickets to the Chicago Stadium had now become the currency of the realm in glamour and power centers all over the country, then a chance to spend a few moments with Jordan carried even more weight. You could live in Beverly Hills or Washington or Manhattan and create a little jolt of envy in your neighbors by casually mentioning that you were going to Chicago for the Finals; to really put them away, though, you would say that you were scheduled to get together with Michael Jordan.

"Does that make you nervous at all?" I asked him.

"Not really," he said. "Why should it?"

"I don't know," I said. "All these famous people wanting their moments with you. And I figure a lot of them were famous way before you were famous. They're scrambling to meet you, and maybe there are some of them who don't realize that you'd be nervous to meet them."

"Nope," he said. "There's no one I would be nervous to meet."

"There has to be someone," I said.

"There isn't," he said. "I see people getting so nervous to meet me, and I know that I'm just some person, so why should they be nervous? If they're nervous meeting me, and I know that they have no reason to be, then I have no reason to be nervous meeting anyone. Because no matter who it is I'm going to meet, that person probably can't understand why he or she would make people nervous, either."

"It's human nature, though," I said. "Everyone gets nervous meeting someone."

"Not me," he said.

"What about if someone came into the locker room and told you that you were going to meet the president?" I said.

"Nope," he said.

"The pope," I said.

"No," he said.

"The Queen of England," I said.

"No," Jordan said.

"Frank Sinatra," I said.

"There's no one," Jordan said. "I'd enjoy meeting Frank Sinatra, but I would know there just was no reason for me to be nervous, because I'd know he had been through the same thing I had."

"There must have been a time when you were nervous about meeting someone," I said.

"There was," he said. "It happened once in my life."

"Who was it?" I said.

"When I first met Coach Smith, I was really nervous," he said.

Dean Smith—the coach of the University of North Carolina basketball team.

"That scared me," Jordan said. "That got to me. But that was a lot of years ago. I was in high school at the time. I can't imagine it happening again."

David Stern, the commissioner of the NBA, stood beneath one basket just before Game 1 of the Finals, chatting with Jordan. Stern was in a dark suit, Jordan was in his white basketball uniform. The sight of the two of them in earnest conversation did not have the feel of an old-time commissioner making a patriarchal visit to some grateful and obsequious athlete toiling in the field, though. Stern and Jordan looked very much like business partners. Together they gazed soberly around the Stadium, at the fans arriving to fill the seats, at the extra press tables that had been jammed into every available inch of the arena, and they might have been examining their accounts book to see what kind of fiscal year their company was having.

Sportswriters and broadcasters from nations all around the globe had arrived in Chicago to cover the Finals. They made collect calls, speaking loudly in English to be heard above the Stadium noise as they gave instructions to American operators—"I wish to talk to Mr. Consueles"—and then in their own languages once they reached their home offices. The basketball players—twelve Lakers, twelve Bulls—prepared to compete. If you're a player, how do you possibly process something like this? Men from countries you've never visited —maybe some countries you didn't know existed—pack their suitcases and update their passports and say goodbye for a while to their families and travel to the United States to watch you play a game.

To see Jordan guarding James Worthy, trying to smother him on defense, was to recognize instantly that nothing that had happened all season, including the playoffs thus far, was going to be anything like this series of games. Jordan and Worthy had been college teammates at North Carolina, they had known each other longer than they had known anyone in the NBA. They were still friends, or so the story went. But the fury with which Jordan pressed Worthy, the pure and basic and vestigial athleticism with which the men competed, was a sign that now we were into something extraordinary.

Magic Johnson loudly called signals to his teammates on the court, and it mattered; they looked to him and paid attention as if he held the key to the most important secrets in the world, secrets they needed to know. With 8:30 to go in the second quarter, Pippen went back in the game for Grant, and on the court Pippen spoke urgently with Cliff Levingston about whom to guard now, making sure both of them were absolutely sure of their assignments. They all understood something: They could not sit back even for a second. One lapse—one blown play, one lazy mistake that might have been shrugged off and forgiven in January or February—could mean the points that would decide the game.

B. J. Armstrong spelled Jordan midway through the second quarter, with Los Angeles leading 39-34, and this was the real test: Would the Bulls be able to remain close with Jordan on the bench? The smiling handshakes and jovial joint TV appearance by Jordan and Johnson to promote the Finals were over. To judge by the expressions on their faces out on the court, they might as well have never met. No grins or hugs, not now; this was business, and life, and in some degree this was being a man.

It was June in Chicago, nearing ninety degrees outside the Stadium, and the lead changed from the Lakers to the Bulls and back again twenty-two times. Jordan could have won the game with a long jumper in the final four seconds, but the ball rattled around the rim and then popped out. The Lakers led the series one game to none. During an intermission there had been the usual chip race up on the scoreboard, but for the first time all year not a player watched.

"Join us next game for the Subaru shoot-the-hoop contest," Ray Clay intoned over the P.A. system.

This was during a time-out in the midst of Game 2. The Subaru promotional contest had just been held, and Clay's script, as always, called for him to invite the fans to watch it again the next time the Bulls played at the Stadium. But there was no guarantee there would be a next time, at least not this season; the teams would be going to Los Angeles for Games 3, 4, and 5 if a fifth game was necessary. No one knew whether the Bulls would be coming back.

I was assigned to the upstairs press box; it was the first time during the season I'd sat there. The beat writers from around the country who were covering the game on deadline were at the courtside tables, so I watched from the high-in-the-arena vantage point. From up here the season just past seemed distant and far off, as if something were departing and I could not touch it or stop it from leaving. Jordan was feeding the ball to his teammates during the opening minutes; they would throw it to him and he would throw it right back. It was as if he had decided that the Lakers must not be permitted to believe that he had been appointed to win a championship by himself. The Lakers had seen his teammates turn automatically to him at the end of Game 1—had seen Jordan take the shot, miss the shot, had seen the Bulls lose.

So he fired the ball to Pippen, he fired the ball to Cartwright, he fired the ball to Grant. There was almost an anger in how he did it, almost a contempt toward the rest of the world, that he should have to go through this drill and prove something he did not think needed proving. Once the elementary concept of the team effort had been established, though, he started shooting. I had seen him do some impressive beyond understanding things during the season, but I had not seen him play at this level. He took eighteen shots from the field during the game and made fifteen of them. Apparently he had determined that the ball was not going to be allowed to miss.

The shot that made eighteen thousand people melt into

their seats came midway through the fourth quarter. Jordan drove toward the basket as if preparing to slam a ferocious dunk shot. The ball was in his right hand, which was extended above his head. But as he approached the hoop, Sam Perkins of the Lakers was in his way. High in the air, still heading for the rim, he brought the ball back down, hesitated for a fraction of a second, shifted the ball to his left hand—he was floating toward the backboard in heavy traffic all this time— then, at the penultimate instant, stretched out his left arm and banked the ball off the glass and into the net.

In the press box, a dozen writers stood up without a word and walked briskly to a TV monitor that was tuned to the NBC broadcast. That swift, reflexive, silent walk was the greatest tribute they could pay to what they had just seen. There was no time to discuss it with one another; they knew they had just witnessed a basketball moment they would remember for the rest of their days, and now they wanted to make sure they hadn't imagined any of it. They stood in front of the TV set, not looking at the court, and watched the replay again and again and again. Somewhere down below on the floor of the Stadium something or other must have been going on. The writers had their backs to it. Within the next year, Jordan's shot would be replayed on various sports broadcasts and game intros literally thousands of times; it would become a new logo for the beauty of professional basketball. Now it was still just a few seconds old, and the writers stared at the monitor, making sure that it had been real.

At 10:45 P.M., the game over (Bulls 107, Lakers 86), Magic Johnson was standing in the basement room that had functioned as the press buffet all year. For the Finals it was doubling as the postgame interview area; Johnson, still in his uniform, was telling the assembled reporters that he had never seen anything quite like Jordan's shot, either. Whether willingly or because he knew he'd have to do it anyway, he served as a play-by-play man after the fact, describing not something he himself had done, but Jordan's shot: "He came down the lane, went one way, put it in one hand, floated it about five more yards, and said, 'Well, I don't know.' Then he changed hands and laid it in off the glass. That's just the kind of player he is. He can do the impossible and unbelievable."

I took a walk down that grungy basement hallway and, unexpectedly, found Jordan. He was already dressed in a business suit (people always granted him the proper amazement for his shooting skills, but what I wanted to know was how he could routinely shower and dress and look like a man on his wedding day in the time it took most of us to get a drink of water); he and Tim Hallam were sitting on two folding chairs inside a little recess in the cement catacombs.

He was committed to addressing the reporters after Johnson had finished and Phil Jackson had had his turn. There was a TV set resting on the seat of a third chair, tuned to the local NBC affiliate, WMAQ, which was broadcasting the press conferences live. Jordan, not fifty feet away from the press throng but almost alone in the alcove, watched the monitor with some impatience.

"I'm hungry," he said to Hallam.

"I know, but you've got to do this," Hallam said.

"I will, I will," Jordan said. He was a public relations man, a de facto coach, a manager, inspirational speaker, interview subject, photographer's model, explainer of strategy, visual symbol of the league, and ambassador for his city. And oh, yeah, he played basketball, too. It was in fulfillment of all those roles that he would stand before the reporters and camera crews, and would allow them to take his picture and ask him questions. That's what he was waiting to do. Mostly, though, he wanted to go to dinner.

As the Bulls prepared to fly to Los Angeles with the series tied 1-1, Jordan had become the national symbol of Chicago. He perpetually was anyway, in one way or another; all year people around the country thought of Jordan and thought of the Chicago Bulls, and they thought of the Chicago Bulls and thought of Jordan. But during the NBA Finals, the man and the city became inseparable. There probably wasn't a citizen of Chicago who could travel anywhere in the United States that week and not be asked about Jordan.

The fact was that Jordan in the years before he had been drafted by the Bulls had nothing at all in common with Chicago. He had grown up in a North Carolina as different from the urban, gritty image of Chicago as you could get. It was a matter of fate that people now connected the city to a mental picture of him. There was nothing inherently Chicago about Jordan, and had some other team drafted him out of college, the connection would never have been made.

"Chicago?" Jordan said. "I don't know if I had any thought of it at all when I was growing up. Big city, probably. If it even crossed my mind, I'm sure I must have known it was a big city. Even as a kid I was never too crazy about big cities."

"Did you have any stereotype of it?" I asked. "The old Capone stuff, or the politics, or anything like that?"

"I don't think I even knew about that stuff," Jordan said. "I probably was just vaguely aware that there was a place called Chicago that had too many people in it. Like New York. I probably didn't differentiate between the two. I definitely never thought I'd end up in Chicago."

"Was there something about the city that made you not want to go there?" I said.

"It was more of a situation where I don't think Chicago even registered in my consciousness," he said. "I was in North Carolina. That's all I knew and all I wanted."

"You never wanted to leave home?" I said.

"I was afraid of a major, major city when I was a kid," he said. "I'd never even been to one. When the Bulls drafted me and I flew to Chicago, the team didn't pick me up at the airport. I flew into O'Hare and there was no one there for me. That was my introduction to Chicago. I got off the plane and there I was, alone."

"Did you see the prices on the room-service menus?" Will Perdue said.

He was the first person I'd run into in the lobby of the Ritz-Carlton Marina del Rey. He was standing by the front door of the hotel, as if preparing to go out.

"I haven't looked yet," I said.

"Man!" Perdue said. "This is a real nice place, but there's no way I'm going to pay that kind of money for a sandwich! I think Bill Cartwright and I are going to take a walk and see if we can find a restaurant around here."

It was not necessarily an observation I would have expected from an NBA player in Los Angeles for the championship series—the world was always being told how much money these guys made—but it was sort of pleasing. When Perdue had started out as a boy tossing balls at a hoop, he could not have known that one day he'd be a Ritz-Carlton traveler; somehow his authentic shock at the room-service prices was an agreeable and genuine touch in the midst of a jumbled week.

"You just get in?" Perdue said.

"Just a few minutes ago," I said. At O'Hare Airport in

Chicago, before boarding my flight to California, I had stopped at a newsstand and picked up a copy of *Sports Illustrated*. Jack McCallum, *S.I.*'s pro basketball writer, had been in Chicago for Game 1 and Game 2; when I had seen him at the Stadium I'd asked him if he thought the article he was working on would be a cover story. He had laughed as if the question was too absurd to even ponder. "I imagine so," he'd said. "All the photographer has to do is get Michael and Magic in the same frame of film, and the picture will make the cover." And of course he was right; an action shot of Jordan and Johnson competing against each other was as good a sales hook as a magazine could hope for, and on my way across the continent I'd read McCallum's cover story, which, six miles in the air, seemed in a way like a letter from home.

Perdue lingered by the front door of the Ritz. Andy Rosenberg, the young director for NBC's television coverage of the Finals, was there, too, waiting to hook up with Tommy Roy and other members of the production staff. "We're relighting the Forum," he said.

"You guys are in charge of the lights at the basketball arenas?" I said. "I didn't know that."

"Technically, we're not supposed to be," he said. "The way the Forum is lit during the regular season is fine for the fans in the seats. But on television, you can see the players, but their faces aren't distinct. It's just not a good look for the Finals. So we're lighting the whole arena the way we want it. The deal is, we're allowed to do it, but the Lakers have the right to approve or disapprove when we're done."

"That's got to be costing you some money," I said.

"An incredible amount of money," he said. "And we do it knowing that if Magic Johnson and James Worthy walk in and decide they don't like it, we'll have to just tear it all down."

In the bar of the Ritz, the traveling family was assembling. Red Kerr, who had been the Bulls' first coach back in 1966 and who would be doing the radio broadcast back to Chicago, said that a limousine had picked him up to take him to an appointment: "I got in, then got out and got in again just so people could see me. I wondered what my old friend Stinky Fryer would have thought of me getting into a limo. That's still how I judge everything—how Stinky back in the neighborhood where I grew up would react." On a terrace outside the bar, with a view overlooking the gorgeous marina, crews from Chicago television stations were setting up for live reports.

Phil Jackson and one of his assistant coaches, John Bach, sat together at the bar, waiting until it was time for Jackson to go onto the terrace and be interviewed. Perdue, apparently still undecided about his meal plans, wandered in to join us.

B. J. Armstrong and Craig Hodges were out in the hallway; they had just been guests on a network talk show, and they said they'd heard that Scottie Pippen had been invited to appear on Arsenio Hall's program. Jordan was turning down all such requests. There was no real need for him to go anywhere for TV appearances; that breathtaking shot from Game 2 was delivering him into every television home in the country—the sports broadcasts seemed virtually unable to stop playing it, it was as if they were addicted to that piece of video. Andy Rosenberg had done a flawless job capturing the shot from every camera angle imaginable. He'd certainly had the lights he'd needed that night. I didn't know whether Jordan even knew him; for however many years that shot appeared on television to augment and amplify the Jordan legend, Jordan would get proper credit for the basket, but Rosenberg was deserving of at least an assist.

"Hello, Will," Phil Jackson said, catching sight of Perdue in the bar.

"Did you see the prices for food at this place?" Perdue said to his coach.

Around two o'clock the next afternoon I walked onto the balcony outside my room. Sailboats and yachts filled the marina. The Pacific Ocean beckoned, blue and inviting.

I stood there looking at the water, and after a while I looked above me, toward the higher floors. Four stories up, another man was out on his own balcony; he, too, was looking at the water. He was alone, seemingly lost in thought. Scottie Pippen.

In a few hours tens of millions of people around the globe would be watching him perform his craft. Now Pippen watched the ocean. The hotel was decidedly formal, with marble floors and mahogany furnishings; it was a place where most of the staff wore tuxedos and every guest was invariably referred to as "Sir" or "Ma'am." On some level Pippen had to realize that, were it not for his skills with a basketball, this kind of establishment, and this kind of life, would in all likelihood have been eternally beyond his reach. It is the essential lure and the essential cruelty of professional sports: If you are among the anointed best, your world will change forever and all of this will be yours. If you are the slightest bit lower on that echelon of skill, you sit in your home, wherever you may live—you sit in your home in the central part of Arkansas—and you observe your athletic betters on a screen.

Earlier in the day I had seen Pippen and his friend Grant taking a quiet walk around the manicured grounds of the Ritz. All of this attention, all of this international scrutiny. They were twenty-five years old.

Now Pippen stood and looked at the water. The entire side of the hotel was in shade; the sun had passed over the roof. So Pippen, on his balcony, was in cool shadows, but the water itself was bright and dappled with California sunlight. Somehow Pippen got here; somehow all of them did. The water was calm, and Pippen stared out at it for a very long time.

"Dr. and Mrs. McCabe?"

The kid on the pay telephone apparently had reached an answering machine on the other end. He was speaking without pausing even briefly between sentences, a sign that there was no actual human he expected to respond to him.

"This is Brian Sacks," he said. "I was wondering if you could tape the Poison concert? We were there for it, and I think you can see us in the audience. We're at the Forum now, so we can't tape it ourselves. The Poison concert is on at eleven, I think, on ABC, I think."

He was an L.A. kid in shorts and high-top sneakers, maybe a high school student, a college freshman at the oldest. This was in the lobby of the Forum, sixty-five minutes before tipoff of Game 3. A classic Los Angeles example of Big Event Overload. In the audience at the network taping of the Poison concert, in the audience at the network telecast of the NBA Finals. A fellow can't be everywhere at once.

L.A. was accustomed to having winners to observe, accustomed to having champions of every sort on hand all year round for the personal viewing pleasure of the people in the seats. As soon as I walked into the arena I felt as if I'd been there before; I had seen so many Laker games on TV, had seen the orange-and-yellow chairs of the Forum and the distinctive spokes of its ceiling on so many album covers for big-name musical groups in live concert. I found the press area, high in the arena behind one basket. Down below, the singer-

of-the-night walked to center court to perform the national
anthem. I thought his voice was very nice.

"Who is that?" I said to the reporter in the next seat. "He's
a pretty good singer."

"Placido Domingo," my seatmate said.

"Oh," I said. Back at the Stadium, the anthem was generally sung by a chunky, earnest Chicago computer technician
by the name of Larry Kornit.

"I guess out here you can pretty much pick and choose
among singers," I said to my seatmate, who worked for a
television station in L.A. "I mean, gee. Placido Domingo."

"The Lakers are probably disappointed," he said. "They
probably wanted the fuckin' Beatles."

There were six championship banners behind me. The fans
were so nonchalant that even tonight, even for a game as
ravenously anticipated all over the world as this one, many
ticket-holders were choosing to show up fashionably late. I
watched the game begin as the NBC cameras dotting the Forum beamed it to the nation, and all of a sudden those November nights at the Stadium for games that meant nothing,
those blizzard-whipped February nights when the name of the
opponent wasn't even important, felt valuable.

Meanwhile Game 3 unfolded. I had been telling myself all
year that the individual games weren't what counted; I had
been telling myself that the feelings of being here were what
would last, that the specifics of what took place on the court
on a given evening were ultimately ephemeral. I still believed
that; I still believed that the small moments, the unexpected
found experiences, were what I would take with me and cherish over the years.

Having said that, Game 3 of the NBA Finals was probably
the best basketball game I had ever seen. Two exceptional
teams pushing each other to the limits of their talents for all
forty-eight minutes of regulation, each player proudly displaying to the world what he could do best, the scoreboard showing the Bulls and the Lakers staying within striking distance of
each other throughout the night. Each man on the court having his great moments; each trip down the floor failing to
answer the question of who would leave the arena as the winner. Vlade Divac of the Lakers sinking a miracle shot as he
stumbled in the lane with less than a minute remaining, the
referee signaling he had been fouled as he had been aiming
the ball, Divac hitting the free throw to complete the three-

point play and put his team ahead 92-90 with 10.9 seconds left
in the game. The Lakers celebrating wildly under their basket,
thinking they had pulled it out.

And Michael Jordan watching the Lakers' celebration, then
calmly, all by himself, bringing the ball upcourt, no one in the
building taking an unlabored breath. Jordan dribbling in front
of Byron Scott of the Lakers, the Laker fans screaming, everyone in the Forum knowing that the Bulls and Jordan were
within seconds of a loss that could devastate their dreams.
Jordan, seemingly no more nervous than if he were at practice
back in Chicago, seeing the clock ticking down over the basket, understanding there was no time to set up a play or feel
out the Laker defense, yet sensing that with the right move he
could throw Scott off balance, then doing just that, as if
he were watching himself on film. His shot sailing toward the
basket with 3.4 seconds left, dropping through the net, the
Forum suddenly going stony silent.

Bulls 92, Lakers 92. The Lakers tried to inbound the ball;
Jordan lunged for it and swatted it away where it could do no
harm. The buzzer sounded to end regulation. In the tumult of
the ensuing overtime he scored six more points, directing the
Bulls to a 104-96 victory and a 2-1 lead in the series.

In my Jimmy Crum years at St. John Arena in Columbus,
every game was a gift to my spirit, every game made me glad.
Only one, though, stands out vividly above all others in my
mind as the best. I can't tell you many of the details. I can only
tell you that with time running out, Larry Siegfried hit a long
shot from the left side of the foul lane to beat Indiana and
end the most exciting basketball game I had ever been lucky
enough to watch, and that for thirty years I had been seeing
that shot in my head. Now that shot and that game had company. I had a notion that in the recesses of my finest memories I would be seeing Jordan hitting that jumper over Byron
Scott for the rest of my life.

I don't know how Los Angeles people celebrate thrilling victories; maybe they're so used to them that they just go out to
dinner afterward and talk about life in general. Chicago
hadn't had all that many nights like this one, however. Back at
the bar of the Ritz, Red Kerr entertained the traveling party
by eating lighted matches. This was a table trick that perhaps
would be frowned upon at Spago, but Red was that happy.
Phil Jackson joined the rest of us and never let the smile leave

his face. Cliff Levingston, who had come off the bench to have one of his best nights as a Bull, walked around allowing people to shake his hand and congratulate him. No one was being cool or detached; the Finals weren't over yet, but nights like this one were rare, and no one was going to pretend otherwise. Red Kerr ate another match, and I had a feeling that Stinky Fryer would have understood.

"I haven't really left my room," Jordan said.

He had not been seen celebrating after Game 3; he was scarcely ever seen around the hotel that week. We were talking in the Bulls' locker room at the Forum just before Game 4.

"I've left the room for practice, and for the game," he said. "But except for about thirty minutes, that was it."

"What were the thirty minutes?" I said.

"Some friends of mine were playing tennis and I wanted to watch them," he said. "So I did go downstairs and I sat next to the court and I watched."

"Right on the hotel grounds?" I said.

"Yes," he said.

"No one bothered you?" I said.

"I could sit there," he said. "No one even came by. I was able to watch them play for almost half an hour. Then some people started to figure it out, and started to come around. So I left."

"What did you do?" I said.

"I went back upstairs," he said. "Other than those thirty minutes or so, I've been in the room."

Jim Cleamons, one of Phil Jackson's assistants, was diagraming plays on a chalkboard, drawing little half-court replicas of the basket and the foul lane, labeling each setup: "Transition," "Sideline 12-12-18," "3 Up," "15," "2 Down." Jordan was still in his civilian clothes, with his red road Bulls uniform laid out on the carpeting; the newspapers had been full of reports that he had injured his toe in the previous game, and that he was going to be playing in pain tonight, with one of his shoes specially modified by team physician Dr. John Hefferon and trainer Chip Schaefer.

A group of reporters entered the locker room. Jordan, sitting coolly near his cubicle, seemed impalpably removed from the notion of some athlete in physical distress. Whatever discomfort Jordan ever felt, he seldom let the outside world see how he was being affected. With him, injuries were something the public might read about on the sports pages, but not something he chose to discuss in any kind of personal detail.

"So," a reporter said to him, "do you have an orthopedic shoe endorsement contract?"

"Nah," Jordan said, playing along. "I don't think there's any profit in that."

"Don't sell yourself short," another sportswriter said. "Seventy-year-olds would snap them up."

Jordan shook his head. An hour from now he would be on the court before a full Forum and a television audience of forty million. The writers were hooked on their toe jokes. "The Lakers are going through a special warm-up drill," one of them said.

"What's that?" Jordan said.

The reporter began stomping his foot down hard on the floor, all around Jordan's injured foot.

"You guys are sick," Jordan said, laughing.

"It's their new kick-the-can defense," the stomping reporter said.

I left the locker room and went to my seat up near the top of the Forum. The Bulls came onto the court for warm-ups, then the Lakers. The correspondents from foreign countries, the same people I'd seen in Chicago, were here in Los Angeles now, screaming above the crowd noise into microphones and telephones, few words understandable to me but several leaping out: "Pippen!" "Magic!" "Paxson!" And, always: "Jordan!"

He scored twenty-eight to lead both teams. Bulls 97, Lakers 82. One game away from the championship.

The foreign voices speaking his name were nothing new to Jordan. It wasn't only the broadcasters from other countries. In the lobby of our hotel one afternoon I saw several guests from Japan who had made reservations in advance and had had no idea this would be the visiting team's hotel during the NBA Finals. Now someone had let them know. I could hear them talking excitedly in their own language. Every few seconds I could make out the words *Michael Jordan*.

"When was the last time you weren't recognized?" I asked him.

"By who?" he said.

"By anyone," I said. "Just a case of being somewhere and no one knowing who you were."

"A couple of years ago, I was in Paris," he said. "I couldn't speak the language. And they're not very basketball inclined in Paris at all. So none of the French people recognized me."

"You could just do whatever you wanted?" I said.

"The French could care less," he said. "When I went to the stores to go shopping, none of the French people bothered me. I'll tell you, I didn't miss the attention. We were all sitting outside at a café having lunch one day . . . it was really nice. It was fun."

"It must have been," I said. "To have one place in the world where they didn't know who you were. To be able to get through lunch."

"Well, I couldn't really get through lunch," he said.

"What do you mean?" I said. "You just said no one recognized you."

"The French people didn't recognize me," he said.

"I know," I said. "And you were in France."

"But there were a lot of Americans and Italians and Spanish people and Germans around," he said. "They recognized me."

"Oh," I said. "So you didn't really get left alone after all?"

"Well, I did by the French people," he said.

"But the others bothered you?" I said.

"It wasn't so much a case of bothered me," he said. "But they saw I was there and some of them came up."

"What I was asking about was the last time that *no one* recognized you," I said.

"You mean no one at all," he said. "You mean not just the French."

"A place you've gone where you weren't noticed," I said. "Where you were pretty sure no one knew who you were."

"No one," he said, thinking.

A few moments passed before he spoke again.

"I can't remember the last time that happened," he said.

On the night the Bulls would become the basketball champions of the world, their locker room before the game felt like the last day of school. The players and coaches and staff were grown men, so they were too old to be passing around yearbooks to solicit each others' autographs, but that's what the loose, friendly, almost giddy atmosphere reminded me of.

The curious thing was, there was still a game to be won. You would think the team would be doing everything possible to avoid tempting superstition—you would think they would refuse to acknowledge what might await them at the end of the evening. It was hardly possible, though; NBC technicians were preparing to hang lights in the room so the postgame celebration could be telecast in the event of a Bulls victory, and Tim Hallam was meeting with NBA officials to determine who would be allowed into the locker room and who wouldn't. The place should have been full of tension. Instead it felt like pure anticipation—like the players were waiting for the home-room teacher to hand out final report cards and let them go home for the summer.

At one end of the room, Scott Williams was watching a television set. On the screen, University of North Carolina coach Dean Smith was being interviewed. A number of his former players were in the Finals—Jordan, James Worthy, Sam Perkins, Scott Williams himself—and a TV reporter was asking Smith about this.

Jordan was all the way on the other side of the locker room, sitting in front of his cubicle. He was listening to music through his stereo earphones. He glanced in the direction of the TV set, took the headset off, and called to Williams: "Hey, Scott, is that Coach Smith?"

"Yeah," Williams called back.

"Who's he talking about?" Jordan called.

"You," Williams said.

"Yeah, right," Jordan said. "Who's he really talking about?"

"He's talking about you!" Williams said.

"No lie?" Jordan said. "What did he say about me?"

He didn't seem to be joking; he seemed a little surprised and flattered that his college coach would be mentioning him, and honestly inquisitive—and, I sensed, hopeful—about what the coach might be saying. No matter how far any of us may get in life, we are likely to remain sensitive to the power and the judgments of the first people who evaluated us before the outside world knew we were any good.

I looked around the room. These twelve guys were about to go out and, before a global audience, attempt to prove that of all the basketball teams on the planet, they were the best. The rest of us could pretend to know them, pretend that we understood. But we didn't; we never would. The only people who would understand what it was like to go through something like this were the twelve in the red uniforms.

The game itself, while close at times, was never really in much jeopardy. The Forum crowd appeared much less despondent than a Chicago Stadium crowd would have been had the home team been on the verge of missing out on the title. But then, L.A. was not Chicago, and never would be. At the Chicago Stadium, on any given night you could see a dozen men who were trying to look like Arnold Schwarzenegger. The difference here in the Forum was that the Arnold Schwarzenegger lookalike down there in a flowered shirt was, indeed, Arnold Schwarzenegger.

But if Los Angeles had the real Arnold Schwarzenegger (and the real Jack Nicholson and the real Arsenio Hall and the real Dyan Cannon, all of them in the good seats tonight), Chicago had the real Michael Jordan. The Lakers made a comeback, and with 6:47 left in the fourth quarter had managed to take a 91-90 lead. During a time-out a tape of "I Love L.A." was played loudly on the Forum P.A. system, and the fans were singing along and waving their fists and hugging each other, and in any other arena on any other evening it might have signaled the beginning of a rally that would put the visiting team away.

A reporter named Jorge Casuso was sitting next to me. I borrowed his binoculars. I looked through the glasses at the Bulls' bench.

"Look at that," I said to Casuso. "He's not going to let them lose."

Later, I would learn that Jordan's father had said the same thing, in almost the same words. He had looked at the bench during that time-out, and he had realized there was no way his son was going to leave the Forum a loser tonight. Jordan on the bench was furious and agitated and talking rapidly to his teammates, sparking them; he was as intensely focused as any person I could ever imagine seeing, even all the way up here there was no mistaking it. The Los Angeles fans sang and swayed in the Forum, used to their championships, and Jorge Casuso looked through the binoculars and said, "He's winning it."

John Paxson was the hero of the final minutes; he had been remarkable from the field throughout the series, and now Jordan and Pippen kept finding him with flawlessly fired outlet passes, and Paxson kept sinking the ball from all directions.

The final buzzer sounded: Bulls 108, Lakers 101. Whenever Jordan had talked in public about how much he wanted to win a championship, the words had sounded uncharacteristically dry and cold; he always said all the right things, but on that subject there was invariably something held back, something missing. I never quite understood why. Now, on a portable television in front of me high in the Forum, I could see the live NBC pictures coming out of the Bulls' locker room underneath the stands, where the team had just dashed from the court. I couldn't hear a word. But there was Jordan, in a scene that would become instantly famous. He was sitting in front of his cubicle, embracing the world championship trophy, weeping uncontrollably as he rested his head against it. Of course he had never been able to put into words exactly what a night like tonight would mean. There are only two reasons for us not to be able to talk about something: When it means nothing to us. And when it means everything.

"All right," Pat Riley said. "I'm leaving. I'm gone. You can tell me the truth."

We were in the bar of the Ritz. Riley, the former coach of the Lakers, had worked all season for NBC; now he had decided to leave the network to coach the New York Knicks. He was directing his comment at one of his producers.

We were at a table in the middle of the room. Bob Costas, whom I'd known for years, had invited me to join him and Riley and Andy Rosenberg and Al Michaels of ABC Sports, who happened to be in town on a different assignment. There were some other NBC people who had pulled up chairs, and they were listening to Riley's exchange with the producer.

"The truth," Riley said. "How many times this season did you see panic in my face?"

He wanted to know if he'd done okay. He was kidding but he wasn't kidding.

"I don't know, Pat," the producer said.

"How many times?" Riley said.

"Barcelona," the producer said.

Barcelona had been a preseason exhibition game, Riley's first appearance as an NBC broadcaster.

"Just Barcelona?" Riley said.

"The All-Star Game with no prompter," the producer said.

Riley had been forced to work without a TelePrompTer at the All-Star Game.

"Just those two times, though, huh?" Riley said. "You really couldn't see any panic any other times? Tell me the truth."

Something was going away here. The Bulls had attended a private team party in the hotel, and then had drifted their separate ways. John Paxson had been in the lobby, checking for messages at the front desk; a large crowd of fans who had descended on the hotel had gathered around him just to look, and Paxson, unaccustomed to being the center of attention, had appeared startled to turn around and find them there. Phil Jackson was celebrating with his wife and children. Stacey King, who had played in only two games of the Finals for a total of six minutes, rode the elevators in his Bulls uniform—the actual shorts and jersey and shoes—for a reason no one was quite sure of. It was one thing to be a world champion Chicago Bull; it was quite another thing, and an eccentric one at that, to mingle among the hotel guests in your game clothes. Jordan, as ever, was in his room.

Bill Cartwright walked with his wife past the periphery of the barroom. Some patrons caught sight of him, and burst into applause and cheers.

"Magic would have walked through the bar," Riley said. "He would have mingled with the people. That's the difference."

Maybe so, but Cartwright's style was not Johnson's style, and it seemed to suit him just fine. Andy Rosenberg, at the table less than an hour after directing NBC's game coverage, was going to sleep here tonight and then head for England to direct the network's broadcasts of Wimbledon. The kid on the pay phone in the lobby of the Forum might have been earning his initiation into Big Event Overload, but men like Rosenberg were past masters of it, and quite hooked: from one huge event to another, often without pause.

After the game tonight the Bulls had filmed a commercial saying they were going to Disney World. They were going to Disney World, Riley was going to the Knicks, Rosenberg was going to Wimbledon. Jordan and the Bulls were champions of the world, but already the world was moving on. It was a world with no attention span and even less patience. As Jordan would learn soon enough.

20

For MOST OF THE SUMMER, things were relatively quiet. After winning the championship, the Bulls flew home for an outdoor rally in Chicago's Grant Park that drew an estimated one million fans. One by one in front of the roaring, sun-drenched gathering, the players were called to the microphone in the park's band shell. It was quite a sight—B. J. Armstrong addressing a million people. For me, the previous autumn—spotting *Garp* in Armstrong's gym bag—seemed suddenly like something out of a dusty old diary. Armstrong was a world champion now, they all were, and it was almost as if each player had suddenly taken on a golden glow, a glow invisible to the eye but powerful in its effect on people.

After that June rally matters settled down. The players went their separate ways for the summer months; you could actually pick up the sports pages and not encounter a word about the Bulls. I found myself wondering whether I would go back to the Stadium when the new season began.

It wasn't that I had lost interest. I hadn't. Ever since I was a kid, though, I had tended to protect myself from liking anything too much. I'm not sure where that came from. But something inside me was always a little afraid to invest too much faith in anything. It was as if somewhere I had learned to believe that if you allowed yourself to acknowledge how much something meant to you, that was a guarantee the thing would go away. I was already beginning to regard the basketball nights at the Stadium as a joyous moment out of time. I wasn't sure if you should try to repeat something like that. Something that good, I half-believed, maybe you're only supposed to see it once.

During the summer I went to the office and did my job,

and, without giving the subject much conscious thought, I started to assume that my days at the Stadium were probably done, and that I wouldn't be going back. In September, an invitation arrived. Jordan was having a dinner party.

The placard in the lobby was discreet. It said that the "MJF" function would be held in a certain room. It was not a sign designed to draw the attention of anyone who didn't know what it meant.

Which was exactly the point. "MJF" stood for the Michael Jordan Foundation, the charitable organization he had founded, and its annual black-tie fundraising event was being held in Chicago's Hotel Nikko. The organizers of the evening had decided that to put Jordan's name and a room number on a sign in the lobby of a public hotel would just be asking for a chaotic situation. So "MJF" it was.

What for most people would be the key event of a day, if not a year—a large function with your name attached to it— was just one of several for Jordan on this Saturday. As the guests who would be attending the party were still at home changing into tuxedos and formal dresses, Jordan and Magic Johnson were in another room of the Nikko, sitting before television cameras, taking part in a live national broadcast announcing the members of the United States Olympic basketball team. The two of them were linked via satellite with the other NBA members of the team; NBC had packaged all of this neatly into a special late Saturday afternoon show.

The main event, at three hundred dollars a ticket, was booked into a ballroom on the lower concourse of the hotel. Jordan's smaller private dinner was in the hotel's first-floor Les Célébrités restaurant, which had been closed to the public for the night. Corporations had been permitted to purchase admission to this more intimate affair, at a cost of six thousand dollars per table. At each place setting as the guests entered the dining room was a china plate with the Jordan Foundation's logo hand-replicated in a sugary glaze. An elegant menu was next to each setting. The evening's meal, the menus informed, would consist of herb crepe of seafood with a lobster mayonnaise and petit salad; roast loin of veal with an herb crust and rosemary wine sauce; scrambled squashes in a pecan filo cup; au gratin potatoes; chocolate bag with assorted fresh fruits of raspberry and crème anglaise. The wines were Mouton Cadet White and Veuve Chilicquot Demi Sec. The chef had signed the menus: "Teamwork is the key to success. Jean Paul."

The Chicago Bulls had a corporate table; Steve Schanwald and Tim Hallam and several other executives, in black tie, were at that table, which was several tables removed from the one reserved for Jordan and members of his family. In this room tonight, it seemed, the Bulls were just another sponsor of Jordan, like Nike and Wheaties and Chevrolet. Security men in tuxedos stood along the walls; a harpist played before-dinner music. I sensed anew that something in Jordan's life was inexorably changing. Maybe not for the worse. But this was a different stratum, a stratum from which there was no going back.

There was a stir in the room. Jordan was entering. The etiquette was uncertain. Were people expected to applaud? That might not be entirely appropriate; this was, after all, a dinner party. Approach him and ask for autographs? That didn't seem right either. So in silence Jordan walked between the tables toward his own.

He spotted Phil Knight, the chairman of Nike, who had flown in from Oregon for the dinner. Jordan made a detour to say hello to Knight, who stood to greet him. I looked around the room. Every eye was on the Jordan-Knight conversation. It had immediately become a spectator event. The two men finished talking, and Jordan walked on. I saw him heading in the direction of where I was sitting, and in a few seconds he was there and extending his hand.

We talked a little bit, and I was aware of the same thing I'd noticed when he was talking with Knight: By the fact of taking part in this conversation, I was the object of scrutiny by every other person at every other table. It wasn't an entirely comfortable feeling; it gave me a hint of what Jordan must feel every single time he ventured out in public.

"Have you been in town all summer?" he said.

"Most of the time," I said. I couldn't help being constantly conscious of the eyes.

"I just flew in from the West Coast," he said.

"I watched the Olympics broadcast before I came over here," I said. "You're having a pretty busy week." For the first time, I wouldn't have minded a conversation with Jordan to be over, right now; the private conversations in the Stadium had been one thing, but the feeling of being observed here was unnerving.

"Yeah, and it's just starting," he said. "I have to fly down to North Carolina tomorrow morning."

"For what?" I said.

"They're naming a freeway for me," he said.

"The Michael Jordan Freeway?" I said.

"Well, it's just a stretch of freeway, really," he said. "It runs near the town where I grew up."

"And then you've got 'Saturday Night Live,'" I said. He had agreed to host the season premiere of the show.

"I go straight from North Carolina to New York for rehearsals," he said. From the freeway christening to "Saturday Night Live"—like anyone else might say they were going from the hardware store to the grocery.

Magic Johnson came into the room with his wife of one week. Jordan said he wanted to go welcome them. "Are you coming to any exhibition games this year?" he said before walking away.

"I don't know," I said. "I haven't decided."

"Have you ever seen one?" he said.

"Never have," I said.

"You ought to take a look," he said. "They feel completely different from the regular season and the playoffs." And he was off to show Johnson and his new wife to their table, followed by the roomful of curious eyes.

Jordan and Johnson were in that logo mode of theirs tonight; they might as well have been AT&T and IBM as two men who happened to play basketball. They took their seats at the table nearest the lectern. Jordan went to a microphone and introduced Johnson to the guests. Johnson referred to having lost the NBA title to Jordan and the Bulls in Los Angeles: "I'm a little resentful of Michael. He got the diamond ring *and* the ten million dollars." It was intended as a funny line, and it got the expected laughs, and it wasn't until a few seconds had passed that I realized this was not hyperbole. After the NBA Finals, Jordan had, indeed, picked up ten million dollars. Eighteen million dollars, actually, in a long-term contract he had signed to endorse Gatorade.

Johnson thanked the guests for their hospitality toward him, even though back in June he had been the enemy. Then he said: "I'd like you all to meet my bride. Cookie, will you stand up?" And, her face happy, his wife did stand, to applause.

Halfway through the dinner Jordan abruptly left the room

for a few minutes. I asked Ann Armstrong, who ran his charitable foundation, what was going on; she said that upstairs, in a hotel suite, a man had arranged to have dinner with some friends. The man paid the $6,000 that a table at the Les Célébrités dinner went for, plus offered to pay an additional $15,000 if Jordan would stop in to say hello. So that's what was happening. For the man in the hotel room, it had apparently been worth $21,000 to show his friends that Michael Jordan was willing to drop in at their dinner; for Jordan, it had been worth $21,000 to his charitable foundation to ride the elevator upstairs for a few minutes.

He soon returned to join the rest of the guests for the remainder of the dinner. Most did not approach him; some did, and he greeted all politely. The only glimmer of annoyance I saw was when a woman slipped behind him while he wasn't looking, and without warning started to rub his head. He wheeled around quickly; that one, I sensed, was just too much for him, and she stopped.

When dinner was over Jordan and the others in the private room went downstairs to the main function, which had already begun. The ballroom was packed shoulder-to-shoulder with a variety of Chicagoans—lawyers, brokers, architects, doctors—who could afford three hundred dollars for an evening within the same ballroom walls as Jordan. He moved through them the best he could, being led to the seat of honor at the front of the room. Although this was all for a good cause, I couldn't help wondering whether things were getting away from him, and then, as if in answer to what I was thinking, I saw Carmen.

She was off to the side of the crowd. Jordan had thought to include her tonight. Doc Spikes was there, too, but it was Carmen who I saw in her party dress.

She said that Jordan had invited her to come to the party as his guest. The invitation she received in the mail had indicated that the evening was formal, she said, so she and her mother had gone to a branch of the Carson Pirie Scott department store and had asked a salesclerk to help them. This was going to be a special night, they had said.

The clerk had showed them several dresses, and the one they had liked was black and white. Carmen's mother had explained that it would be difficult for Carmen to try the dress on in the store; she would have to lie down to have it put on her. Would it be all right to take it home to see if it fit? The clerk said that would be fine.

So Carmen tried the dress on at home, and it fit her beautifully. Tonight her father, in a tuxedo, had escorted her to the party. Which is where I saw her in her motorized wheelchair amid all the other men and women. She was looking toward Jordan as the security people helped get him through the room, and with all the people pressing toward him, trying to have a word with him, of course she was the one toward whom he headed, of course she was the one to whom he brought Johnson and his wife, of course she was the one he made feel special.

"Magic, Cookie," Jordan said, turning to the Johnsons. "I'd like you to meet someone. This is my friend Carmen."

Magic and Cookie Johnson reached their hands toward hers, and they told her it was a pleasure to meet her. The night was filled with entertainment and songs; in newspaper sports departments all over America, writers were busy analyzing the Olympic team selections that had been announced only hours before. Would the team be able to work well together under Coach Chuck Daly? Would the omission of Isiah Thomas from the team prove to be a mistake? Was letting professionals compete in the Olympics really such a good idea? The details of the Olympic announcements were still fresh, they were big news still in the process of being written up for the Sunday morning papers, but in Jordan's universe that was way back this afternoon, that was something he had already moved well past. He was in the Nikko's ballroom tonight, and "Saturday Night Live" lay ahead, and in the morning he would be flying south toward the Michael Jordan Freeway, moving all the time.

Seeing Jordan in the off-season had been a funny feeling. It was unusual to see him outside of the context of the Bulls, even though there were no games being played yet. I had this vision of Phil Jackson touching base with him all the time, checking up on him and talking basketball and basically keeping tabs on his star.

"Does he call you at home a lot?" I asked.

"Hardly ever," Jordan said. "Not unless he has to talk to me about something important."

"Well, who does call you?" I said.

"No one from the Bulls' office," he said. "When they do, it's always for a reason."

"But they have your number," I said.

"They have *a* number," he said.

"Not your home number?" I said.

"My second home number," he said. "I have two lines."

"So how does it work?" I said. "You can tell by which line is lighting up whether it's someone you want to talk to?"

"Either by that, or by letting the answering machine answer," he said. "Everyone in my house knows which line is which. The second line is for business. The first line is for people I want to hear from. Family and friends. If I see it's the first line ringing, I'll answer it right away. The second line I don't always pick up."

"Even if it might be someone from the Bulls' office or coaching staff?" I said.

"We see each other every day eight months a year," he said. "I don't need to talk to them on the phone. I don't especially like the sound of the phone ringing."

Jordan was right about the preseason games; they had a completely different feel from anything I'd seen last year. Of course, that may have been because of all the strangers in Bulls uniforms.

I went to the Stadium in early October for an exhibition game against the Los Angeles Clippers. There, in the familiar white uniforms, were men who had been signed on just for the one month before the real season began. A man named Ken Redford was in uniform; so was a man named Chris Munk, and a man named Anthony Bowie. Oliver Taylor, a little guy, warmed up on the court, as did Chuck Nevitt, an extremely tall and thin fellow with a moustache. Different faces, different haircuts; to observe them doing layup drills on the Stadium court with the Bulls was like watching a favorite movie you've seen a hundred times and suddenly finding extra actors on the screen. *Casablanca,* starring Humphrey Bogart, Ingrid Bergman, and Chuck Nevitt.

There were no names on the backs of their uniforms. The word "PAXSON" still appeared above the numeral 5 on its owner's jersey, the word "GRANT" above the numeral 54. Nevitt, Taylor, etc., though, were not bequeathed the perquisite of having their names displayed to the Stadium crowds;

the presumption was that they were just passing through, guys trying out.

The real Bulls—that's what they were inevitably called—came back from summer vacation changed in ways small and not so small. B. J. Armstrong—always "Little B.J." to the fans —was suddenly muscular and brawny. It wasn't a matter of vanity; he had made a business decision that to endure in the NBA, a person had better add bulk. Scottie Pippen was suddenly more talkative; he still wasn't exactly Dale Carnegie, but his impressive showing in the Finals, his selection for the U.S. Olympic team, and his featured role in a popular Nike commercial parodying "The Twilight Zone" seemed to have given him measurably more social confidence.

The change that really counted, though, was contained in Ray Clay's reading of the spotlight introduction. There was a two-word addition to the script this year: "And now, the starting lineup for your *world champion* Chicago Bulls. . . ."

I asked Joyce Szymanksi why the Bulls with no names on their shirts had been hired as temporary help; there were going to be no available spots on the team once the season began. She said it was to provide competition for the real team during two-a-day workouts: "We've got to have guys to practice with."

They'd all be gone by the time the first regulation game tipped off. For now, though, they were running onto the court of the filled-to-capacity Chicago Stadium, they were hearing the same cheers that Jordan heard, they were, for a twinkling, members in good standing of *your world champion Chicago Bulls.* Maybe they were, indeed, around mainly to help out at practice. But I had a hunch that, thirty or forty years down the line, that's not necessarily the version of the story they'd be telling their grandchildren. And could you blame them? "What did you used to do, Grandpa?" "Oh, I played a little professional basketball." "Was your team any good?" "We were very good. You've heard of Michael Jordan? He was my teammate."

I flew down to New Orleans, switching planes in Dallas. The Bulls were scheduled to play an exhibition game against the Denver Nuggets in the Louisiana Superdome, a massive structure designed for football. I wanted to see what a basketball game in the huge dome would look like.

The cab from the airport took me past the dome. I looked

up at it in the darkness and realized that the only reason it would be open tomorrow night was because Jordan was coming to town. You can't put a virtually meaningless preseason basketball game in a football stadium like this—unless there's a reason that fans might want to show up that has nothing to do with the contest itself.

At the Fairmont Hotel at 10:30 P.M., a bellman told me that his shift was over, but that he was going to wait around "just so I can get a look at Michael." I said the team wouldn't be arriving at the hotel until 1:30 A.M. at the very earliest; they were playing a game against Portland tonight in Chicago, and would get on their plane for New Orleans only after that game was over. That was all right, the bellman said; he'd wait.

I glanced at my watch as I talked with him. In Chicago right at this moment, the game had probably just ended; Jordan was in all likelihood sitting in front of his locker in the Stadium. I went to my room and made a long distance call to the *Tribune* copydesk that handled my columns; the woman in charge tonight, Nancy Watkins, answered, and I asked her to check her computer for an Associated Press report of the Bulls-Blazers game. I could hear her hitting keys. "The Bulls won," she said. "It looks like Jordan had twenty-two." The news of the results of the game had already been flashed via the AP wire all around the world, and Jordan almost certainly hadn't even put on his overcoat to leave the building yet.

I watched some television, then drifted off. I dreamed that I was hearing people scream as if they were at a rock concert. When I woke up, though, it was no dream. The clock by the bed said that the time was 2:20 A.M. Five stories below me, on the street, the Bulls' team bus had just arrived from the New Orleans airport. The screams were real. Almost two-thirty in the morning, and the frantic, plaintive voices from the sidewalk: "Michael! Please! Look at me, Michael!" The voices rose to a crescendo, then suddenly stopped. The team was safely inside the hotel. The night was soundless again, but it was a while before I was able to get back to sleep.

"If there are people in the room with me, a lot of times I'll zap to a different channel," Jordan said.

We were in the Superdome. The arena would not be open to the public for another five or six hours; I had gone over for the Bulls' brief practice session at midday, and Jordan and his teammates were alone on the floor of the gigantic arena. A basketball court had been laid down over the artificial football turf. You could walk across the thirty-yard line, the thirty-five, the forty, and abruptly you'd find yourself on hardwood underneath a basketball hoop. Even when Pippen or Grant lofted the ball as high as they could, it was just a tiny, impotent-looking arc beneath the towering dome.

Jordan and I were talking about television because, when I had awakened in the hotel in the morning, I had switched on the TV set in my room and had been greeted by a cartoon version of him cavorting on the screen. The show was a Saturday morning entry called "ProStars"; there was a cartoon Jordan, a cartoon Bo Jackson, and a cartoon Wayne Gretzky—a kind of sports-oriented Justice League of America for the modern age, the threesome winning championships while doing daring deeds. After the cartoon show, I had seen Jordan himself on an Ahmad Rashad–hosted program called "NBA Inside Stuff"; Jordan talked with Rashad on videotape about what he had done over the summer. At some point in the morning I'd seen a Jordan commercial for Wheaties. So by the time I saw him in person today, I had already, without looking for him, seen him in three separate television embodiments.

"If you're in the room and you come onto the TV screen, what do you do?" I said.

"I guess I look at it when I come on," he said. "I've seen myself so much now that it's not a surprise when I come on. If it's videotape from a game, I criticize myself. I look and I ask myself, 'Did I do something right there?' "

"Are you as interested in it as you once were?" I said.

"I don't watch myself as much as when it was new to me," he said. "I won't watch replays of games as much. I used to, but by now I know pretty much what it will look like. I played in the game. I'll watch now if it's a commercial I've done. I'll look to see how I followed the directions they gave me.

"Sometimes, though, I'll just zap the channel when I see me. I mean, how many times can you look at yourself? If I'm watching and it's a commercial I've seen a lot, I'll go to another channel. That's what I was telling you, about when there are people in the room. When that happens, I'll usually zap right away."

"You don't think they want to see?" I said.

"I don't want to keep putting my picture in front of people," he said. "Think about it—sitting there and making the people in the room watch you on TV, and you're there watching them watch? It's a little embarrassing. So with other people, I zap as soon as I see my face come on."

"A lot of people never get a chance to see themselves on television," I said. "I guess that's a little different now, with VCRs and home video cameras. But a lot of people, probably most people, will never be on a real television show in their lives."

"There must have been a time before I'd seen myself on television," Jordan said. "But right now I can't even remember what that was like."

The practice at the Superdome was low-key. It was really just to keep the players limber after the long late-night plane trip south. Even though the building was locked and secured, there were probably a hundred people—friends of the game's promoters, children of the arena executives, girlfriends of the security guards—on the outskirts of the court, wanting to catch a glimpse of Jordan. Morten Andersen, a star placekicker with the National Football League's New Orleans Saints, had made a special trip to the dome, his own place of work, to watch Jordan practice. He stood amid the others who wanted the same thing.

On a chair next to one out-of-bounds line, Horace Grant rested his chin in his palms and said his head hurt. "It's been bad for a day now," he said.

"Go on home," Tim Hallam said, knowing that Grant wouldn't. "Go on back to Chicago."

"Can't," Grant said. "Can't miss Bourbon Street after the game tonight."

What a life. You play basketball in Chicago before a full house on Friday, you fly to New Orleans in the early hours Saturday, you play another game in the Superdome Saturday night, you go to Bourbon Street to unwind with your friends after the game, you fly out in the morning heading for more basketball. And the whole world knows your name.

Phil Jackson declared the practice over. The rest of the Bulls walked swiftly to the waiting bus. But Jordan was trapped by the crowd—the hundred or so who had somehow gotten into the dome pressed in on him, wanting pictures, wanting autographs, wanting a moment. A man from a radio station stuck a microphone in front of Jordan's mouth. He was surrounded and trapped by the crowd. And this was relatively secure; this was relatively private.

So his teammates waited on the bus, and Jordan moved about six inches every thirty seconds. Tim Hallam, who had traveled with him more than anyone else in the world—he had been the Bulls' PR man from the moment Jordan joined the team—called to him: "One step forward, Michael. One step." It was a daily signal between them, had been for years. One step forward. Enough single steps and you'll get to the bus.

Which Jordan finally did. The people who were left behind called to him and screamed his name and cried their good-byes. He had never met any of them before. Hallam waited by the front door of the bus until he saw Jordan climb on. Then, before getting on himself, he said in a bemused and weary tone: "Elvis has left the building."

I had been telling myself for so long that what I was seeing with Jordan was a parallel to Elvis '56 that I had managed to put out of my mind what had happened to Elvis in '57.

In 1956 Presley had excited the country in ways it didn't even fully understand. He became so famous in 1956, so idolized and so pursued, that everyone from historians to sociologists to anthropologists were busy analyzing why the phenomenon was taking place and what it said about the culture. There had been doldrums in the public life before he came along; in 1956 he gave the country what amounted to an electrical shock.

In 1957, though, things began to become unmanageable. He could no longer play the auditoriums and dance halls that had provided his springboard to fame. He was much too sought after for that by '57. Now he was booked into the republic's most gargantuan arenas, places meant for political conventions and trade shows. The fans who came to the concerts could no longer see him clearly; the places were too huge, and he was too far away. He had always taken pleasure in meeting people, but by 1957 the public's desire and communal lust for him had become something frightening, and meeting new people who were guaranteed not to be a potential commotion or a potential threat was suddenly a difficult proposition. Presley had been anointed as a singular and powerful force in 1956; by 1957 his popularity was so extreme that the people who knew him best were said to be afraid that no one would ever get truly close to him again.

We went back to the hotel in New Orleans after practice. The afternoon was devoted to rest; the bus for the game was supposed to leave from the street right outside the lobby at 5:30 P.M.

Will Perdue came downstairs early, and Craig Hodges, and Cliff Levingston. One by one the Bulls walked off the elevators and made their way out the doors of the hotel and onto the bus. An uncomfortably large crowd was forming in the lobby. No one in the hotel seemed to be in charge of keeping an aisle free. Grant rode an elevator car downstairs, then Pippen. They were able to get to the bus with minimal impediment. No one was following them; everyone was waiting, staring at the elevator doors. There was a young man standing next to me in the crammed lobby, a disconnected and agitated look on his face. His voice was filled with the kind of unfocused passion that has the capacity to chill. He handed a camera to a woman who was with him. He said to her, "When he gets off the elevator I'm going to get next to him, and you just aim and unload it. Do you understand? Keep shooting. Don't stop for anything. Aim it at us and keep shooting until there's nothing left."

Phil Jackson emerged from an elevator car. "Has Michael come down yet?" a woman shouted. Jackson smiled in an almost indecipherable way and said softly, "No, he hasn't come down yet." He continued to the bus. Everyone but Jordan was on board and ready to go.

When he came out of a far elevator he was completely alone. That was what seemed to surprise the horde that had gathered. Apparently they had expected a retinue, a flying wedge of security officers. But there were only three hotel security men in sight, and as soon as they saw Jordan they did not move to help him; instead they pulled cameras out of their own pockets and started firing.

The young man I had overheard while he was standing next to me lunged toward Jordan. So did dozens of other people. Jordan, his stereo headset clamped down over his ears, moved as quickly as he could. People were lurching against him, tearing at his clothes, hollering in his face. Jordan wore a small smile and kept moving forward. His eyes looked neither right nor left.

"I put my phone number in his pocket!" a teenage girl called out to her friends who had been unable to get close enough. By now Jordan was on the bus, and the bus was pulling rapidly away from the curb. As always, the bus, like the plane, was for team members and the Bulls' staff only; I grabbed a cab for the Superdome.

By the time I got there the Bulls were in their locker room. The first person I saw was John Paxson. I asked him if this was markedly different even from the fury of last season.

"This is different," he said. "I've been playing next to the guy for six years now, but this is a whole different level. The time I really stop and think about what is going on is when he steps to the foul line and all those hundreds of lights start flashing.

"Watch what happens tonight. Michael will be at the free-throw line, and just as he's getting ready to release the ball, there will be hundreds and hundreds of lights flashing all over the arena. I've never seen anything like that before, and now we see it every night. It's all the people with their cameras, trying to capture the moment they saw Michael."

Amazingly, in the domed football stadium tonight, in a city in which neither the Bulls nor the Nuggets were the home team, for a game that was really just an exercise session for the two squads, more than thirty-one thousand people had purchased tickets. This was a night when a World Series baseball game was on TV; this was a night when, up the road in Baton Rouge, Louisiana State University was playing football against number one Florida State, in a game that was also nationally televised. Any sports fan in Louisiana would have had every excuse not to be at the Superdome.

And more than thirty-one thousand were coming. That was more people than had seen any single National Basketball Association game during either the regular season or the play-offs last year. Horace Grant, getting dressed, said, "The people come out to see us because we're the world champions now, yes, but we're all aware of the real reason they're here." He nodded across the room at Jordan. "When he comes to town, you'd better get the biggest building you can find." B. J. Armstrong, sitting within hearing range of Grant, said, "It's become something different from basketball. It's like we're on tour or something."

Next to Jordan's locker was a set of steel doors. Apparently they were fire doors, leading to either the outside of the

Superdome or to a public corridor inside. From the sound of it there were hundreds of people on the other side of the doors. They were pushing against them, banging and shoving. You could tell that they weren't trapped or in danger; they just wanted in, wherever in was. Whoever was doing it did not likely know precisely where the doors led to. Jordan was only about five feet from the set of doors. The doors bulged toward us, then receded, then bulged again, as if they might give. In here, save for the din of the feet and fists on the doors, it was quiet.

We sat and talked, but it was a difficult conversation to have, with the harsh, hollow, metallic noise of the pounding against the doors. I asked Jordan if what I'd seen at the hotel was his routine—to travel essentially alone, with no assistants or personal staff to shield him from the kind of thing I'd witnessed in the lobby.

"Yeah," he said. "I can't have anyone do that. We're a team. We have to travel like a team."

"So there's no one in your room except you when the room service waiter or the laundry person comes?" I said.

"Usually it's just me in there," he said.

"What do they expect when they knock on your door?" I said.

"They know that it's my room," he said. "What happens is that I'll open the door, and the person with the food or the laundry will be there, and even though they knew it was my room before they came up, they're surprised that I'm opening the door myself."

"So what happens then?" I said.

"I try to let them know, without saying it out loud, that I respect them as people for doing the jobs they're doing," he said. "Both of us are just human beings doing different jobs. I usually roam around my room in a pair of shorts or whatever, and if I hear a knock on the door I don't try to make myself look better. I know they're looking at me when they come in, but the way I figure it, I'm just like most hotel guests, and most hotel guests don't get dressed up for the room-service waiters."

The banging was not letting up. Every minute or so Jordan would glance over at the double doors, which would swell inward, then bounce back, then swell again.

"Do the hotel people want to stand around and talk with you?" I said.

"Most of the time," he said. "Sometimes I can tell that they've been instructed not to. We'll usually talk for a few minutes. It's easier if you don't make a big deal out of it. I'm just a guest in a hotel."

More banging and pounding. More fists and feet against metal. The doors continued to bulge and jut, but they were strongly constructed, and they did not pop open. Jordan crossed his legs and bent down to pick up the pair of basketball shoes he would wear tonight. Had he stood and taken two strides, he would have been at the metal doors. They were that close. But he didn't stand. He did his best to ignore the doors, and what was happening. I found myself wondering whether the people outside, whoever they might be, would ever have any idea of how near to him they were.

The game was not a very competitive one. The Bulls took an early lead and went on to win easily, 135-108. Those in attendance did not seem to have come with the expectation of beholding a tightly fought basketball contest. They were here to see one person.

The official attendance was announced as 31,278. The audience filled the seats all the way to the top of the dome. Jordan appeared disconcerted by only one thing. The promoters of the game had sponsored a Michael Jordan look-alike contest, and the winner, a man with a shaved head, dressed in a facsimile of a Bulls uniform with the numeral 23, had been walking around inside the Superdome all night. Part of his prize was a seat next to the Bulls' bench. His presence seemed to irritate Jordan. He did not look at the man during the game, and chose to sit far down the bench, away from the impersonator.

Every time Jordan touched the ball the 31,278 roared in approval. Every time he dribbled downcourt they leapt to their feet. And the first time he stepped to the foul line, the lights flashed from every corner of the dome, just as John Paxson had said they would. Hundreds of lights, maybe thousands, all the way up to the roof, flaring like so many ceremonial fires in the night.

After the game, Jordan did have protection; unlike at the hotel, police officers inside the Superdome had been sent to assist him on his way to the bus.

It was a wise precaution. Several hundred fans, young and

old, had congregated outside the Bulls' locker room, and they displayed no intention of leaving until Jordan came out. The pattern repeated itself: Paxson and Stacey King and Bill Cartwright and the others left the locker room, and then Grant and Pippen together, and last came Jordan.

The police officers were in a circle around him, with additional security men in front and behind. Because of the setup of the Superdome, the team bus was parked in an interior corridor all the way down at the other end of the building, past the basketball court that had been assembled atop the football field. So Jordan, the men in uniform on all sides of him, walked briskly the length of the court on which he had just played. The people who had waited for him to get dressed jogged alongside the moving cocoon, calling his name.

His attire was the customary suit and tie; over the top of his head once again were the earphones that may or may not have been playing music. Just before he got to the bus, his path took him close to two very little children, really tiny, probably no more than four years old. The boys were dressed in scruffy, raggedy clothes, and there was no adult visible who appeared to be supervising them; it was puzzling that they would be here so late at night. They said nothing until Jordan was within a few feet of them, and then it was as if they had planned the moment and rehearsed their lines.

"I want to be like Mike," one of the boys called, with no smile on his face and a desperate tenor to his voice. "I want to be like you, Mike," the other boy called, frantic.

Over the summer, Jordan had switched his beverage endorsement contract from Coca-Cola so that he could sign the Gatorade deal. The Coke commercials, with Jordan floating past the moon, were gone; they had been replaced by a new Gatorade campaign featuring a bright, bouncy jingle with the multiply-repeated tagline "I want to be like Mike." The commercial had been on the air for only a few weeks by now, but it had reached these little boys in Louisiana.

The police officers hurried Jordan forward. "I want to be like you, Mike," one of the boys called again, almost crying. "I want to be like Mike," his companion shouted in the smallest of voices, over and over and over, not taking a breath. It was as if the boys believed that, were they to catch sight of Jordan and recite the magic words, something good might happen to them. But the boys were pushed aside by the rest of the crowd as the police phalanx moved onward.

The police hustled Jordan farther along, toward the bus, and the boys, by necessity, shortened their phrases. "Be like Mike," they called to him. "Be like Mike." It was a plea; there was no joy in it, no gladness. It sounded like heartbreak, it was almost a mournful demand to him: "Be like Mike."

The police pressed through the crowd, Jordan in the midst of them. I don't know whether Jordan saw the boys; the closest objects to him, anywhere he turned, were the shirts of law-enforcement uniforms. I don't know whether he heard the boys. If he had his music turned on, he couldn't have.

The police officer behind him had a hand on his left shoulder. The police officer in front of him was pulling at his arm, trying to get him to the bus. Tim Hallam was waiting up ahead. Hallam motioned to Jordan. "One step forward," Hallam called. Most of the crowd had moved along with Jordan, and thus had passed by the two boys, who were by themselves on the floor of the Superdome now. One of them tried it once more at Jordan's retreating figure: "Be like Mike."

The police escort delivered him to the bus. I saw him just before he got on. For one of the first times since I'd known him, I could see in his face and in his eyes something that looked very much like confusion.

21

"AFRAID OF IT?" he said. "Why would I be afraid of it?"

"Not literal fear," I said. "It's just that you're making your living in an occupation that so obviously values youth. I just wondered whether you've ever tried to envision what your life will be like when you're an old man."

That's what we were talking about—Jordan the old man. Jordan in his seventies or eighties, when all around him are people in their teens and twenties who are strong and full of energy and able to run full speed for hours on end.

"Being an old man is actually something I look forward to," he said. "When I imagine it, I see myself playing around with my grandchildren all the time, being this old guy who's a lot of fun, and who the kids love to be around. I see myself telling a lot of fables and tales and lies. A lot of exaggerations that the grandkids let me get away with."

"And that appeals to you?" I said. "The knowledge that some day that's going to be your inevitable role?"

"I think it sounds fun," he said. "I get a hint of it now, when I sit around with older men from my family and from my wife's side of the family. We'll be sitting around, and I'll notice that I'm the only one at the table who doesn't have glasses on. I think to myself what it would be like to be them instead of me. It doesn't sound too bad at all."

"The thing about older people in our society is that they get patronized so much," I said. "When a man or a woman gets old enough, sometimes younger people treat them like children. Like they have to be talked down to. That has to drive them crazy."

"I don't think it always has to be that way," he said. "When you're an old man, sometimes I think you're made to feel welcome. You can be patronized, sure, but it can be in a good way—when the younger people in your family pay so much attention to you, it can make you feel important. When I ask the older men in my family questions about something they've lived through, I can tell that they love doing it—they love searching in their memories and giving detailed answers. By giving the answers, it makes them know that the lives they've lived have some importance."

"That happens in your family?" I said.

"Certainly," he said. "The older men on my wife's side of the family, for example—they love to tell me about Chicago before I was around. They love explaining to me about the first Mayor Daley, and what Chicago was like before I knew anything about it. About all the politics and all the goings-on and all the big events. So when I'm an old man I can envision myself telling all the kids at the table about Chicago during the time the current Mayor Daley was mayor."

"It does sound like fun, in theory," I said. "Sitting around telling stories to grandchildren. But if being an old man is really like that, then I wonder why so many old men seem so bitter."

"You're only bitter if you reach the end of your life and you're filled with frustration because you feel that you missed out on something," Jordan said. "You're bitter because you regret not accomplishing the things you could have accomplished. I know I'm not going to be a bitter old man."

The world championship banner was raised during a November ceremony before the opening game of the 1991–92 regular season against the Philadelphia 76ers. The Stadium lights were turned off, and a spotlight was trained on the white banner, and it was hoisted to the ceiling. It looked kind of lonely up there; although it was in celebration of a great achievement, the fact that it was the first one—I thought of all those championship banners in the Forum in Los Angeles—emphasized the emptiness of the space around it.

The players, introduced by Red Kerr, each came to center court to receive their championship rings. The fans were on their feet the entire time. Because of all the advance promotion in the newspapers and on TV about what a memorable night this was going to be, for an instant right after the ceremony had ended and the banner was in place there was almost a sense of hesitation in the building. Okay—now what happens?

What happened was a resounding 110-90 victory for the Bulls, which was a reminder both of just how good they could be and of the fact that this whole cycle was beginning anew and that eighty-one regular season games lay ahead. To me, the most telling moment of the evening happened in front of the Sixers' bench, and it came and went so unexpectedly and so quickly that it was easy to miss.

There had been a flurry of stories in the news about a controversy in Philadelphia involving Charles Barkley. The 76ers were on the verge of having to trim their roster. Only one of the players on the team—a man named Dave Hoppen—was white. Barkley, the team's star, predicted that Hoppen would be kept on the team even if a black player was more deserving of the spot. He said that this was a sign of racism; he said that the team's owner would not dare to field twelve blacks and no whites in Philadelphia.

I initially thought the controversy was overblown; Barkley was known for stirring things up, and I assumed he was just trying to get a rise out of people. It seemed to me an ill-advised move—the last thing the country needed was more racial divisiveness—but I figured Barkley probably had nothing against Hoppen as a person. Whatever the validity, or lack of it, of Barkley's opinion, this situation wasn't Hoppen's fault, and Barkley had to realize it. Hoppen was just a guy trying to make a living.

Tonight Hoppen was still on the team. Eleven black players and Hoppen. The 76ers' starting lineup was introduced, and as the five starters headed back to the bench the rest of the team extended their palms to greet them and wish them luck.

Barkley slapped the palms of all the other 76ers. Hoppen held his hands out toward Barkley. Barkley walked right past him, leaving Hoppen with his hands in the air.

Some of the other 76ers saw this happen; they looked at Hoppen and rolled their eyes to signal to him that they thought Barkley was acting like a jerk, and a couple of them patted Hoppen on the shoulder. Several of them walked over to whisper words of encouragement to Hoppen. Barkley went out onto the court for the tipoff. Sometimes you find out all you'll ever need to know about a person in the course of a few seconds. I now knew all I ever cared to know about Barkley.

* * *

"Whenever you start thinking about how good life in the NBA is, you should always remember something else," B. J. Armstrong said. "This is a very cold business."

The Bulls were playing Golden State in the second home game of the new season, on a Tuesday night. The day before, Dennis Hopson, who had never quite been able to fit in with the team, had been traded to Sacramento. Just like that—he'd been at the Stadium for the Philadelphia game, had picked up his world championship ring in front of the 18,676, and now, before the next game could be played in the building, his cubicle was empty. He was gone from Chicago.

"I sat up with him last night," Armstrong said. "I told him I'd help get his stuff sent out to California. He was going to leave on the first plane this morning."

For Hopson, the Sacramento Kings had given up a guard named Bobby Hansen. I had seen Hansen up on the court when I arrived at the Stadium; he was shooting jump shots, getting used to his new place of work. There was a snag, though. Hopson, for some reason, had not yet turned up in Seattle, where his new team was playing the Supersonics tonight. So Jerry Krause, the Bulls executive who had engineered the trade, hurried onto the court and told Hansen to get off. League rules specified that until Hopson had reported to his new team, the trade wasn't valid. Krause did not want Hansen doing anything remotely approximating playing basketball until the trade was officially consummated.

Thus here was Hansen, sitting in the locker room, waiting to be told what to do. In the newspaper he had been described as "a proven defender [who] has shown range as a shooter," which in all likelihood was true enough. But tonight Hansen the person, as opposed to Hansen the basketball player, looked a bit cast adrift. If at the end of the previous season the twelve Bulls had seemed like kids on the last day of school, then this evening Bobby Hansen resembled nothing if not a new kid in school whose parents have to register him a week or so after the first day of classes. Everyone else here knew each other, from the players to the coaching staff to the equipment handlers to the sportswriters. And here was Hansen, fresh off the plane from Sacramento, looking across the room at Jordan, looking to his left at Cartwright and Grant and Pippen, looking over at the perpendicular row of cubicles where Paxson and Perdue were putting on their uniforms. No one knew quite what to say. Krause had requested the sportswriters not to ask Hansen any questions, so he was sitting in total silence.

It was time for the game to begin. The Bulls went upstairs, leaving Hansen behind in the locker room. There was a phone on the press table that I often used to call my office; I picked it up to dial, and Joyce Szymanski said, "We've got to keep that one free tonight. It's the one the Kings are going to call Jerry on when Hopson shows up."

Every time the phone rang, Krause looked anxiously at it. There were several false starts. Finally, though, it rang and it was Krause's counterpart with the Kings. Hopson had reported for duty and was officially a member of the Sacramento club. Which meant that Bobby Hansen was free to put on a Bulls uniform and come up for the second half.

Which he did, looking more than a little bewildered. In a period of less than twenty-four hours he had gone from being a member of a cellar-dwelling team in Sacramento to being one of the twelve world-champion Chicago Bulls. These men may have been wealthy stars, but a night like tonight was evidence that in the broader scheme of things they were basically so many interchangeable parts. As the Bulls came upstairs for the third quarter, Hansen was careful to follow Horace Grant's back so he would be sure to trot to the correct bench.

The arrival of Hansen completed the Bulls' roster for the new season. Paxson had been given a new contract (during the summer Jordan had arranged for his own agent, David Falk, to represent Paxson, too, and once Falk stepped in Paxson was given a much richer deal than he'd ever had before in the NBA); Bill Cartwright and Cliff Levingston and Scott Williams, the Bulls whose contracts had left open the possibility of their leaving the team, were re-signed or were in the process of being re-signed, too. The preseason Bulls—the Chuck Nevitts and Oliver Taylors—had all departed on schedule. So with the exception of the Hopson-for-Hansen trade, the team that took the Stadium floor in November was the team that had won the championship in June.

Jordan's role in getting Paxson a new contract was not without its symbolism. He liked Paxson, not only as a person but as a running mate who always knew exactly where Jordan was on the playing surface. One of the things Jordan valued most about Paxson the basketball player was that Paxson understood precisely how Jordan liked to receive the ball. When Paxson spotted Jordan open for a shot, Jordan was confident that when the ball floated into his hands he would usually have to do no adjusting at all—it would arrive at the height he preferred it and with the velocity that enabled him to propel it toward the basket in one uninterrupted motion. A seemingly small thing to those of us who didn't play basketball for a living, but essential in Jordan's and Paxson's business; if Jordan had to think about where and at what speed a fellow guard was going to deliver the ball to him, it would develop into a constant annoyance.

But the fact that, in order to keep Paxson as a member of the Bulls, Jordan hooked him up with his own personal agent, was another example of the ever-veering balance of power on the team. It mostly took beneficent forms—Jordan bringing the entire squad onto the floor with him to accept his MVP trophy, Jordan insisting that the Bulls' starting lineup share in his Disney World endorsement (and the paycheck that came with it) following the championship—but in every instance it was a reminder, as if a reminder was necessary, that he was different from them. He was not John Paxson's employer—they were teammates who were genuinely fond of each other—but there was no getting around the fact that, by arranging for Falk to represent Paxson, Jordan was saying to the Bulls' front office: If you make John unhappy you're making me unhappy. Thus Jordan in large measure was responsible for assuring that the man he wanted playing next to him in the backcourt was rehired at a salary that was pleasing to Paxson. For Jordan to take that kind of middleman's role in dealings between a team and a fellow player was a highly unconventional position for an athlete to be in, to say the least.

When the McDonald's restaurant chain brought back a sandwich called the McJordan Special, which it had introduced the previous season, people who watched the television commercial promoting it thought it was a cute ad. The previous year Jordan himself had starred in the TV commercials for the sandwich; this year the commercials featured B. J. Armstrong, Craig Hodges, Cliff Levingston, and Stacey King, all dressed nattily in the 1930s style of Eliot Ness and the Untouchables. The four of them sang a jazzy song with the payoff phrase: "The McJordan Special is . . . back in town!"

The concept of the commercial was charming—the four Bulls doing the unexpected vocalizing, in getups no one had seen them in before—and the ad campaign was such a success that there wasn't much public comment concerning the most unusual thing about it.

Which was that Jordan's four teammates were singing in praise of his sandwich—while Jordan himself did not even appear in the commercial. It was a pointedly impressive display of the power of his name to sell a product. It may have been the first commercial designed to capitalize on a celebrity's persona in which the allure of the celebrity was so strong that he was not even required to show up. At the end of last season, in a road game at Charlotte, Jordan attempted—and made—a free throw with his eyes closed. Just to show that he could. The McDonald's commercial for the McJordan Special was the business-world equivalent of that free throw. Any famous athlete could get a product endorsement. Only one could get the endorsement and send his teammates to make the commercial for him.

"I think I could do it," Jordan said, which surprised me.

We were talking about the "Michael for President" signs that had been popping up in the Stadium and around the league since the Bulls had won the championship. The signs were whimsical and they weren't; the people who drew them and brought them to the games probably were not thinking seriously about Jordan running for elective office—it was, of course, just their way of expressing their high regard for him. So when I asked him if the signs ever gave him any ideas, I had not expected him to answer yes.

"I never would actually do it," he said. "But could I do it? Yeah, I think I could do it. I think I could try to be a politician and do all right."

"What makes you think that?" I said.

"We're just talking in theory, right?" he said.

"Right," I said. "But even in theory, what makes you think you could pull it off?"

"Because I think I could try to be a politician who is fair to everyone," he said. "Most people who run for office, their ego has to be a factor. Don't you think? Part of their running for office has to be a need to satisfy their egos. But athletes have been going through the need to satisfy their egos all their lives

—so all that would be behind me. The ego part wouldn't apply."

"Are you even considering the eventual possibility of doing something like this?" I said.

"It wouldn't be worth it," he said. "Because you pay for it with your privacy. Politics just seems like such a nasty business to me. Your whole life goes on trial. Even if your reason for being in politics is that you want to help people out, you're on trial all the time. Is your bank account overdrawn? Did you bounce a check at a certain point in your life? Did you do something when you were twenty-one or twenty-two that was embarrassing? Even little neighborhood things, they try to find those things out."

"It's not like your life is exactly private as it is," I said.

"I can expect boos when we're on the road," he said. "But running for office would be different."

"The loss of privacy isn't even the strangest thing," I said. "To me, the strangest thing is the thought of all those people going into a secret little room—the voting booth—to say whether or not they like you. The only people in the world who face that particular kind of judgment are politicians."

"Even if I won, even if I got fifty-one percent of the vote, I think I'd feel bad," Jordan said.

"You would?" I said. "Why?"

"Because that would mean that forty-nine percent of the people didn't like me," he said.

"That sounds like the comedian who goes on stage and everyone is laughing except one guy at a table in the front," I said.

"What do you mean?" Jordan said.

"The guy at the table is sitting there frowning with his arms folded, and even though everyone else in the room is howling, the only person the comedian can see is the man who's not laughing. It doesn't matter how well the comedian is doing with everyone else. To him, the man who isn't laughing is the only person in the room."

"I know," Jordan said. "I know. I go through a big part of my life seeing that guy who isn't laughing."

Because I had never seen Jordan sad, when it happened it was all the more jarring.

The sadness was not something that was being reported as such in the newspapers; the word that most often appeared in print to describe what was going on with him was "controversy." That's a journalism term, though, used conveniently to describe a number of things. There were thirty or forty controversies a day in the average morning edition. Controversies I was used to. Jordan being so distressed I wasn't.

Some of what was vexing Jordan had been building, some blindsided him, and all seemed to combine to suddenly sap him of part of his spirit. It had started with reports that he wasn't sure whether he wanted to play on the U.S. Olympic team. The reports said that, in light of the fact that he'd won an Olympic gold medal in 1984 when he was in college, he was considering sitting out the 1992 Games. The day the invitation was issued he accepted it immediately and denied that he'd ever had second thoughts. But when the speculation had appeared in print that he didn't wish to play, he was called unpatriotic and selfish, which was something he was unaccustomed to. In his public statements he seemed a little defensive and on guard for the first time.

Then he didn't travel to the White House when President Bush invited the team there for a brief photo session. This time the criticism was harsher. Who was a basketball player to snub the president of the United States? Jordan, who claimed to have private reasons for not going, appeared taken aback by the forcefulness of the criticism. "It's none of your business," he said angrily to a cluster of reporters who approached him after his teammates had returned from Washington. The tone of voice was not one that many people had heard from Jordan; I was surprised at his demeanor as I watched the impromptu interview with the group of reporters on television: "If you want to ask me what I did, I don't have to tell you. I have to live my life the way I want to live it. I might want to know what you did, but I'm not asking you. That's only respect."

Then, less than a week into the new season, Magic Johnson made the announcement that he would have to retire from the Los Angeles Lakers because of medical factors that, thanks to the power of live television, the entire world knew the details of at the exact same instant. In June, Jordan and Johnson had competed at the highest and most thrilling level of basketball skill; in September, Johnson and his new wife had come cheerily as guests of honor to Jordan's dinner. In November, this.

So Jordan was wary and more than a little somber about

what was going on around him, and the thing that was to affect him most hadn't yet happened. That would take place during the second week of November, when a book by Sam Smith, the Bulls-beat writer for the *Tribune*, was published. On November 11 there was a story about the book on the front page of the *Sun-Times*, with the headline: BOOK DEPICTS TYRANT JORDAN AND IRRITA-BULLS. According to the story, in the book "Jordan is depicted as a dictatorial figure whose team-mates dislike him and ridicule him behind his back."

The *Sun-Times* story was one of those media goads that takes on a life of its own. Reporters who had known Jordan for years felt compelled to approach him with microphones and ask him if he was a "tyrant." He didn't seem to know how to answer; in many cases the reporters asking the questions were familiar faces to him, he had talked with them at length numerous times, yet they didn't seem to be kidding. The thing that surprised me the most about the reports about the book —no one had yet seen it, and Sam Smith was saying that it was being characterized out of context—was that in all the times I'd talked with Sam, he had never said a mean-spirited word about Jordan. I couldn't claim to know Sam exceptionally well, but we'd had dozens of conversations during the previous season—in California during the Finals he had given me a ride every night from our hotel to the Forum—and I was genuinely perplexed to hear that he apparently had such a low opinion of Jordan. He had always spoken of Jordan in generally admiring terms.

The specifics of what was being said about Jordan, though, interested me less than the way he was reacting to it. All of a sudden, for the first time since I had known him, he seemed to be avoiding people. He no longer sat around the locker room before games, talking to anyone among the sportswriters who cared to drop by; now as often as not he wasn't anywhere to be seen until the team came upstairs for the introductions. Tim Hallam and John Diamond reported that on the road local reporters would pepper Jordan every night with questions about the Olympics, about the White House trip he hadn't made, about Magic Johnson, about the allegations that he was an unpleasant bully whom his own teammates shunned. He seemed not to be having fun, Hallam and Diamond said; for the first time they could remember, he often seemed to wish that he was somewhere else.

That's what was defining the new season, as far as I could

sense. For Jordan, a man who was usually as full of energy and life as anyone I had ever been around, it appeared to be turning into a season of sadness. I'd watch him come upstairs with his teammates to get ready for the tipoff, and his countenance was that of a man with troubles he couldn't seem to resolve or even fully understand. He would score his thirty or thirty-five points every night, and his team would almost always win. There would be 18,676 people in the Stadium, and he didn't seem to be one of them.

The thoughts I'd been having over the summer—the thoughts that maybe it was time to stop going to the Stadium—were strengthened by the uneasy mood of this new season. Contention and conflict weren't among the things I sought at the Stadium. I went there for something else, and the difficulties that had developed by mid-November made me guess that maybe my nights in the arena had run their course. Maybe it was time to go back to real life full-time.

I had an urge to say something to Jordan before I did, though. All of us who write or broadcast for a living are expected to embrace the canard that we must be dispassionate and removed from the people we are observing; the notion is that if we are not permitted to care about anything, then we can be more effective as reporters.

Since Jordan's troubles had begun, I hadn't spoken much with him. I'd observed the postgame questioning of him night after night. He was a public figure; he was fair game for anything, and he knew it. Those were the rules he played under.

I sensed that all those Stadium evenings of talking casually before the games had become past tense now; this was Elvis '57, all right, or so I thought, and I could sense the distance widening between him and the outside world. The Bulls were on an extended West Coast trip. I knew I risked appearing foolish by making the phone call, but it was something I wanted to do.

I got the number of the hotel where the Bulls were staying in Los Angeles; one morning I spoke with the clerk at the hotel's front desk, and asked him to leave word for Jordan that I'd called. I left both my work and my home numbers. I had no idea whether Jordan was even given the messages that came in for him, or whether he ever responded to them. I had never talked to him on the phone.

An hour or so later someone at my newspaper office stuck

her head in the doorway and, somewhat disbelieving, said that Jordan was on the line.

"Hi," he said. "Did you call?"

I think he was expecting me to ask for his responses to all the controversies. Everyone else in the world had been asking him to react; he was doing me the courtesy of making himself available for my questions.

That's not why I had called, though. I said, "I just wanted to tell you I'm sorry about everything that's going on. I'm sorry you're feeling so down." I felt as foolish saying it as I'd felt thinking about saying it.

There was a silence on the other end. Then he said: "Thank you so much. That's why you called?"

"Yeah," I said. "I know you don't need to hear it from me, but you'll get through this."

There was another pause. "Listen," he said. "I can't talk right now. I just got up and we have to get on the bus to go to practice."

"That's all right," I said. It felt awkward; it felt nothing like all the loose conversations we'd had over the past year. "That's all I wanted to say. Thanks for calling back."

"No, it's just that I have to get on the bus," he said.

Which was fine. I'd said what I had to say. It wasn't the kind of call I was accustomed to making—actually, I couldn't remember having made a similar call. It's always easier not to say what you're feeling. At least it always has been for me.

That was on a Monday. Thursday was Thanksgiving Day. I was at home with my family, getting ready for a late-afternoon dinner; some friends would be coming over to share the meal with us. It was a typical Thanksgiving—lazy, groggy, disconnected from the rest of the week. I was in the bedroom, half-dozing, half-watching a football game on TV, when the phone rang. I picked it up.

"Bobby Greene," the voice on the other end, deadpan, said.

"Yes?" I said.

"Michael Jordan," the voice said.

He was spending his Thanksgiving in a hotel in Portland; the Bulls would be playing the Trail Blazers the next night, so that's where he was having his holiday. "I'll most likely end up eating Thanksgiving dinner in my room," he said.

We were on the phone for more than an hour. It was just two people talking; certainly there had been enough times in my own life when, sitting in a hotel room looking out the window, I'd picked up the telephone out of boredom or out of restlessness, just to break the silence. So I didn't want to ascribe any undue significance to the call. For whatever reason, he'd decided to make it.

We talked about a lot of things. I'd already heard all of his well-reported explanations about the various turmoils in his life. Every time someone with a microphone and a camera crew challenged him about the controversies, he went into his oft-repeated and by now familiar catalogue of responses: He was looking forward to going to the Olympics; he had meant no disrespect to the president; if his teammates didn't like him it was something he was unaware of. On Thanksgiving Day I really didn't need to hear him tell me any of that; whatever his impetus for choosing to call on this particular afternoon, I doubted that it was because he felt a compulsion to run through all of that again. So we just talked. It was a conversation about everything and about nothing; we never discussed head-on the matters that were troubling him, but in a way they were the very reason for the conversation. It was as if his troubles were underlying everything, and that this conversation was a way to quietly certify that he could get away from them, at least temporarily.

I touched upon the subject a little bit by alluding to the public image he always seemed so afraid of sullying. "Maybe you ought to look at how the professional wrestlers make their livings," I said. "In wrestling, the bad guys are just as famous as the good guys, and they make just as much money. But they never have to watch what they say or do. Maybe your life wouldn't be so complicated if you had just decided to sell yourself as a bad guy."

"I know," Jordan said, laughing only slightly. "That's just the discipline that I have to live with. The way people look at me, they're going to be paying close attention to everything I say. I guess I asked for it."

"Your friend Barkley seems to be doing all right the other way," I said. "He acts like he doesn't care what people think about him, and he's one of the richest and most famous people in your sport."

"That's the truth," Jordan said. "With Charles, whatever he says, people accept it for its shock value. And they accept it on that level, and that's that. If I were to say the same things, people would be talking about it for weeks, all over the world.

But that's okay. The financial situation I'm in wouldn't be available to me if I presented myself as a bad person. When a man plays the role of the bad guy, everyone hates him, but he always has the out of telling himself, 'Well, everyone's going to hate me anyway, so what does it matter?' "

"Is it just a marketing decision?" I said.

"I like to be considered a good person," Jordan said. "And I hope that I am. But I also realize that from the marketability standpoint, I really don't have any choice anymore. That's all gone, having that choice. I can't do things or say things that maybe some other people can. I accept that—it's a choice I made, and the rewards are great, and I live with that choice."

"Someone told me that if you go out to dinner, you won't even allow yourself to order a glass of wine with your meal," I said. "Because if you do, you know that the people at the next table will probably be going around the next day telling all their friends that they saw Michael Jordan drunk."

"I used to worry about that," he said. "But I'm deciding now that I have to live my life, and I can't let other people determine how I do it. If I'm out to dinner now, and I want to have a glass of champagne or a glass of wine with my meal, I'll allow myself to do it. It's true that I used to not do something like that, because of my concerns. But now I really do think that I have to start letting go."

"Letting go in terms of wanting things, too?" I said.

"Wanting what things?" he said.

"Just everything," I said. "You're so used to having so much —but how much is enough?"

"I really don't know," he said. "I guess I've reached the point where everything is enough, and now maybe it's time to live my life to enjoy the people in my life."

"So you don't feel a compulsion to earn even more money by putting your name on even more products?" I said.

"I'm cutting back on my endorsements," he said. "I'm not looking for any more endorsements. I'm happy with what I have. I don't need to earn more money. If there are players in the NBA who make more money than I do, that's okay, they can have it. If someone wants to get more endorsements than I do, that's okay, go ahead."

"Does the having enough apply to games, too?" I said. "It must be difficult at this point in your life to think of any game as being a big game, because you've been in so many games that were defined in advance as big games."

"Each game is a bigger game," he said. "Each game is the biggest game."

"Isn't that just the kind of thing that athletes say automatically?" I said.

"No," he said. "I don't know about anyone else, but I mean it. Every time I step onto the court, if you're against me, you're trying to take something from me. I don't want the other team to win. I just do not want them to win."

"And it doesn't matter who the other team might be, or what part of the season you may be in?" I said. "There are so many games in a season that seem almost like throwaway games."

"I never want anyone else to win when I'm playing," he said.

"Even at this point in your life?" I said. "I guess that's one of the things I meant by 'how much is enough.' You've won a world championship now. Why would an individual game in an eighty-two-game season mean as much to you now? You say you want to win every game and that every game is the biggest, but why is that?"

"That's why," he said. "The question is the answer. Because I want to win. I want to be the one who wins."

As we talked, I kept looking at a clock on the table next to me. I didn't know what the conventions of this conversation were supposed to be; getting the call from Jordan had been so out of the ordinary that I wasn't entirely sure how to approach it. But he didn't seem to be in any hurry; he seemed content just talking away. He told me that he missed being with his children on Thanksgiving, but that he had become accustomed to spending holidays on the road; he said he called home all the time when he was traveling, but that hearing his children's voices on the phone was no substitute for seeing their faces.

"On the road, after a game I know there's just another game ahead," he said. "Traveling takes on a routine of its own, but there's very seldom a peaceful feeling after a game. In Chicago, my mood after a game will depend on whether we won or we lost. But the drive home after the game is peaceful for me in a way that getting on an airplane after a road game isn't. I like to drive myself. Sometimes I think about the traffic around me and sometimes I don't. If a car pulls up next to mine and the people in the car see who I am, then I find myself always looking behind me the rest of the ride, to make sure they're not following. But that doesn't really preoccupy me. I like that drive home. I listen to music, and it's a nice feeling."

"Maybe on the road you could just go out and take a walk by yourself sometime and get the same feeling," I said, knowing as soon as I heard my words that they weren't very practical.

"It's been a long time since I've done that," he said.

"How long?" I said.

"Since I've just gone out the door for a walk by myself?" he said. "Probably not since high school."

"Really that many years?" I said.

"My life changed after high school," he said. "In theory, it sounds like it would be very nice. Just go out and take a long walk with no one else around, and think my thoughts. But I couldn't do it on the road—if I decided to do it even this afternoon, even on Thanksgiving, I'd be stopped by people. And I can't do it in Chicago—I'd probably be stopped by even more people there. It sounds like something I'd very much like to do. It sounds very peaceful—a park or something like that, and just walking by myself for hours. But it wouldn't be as peaceful as I'd want it to be."

"Is it worth trying?" I said. "Just to see?"

"I've just never done it," he said. "It's just not an option for me. It's not something I've ever entertained to do, at least in recent years."

"It's a fairly simple pleasure for a person to give himself," I said.

"Well, simplicity is one of the things you sometimes have to give up," he said.

The content of our conversation seemed not as important as the fact of it. I told him that maybe someday, when he was no longer quite so famous, he could take his walk. Someday the simplicity would return.

"Oh, it will happen," he said. "When you're on the pedestal, you know that someone will replace you on it eventually. You don't know when it will happen. But you can be sure that it's going to happen, and that when you're off the pedestal there will be someone else to take your place."

I wished him a happy Thanksgiving, and he did the same. He asked if I planned to keep on going out to the Stadium during the year, and I said that I did. The thoughts I'd been having of staying away had been altered during the course of the time on the telephone. I wasn't quite sure what it was I was hearing in his voice, but it was different from what I'd heard before. And I didn't know what the new season would bring, but now I knew that, at least for me, it would be distinct from the last. Our guests arrived for Thanksgiving dinner, and halfway through I found myself thinking about a traveler eating a room-service supper in Portland.

22

THERE WAS ONE THING I kept remembering all during the new season, as an undeniable backlash against Jordan grew.

In the years I had worked for newspapers, I had seen parallel backlashes in virtually every field of public endeavor—politics, entertainment, literature, sports. Once a man or a woman was elevated to a lofty enough position in the public eye, attempts at demolition inevitably began. The demolition served the purported function of reminding the world that its heroes are human.

So while Jordan answered questions every night about what were now being seen as his personal failings, I kept recalling a phone call I had received early in the previous season, when I was first coming to the Stadium. I had written a column about a random act of kindness I had seen Jordan do for a child outside the arena. It was when all of this was new to me, before I knew that he did this kind of thing all the time.

The day after the column ran I got a call at work from a man who said he lived in a western suburb of Chicago. He said: "I read what you wrote about Jordan, and I thought I should tell you what I saw."

Here it comes, I thought. It always does. Write something nice about a person, and people call you up to say that the person is really a callow creep.

What the caller said, though, was this: He and his wife had been to a Bulls game, and their car had broken down. They'd had to wait about forty-five minutes after the end of the game to get a cab ride to the suburbs.

"We were four blocks from the Stadium, in a bad area, and at a corner under a streetlight was Jordan's car," the man said. "He was standing outside the car, talking with some boys from the neighborhood. It was late at night, and they were just talking. I thought it was nice of him, but I wonder why he stopped."

I didn't know what to make of the story. A few weeks after the phone call from the man, Jordan and I were talking about something else before a game, and I brought up what the man had said. Was the man right? Had Jordan really been talking to those two boys in that grim neighborhood?

"Not two boys," Jordan said. "Four."

And he named all four of them.

"How do you remember their names?" I said.

"Because I see them every night," he said.

"The same four boys?" I said.

"Yes," Jordan said.

He said that the year before, he'd seen them waiting outside the Stadium in terrible weather, wanting a glimpse of the Bulls as the team arrived for a game.

"I said, 'Don't wait out there, come inside,'" Jordan said. "I brought them in with me to the game."

The boys, he said, lived four blocks away from the Stadium, in that dismal and dangerous area that basketball fans from the affluent suburbs drove through only on nights of games. No matter how many times you visit that area, you are always struck by how little hope it offers the young people who live there, if indeed it offers any hope at all.

"Now they wait for me on that corner every night," Jordan said.

And after games some nights he stops?

"Every night," he said.

Every night? Why?

"If I don't stop, I'll go home knowing that they're waiting for me anyway," he said. "If you knew my four guys you'd know that they're going to be out there if it's raining, if it's snowing . . . they're there."

I asked him what he talked about with the four boys.

"Everything," he said. "Anything. They're just kids who seem like they really need someone to talk to."

I said I found it surprising—that after performing for all those people every night, after giving all that effort, he took the time to see those four boys.

"What does it cost me?" he said. "A couple of minutes? It's on my way anyway. And if I went home or went out to dinner knowing that they were standing there waiting and I hadn't shown up, it would ruin my evening."

A few nights after I'd had that conversation with Jordan, I ran into his wife, Juanita, at the Stadium. I asked her about the boys.

"It's really a thing with Michael," she said. "Those four boys are on that corner every night. I think Michael is concerned that they may be letting it take over their lives. So lately he's asked to see their grades, just so he can check to see they're paying attention to their schoolwork. He's told me that if it turns out one or two of them may need tutoring, he wants to make sure they get it."

Had the newspaper reader from the suburbs—the man who'd seen Jordan talking with the boys—not called me to tell me what he'd witnessed, I would never have been aware of the boys' existence. Now, as Jordan's mood darkened and the criticism of him sharpened during the new season, I couldn't help but recall that story. Not a headline story; not a piece of urgent news. Just four boys under a streetlight, waiting for the man they knew would come. For someone they could depend on.

The season itself was going prodigiously well for the Bulls. Through December and into the first weeks of January, the team built up a 28-5 record, on pace with the best records in the history of the NBA. The fans were not only satisfied, they were close to delirious. What had seemed impossible at the beginning of last year was now taken for granted: The Bulls were the best basketball team in the world.

That assumption was one of many factors that made the Stadium feel different. A year ago the starters had trotted onto the court each night as one NBA team among twenty-seven, five men who never knew on a given evening whether they might win or get blown out. Now the expectations had changed; now the fans anticipated a win each game, and the opposing teams stood at center court before tipoff, looking with a combination of nerves and defiance at Jordan and Pippen and Grant and Cartwright and Paxson, knowing that if they beat the Bulls it would be big news back home, cause for celebration. The Bulls were now the mountain that everyone else wanted to climb.

The faces along press and broadcast row had changed, too. Jim Durham, the Bulls' radio and TV play-by-play man for eighteen years, had had a parting of the ways during contract negotiations with the team's front office, and he was out. There also had been switches in the newspapers' coverage of the Bulls. Dave Hoekstra had been transferred to another department at the *Sun-Times*, and the Bulls beat had been given to a sportswriter named Mike Mulligan. At the *Tribune*, Sam Smith had been assigned to be an overall NBA writer, Paul Sullivan had switched to Chicago Bears coverage and college athletics, while sports reporter Melissa Isaacson had been given the daily Bulls beat. Mike and Melissa were bright, talented people, and good company on game nights, but it was strange for me, no longer feeling quite so junior at the Stadium to the beat writers. Feeling junior had been one of the main attractions for me last year.

I called Dave Hoekstra one day just to see how he was doing. He said he had been driving over to Rockford, Illinois, two hours away, to watch the games of the Rockford Lightning, a team in the minor-league Continental Basketball Association. He wasn't covering the team for his paper—he would just show up at the Rockford Metro Center on game nights, buy a ticket, and sit in the stands. Even though last year he'd covered the Bulls' path to the world championship, he said that he found going to the Rockford games fun and interesting. He said he was becoming a fan.

Carmen was still at the Stadium almost every night, but Daniel Spikes was often missing. Carmen said that Doc's illness—his underlying disease was lupus—had flared up badly, and that he was too weak to come to the Stadium most evenings. He was in and out of the hospital, she said, trying to get stronger.

There were other changes, some important, some frivolous. Coaches had come and gone on several teams, so when the visitors showed up at the Stadium there was a new cast of characters on the sidelines. The rights to the dot race had been sold to a different merchant—now the colored lights skittering around the scoreboard were supposed to be M&M's candy instead of corn chips—but Levingston and Perdue and King still watched during time-outs as if each race was the Kentucky Derby. A new musical jingle, "Chicago Bulls Boogie," had been commissioned, and was played before each night's game.

All the changes had served to make this season feel disparate from the last. The biggest change in the hours before the games, though, was the nature of Jordan's presence in the Stadium, or, more precisely, the lack of his presence.

"There's only been a handful of times in my career when I've heard them," John Paxson said one evening.

We were talking about the play-by-play broadcasts that were done from courtside microphones each game. To people listening in their bedrooms and on car radios, the announcers' voices defined the games. There was the roar of the crowd, and the excited shout of the play-by-play man: "Here comes Paxson dribbling downcourt, there are ten seconds left in the quarter, he's looking for Jordan. . . ."

"I really never hear it," Paxson said. "I know the broadcast guys are there, but even when I'm dribbling right next to them, I'm not aware of what they're saying. . . ."

"I don't hear the broadcasters, and I don't hear the music playing," Bill Cartwright said. "It's so loud out there that you can't hear anything but the crowd. Sometimes you want to wear earplugs. That's why we have our hand signals out there, because there are many times that there's no chance at all that we can hear each other, even if we're right next to each other and yelling."

The Bulls were sitting around the locker room, as always, before a game, this one a Friday night contest in January. It would have felt very much like the year before, except that Jordan was not at his cubicle. He was back in the trainer's room, and he wouldn't be coming out until all of the reporters were gone. It was like this almost every night now.

Horace Grant, talking about catching sight of the Stadium on his drive to work, said, "When I get off the expressway, the reality sets in. It's not so much that it's a feeling of home. On nights when we have games, it seems like I'm going to a concert. But a concert that I'm in."

"You don't think of the building as ugly," Cartwright said. "It's quaint. As a player, it's just a feeling of going to work."

"I've driven by on nights when there isn't a game, and it seems like a ghost town," Grant said. "Like a spooky place."

"Is it as physically cold over the ice rink to you guys as it is to those of us who don't play?" I said.

"The place I feel the coldness is my hands," Grant said. "I feel like I want to put something on them. You feel it in your feet, your hands, your face, everywhere. But when I think about how I feel on the court, it's my cold hands that I think of first."

"Does it seem odd for you to read newspaper accounts of the games the next morning?" I said.

"Some people like to read the paper," Cartwright said. "I don't. I say to my wife, 'What are you reading that for? You were there.'"

"So you're not interested in seeing how the sportswriters analyzed the game?" I said to him.

"I have no curiosity at all to read a story about the game we played the night before," Cartwright said. "The stories aren't written by basketball players. We all know each other. We know the game. We know what happened."

It was a pleasant and instructive way to pass the time before a game, and one that Jordan used to be a big part of. Now, though, in the wake of the negative stories about him, he was seldom seen. Phil Jackson closed the locker room to the press forty-five minutes before the start of each game, and after the reporters had left, Jordan would join his teammates. He was required to be present for questions after the games. But the pregame banter with groups of reporters was over, except for rare occasions. So was the solitary shooting practice in the locked Stadium early each evening, the thing he had seemed to take such pleasure in. Now he didn't want to see anyone. He never came upstairs to shoot until the arena was filled and it was time for the tipoff.

In their public statements his teammates had stood firmly behind him during the various controversies, but he was no longer sure exactly whom he could trust. He was convinced that more than a few of the negative things that had been written about him had come from some of the men he played with, men he felt were betraying what he considered to be locker room confidences and talking behind his back. He was feeling more separate from the rest of the world than ever. The Bulls were doing well in the basketball games, and Jordan had apparently decided to just leave it at that.

Of all the alterations at the Stadium since last season, perhaps the most symbolic was a bare wooden door constructed between the locker room and the trainer's area. The short hallway between the two used to be a place where anyone could wander; technically the trainer's area was off limits to nonplayers, but last year when Jordan was getting taped there before games anyone could look in and say hello to him or ask him a quick question. As this year wore on, when he was back there the new door stayed always closed.

Jordan's apparent confusion about what was happening in his world was exemplified by a pair of journalistic endeavors—an edition of a magazine and a newspaper wire story.

The magazine was *Sports Illustrated,* specifically the publication's annual Sportsman of the Year issue. Jordan received the honor at the end of December; the edition was proving to be a collector's item. News dealers around the country were keeping it on the stands all through January, even as other weekly issues of *SI* were published. The reason the issue was such a favorite with sports fans was that the cover was no mere color photo of Jordan—it was a hologram.

The hologram, in startlingly realistic 3-D, featured Jordan in a red-and-white warm-up jacket. The holographic image was constructed from a two-hundred-frame strip of film, in which Jordan went from looking to his right with a straight-faced expression to turning to his left and breaking into a wide, winning smile. The magazine offered helpful instructions:

> To appreciate the full effect of the image, hold the cover of your *SI* about 16 inches away from your eyes and look at the center of Michael's face. A clear light source—such as a halogen track light—should be behind and above you, about eight feet away and at a 45-degree angle. Bright sunlight works too. At the correct angle, Jordan's jersey will appear bright red and the background a deep blue. By tilting the cover left and right, you will see Jordan break into a dazzling smile.

More than 4.1 million of the foil holograms had been printed up; the magazine's editors quoted holographic artist Sharon McCormack as saying: "It's the closest thing to having Michael right in front of you."

So there it was: Jordan as a literal graven image. The ultimate result of a human being turned into an icon. The newspaper wire story conveyed a somewhat different mood.

"Federal investigators in Charlotte have seized $57,000 from a convicted cocaine dealer in a golf betting case," the story, based on reporting by the Charlotte *Observer,* began.

"But James 'Slim' Bouler, a Union County businessman, says the money didn't come from a bet but was a loan from the Bulls' Michael Jordan."

The story continued: "Bouler's court file includes copies of a certified-mail envelope from ProServ of Arlington, Va., and a $57,000 cashier's check dated Oct. 17, 1991. ProServ is a management company that represents Jordan and other athletes. Officials said Jordan is not a subject of the federal probe. There is no evidence that Jordan knows about Bouler's background, investigators said. . . . In 1986, Bouler pleaded guilty in Union County to selling cocaine and possessing cocaine with intent to sell."

A smiling hologram on living-room tables all over America; a figure in newspaper stories about a federal investigation. Jordan stayed in the trainer's room most evenings and came out only when the 18,676 were in place. He may have been smiling in the hologram, but he wasn't smiling much in Chicago.

One evening, with the locker room full of sportswriters and broadcasters, he came walking briskly from the lavatory part of the complex toward the brown door that would seal him in the trainer's room. I hadn't spoken more than a few words with him since the Thanksgiving Day call.

He paused to shake hands, and I asked him how he was doing. He looked around the locker room and said, "I can't . . . I have to go get taped. I'm not staying out here." I had not seen him so skittish before. It was as if the locker room used to be his home, and now it wasn't.

"Do you ever feel like talking?" I said.

"Not here," he said.

"Is there someplace that would be better for you?" I said.

He paused for a moment. "Is it a problem for you to travel?" he said.

"Not really," I said. "I could do that."

"It's just easier for me on the road," he said. "I'm just in my room all day."

"Do you have a specific city in mind?" I said.

"Where are we next week?" he said.

The schedule said that the Bulls would play in Cleveland between home games against Philadelphia and San Antonio.

"Is Cleveland okay with you?" he said.

"I can be in Cleveland," I said.

"That's fine, then," he said. "Let's get together on the day of the game. We'll probably practice in the morning. I'll meet you at the hotel right after practice."

And he ducked behind that door and closed it hard. A few minutes later all of us outsiders left the locker room so that the team could be alone before the game. He came upstairs just before the spotlight introductions and scored thirty-seven points to lead the Bulls to a 105-90 victory over the Utah Jazz.

I made a reservation to fly from O'Hare Airport to Cleveland, but a blizzard and ice storm shut down all the runways during the day, and my flight was canceled. No one was sure whether the airport would resume regular operations by nightfall.

I tried to figure out how to get to Cleveland in the storm, and I thought of the train. I called Amtrak; it turned out that the Capitol Limited would be leaving Chicago late that afternoon, and was scheduled to arrive in Cleveland at a minute after midnight en route to its final destination in Washington. I'd never ridden a long-distance train before, but now it seemed to be the only choice. I reserved a bedroom, took a cab to Union Station, and got on the train.

We rolled out of Chicago right on time. I read a book in my small, cozily designed compartment. The Capitol Limited roared through the snowstorm, its whistle announcing our presence to the towns and cities we passed.

A little boy giggled in the bedroom next to mine. I could hear him through the wall, but I didn't mind at all. He was traveling with his mother. The whistle sounded again, soft then loud then soft, trailing off. The boy and his mother played a card game and sang a song together. His voice was filled with wonder and the sense that he was seeing something new.

This was beginning to seem all right. "*First* call for dinner in the dining car," the conductor intoned as he walked down the corridor beside my bedroom. "*First* call for dinner in the dining car." I heard him open the door that led to the next car. A rush of cold air swooped down the hall.

I had dinner in my bedroom, and read some more of my book, and sometime after 10:00 P.M., after I'd walked through the train for a while, up and down from one end to the other, I returned to my room and turned all the lights out.

The blizzard was still picking up, but we were moving steadily. There was no way we were going to make our scheduled arrival in Cleveland—the weather had been far too severe to allow that—but we weren't going to be all that late. The loco-motive's whistle was singing in the night, and we were chug-ging across northern Indiana.

The window in my room was wider than it was tall. I pulled the bed down, found a pillow, and in the darkness started to watch the window.

All the houses, all the little stores. We were rolling through America's backyard; few people construct their houses to face the train tracks. So what we were seeing was a view that the homeowners and business operators did not consider the most flattering view; what we weren't seeing was the front doors and front lawns. It didn't matter. It was sort of beautiful any-way.

This is what you miss when you fly over America. You even miss it when you drive, because the superhighways bypass so much. On the Capitol Limited, on this snowy nighttime run, there was no skipping any towns, no fast-forwarding. Every little town along the way, every half-forgotten hamlet, passed by my window.

Seven hours is a long time to ride, but some people watch television for seven hours without thinking twice, so with the lights off I lay in bed and watched that window as if it were a TV screen. The show was a marvelous one, and if the plot wasn't obvious, there was all kinds of hinted drama just be-neath the surface.

In the smallest of villages the crossing gates dropped to horizontal as we approached, and the red lights flashed, and the bells clanged, and as we rolled past I could see the auto headlights at the intersections, waiting for us to be on our way. There was nothing very majestic about our journey, it was the essence of the ordinary, but for a few minutes in one town after another we broke through the silence, we broke through the cold.

At so many houses in so many towns, cars had been pulled into the driveways, next to the back doors for the night. Nine or ten hours from now, when it was early morning in these towns and it was time for the people in the houses to go to work, they weren't going to want to walk very far in the wintry air. These weren't the most luxurious homes, not in any of the towns; in each of the homes in each of the towns the people inside, when explaining where they lived, were undoubtedly obliged at some point to say "down by the tracks." But the houses looked warm and secure as we approached them and then were gone, and in the driveways the cars were ready for morning.

In hundreds of houses there were lights in the windows. One of the oldest phrases in American life, but town after town it was true: Someone was leaving a light in the window for someone else. Someone was waiting.

A billboard for a health-care service, canted away from the tracks but still at an angle where we on the train could just make out the words, bore the message: "We Wish You Well." Outside a service station, closed for the night and its lot now covered with snow, a red-and-white Coke machine glowed from its light within, one of how many machines on how many corners in how many American towns. In a car parked near the railroad grading I could see a man and woman kissing.

In an MTV, CNN, VCR land, the rumbling sound of the Capitol Limited was at the same time ancient and entirely new. One town after another, town by town, and as I lay in the dark and watched the window it was like a wonderful television show, all right, it was pay-per-view and the price was right and I had not the slightest desire to turn the channel or turn it off.

We rolled softly through Bryan, Ohio; I knew because out the window I could see the town's neatly inscribed water tower, lighted and shining bright in the freezing, empty night. Outside the town the telephone wires were coated with ice. Satellite communications and computer-chip technology have conspired to make our world seem tiny at times. Tonight I looked out that window from my warm and darkened room on the Capitol Limited, and I could tell where I was by the words painted on the sides of yellow school buses, parked in frosty lots until the dawn. Town after town after town. This used to be a big country.

In the Cleveland suburb of Independence the desk clerk handed me an envelope along with my key. Inside the envelope was a room list for the Bulls' traveling party, so that the players, coaches, staff, and reporters would be able to dial room-to-room. It was peculiar to see those box-score names, familiar to sports-page readers all over the world, reduced to first initials, last names, and room numbers on the letterhead stationery of the Cleveland Hilton South:

B. CARTWRIGHT	230
H. GRANT	424
S. PIPPEN	425
C. LEVINGSTON	402
B. J. ARMSTRONG	430
J. PAXSON	420

And all the rest. M. JORDAN, according to the room list, was staying in rooms 426–427; other than Phil Jackson, in rooms 535–536, Jordan was the only member of the traveling party who had a suite. By the time I arrived at the hotel it was almost 2 A.M.; there was no activity in the lobby, and I went straight to my room and then to sleep.

Early in the morning my phone rang; it was John Diamond. "We'll be coming back from practice a little after eleven," he said. "Michael knows you're here. The best thing for you to do is wait on the first floor for the bus to pull up, and then get right on the elevator with him."

"The main lobby where I checked in?" I said.

"No, that's one of the reasons I'm calling," he said. "To avoid having the team walk through the people in the lobby, we're going to pull up to a back door. You'll see it—get off the elevator and instead of turning right toward the lobby, turn left. There's a little glass door that opens onto a back parking lot. That's where we'll be."

I went downstairs a few minutes before eleven. It was a subfreezing morning in northern Ohio, with ice caked on the windows and snowdrifts on the ground. Apparently word had started to get out in the hotel that the Bulls would be coming in the back way; a few people, both guests and employees, were lounging around the hallway with posters and Bulls caps in their hands, waiting for autographs.

The bus came crunching through the snow to the rear door of the hotel. Tim Hallam was the first person into the back hallway, then Phil Jackson, then Pippen and Grant together. They got on the elevator, followed by Craig Hodges, and then came Jordan in a ski cap out of the cold and into the hallway.

The people who had been waiting moved toward him, thrusting the items into his hands. He signed as he moved; he caught my eye and motioned with his head for me to get on the elevator. More pictures and pieces of paper were shoved at him as the elevator door closed.

In the crowded-to-capacity elevator car I stood between

Armstrong and Pippen. "Did your plane just get in this morning?" Armstrong asked.

"I took the train last night," I said.

"A train from Chicago?" Armstrong said. "I've never done that."

"It was actually pretty nice," I said. "Going through the blizzard at night."

"Did it go real fast in the snowstorm?" Pippen said.

"It did," I said. "I was surprised by how fast it went."

"I wouldn't want to do that," Pippen said. "Not in the snow."

The car stopped on four. Most of us got off. Jordan said, "It's this way." I followed him down the hall, accompanied by Pippen. Pippen let himself into his room, and Jordan slipped his key into the lock of the next door down.

"I keep it hot in here," he said, almost apologetically. It was exceedingly warm in the room; we walked through the bedroom part and into the living room. He had left the television set on. He sat down on the couch and I sat in a chair by the window. He propped his feet on a small table.

I realized it was the first time I had seen him completely alone.

"I know it's hot," he said again. He said that he was subject to catching colds and flu bugs all during the winter, and that one way he tried to fight it was to jack the thermostats in his hotel rooms up. It was so quiet in the room; even at the Stadium when we'd talked in relative privacy there was always the likelihood that someone was going to come walking around the corner with a request or a message, or that someone was up in the stands, watching. Here it was as if he had allowed himself to let out a breath. Here he was a man with the door closed and locked.

The logistics I'd gone through to meet him here—the planning in advance, the call in the morning from John Diamond, the carefully arranged hookup point on the first floor so that I could get onto the elevator at precisely the right time—pointed out once again the difference between his world and the world the rest of us inhabited. Later I would see this orchestrated meeting routine happen with old friends of his from North Carolina, and even with family members—the need to wait for him at a preordained spot, to spend minutes watching a doorway for his arrival, to move onto the elevator as the door was sliding shut. It was not the most natural way for people to greet each other; it was destined to color the nature of the meeting every time. Yet it seemed, under the circumstances, necessary.

"It's the one way to do it that works for sure," he said. "At most hotels they don't ring my calls through to me, or at least I can't count on getting them. There are security guards near my room a lot of the time. Sometimes they'll have me on floors that are blocked off, where you need a special key to get there. So if I just tell people to meet me in my room, a lot of times I'll end up not knowing where they are because they can't get up to see me. If we meet up with each other in the lobby and get on the elevator together, we're set."

"That just seems like it might be such a strange thing for you," I said. "For you to know that everyone is always waiting for you, and that you're never going to be the one who's waiting."

"Not any more, I guess I never am," he said.

"Everyone waits for people," I said. "It's just part of life."

"I remember when I went to apply for my first job," he said. "I waited an hour and a half for the boss to see me. It was for a maintenance job at a motel. It was changing air conditioning filters, fixing broken windows, some painting—general maintenance work. I guess I was thirteen years old.

"I showed up and I said I was supposed to see the boss. They said the boss wasn't there. So I waited one and a half hours. I just sat there and didn't say anything and I waited. It was frustrating because no one spoke to me, and I didn't know what to do. It was the first time I had ever gone to apply for a job, and I didn't know whether you always had to wait that long."

"Had you read about the job in the paper or something?" I said.

"No, my mother was working at a bank, and she heard about this job at the motel," he said. "I was supposed to go and ask for this man. I was supposed to show up at noon. But he'd gone to lunch. He had just left, but no one told me that. So I sat there for the hour and a half, not saying a word, and no one telling me that he was at lunch."

"Were you in his office?" I said.

"Actually, it wasn't a room by itself," he said. "It was behind the front desk of the motel. So people could have told me what was going on, but they didn't. I was very nervous. I think part of me was happy that he wasn't there, so I could relax for a while. When he did come back he asked me what I was doing there. I said I had come about the job. He seemed surprised at how long I'd been waiting. What I remember most was sitting there for the hour and a half, and no one talking to me. They were looking, though, like, 'Who is this boy, and why is he still here?' But they never spoke to me."

"Do you ever wait for anyone these days?" I said.

"Not really," he said. "It doesn't come up very often. And when it does happen—when I go somewhere I'm supposed to be, and the person isn't there—I turn around and go sit in the car by myself rather than wait where there are people."

"It's more comfortable in your car than with the people?" I said.

"Not physically more comfortable," he said. "But if there are people, it always turns into a situation that's a little out of hand. So I'll just go back to my car and sit by myself."

Jordan in his hotel room was as free of tension as I had ever seen him. At the Stadium, on some nights he had appeared calmer than others, but this was something else. His life was so continually conducted under the observation of strangers; I had long wondered what happened when he finally chained the door shut and hung out the Do Not Disturb sign. The ultimate answer to that I would never know—no one would. As long as there is one other person in the room, a man can't act the way he might in complete solitude. But this was likely as close as it got. Even the voice was subtly different; the voice today had no edge at all, he sounded like a man at the breakfast table, talking about something he'd seen on a morning TV show or overheard from the neighbors' house when he'd gone outside to pick up the morning paper off the front stoop.

It was as if he didn't have to think about who might be staring at him, or who might be poised to approach him for an autograph or an entreaty for Bulls tickets. I had seen him in so many of those public situations, surrounded by law officers with guns on their hips. Whenever Jordan went out these days, it seemed, he was guarded as if he were some priceless piece of sculpture. Did the constant sight of all those guns affect him in any way?

"I used to be afraid of guns," he said. "But in the last couple of years I've gotten over my fear. I went to a range and I learned how to shoot. I was taught how to handle guns properly, and how to clean them. I couldn't even imagine taking another life with a gun, but I used to look at a gun and be afraid even to touch it. You hear about kids with guns all the time now, but when I was a kid, the sight of one really frightened me."

"There had to be a lot of people with guns in North Carolina," I said.

"Of course," he said. "The fear of them was just something with me. I remember once, my grandfather and some other older people went hunting, and they took me along with them. I was just a kid; I had a knife. They were going to go into the woods with their guns to hunt, and I was afraid to walk along with them."

"So what did you do?" I said. "Just stand there?"

"I sat on the truck," he said.

"They left you there on the truck?" I said.

"Well, they would have taken me with them," he said. "But I was afraid to go into the woods with the guns. There was a dirt road right next to the woods, and that's where they parked the truck, and I sat on it and watched them disappear into the woods."

"Did the men say anything to you before they left?" I said.

"They were kind of kidding me," Jordan said. "My grandfather said, 'Let us know if you see a deer or a bear.' And then they were gone."

"Were you scared to be by yourself?" I said.

"A little," he said. "I figured that if I got scared enough, I would get into the cab of the truck and lock the doors. I don't know how many hours they were in the woods. I just remember me sitting on the truck, and them coming out when they were finished and saying to me, 'Did you see anything?' and me saying that, no, I hadn't."

We watched some television and talked about the basketball season, and still unspoken was the subject of the troubles that had come upon him recently. I was wondering how to bring them up, or whether to bring them up at all, and what I found myself saying was, "Do you ever get your feelings hurt?"

He looked at me. After a few seconds he said, "When we would play Detroit, it would hurt my feelings, knowing what they were doing. Stopping me and totally humiliating my teammates. Knowing that if they could stop me they could stop the rest of the team."

"I don't mean that," I said. "I don't mean getting your feelings hurt by the Detroit Pistons."

He paused again. "Have my feelings ever been hurt?" he said. "If they have been, that's not the kind of thing I would ever let anyone know about."

He pointed to his head, and then to his heart. "If something hurts you badly enough, you have to keep it right in here," he said.

I didn't say anything. He had lowered the volume on the television set until it was all the way down, and I looked at the screen and watched a soap opera with no sound. He watched it too. We did that for thirty seconds or more.

"Well, my feelings are hurt right now," he said.

I looked over to see him still staring at the screen. He didn't turn.

"I've tried so hard to be a respectable person. . . ." he began.

The next couple of minutes were almost surreal. "I suppose that if I had thought in advance about hitting Will Perdue that day at practice," he said, addressing himself to an altercation that Sam Smith had reported. Then: "I had already met President Bush the one time, and I didn't think . . ." Then: "I really never did say that I wasn't going to the Olympics. . . ." Then: "As far as not throwing the ball to Bill Cartwright . . ."

That last one was in reference to another allegation of his shortcomings: that he didn't want the ball thrown to Cartwright at the end of close games, because he didn't regard Cartwright as a great shot-maker. This is what Jordan was doing: He was sitting there trying to remember every single negative thing that anyone had said about him in the last six months and attempting to respond to each of them, one by one. There were moments that bordered on being poignantly preposterous—he was addressing his distrust of Cartwright's shooting ability as if the revelation of that was a mortal wound; he was speaking about a scuffle with Perdue in practice as if he believed the world thought that a flare-up between two young athletes made him unworthy of its admiration.

I listened for a while. None of us will ever know what it's like to be him; to pretend that we understand the pressures a person like Jordan is under would be naive and presumptuous. He was still only twenty-eight years old, though; the rest of us might never come close to feeling scrutiny anywhere near the level that he feels it, but many of us have lived more years than he, and have had our own share of sorrows. I heard him saying all these things.

"Think of the worst things anyone has ever said about you," I said.

"I am," he said. "Believe me, I am."

"All right," I said. "Keep all of those things in mind. And now think about the things you wake up terrified about in the middle of the night. The things you stare at the ceiling thinking about, that only you know about yourself."

He nodded his head.

"Those things that wake you up in the night," I said. "Are any of them the things that other people have said about you?"

"No," he said. "The three-o'clock-in-the-morning things are much worse."

"I know," I said. "It's not just you. It's everyone. The worst things that anyone else could ever say about us don't come close to being as bad as the worst things we think about ourselves."

Outside the window there was only snow and January ice.

"If people knew those things, then they really wouldn't think very highly of me," he said.

"That's where you're probably wrong," I said. "There's not a person in the world who doesn't have those three A.M. terrors. All of our secret terrors are different terrors, but every one of us has them."

How do you tell another person how much you think of him? How do you verbalize the kind of thing that seldom gets said from one adult to another? You don't, usually; you just tell stories and dance around it and hope the point gets made.

"Do you remember that letter I gave you down in New Orleans?" I said.

"From the woman?" he said. "Whose daughter . . . ?"

"Yes," I said. I had received an agonizingly moving letter from a woman whose three-year-old daughter had been killed in an awful and random traffic accident. In her despair, she had written to me; she knew that I knew Jordan. In the envelope she had enclosed the letter to me, and a separate letter to Jordan. In her letter to him she said how much his grace on the basketball court, and his dignity in the way he conducted himself in public, had meant to her family for so long. She said that she didn't know why she was writing to him, except that somehow in her grief it would help her and her husband and her other children just to let him know about this. She wanted nothing in return; she didn't even want him to write her back. She signed her name, but purposely didn't put a return address on the letter to him, so that he wouldn't feel compelled to respond. In her letter she enclosed a mass card from the funeral of her daughter. She wanted Jordan to know that her child had once been alive.

There was no way I wasn't going to pass the letter on to Jordan; I'd taken it down to New Orleans with me and explained to him what it was, and he had taken it back to his room and read it that night. Now, in Ohio, he said, "Do you know how the family is getting along?"

"I called her," I said. "It was either the day of Christmas Eve or the day of New Year's Eve. For some reason I was thinking about her, so I picked up the phone. I had told her husband that I was going to give you the note, but I called her that day to tell her that I had, and that you'd read it. She was having a very rough day. You don't know what hearing that you'd read her words meant to her."

We were on new ground here; this was not the way a person who writes for a living customarily talks to a person who is written about. But these were things I thought he ought to hear.

"There's something I didn't tell you about when it happened, but I want to tell you now," I said. And I related to him the story of a coach from the southern part of the country who, like that woman, had sent me a letter.

When I first met Jordan I had written a column about how his coach had cut him from his high school basketball team. It was almost a year after that column ran that I heard from this other coach, who had never met Jordan and figured he never would.

He had a daughter, it seemed, who was not as adept an athlete as she wished she was. It was especially difficult for her because her dad was a coach. She tried to do better, and he tried to help her, and one day, when she was feeling especially low, he took her aside and told her something. He told her that when she was feeling the most despondent, and thinking she would never be as good as the others, there were four initials he wanted her to repeat to herself. He told her to use the initials as she would a talisman; to use the initials to make herself persevere. The initials were M.G.C.T.

She did work hard during the year, he wrote me, and he worked with her, and by the time he mailed me the letter she was doing just fine. She wasn't the most coordinated girl in her school, or the most physically gifted, but she had made herself better. He wanted to thank me, he said, because it was the story told in the newspaper column that had inspired him to come up with those initials and to present them to his daughter almost as a gift. The initials were a secret code between them, designed to make her feel not so alone. He wanted me to know about them, and what they stood for: M.G.C.T. Michael got cut, too.

Whatever was or wasn't wrong in Jordan's life—and like all of us, he knew what his faults were far better than any outsider knew—the strength of what he had come to mean to people he'd never even meet was something precious, something for him to cherish. He was aware of that, of course; he saw evidence of it every day of his life, which may have had something to do with why he always seemed so afraid that he might screw everything up and let everyone down. *I've tried so hard to be a respectable person.* Somewhere down the hallway a radio was playing.

We got off that and onto a number of other things, which may have been less compelling but were certainly more comfortable. He seemed so free of nerves, waiting for the night's game with the Cavaliers; I had heard that the Richfield Coliseum was one of the few arenas in the NBA where Jordan was routinely booed, and I was curious why the prospect of a night full of hostility did not appear to have him on edge.

"I like it," he said. "So many arenas we go into this year, the home teams' fans cheer for us almost like *we're* the home team. In a way, I like this better. If they hate me, that only energizes me. I look forward to them booing me. It makes me better."

"I would just figure it would build up," I said. "The combination of being pursued all day long everywhere you go, and being booed at night in places like Cleveland, and being approached by strangers every time you stick your head out the door . . . I would just figure that there are times when you want to lose it, or get drunk, or scream at someone who comes up and pulls on your sleeve."

"I do do that," he said.

"When?" I said.

"I try to do it in a polite way, but I do it," he said. "If I'm in a public place with my family, and someone wants to talk, I explain to them that I can't do it right then."

"That's hardly the same thing as screaming at someone and telling them to get lost," I said.

"I'm too regulated a person to yell 'Get out of my face' at someone, even if that's what I'm feeling," he said. "I can never do it. There may be that little voice telling me to do it, but I keep going on an even level. I don't let that little man get his way and interfere with my future.

"Because if I go crazy for a moment, if I say 'Get the fuck away from me' to someone or I push someone away who's bothering me, it's not going to be good enough for me to explain later that ninety percent of the days I'm feeling fine, but that on ten percent of the days I'm not feeling so fine, and that someone just happened to catch me on one of those ten percent days."

"I suppose you could explain that," I said.

"That's not going to work for me," he said. "I can't afford to have any of those ten percent days. I don't have that luxury. I know I can't have them."

The afternoon had the illusory feel of time spent with a person who had nothing pressing on his schedule. Jordan seemed the opposite of rushed; as we talked and watched television and sometimes merely sat around, he might have been just another guy on the road, having to kill the day in a hotel room before some requisite business appointment at night. Three or four times I tried to give him an out; I asked if he needed to rest up for the game, or whether he wanted to make phone calls in private, or whether he simply wanted to be alone. "No, that's all right," he said. "We're fine. I don't have anything to do." In the end I took it upon myself to leave; I had a feeling that if I hadn't gotten up, we would have been sitting there until it was time for the Bulls' bus to depart for the arena.

I told him how much I'd enjoyed the afternoon; he said days like this—sitting behind the locked door—were pretty much the story of his life lately. The Bulls were going to go back to Chicago for a few games, then embark on a trip to Texas and stops farther west. I asked if he'd be in the mood for having company again at any point in the trip; he said sure, it was just going to be more hotel rooms, and we made tentative plans to meet in Houston.

He was watching the television set as I left the room. For that one second the illusion was intact, the illusion of just some guy on the road. But when I stepped into the fourth-floor corridor I saw a uniformed security officer sitting with his back to the wall several feet from Jordan's doorway, on sentry to keep curiosity-seekers away. In a few hours, more than twenty thousand people would pack the Cavaliers' sold-out-for-months arena to watch Jordan work. I rode the elevator down to the lobby. In the gift shop were multiple copies of a magazine with a cover featuring a hologram. The man in the hologram was smiling joyfully, the grin seemingly uncomplicated, his three-dimensional face eerily alive. If you walked past the magazine rack and the light was right, his eyes appeared to be following you, as if he wanted to ask a question, or perhaps to say something.

23

ONE NIGHT AT THE PRESS TABLE I was sitting next to
Melissa Isaacson. She was taking notes for her story about the
game that would appear in the next morning's *Tribune*. Out on
the court Jordan did a fancy little step back around the foul
line, feinted toward the basket with one knee, then, his defender off balance, took off the other way, shifted the ball
from hand to hand, and laid it into the hoop while nine other
men just stood and stared.

"Sometimes I don't think I describe his shots enough," Melissa said to me.

I knew what she meant. The printed word was not always
sufficient to capture what was so special about Jordan on the
basketball court; the things you could see with your own eyes,
both at the Stadium and on television at home, were often
more eloquent than written accounts of his accomplishments.
It was especially tough in game stories for the daily papers, in
which all the statistics and evaluations of the flow of the forty-
eight-minute contest had to be included. With the space limitations intrinsic to daily newspapers, there wasn't much of a
chance for the beat writers to include long, vivid explanations
of what exactly Jordan did out there.

And of course it was what he did out there, as opposed to
the final score, that made the nights at the Stadium so exceptionally satisfying. When people went to work the day after a
Bulls game, they didn't talk about the score; they talked about
what they had seen Jordan do on specific plays.

That's why, on the long January and February nights,
against opponents whose positions in the NBA standings
didn't matter, I never had the urge to skip a game. There was
no such thing as an important game or an unimportant game

—there were only opportunities to see Jordan do things that perhaps he had not ever done before, inventing them every time he came down the court.

I had somehow never read the famous, much-anthologized John Updike essay on Ted Williams' last baseball game at Fenway Park. When I did get a copy of it during this season, I immediately recognized the wisdom of something that Updike had written about Williams:

> I remember watching one of his home runs from the bleachers of Shibe Park; it went over the first baseman's head and rose meticulously along a straight line and was still rising when it cleared the fence. The trajectory seemed qualitatively different from anything anyone else might hit. For me, Williams is the classic ballplayer of the game on a hot August weekday, before a small crowd, when the only thing at stake is the tissue-thin difference between a thing done well and a thing done ill.

The tissue-thin difference. That's why we were all there. Jordan may have been hearing the applause from the 18,676, but we weren't the ones he was playing for. He played not to please strangers, but to honor the pride within himself. A thing done well and a thing done ill, and that tissue-thin difference in between. If he didn't honor the difference each night, perhaps no one else in the arena would know. But he would.

On a lot of nights at the Stadium, former Chicago professional athletes—Bulls, Bears, Cubs, White Sox—would show up and hang around the floor. It wasn't the same as if, say, a retired New York Yankee or Los Angeles Ram had shown up at the Stadium. The fact that these particular athletes had once played for Chicago teams, and were now here as spectators among the same spectators who had cheered for them, only emphasized the breach between what they used to do, and what they didn't do anymore.

It was perfectly understandable, of course, that they would want to come to the games. They had made their livings on the field of play, and the lure of an arena still had to be overpowering. But I tried to envision Jordan coming back, wandering around the periphery of the court before game

time, shaking hands with players who might patronize him just
the slightest bit and with fans who might inadvertently talk
about him in the past tense . . . I couldn't really picture it.

"I'll be around," Jordan said, which was not the answer I
expected.

"I thought you always said you were going to walk away
from here so fast that it would make people's heads spin," I
said.

"I won't come back immediately after I retire, because right
then I'll just want to get away," he said. "But I'll be back at
the games."

"I don't know," I said. "I see some of these players, and
they walk into the Stadium and sometimes they're recognized
and sometimes they're not, but it makes you wonder if they
really make the right decision when they decide to come here.
Whether they should just let the memories live here."

"It won't matter to me," Jordan said. "I'll come to games
when I feel like it. It won't be anything for me to worry about.
I won't be a player anymore, and maybe there'll be nights
when I feel like watching people play a game. I'll do that. I
won't have any problem doing that at all."

I arrived at the Westin Galleria hotel in Houston the night
before the Bulls were due in town. This was on a Tuesday in
late January; they were over in San Antonio for a game
against the Spurs. When I got to my room and switched on the
television set, one of the local sports anchors was narrating a
piece of videotape that had just come in from San Antonio.

Jordan had apparently had an appointment of some sort
during the day, and a limousine had been sent for him. The
shot on the Houston newscast opened with only the limousine
itself, and not its passenger, visible.

"Who do you suppose is inside the big stretch limo down in
San Antonio this afternoon?" the sportscaster said. "Davy
Crockett? Former mayor Henry Cisneros?"

The door of the car opened and Jordan stepped out and
saw the camera lens.

"Why, it's *Mr. Jordan*," the sportscaster said, his tone of
voice reflecting the new snideness toward Jordan that was
now becoming fashionable. "It must be tough, having to go to
practice on the day of a game."

But if television takes away, it also gives. The San Antonio
game was on a cable channel not available in my hotel room,

so I went to a sports bar in the adjacent Galleria Mall to watch it. I had to ask the waiter to put the Bulls-Spurs game on the screen closest to my table; this was one of those establishments that have satellite hookups capable of picking up dozens of contests in many sports.

At the next table were two women who had not planned on watching the Bulls game; they just happened to be in the restaurant, and they saw that the TV set was tuned to Chicago–San Antonio. I could see them watching all during the first half, getting interested, reacting visibly to Jordan's moves. At halftime one of the women went out into the mall. Her companion waited. She was back at her table by the time the second half was ready to start. She had a package with her. She had found a sporting-goods store in the mall, and she pulled out a Wilson autograph-model Michael Jordan basketball, which she displayed like a prize. He'd made another sale, and he wasn't even in Houston yet.

The Bulls flew over from San Antonio in the morning. They had lost to the Spurs, 109-104, ending a thirteen-game winning streak; Jordan had scored thirty-nine points in the loss (the woman in the sports bar had showed no indication of wanting to return her basketball). Before the Bulls had left San Antonio, I'd talked on the phone with Tim Hallam; he said that when they arrived in Houston they were going straight from the airport to practice at the Summit arena, and would not be checking into the hotel until afterward. He gave me a time that Jordan was expecting to meet me in the lobby.

The bus rolled up right on schedule. Phil Jackson and John Paxson and Bill Cartwright and most of the other players walked into the lobby, as did Chip Schaefer and John Bach and Tex Winter and the rest of the coaching and support staff. But several players, including Jordan, were missing.

"Did he go in a back way?" I asked someone in the traveling party.

"No, no," the person said, shaking his head and smiling sardonically. "Jordan and Pippen and Grant are still on the bus, playing cards. We warn Pippen and Grant every time— *don't play cards with Michael.* He's better than you, and he's just going to take your money. But they never listen. They always think the next time is the time they're going to beat him."

I looked out into the street. The bus was still there, all right, its engine running.

"The thing is, it's a five-minute bus ride from the Summit to the hotel," the person told me. "I mean, how much willpower do Pippen and Grant have to have to refuse to play cards with Michael during a *five-minute ride*? And now he's making the bus driver sit there while he wipes them out."

More minutes passed, and then Pippen and Grant, hangdog expressions on their faces, came trooping slowly into the hotel. A few steps behind them, beaming, was Jordan. I figured out who they reminded me of—three soldiers in the motor pool at Fort Baxter, Kansas. Pippen and Grant were Rupert Ritzik and Dino Paparelli, busted flat once again in a barracks poker game. Jordan, jaunty and counting the cash in his head, was Sgt. Bilko.

I was going to joke with him about it that day, but when we talked later I forgot to bring it up. Events that would occur soon enough in Jordan's life would make the humor suddenly less than sidesplitting, and I never did mention the Bilko connection to him.

For now, though, he came into the lobby, stopped not even for an instant—he had learned that he could never halt in his tracks in a public place if he didn't want to be stuck for fifteen or twenty minutes—and we walked off together. We rode up an escalator leading to a bank of elevators, people's eyes focused on him every foot of the way.

His room was down a long hallway high in the hotel. This did not seem to be a team floor—it was not reserved for the sole use of the Bulls—and as we walked past an open doorway, a woman caught sight of him and screamed as if she had witnessed a crime. It wasn't the kind of studied, rehearsed scream that fans favor the celebrity-of-the-month with; hers was almost a scream of alarm, as if she had suddenly happened upon something she wasn't supposed to. Although I am certain that, in retrospect the next day, she was glad to have encountered him, the shrill and troubling *"MICHAEL JOR-DAN!"* that emerged seemingly without bidding from deep within her had the sound of something out of a nightmare, and other people up and down the corridor flung open their doors as much at the urgency of her wail as at the name she had cried.

Jordan showed no reaction to this. Evidently this was what

walking to a hotel room entailed for him. He unlocked the
door, said "Hot again, I know," and once again we walked
through the bedroom, once again we settled into the living
room.

Like his accommodations in Cleveland, this was a very ordinary set of connecting rooms; Jordan might get a suite while
his teammates got single rooms (he said that he paid for the
upgrades himself), but a Hilton or a Westin is a Hilton or a
Westin; someone else slept here last night and someone else
would be sleeping here tomorrow night, and I could see that
what Jordan experienced behind these doors every away game
day of the NBA season was something he considered to be the
cheerless opposite of glamour.

Once again as soon as the door was shut he seemed to
visibly slow down; as soon as the double-lock was secured, the
scream from the woman down the corridor, and all it represented, were pushed aside for a while.

I looked at the locked door and thought of the morning
paper that many hotels customarily slide into the rooms of
their guests at 6 A.M. or thereabouts. I asked him what it was
like to know that whenever he was traveling and the hotel
staff slid the local newspaper under his door, he was going to
be in it.

He shrugged. "Sometimes I read it, sometimes I don't," he
said.

"Does it strike you as at all odd that you're always going to
be in the morning paper?" I said. "That the fact of your coming to town is big news?"

"If I thought about it enough, I suppose it would," he said.
"But that's something you get used to. I know that someone
will have written something about me, but I'm not compelled
to read it. If I'm in the mood to look at the paper, I might
check out what they've said about me. If I'm not, or if I'm in a
hurry, I let it lay there."

He seemed irritated that the team had lost last night; it was
no way to start a road trip. I asked him what, of all the things
he did on a basketball court, provided him the most pleasure.
I had seen the people in the sports bar last night marveling at
every skill he demonstrated during the game, and I'd wondered what, among those feats, gave him a special jolt of happiness.

"You mean happiness other than accomplishment?" he
said. "Other than professional satisfaction?"

"Happiness like anyone else would define it," I said. "Happiness that makes you feel good."

"A blocked shot, probably," he said.

"When you stop someone else?" I said.

"Yeah," he said. "I love that."

"And that makes you happier than making some spectacular shot yourself?" I said.

"I've been given a lot of credit for a long time for being able to make baskets," he said. "But I'm not really known for my defense. Which is why when I block a shot I feel so good about it. Because that's not what people are necessarily expecting to see from me.

"The shots that I make are shots that I intended to make. There's a difference between that and when I block someone else's shot. I like to see some guy going up to make a basket, and he thinks he's going to make a beautiful play, and he doesn't see me coming. And I swat the ball away and his beautiful play is over. It didn't happen. The big guys, especially, really get pissed off. Oh, it pisses them off. It makes them look bad in front of all those people."

"Is that the reason you enjoy it so much?" I said. "Because it makes them look bad?"

"No, not really," he said. "What I like about blocking a shot is that it's all guessing. Defense itself is all guessing, but especially a blocked shot. And when you block it right on the money, it shows that you guessed right. You guessed exactly what he's going to do with the ball, and you guessed correctly, and his shot doesn't happen. You're thinking so fast, trying to figure out what he's thinking, and you're right."

"I assume that can be fairly humiliating for the other player," I said.

"It's supposed to be," he said. "Sometimes after I block the shot I'll say to the guy, 'Get that shit out of here.' Like, don't try to make that shot while I'm around."

"And that's more fun for you than making some creative dunk," I said.

"Yeah," he said. "Because I don't get much credit for being good at blocking shots, and I think I'm pretty good at it."

" 'Get that shit out of here,' " he'd quoted himself as saying. That was today; in Cleveland he had told me how he never allowed himself to say "Get the fuck away from me." It wasn't a case of Jordan being relentlessly profane in private; he wasn't. What struck me about it was not the fact that he occasionally used off-color language behind closed doors, but rather the control he exhibited by virtually never cursing in public settings. In the season and a half that I'd been seeing him regularly at the Stadium, I couldn't recall him lapsing into obscenities even once when groups of people were around. It was as if he had a built-in governor; he was so disciplined during every public situation that he apparently didn't even need to think about monitoring his language after heated games and angry losses. There was simply a certain way he did not talk in public, even in the locker room when non–team members were present.

Whether that was out of respect for people who might be offended by pungent language, or whether it was just a wise business decision—it's safer not to be publicly obscene when you're endorsing products for companies with some of the most wholesome corporate images in the world—I wasn't sure. But if it was the latter, it was yet another way in which he seemed instinctively sure of himself about business. When he had been endorsing Coke, or so I had been told, he had been in public settings where Pepsi was being served, and although he was thirsty he refused to drink it. He knew that if a photograph were to be taken surreptitiously showing him wetting his throat with a Pepsi—even though that's all that was available—or if someone in the room talked later about him having one, it might show up in some newspaper somewhere. Obviously he could explain it away—he could say he hadn't had anything to drink for hours, and Pepsi was all his hosts had to offer him—but he was that careful; he just didn't do it.

"You know, I think there are some people who love the fact that you're a successful basketball player, but resent the fact that you're a successful businessman," I said.

"Who resents it?" he said.

"Other businessmen," I said. "At least some of them. Some of the people in the expensive seats in the Stadium."

"When I came into the league, I didn't know how to do anything as far as business went," he said. "All I thought about was basketball. Now I know enough that I can make some decisions about business. I'm pretty sure about the decisions I make. But why do you think anyone would resent that?"

"It's probably just human nature," I said. "You have some people in the two-hundred-dollar seats, and the hundred-dollar seats, who can accept the fact that you're a better athlete than they'll ever be, because they know they're not athletes. It's not how they define themselves. They do define themselves as successful businessmen, though, and I just get the impression that it's hard for them to accept that you're better at being a businessman—at being what they define themselves as—than they are."

"What do they say?" Jordan said.

"Oh, I've heard some of them say that your agent must be a good negotiator, but that you probably aren't all that smart at it," I said.

"If when they sit down with their friends they say, 'He's a good basketball player but I'm a better businessman,' they may be right," Jordan said. "I've started to see that attitude a little bit—maybe they're saying, 'I'm tired of seeing Michael Jordan in all these commercials. He's just a basketball player.'

"Who knows? Maybe they're right. For my own situation, maybe I'm a good businessman, but maybe I couldn't do it in any other situation. I just learned it as I went through it."

"You can understand, though, that a wealthy businessman's ego may not be threatened by your basketball success, but it might be threatened by your business-world success," I said.

"Those people probably *are* better businessmen than I am," he said. "I still don't really understand the stock market. I can read the stock tables in the newspaper, but I don't understand why there is a stock market. I was talking to a guy from the Board of Trade, and he was explaining what he did every day, and he might as well be in Las Vegas.

"He told me that in a day he might make a million dollars, or lose a couple of million dollars. I told him, 'What you're doing, basically, is gambling with other people's money.' That's why I still don't understand the stock market—it just seems to be gambling on which way the market will go. I don't know how you do that. I have a lot of confidence in what I do —but if I had to handle someone's stock portfolio, I don't think I could handle it. So maybe those people are right—I'm not as good at business as they are. It's very foreign to me."

The juxtaposition of Jordan the basketball player and Jordan the person was intriguing enough, but there was also the juxtaposition of Jordan right now and Jordan when he first came into the league. It hadn't been all that long; his first year with the Bulls was the season of 1984–85.

Yet in many aspects that first season seemed like ancient

times. I hadn't followed the NBA back then, but since getting to know Jordan I'd looked at copies of several of the videotapes that were marketed about him. One, "Come Fly With Me," based on Jordan's earliest days in the league, showed someone who in a lot of ways would be unrecognizable if he were to be placed next to the man in the Houston hotel room. The Jordan of '84 was a skinny kid, a hotdog, a wiry show-off who would squat theatrically and pump his fists after making a shot. He not only looked different from the man in the room, he behaved like a different man.

"I know," Jordan said. "I've watched the tapes, too, you know."

"What do you see when you see that kid?" I said.

"I see a very young, very motivated, very egotistical person," he said. "I see a person who is trying to create an identity for himself. I see a person who is trying to energize a city, and is teaching himself to do it as he goes along."

"So what changed?" I said.

"Now I think I'm a more reserved person," he said. "I made a decision to calm down and stop all that pumping of the fists and showing off."

"Everybody changes over the years," I said. "But the rest of us don't have videotapes in millions of homes to remind the world of who we used to be. When you see that guy on the videotape, do you feel that it's you, or that it's somebody else?"

"It's me," he said. "It's like when you see baby pictures of yourself. Is it you, or is it something that you can't quite figure out, but that turned into you eventually? I'm still that person who's on the videotapes. But on the other hand, I'm not. He's just someone I used to know. He's him and he's me. He's me off in the distance."

"He even looks like someone else," I said.

"The physical guy is gone," Jordan said. "I weighed 185 then. I weigh 213 now."

He said the words as if he'd undergone a sudden and unexpected late growth spurt or something. In fact, Jordan's carefully planned physical transformation was one of the most dramatic testaments to his ambition. He was already being called the greatest basketball player who ever lived when he made the decision that to have a long and prosperous career in the NBA a man must be muscular in his upper body, to absorb all the blows that come from driving the lane against huge opponents. Thus, working with a weight coach, he totally rebuilt the shape and composition of his chest and arms and shoulders (he left his legs alone). Twenty-eight pounds of muscle that didn't used to be there, because he had a hunch he'd need it. His decision to do that was tantamount to a John D. Rockefeller or an Andrew Carnegie being told he was the richest industrialist in the world—and then ignoring that glowing evaluation and enrolling in a rigorous business school because he feared that his powers, as they stood, might soon be obsolete.

"So when you look at that skinny guy?" I said.

"Before and after," Jordan said. "Before and after pictures. I know him. He's changed a lot, but I know him. Sometimes I wish that I still had some of that stuff that he has. There are days I wish I was still him. He was a very naive person. But he sure had a lot of energy, and he sure knew what he wanted."

When I had met Jordan in the lobby, I had noticed a fellow standing anxiously by the front door, waiting for the bus to unload. After I'd left Jordan's room I went back to the lobby and saw the man still there.

"Have you seen Tim Hallam?" he said to me. The story he told me pointed out once again the utter difference in the lives the NBA stars lived and the lives the rest of us live.

The man was a producer with NBA Entertainment, which is a subdivision of the league office that deals mostly in television productions. Along with a full crew, he had flown here from New York to prepare a special feature on the Bulls for use during the following Sunday's nationally televised game against the Los Angeles Lakers.

The centerpiece of his story was going to be interviews with Pippen and Grant. To make it easy on the players he had rented a suite close to theirs, had hung a backdrop in the suite so that it would look like they were in a TV studio, had set the cameras up well in advance, and had his crew in place and ready to roll tape as soon as the Bulls got to the hotel.

And Pippen and Grant, prompted by Hallam, had, indeed, gone up the elevator and to the room. But there was a slight holdup in the taping schedule, and they had walked out the door, promising they'd be right back.

They never came. "They just disappeared," the producer told me. "To their credit, they did call me. They said, 'Sorry, we just can't get it together.' So our whole day is a wash."

He was looking for Hallam so that he could try to reschedule something the next day. That Pippen and Grant might stiff the press on occasion did not surprise me, but to stiff NBA Entertainment made no sense at all. This was not exactly Mike Wallace showing up with a crew from "60 Minutes" and a legal pad full of indicting questions; NBA Entertainment was devoted to glorifying the league and its players. To stiff the crew from NBA Entertainment was akin to holding a hat over your face while your father takes snapshots at a family picnic.

Yet perhaps the two players' blowing off the camera crew said more about the curious subuniverse they lived in than it did about their manners. Grant, especially, was as kindly a person as you'd ever want to meet; I'm sure if he were told that he was being impolite to someone, he would go out of his way to try to make it right. But to Scottie Pippen and Horace Grant, what they had just done was not impolite; a television crew flying in from out of town to interview them meant something totally different than it would mean to you or me.

For most of us, the thought of a producer from New York lining up a crew and jetting down to Houston to do a laudatory interview with us would be flattering and maybe even thrilling: Our own thoughts about our jobs, presented in the best possible light on network television. Unlike us, though, these basketball players *existed* on television. When they arrived at the arena each night, they knew for a fact that dozens upon dozens of television technicians had been there for hours, firing up the equipment and testing the camera angles and checking the satellite uplinks, all so that the players' next shift at work would be beamed into homes across the city and across the nation. Television? Television to them was like the office watercooler was to everyone else: It was there. Big deal.

Thus I was sure it never crossed Pippen's or Grant's mind that this guy had made the trip from New York, and had readied his crew, and had set the shot up just right, all in an effort to make the two players look good—and that he might be personally upset that they had decided not to walk across the hall and do the interview. Fly into town and set up cameras? That's what people did for them every night. Their job was to play basketball, and other people's jobs were to televise them while they did it.

"I knew as soon as they left the room that I had a problem," the producer said.

* * *

I told the producer I hadn't seen Hallam lately, and I went for a walk through the mall. I passed a Foot Locker sporting-goods store. In the window was a big cardboard cutout featuring Jordan and Bugs Bunny.

It was part of a new Nike advertising campaign that had premiered on the telecast of the Super Bowl. "Air Jordan vs. Hare Jordan," or something like that. Now, thinking about the man I had just left in his room, I had to smile as I looked at the giant cutout with his likeness on it and thought about the weirdness of our world.

Two of the salesmen, wearing striped referee-type shirts, apparently saw me standing there staring, because they came out of the store and made me an offer in tones purposely soft enough that their store manager couldn't overhear.

One of them pointed to the cutout and said to me:

"Five dollars to have your picture taken with Bugs and Mike."

In the mall early that evening I saw Bill Cartwright, looking at a display of Western-style jewelry; Craig Hodges, just taking a stroll and window-shopping; Cliff Levingston, stretching his legs by walking the length of the giant retail center and back. There was an enclosed ice-skating rink on the bottom level of the mall; Hodges tarried for a moment or two to watch the skaters.

Being out among the shoppers didn't seem to present any hindrance to any of them. It's not that people didn't notice them; Cartwright, at seven foot one, was going to be conspicuous wherever he went, but he was free to pass his time undisturbed in the Galleria. I lost my bearings and asked him how to get back to the hotel; he pointed me in the right direction, and although clearly the people around us knew he was a basketball player—and maybe knew that he was Bill Cartwright of the Chicago Bulls—that didn't get in the way of his privacy. He had no more trouble walking around the mall than did anyone in the Houston after-work crowd that passed by him.

Bugs Bunny's partner, on the other hand, knowing that he would not be granted the same leeway, remained upstairs and out of public view.

* * *

The Bulls lost the game to the Houston Rockets the next night, 105-102, and afterward a group of writers waited outside the locker room at the Summit arena, biding their time until Phil Jackson allowed them in. Several among them were talking about Jordan to each other.

Their topics of discussion were the usual ones that had been addressed all season, with a couple of additions. The story about the check from Jordan showing up in the convicted felon's bank account was gaining momentum, and rumors were growing that Jordan had a little stronger taste for gambling on games of golf and cards than people had been aware of. In addition, the news had just broken that Jordan was taking over the rights to the marketing of his own name and likeness on items of clothing; the NBA had always sold T-shirts and paraphernalia featuring pictures of its players, but now Jordan was telling the league that he was going to be the one who controlled and profited from the sales of any Jordan garments.

So a group of the sportswriters were talking about the fifty-seven-thousand-dollar check, and what it might lead to; about what the NBA's legal response was likely to be to Jordan's notifying the league that it could not sell Jordan clothing; about the various other controversies surrounding him. For some reason, as I stood with them and waited for the locker room to open, I thought of a quote attributed to the late Earl Warren, chief justice of the United States Supreme Court. Warren was asked about his reading habits, and said: "I always turn to the sports pages first. The sports pages record people's accomplishments, the front page nothing but man's failures."

There had been occasions when I'd been tempted to try that quote out on my press-row colleagues, just to solicit their reaction, but I never did because I figured some of them might be insulted by it. The sports pages of Earl Warren's day no longer existed, and what he'd said about why he took such pleasure in reading about sports might be deemed by today's sportswriters as a demeaning comment on the seriousness of their craft. You don't have to be all that voracious a newspaper reader to realize that man's failures long ago expanded off the front page, and have found themselves a secure and spacious home in the sports section, too.

That isn't likely to change; once a barrier falls, it's generally down for good. Sports is big business, sports is law, sports, in a way, is politics, and anyone who expects it to be covered just as games is going to be disappointed. Were Earl Warren to pick up the daily sports section of his favorite paper today—with the coverage of contract arbitrations, and drug arrests, and stadium bond issues, and threats by agents—he might throw it to the floor in dismay.

Tonight a writer made a joke about Jordan and gambling, and the fellow he was talking to estimated how many millions of dollars the league would lose if it failed to challenge Jordan's assertion that he owned the right to his own name and likeness, and all the while they waited for the door to open so that they could go inside and ask the players and coaches about the basketball game they'd just seen.

The door did open, but just a few inches. There had been this boy hanging around the hallway—he was the ten-year-old son of a former basketball player who had overcome a narcotics addiction and who now ran a substance-abuse rehabilitation center devoted to helping athletes in trouble. The man had brought his boy to the arena—and a hand reached out the doorway to give something to him. In the hand that reached out from the locker room was the pair of shoes Jordan had worn in the game just ended. Someone had gotten word to Jordan about the boy; Jordan was going to stop to say hello to him on the way to the bus, but he'd decided to send his shoes out first, as a gift.

I took in the parallel scenes: The group of writers in the hallway debating which of Jordan's recent mistakes was the most damning, the father kneeling down and presenting the shoes to the boy and explaining where they'd come from. I wasn't quite sure what this little twin tableau proved; maybe only that the world around us is an endlessly variegated place, and that there's never a single way to look at it.

The Bulls would be going straight from the arena to the Houston airport for a late-night flight to Dallas, where they would play the Mavericks tomorrow. Before I left the Summit I asked Jordan what he planned to do on the short flight. Did he ever pick up a paperback novel at a hotel newsstand or at an airport, just to give him something to pass the time?

"I don't read novels, really," he said.

Never? He never saw the cover of a paperback book, thought the story might look inviting, and grabbed it to take along with him in the hopes of making the trip more interesting?

"I don't read fiction at all," he said. "Fiction doesn't appeal to me."

But fiction is great escape—fiction is a wonderful way to take you out of your own surroundings and put you in another place for a few hours.

"I'm not a person who wants a lot of escape," he said. "I have to give all my attention to the things that are really happening."

The thing I remember most about going home from the Ohio State basketball games during the Lucas-Havlicek-Siegfried years is how alone I felt. For a couple of hours I had been in the middle of all those thousands of screaming, happy people, I had sat next to Jimmy Crum and heard him shouting the description of the game into a microphone that would carry his voice into tens of thousands of houses all over central Ohio, I had watched those incredibly talented basketball players performing on the polished floor down below.

And then it was over, and I would walk out of St. John Arena, and I would just feel so alone all of a sudden. I had been a part of something big and all-enveloping and welcoming, and now that something had come apart and I was just one person, a twelve-year-old person at that, and the illusion was gone for the night. Whatever sense of communal happiness the basketball game had represented was fleeting, the community had disbanded the moment the final buzzer sounded, and fifteen minutes after the Ohio State Buckeyes had departed the floor the arena lights were already dim and the seats were empty and Jimmy Crum was packing his briefcase. I'd say goodnight and walk out of the arena toward home.

Tonight in Houston the Bulls' team bus was parked in a basement level of the arena. It would be pulling up a long cement incline toward the street that would take it to the airport. The whole team wasn't on board yet—Jordan was still answering reporters' questions in the locker room—so the bus idled until it would be time to pull away.

The night was chilly; even in Houston, January is January. Red Kerr and fellow broadcaster Tom Boerwinkle stood on the surface of the ramp, a few feet from the open front door of the bus, talking quietly with each other and waiting until the last minute before getting on the stuffy coach for the ride to the airport.

I started to walk up the ramp.

"You going to Dallas?" Kerr asked me.

"No, I'm going home in the morning," I said. "I'll see you back at the Stadium."

I continued up the ramp, looking toward the street for signs of an empty cab to take me to my hotel. Everything's supposed to change once you get older, so why did I know this feeling so well?

24

"LET ME GIVE YOU A LITTLE TIP," Jerry Reinsdorf said.

I waited.

"The raisin bread," he said.

I did not immediately understand.

"Go with the raisin bread," he said.

He gestured to the basket on the table in front of us. "The best raisin bread in the world," he said.

We were having dinner in the Governors Room at the Stadium. I had arrived early and had been sitting on press row, making some notes; Steve Schanwald, passing by, had asked me if I'd like to join him in the private dining room. Inside its doors, just a few feet through the tunnel and across the hallway from the south sideline of the court, investors and corporate sponsors of the Bulls dined.

Schanwald and I had been talking at the table when Reinsdorf had sat down. He'd asked whether we minded, which was a pretty silly question; he owned the Bulls.

He owned the White Sox, too. He had partners in each of the athletic enterprises, but Reinsdorf was the main guy. He did not have the look of a tycoon or a business baron—his physical appearance was a cross between Peter Sellers and John Chancellor with a sour stomach, and he often came to the Stadium in plaid shirts and dress pants. A friend of mine had once seen him stopped by an usher as he tried to get onto the main floor. "The usher is telling Reinsdorf that if he doesn't have a ticket, he can't come through the gate," my friend said. "And Reinsdorf is trying to convince the usher who he is. Finally Reinsdorf pulls out his wallet and shows the usher his driver's license, and the usher lets him in."

We ate our raisin bread. Reinsdorf told stories and offered opinions about John F. Kennedy and Jack Ruby, about NBA commissioner David Stern and the owners of other NBA teams, about cable television versus over-the-air broadcasts. It was just table talk.

But I couldn't help thinking, as we sat there, how everyone marvels and shakes their heads over the huge salaries that professional athletes are paid. This basketball player makes four million dollars a year, that baseball player makes seven million. No one marvels over a fellow like Reinsdorf, who writes the checks. Every wealthy player on the White Sox, every wealthy player on the Bulls, and this guy pays them all every week. In a way, that's as amazing a concept as the idea that the average NBA player makes more than a million dollars a year. Whatever there is that separates an NBA player who can soar into the air and cram the ball through the hoop from the rest of us, there's also something that separates a guy like Reinsdorf from the rest of us. We know that we will never be able to win a basketball game at the buzzer in overtime in front of eighteen thousand screaming fans—or to sign Michael Jordan's paycheck without blinking.

You can't see the burning ego and raw ambition in a man like Reinsdorf as easily as you can see it in a man like Jordan or Pippen. It isn't as visible to the eye. But somewhere beneath that plaid long-sleeved shirt it has to be there, as unmistakable as a numeral emblazoned upon a jersey. "Am I right about the raisin bread or what?" Reinsdorf said.

Reinsdorf's wife, Martyl, a jewelry artist by training, had designed the Bulls' ornate world championship rings.

I had never seen Jordan wearing his ring. Not once.

All those years of talking about how much a championship ring would mean to him, how it represented the loftiest goal he had ever set for himself—and his fingers were bare. I asked him about it; was I just happening to see him during those times when he decided not to wear it?

"No, I've never worn it," he said.

"Any particular reason?" I said.

"I know it's ironic," he said. "Something I worked so hard for, and wanted so badly. But it's just something I don't want to wear."

"Are you less proud of it than you thought you'd be?" I said.

"I am so proud of it," he said. "The pride I have in it is why I don't want to wear it. My not wearing it has nothing to do with being afraid of losing it. And although I plan on giving it to my children, my not wearing it has nothing to do with wanting to keep it in perfect condition for them. The reason I don't wear it is because I want to win another one."

"And wearing this one would get in the way of that?" I said.

"Keep it away from me," he said. "I don't want to see it. If you see a championship ring on your hand, you have a championship. If you have a championship, you don't have the same hunger for happiness. The ring tells you that you have the happiness already. If I can't see it, I don't have it. If I have a championship ring on my hand while I'm playing a basketball season, what reason would I have to want to win one?"

"Would wearing it give you any pleasure at all?" I said.

"If I want it, I can go see it," he said. "I have it in a safety box. It's not like I threw it away."

The championship had brought lucrative endorsement opportunities to many members of the team. Jordan, of course, already had plenty of commercials; he was the most sought-after commercial spokesman in the world. Scottie Pippen got a Nike commercial and a Coca-Cola commercial (the spot had opened up after Jordan's switch to Gatorade). John Paxson was doing a toothpaste commercial, and Horace Grant appeared on billboards advertising designer eye wear. B. J. Armstrong was on the sides of buses promoting a shoe store.

The Bulls as a merchandising entity were huge. There was a worldwide fascination with any piece of paraphernalia associated with the team. The National Basketball Association was doing $1.2 billion a year in the sales of NBA merchandise; of that, an astonishing 40 percent—or $480 million—was said to be in Bulls items.

To me, though, the biggest measure of the Bulls phenomenon was not the number of endorsements that Jordan had, or the hundreds of millions of dollars in Bulls T-shirts and caps that were being sold. The most symbolic piece of news about the scope of the Bulls as a business was that Ray Clay now had his own commercial.

Now, there have been television and radio broadcasters who have been given contracts to do commercials. But a public address announcer?

"I can hardly believe it myself," Clay said. "A couple of

years ago I was a guy who watched the Bulls on TV and listened to them on the radio. And now I've got this commercial."

The endorsement was for a fried-chicken company; in the TV commercial he utilized the same shrieking voice he used for the spotlight introductions at the Stadium. Clay was not seen in the commercial; the voice was the gimmick. "The interest starts with Michael Jordan and eventually, I guess, it worked its way to me," he said.

"Is this paying off in other ways?" I said.

"Several corporations have hired me to introduce their executives at meetings," he said. "They want me to introduce their vice presidents or their boards of directors in the same style in which I introduce the Bulls. At one place they turned the lights off in a conference room, and some ladies waved flashlights around to make it look like the spotlight introduction.

"I've done a couple of weddings. The receptions, actually— when the newlyweds come in the lights go down and I yell, 'And *now,* the *bride* and *groom* . . .' I did a bar mitzvah. The lights went down and I introduced the boy's parents and then his little brother came in and I yelled, 'At *four* foot *three* . . .'"

One night in the locker room before a game several of the players were discussing their superstitions. Clothing was mentioned, and meals, and routes to the Stadium.

Pippen, out of nowhere, said, "I don't stand under the scoreboard when someone's shooting a free throw."

There was a momentary silence in the room as people waited for him to continue.

"It might fall on my head," he said.

He was referring to the big four-sided scoreboard that was suspended above the floor.

"You think the scoreboard is going to fall on your head?" someone asked.

"It could happen," he said.

As the season proceeded and the Bulls continued to lead the NBA in victories, Jordan was still rarely seen at moments like those. An hour or so before one game I was walking down a back hallway of the Stadium basement, and I ran into him. He was dressed in his white game uniform, and he was accompanied by three off-duty Chicago police officers wearing yellow Stadium security slickers.

He and they were heading in one direction in the basement, and I was going in the other. He stopped to talk; he said the Bulls' publicity office had asked him to pose for a magazine photo, and he'd agreed to get the task out of the way before the game tonight. A backdrop had been set up, and the photographer had sent for him when all the lights were ready, and he'd gotten it done.

As we stood there having the brief conversation, this odd feeling came over me. Jordan out of context—Jordan standing here in the basement corridor in the white shorts and sleeveless jersey—seemed like a cartoon character. Not in a funny way, not in a frivolous way; this figure in white and red, the figure from so many telecasts and posters and Wheaties boxes, just seemed somehow removed from the man Jordan was. He put a hand on one hip and he wasn't smiling, and as we talked it was almost as if this was Jordan the confection, this was the thing that was for sale. It was as if the person was wearing his Michael Jordan costume.

We agreed to meet in Minnesota. It was the first week of March; he said that he didn't have anything planned for the afternoon before a game against the Timberwolves. If I wanted to come to Minneapolis and spend the time with him, that would be okay.

My best friend—his name is Jack Roth, and we have been best friends since we were five years old—had moved away from our hometown and lived in Minneapolis now, and when I called him to tell him I was coming he said without my asking that he'd pick me up at the airport. I told him that it would probably be a late-night flight; he said that was fine with him.

So as the plane pulled up to the gate at the Minneapolis airport—it had been delayed, and we were getting in even later than I'd anticipated—I knew that Jack would be waiting inside. And he was; the airport was close to empty so late at night, and his face was the first one I saw as I stepped into the main building.

"I'm sorry for the holdup," I said. "I could have taken a cab downtown."

"That's all right," he said. "You don't need to take a cab." We walked to his car. I had told him why I was in Minnesota;

on the way to the hotel I tried to explain to him what the last two years had been like. As we talked, I found myself reviewing for him the events that had led up to my starting to go to the Stadium.

Some of them had changed and evolved during the time that had passed. Cornelius Abraham, for example, whose courage in surviving the torture that had killed his little brother, Lattie McGee—he was doing better now. Jim Bigoness, the assistant state's attorney who had prosecuted the case and had gone to the game with Cornelius and me, checked up on him regularly and said that somehow he was beginning to thrive. After I'd written about Cornelius, people had sent money to me in care of the newspaper, asking that it go for his future well-being; Bigoness and I had put the money in a trust fund for the boy, and there was enough waiting for him in the account to pay for his college education once he became old enough.

The story of the foster child about whom I'd written during so much of the time I was going to the Stadium was more involuted, but also hopeful. She had started regular visits with the man and woman who had brought her up, the foster parents from whom she'd been taken; two prominent children's psychiatrists were in charge of trying to help her heal and to make the visits work, and although the situation was confusing and difficult for her, the therapists reported that they thought her life showed promise of being made close to whole again. She was still living with the woman who had given birth to her and with the woman's boyfriend; the Juvenile Court judge who had presided over the second set of hearings, while expressing horror and revulsion at what had been done to her in the name of justice, felt that to abruptly remove her from the second house at this point would only throw her into deeper turmoil. The judge promised that he would do everything in his power to make sure that she would go through the rest of her childhood receiving the love he said she so clearly deserved. Implicit in his ruling was that the child had been so grievously damaged by what she had been put through that no decision from the bench could ever come close to fully undoing the destruction.

I told Jack about all of this, and we got lost on the one-way streets of downtown, and when we finally pulled up to the hotel he left the car in front and accompanied me to the registration desk. I got my key and my room list, and we went to the hotel's coffee shop, which was just about to close.

We ordered some soup and sandwiches, and we talked about old things and new. We were the only customers in the restaurant. The Bulls had arrived earlier in the evening; John Ligmanowski, the equipment manager, was walking through the lobby, and he waved and then came over to sit with us. Will Perdue got off an elevator with Mark Randall; Randall was a rookie who had been signed by the Bulls at the beginning of the season, had made it onto the roster for a few games, and then, in a move that was said to have devastated him, was dropped from the team. It was the first time in his life as a basketball player that anyone had told him he was not good enough.

He had caught on with the Timberwolves, though, and had made their roster, and now he was an NBA player after all. His team would be playing the Bulls tomorrow night. Perdue had gotten in touch with him and gone out to dinner with him, which I thought was a very nice gesture. Now they were back at the hotel. They came over, and I introduced them to Jack, and they joined us for a little bit.

The hostess in the restaurant came up and said, "Michael Jordan touched me."

It was a statement to which there was no proper response. I said to her, "Was this something that happened recently?"

"Tonight," she said. "The team got to the hotel, and the motor entrance is on the street, and the plan was to take them on the elevator to six and bypass the lobby so people wouldn't bother them. But they got off on the lobby floor by mistake, and there was Michael, just looking around like he was lost. So I said to him, 'You just follow me,' and I held out my arm to lead him to the right place and he touched my arm. No one believes me, but it happened."

In the morning I met Jordan at the customary moment, during those six or seven seconds when he was moving from the bus through the hotel lobby and onto the elevator. He was on a floor to which no other Bulls were assigned; when he told me the room the hotel had put him in—2323—I said, "Do you figure they did that on purpose?"

"I don't know," he said. "They could have."

"Do hotels put you in rooms with 23 in the number all the time?" I said.

"No one has ever put me in a 2323 before, at least not that I can remember," he said.

It was probably nothing more than this hotel manager's version of a bowl of fruit or a vase with fresh flowers in it: a signal of welcome to the esteemed guest. He unlocked the door, and as we walked in I said, "You don't have to say it. I know. It's hot."

"Actually, I may have left it too hot," he said.

Television set on, curtains drawn, room service breakfast tray still on the table with the dregs of a meal for one. The scene in the room would be familiar to any business traveler who's ever been alone on the road: The bed was queen-size, but the blanket, top sheet, and cover had been pulled back only on one side, the side where he'd slept last night; the other half of the bed was fully made, untouched and unused. The message light on his telephone was blinking. He picked up the receiver, dialed "0," told the operator he was Michael Jordan, the guest in room 2323, listened for about thirty seconds as she read him his messages, wrote none of them down, asked her not to ring any calls through unless they were from his family in Chicago, then joined me across the room.

Since I'd seen him last, a number of things had happened to put him in the headlines, although that's probably an imprecise phrase, because he was in headlines every day anyway. But on the basketball court he'd had a rare angry confrontation with a referee that had resulted in his being ejected from a game. It had taken place in Salt Lake City, near the end of a terrific triple-overtime contest against the Utah Jazz. As the clock was running down, Utah's Jeff Malone drove for the basket and a foul was called on Jordan. Jordan exploded at referee Tommie Wood—he knew that Malone's ensuing foul shot would win the game—and when Wood walked away from him, Jordan followed, arguing heatedly with Wood and, according to Wood, bumping into him. A technical foul was called on Jordan, he was thrown out and sent to the locker room, the Jazz did indeed win, and the league office in New York fined him and suspended him for the next game, which was against the Phoenix Suns in Phoenix.

Jordan had made very little comment to the press about the incident. He had seemed not only angry but almost mortified about being banished from the court; after the game, when reporters in Utah went into the locker room, they found Tim

Hallam sitting next to Jordan, who would not speak. "You don't want to hear what he's got to say," Hallam said.

The Phoenix game was going to be the last one before the All-Star break; Jordan was not permitted into the arena in Phoenix because of the suspension, and rather than watch the game in his hotel room he flew down to Orlando, the site of the All-Star weekend, early. In his absence his teammates lost to Phoenix; it was the Bulls' sole visit to the Suns' arena during the season, and fans held up signs protesting what the NBA had done to them by denying them their one chance of the year to see Jordan play.

"The flight down to Orlando must have been an unusual feeling," I said. "Your team's in Arizona getting ready to play a game, and you're traveling somewhere else by yourself."

"I found it very peculiar," he said. "On the day of a game I was flying away from work. My second year in the league I hurt my foot and I was out for most of the season and I was away from the team then, so I had a memory of what it was like for the team to be playing and me not to be there. But this time was different because I was healthy.

"What happened was, I got up in the morning in Phoenix and I called all my teammates and I told them I was leaving and wished them luck in the game. Then I called the pilot and told him, get it ready, let's go. I was going to fly a charter down to Orlando anyway, because of the All-Star Game. So the pilot was already in Phoenix.

"It was a little jet, a Falcon 20. You know what? It was very peaceful, to be alone and away from the team on the plane. It was a little bit of freedom. No one bothered me. When I got on the plane I told the crew that I didn't want to talk about basketball. I just wanted to forget basketball. So no one brought up what had happened, and the word 'basketball' wasn't mentioned the whole flight.

"It was a nice flight. I watched a movie, read a magazine a little bit, looked out the window a lot. I was just looking down at the country. I was looking for golf courses along the way. I knew that I'd have a chance to play golf once I got to Orlando, so I wanted to see courses along the way to remind me of what was waiting for me on the other end."

"Did the courses you saw look good?" I said.

"I didn't see any," he said. "We were too high. But I tried. I found the flight very relaxing. Everything else seemed like a long way away. I knew that the team was on their way to the arena in Phoenix for the morning shootaround, and I was on my way to Florida. The plane stopped in New Orleans for gas. The team was at practice and I was fueling up in Louisiana."

"What was it like for you to watch the game that night?" I said.

"I didn't watch," he said. "It wasn't being carried on any TV station I could get in Orlando. There was a North Carolina game on TV that night, and I watched that, and every once in a while they would flash other scores from around the country on the screen. I saw that we were losing in Phoenix, but all I got was the score."

"What did you think?" I said.

"It was a mixture of feelings," he said. "When I talked to my teammates before I left Phoenix, I told them they were on their own, and that was true. I wanted the team to win, but there was also a voice inside of me asking: 'Are you as valuable as you used to be?' Because if the team went out and won in spite of me not being there, maybe I wouldn't know the answer to that. So before the game started, I was thinking, Are we going to win? Get killed? If the team wins will people be saying that I'm not so vital to this team after all?

"And then when the score of the game was flashed on the screen during the North Carolina game—we were down by seventeen or something like that—I thought, 'Oh, shit, they're going down the tank.' I thought that people would be writing that the Bulls are still a one-man show. And I'll tell you, my reaction was a little divided. You want your team to win the game, but you also want to believe that you're very important to them. So I suppose I could tell you that I was terribly upset that they lost a game because I was suspended, but the truth is, I was pretty torn in my reaction. Because if they'd won, people would have been saying that they didn't need me as much as they used to."

"How upset were you about the suspension itself?" I said.

"Oh, it's like when you're a kid and you get a spanking," he said. "You're so mad that you say you're not going to speak to anyone anymore. And then it fades away. The plane ride to Orlando was a nice little break. Nothing to think about, nothing to worry about, no one to bother me. Looking out the window, looking at the movie that was playing on the VCR. I think it was *Die Hard 2*."

* * *

The phone rang. The hotel operator was telling Jordan that some people he knew in Minneapolis were insisting that they were supposed to have lunch with him, and that they absolutely had to get through or he'd be left hanging about where he was scheduled to meet them. Jordan told her to go ahead and put them on the line. He had, indeed, indicated to them that he'd eat with them.

I could only hear Jordan's end of the conversation, but it was apparent what was going on. "You did?" he said. "It's probably better if you all just come up here and we order room service." A pause. "You probably should cancel the reservation." Pause. "I know, I'm sure it's a great place. It will probably just be easier on all of us if you come here." Pause. "There will be four of you, right? That's okay, the room's big enough. Tell the place I appreciate it a lot, but you really should cancel the reservation."

It wasn't hard to surmise what had happened. The people he knew in Minneapolis had told the restaurant that Michael Jordan was coming to lunch. The restaurant staff had gotten excited about it. Jordan, knowing what would happen if he walked into a public place in the middle of the day, called it off. The people in Minneapolis were going to feel bad to have to phone the restaurant and say that Jordan wouldn't be coming after all; the restaurant owners were going to feel let down that they weren't going to get to meet Jordan; and Jordan was going to eat yet another meal in his room. He knew that every person who had the whit of a chance to come in contact with him—fans, police officers, restaurant owners—would do everything they could to make sure that chance came true. It was understandable, but something he had to keep in check. My favorite line of the year was something Tim Hallam had said when the Bulls were in Washington playing the Bullets, and the crown princess of Saudi Arabia had showed up and asked to be taken to meet Jordan in the locker room. Her request was turned down. When reporters asked Hallam why Jordan hadn't agreed to meet the crown princess, Hallam said: "There's a crown princess in every city he goes to."

Jordan put the phone down and came back across the room. It wasn't a suite today. "Doesn't matter," he said. "We got in late last night and we'll leave town right after the game tonight." We resumed the conversation, and I brought up a recent pay-per-view event that featured two former great

NBA players, Kareem Abdul-Jabbar and Julius Erving, competing in one-on-one basketball at an Atlantic City casino.

"What a joke," Jordan said.

"You didn't watch it?" I said.

"I didn't watch it when it happened, I didn't tape it, I didn't watch anyone else's tape of it," he said. "I never saw any reason that I should watch it."

"So it's not the kind of thing you can ever imagine doing?" I said.

"Doing?" he said. "I can't even imagine watching it. I really admired Julius Erving for staying away from the game. He moved on with his life. And then I heard about this thing and I thought, why? Why is he doing this?"

"Obviously he has his reasons," I said. "Both of them must. It wasn't really hurting anyone that they did it."

"Once I step away from the game, that's the last people are going to see me on a basketball court," he said. "Going to watch a game is one thing. But playing one-on-one on pay-per-view? What would people think of me? 'He must need the money'? 'He must miss the cheers'? I don't ever want people seeing me doing what I used to do, and knowing that now I can't do it anymore."

"I'd have thought you might watch Erving and Abdul-Jabbar just out of curiosity," I said.

"I would pay $19.95 to watch that?" he said. "We were on the road the night they played it, so I didn't have a way to get it on pay-per-view anyway. But I called home and my wife said she was thinking about watching it. I told her, 'Don't watch. Before you even entertain the idea of watching this, don't do it. It's not a game. It's stupid. It's embarrassing. Don't watch it.' "

"Did she watch?" I said.

"She told me she didn't," he said. "I try to think what I would feel like if an offer ever came up to do that. I see it as off in the distance now, but I try to imagine. And I cannot imagine when I'm forty doing that and letting people watch me do it."

He asked me about my trip up to Minneapolis, and when I told him about Jack picking me up at the airport I could see his attention perk. With Jordan it was always fairly easy to tell when he was just passing the time, as opposed to when a subject interested him.

"So your friend was there right on time?" he said.

"I knew he would be," I said.

"He's been your friend for a long time?" he said.

"Longer than anyone else in the world has been my friend," I said.

He sat there.

When he didn't say anything I said to him, "I imagine in your situation, there must be times when you figure that it would be difficult to make any new friends."

"It's so tough to make new friends for me now," he said. "You always think to yourself, 'Would these guys want to be around you if you weren't playing basketball and if they didn't know anything about you?' The frustration of trying to find a genuine friend in a situation like mine . . . There are a lot of times when I think that it won't really be possible to make any new friends until this part of my life is completely over."

Virtually all of the friends I'd seen around Jordan were old friends, predating his professional basketball career. He'd made them all in the days before he'd come to Chicago to be a Bull. George Koehler, who seemed to be Jordan's most recent good friend, was a man who was running a one-person limousine service on the day Jordan arrived at O'Hare by himself from North Carolina to report to the Bulls. Koehler had volunteered to drive Jordan into the city, and the two remained very close. His other friends were all men he'd known in North Carolina—three of them were fellows named Adolph Shiver, Fred Whitfield, and Rodney Everhart. None of them were celebrities or athletes, none of them lived in Chicago; he saw them when he could.

"Your friend who picked you up last night," he said. "This guy Jack. You didn't call him up and ask him to meet your plane at the airport?"

"I told him I was coming in," I said. "I didn't have to ask him."

Jordan shook his head.

"What's wrong?" I said.

"Nothing," he said. "It's just nice."

"What about you?" I said. "If you were flying into a city late at night, and you didn't have a way to get downtown, and your teammates on the Bulls knew about it, how many of them do you think would show up at the airport to get you?"

"None," he said.

"You really don't think so?" I said.

"My friends I grew up with all would," he said. "But it just wouldn't occur to my teammates on the Bulls. Oh, Cliff might, if I asked him. And John Paxson definitely would. John's personality, you know, he wouldn't come up to me and tell me that he was willing to do it. But I know he would come to the airport if I asked him to."

"As you get older, I think you start to realize how rare real friendship is," I said. "You start to value the friends you can trust not to let certain things go any further than between the two of you."

"There aren't many of those," he said.

"There's this phrase," I said. "I don't know if you've heard it. 'D.T.A.'"

"What's that mean?" he said.

"'Don't trust anybody,'" I said.

"I know that feeling," he said, laughing briefly and without mirth. "Where you tell yourself that you should never let anyone know what you really feel."

"So how would you define what the connection is between you and the eleven men you play with?" I said.

"They're not my friends," he said. "They're my teammates."

"Isn't it possible to be both?" I said.

"You have to understand about players in the NBA," he said. "It's a constantly competitive situation. Even when you're not talking about it to each other, it's competitive. To exist on this level, you've got to have been some sort a star at some point in your life. All of the players on every team were the biggest star on their team when they were in college. They were the guy. And when I look around the locker room every night, I'm aware that every one of those eleven is aware that he's not the guy anymore. And while we all may accept that professionally, it's hard to accept personally. It's not something that's conducive to friendship."

"Even so, you have to be very, very close with them," I said.

"We've done a lot of terrific things together," he said. "We've spent a lot of hours together. But we are teammates. We are not friends. What is a friend? Someone you can confide in when something is really troubling you? And know that it won't go a step further? Not these guys. This is a little gossip factory. A little whispering gossip factory. If I were to entrust something to someone on the team? What do you think would happen the next time they got mad at me because

I didn't pass them the ball on a break? They'd turn on me right away. They'd be saying to each other, 'Do you know what Mike told me?' "

"If you woke up at three o'clock in the morning on some road trip, in some hotel," I said, "and you had one of those three-o'clock-in-the-morning terrors—if you had something like that on your mind, would you ever consider picking up the phone and waking one of your teammates and telling him about it?"

"There's not one of the eleven I'd call," he said.

"So you'd never call Scottie Pippen or one of the others and tell him there was something you needed to talk to someone about?" I said.

"Are you kidding?" he said. "I'd rather lie awake and stare at the ceiling the rest of the night."

"What about your friends from North Carolina?" I said.

"That's easy," he said. "Yes. I have called them at three A.M. More than once. It's just different with them."

"Do you think you'll consider this differently twenty years from now?" I said. "Maybe twenty years from now the guys you're playing with on this team will seem, in retrospect, like very good friends. Maybe even the best friends you've ever had."

"No," he said. "Twenty years from now I'll look back on this, and I'll think of them as my teammates. We have a very good basketball team. We have accomplished a lot. That's what it will always be with them and me. We were teammates."

When he would talk like that, sometimes I would stop to think about what his words would look like in sensation-splashed headlines: JORDAN: I HAVE NO FRIENDS ON TEAM. That hadn't been the spirit of what we were talking about at all, of course. What Jordan had been trying to express was something infinitely more complicated than could be summed up in two-inch-high banner type. He, like the rest of us, understood the subtle and sometimes melancholy differences between the relationships we form as adults working side-by-side daily with other adults, and the relationships we form when we are younger, spending our days and nights with people not because we have been hired by the same company, but because we are drawn to them and we choose to be with them and we come to love them.

The difference is a delicate one, and not something that can necessarily be summed up in a phrase or two. Yet when Jordan woke up each morning he knew that every public word he uttered had the potential to be tossed back at him, that before a sentence had even left his mouth he'd better be prepared to justify it and defend it before millions. In the particular world he lived in, thoughtfulness and reflection were qualities to be indulged in at his own peril, and conversations like the one we were having about his friendships only made me understand that more acutely.

Several weeks before, in a game at the Stadium against Cleveland, a situation had occurred that plainly pained Jordan. But after the game was over the quotes that he gave to reporters revealed very little of what I assumed he was thinking. It clearly was a case in which he knew that to speak what was on his mind would be more trouble than it was worth.

The game was played on Jordan's twenty-ninth birthday. His shooting was brilliant, and the game was thrilling. There were twenty-three lead changes and ten ties during the forty-eight minutes, and every time the Bulls were in trouble Jordan came back with a spectacular shot. Going into the last minute of the game he had forty-six points and seemed exhilarated about what he was doing.

With thirty-four seconds left and the Bulls trailing by three, Jordan had hit a fadeaway jump shot to make it Cleveland 113, Chicago 112. The Bulls got the ball back with 6.2 seconds on the clock, and called a time-out. Phil Jackson gave them directions in the huddle, and as they broke to return to the court you could see the anger and dismay on Jordan's face. If you were watching him closely enough, you knew he wasn't going to get the ball. That's what he had to have been told in the huddle.

Indeed, when the game started back up Horace Grant passed the ball in not to Jordan, but to Pippen, who took a jump shot from the left side of the foul line and saw the ball clang off the rim. The buzzer sounded with the Bulls losers. Jordan's comments to the press were diplomatic and devoid of passion; he seemed not to want to talk about what had happened.

Now, in room 2323, I asked him what had gone on that night.

He exhaled audibly. "That was one of those situations where Phil outcoached himself," he said.

"It was a conscious decision not to give you the shot?" I said.

"That's what happened during the time-out," he said. "Phil called us to the bench and said that everyone in the building was expecting me to get the ball. He said, 'We're going to use M.J. as a decoy.' He said I was going to break across the court as if I was looking for the ball, but we were going to give the ball to Scottie instead. I'm standing there listening to this and I'm thinking, 'That's crazy.' "

"Did you say that?" I said.

"I didn't have to say it," he said. "He knew what I was thinking. And I shouldn't have to say it. I should have to say out loud that I deserve to take the last shot? I was really upset. I'm the guy who got you to this point. The way I'm shooting is the reason we have a chance to win this thing. I want that last shot. I can make it. But he's the coach. I kept my mouth shut."

"When the time-out was called, did you see this coming?" I said.

"No," he said. "I was totally surprised. Phil's theory was that everyone in the gymnasium was expecting me to get the ball, so that's why we wouldn't give me the ball. But I don't care if everyone knows I'm going to get it. I could care less. I think I can make the shot anyway."

"And when Pippen's shot went up?" I said.

"I hoped that it went in so that we could win the game," he said. "But half of me was saying, no, I hope it doesn't go in. It really pissed me off. I knew I could win the game. It was my birthday, and I was shooting great, and I think I had a better chance to make the shot than most players."

"So what do you think should have happened?" I said.

"You show some faith in me," he said. "You let me try to win the game for you. Instead we go to the bench at the time-out and I hear him saying, 'Michael, you're going to come up and be a decoy, and we'll look for Scottie off to the side and hope he gets a shot.' "

"I suppose that plan could have worked," I said.

"I was playing well enough to win it," he said. "It was my birthday."

Down in the hotel coffee shop, Phil Jackson was having a sandwich with a friend. There was a book on the table in front of them. I stopped to say hello, and Jackson said that people from all over the country had started to send him books.

"They hear that I read books, so they mail their favorites to me," he said.

On the surface, it was a pleasing thought: that basketball fans, learning that Jackson reads books to pass the time on the road, send him stuff they think he may like. And in the cable-ready, video-saturated age in which we lived, the fact that Jackson truly did enjoy relaxing with serious works of literature and philosophy was, indeed, a heartening signal to be sending out. You could be a man who had played in the NBA and had been a member of a world championship team, you could be the coach of the current world champions, and still you could choose to nourish your soul and better yourself through books.

Yet the fact that people were sending Jackson books pointed out another, not-so-heartening, fact: that the reading of books is slowly becoming something outside of the mainstream, something mildly quirky. When people heard that Jackson regularly read books, they considered that to be something interesting about him, something that set him apart. It was like hearing that he enjoyed lemon-flavored jelly beans, or that he rebuilt old sewing machines. It was something sort of cute. Subtly but inexorably, the habitual reading of books was beginning to be considered not something that the great masses of the citizenry did as a matter of course, but almost a cult activity. It was one of those immensely important changes that happen to a culture so gradually that by the time anyone really notices, the shift is already completed.

"Do you read the books the people send you?" I said.

"I try to," Jackson said. "But it's getting to the point where there are too many of them."

At the Target Center that night the public address system played the "I Want to Be Like Mike" theme from the Gatorade commercials. This was becoming increasingly common in NBA arenas when the Bulls came to town; the playing of the song inevitably ended with a joke—in some arenas it was the sound of a cannon shot, in some it was the triumphant entrance of the team mascot to the floor as the song was precipitously cut off—but always behind the gag there was an aura almost of celebration that Jordan was in the city and on the premises.

Here, as in Houston, the majority of sweat shirts, T-shirts, caps, and other items of basketball-related clothing being worn by the crowd was Jordan clothing. Some appeared to have been manufactured by licensed merchandisers, some appeared to be bootlegged, all in sum depicted Jordan in a startling array of poses: smiling, grimacing, flying, dunking, flexing, sitting, shouting, soaring. There were garments that had been put together artistically, and there was some stuff that was cheesy-looking almost beyond belief. The monetary aspects of Jordan's clothing-rights dispute with the NBA aside, it was hard to look up into the stands and behold the sea of Jordan items, as he looked up into the stands and beheld them every night, and not comprehend that he might be thinking: Since it's my face they're all wearing, I believe I'd like to have some say in this.

The place was full until the clock showed 2:35 remaining in the fourth quarter with the Bulls leading 109-96. Then the voice out of the ceiling announced: "For Chicago, Bobby Hansen in the game for Michael Jordan." He walked slowly to the bench and the building emptied out like a bathtub. The ceiling might just as well have erupted into flames.

Jordan's reluctance to spend inordinate amounts of locker-room time with the sports reporters assigned to games at the Stadium was not going unnoticed by them, and when, on a Friday night with the Los Angeles Clippers in town, he left the premises after the game without speaking to the press at all, some journalists were predictably miffed.

He had scored only fifteen points, and several broadcasters went on the air to attribute his hasty departure to a sense of embarrassment that he had played poorly. I figured that he was just sick of talking by this point in the season. But it turned out that I was wrong about the reason behind his haste, and so were the broadcasters.

I found out about this inadvertently. I called Carmen to see how everything was going with her, and I mentioned that Jordan had left the Stadium in an unaccustomed hurry.

"I know," she said. "He went to see Daniel."

Daniel Spikes had been coming to fewer and fewer games; in an effort to help him get stronger, his physicians had been keeping him in the hospital for weeks at a time.

"Michael told you he was going to see Doc?" I said.

"No, he didn't say anything," Carmen said, that voice of

hers a labored gasp over the telephone line. "But when we were driving home from the game, Michael's car was parked outside Presbyterian–St. Luke's hospital, with all these policemen guarding it."

"You're sure it was his car?" I said.

"Of course I'm sure," Carmen said. "How many other cars do you think would be surrounded by cops and security guards to keep people from messing it up? Besides, I called Daniel. He said that Michael came up right after the game and sat with him until after midnight."

"How is Daniel doing?" I said.

"He sounded really happy," Carmen said. "He sounded like Michael really cheered him up. He couldn't stop talking about it."

In the middle of March, heading toward April and the playoffs, the Bulls owned a 55-12 record, the best in the NBA, on course to be one of the best in the history of professional basketball. Jordan was leading the league in scoring by a wide margin. One morning it was reported in the newspapers that a North Carolina bail bondsman and nightclub owner named Eddie Dow had been found shot to death in his rural home. His killers had pried open a stainless steel briefcase owned by Dow and had stolen an estimated twenty thousand dollars in cash. Left behind in the briefcase were Dow's personal papers and documents. When police officers went through the papers, they found among them photocopies of three checks totaling $108,000. The checks had been signed by Michael Jordan.

25

"**Y**OU'RE SURE you don't just want to be by yourself?" I said.

"No, it's fine," Jordan said. "I'd tell you if it wasn't."

The last week of the regular season was coming up. The Bulls would be making a trip to Cleveland and then down to Atlanta. Earlier on he had said I'd be welcome to come along on that final trip of the year, but his offer had been made before the gambling stories broke. I didn't want to hold him to it if he simply wasn't in the mood for company.

"So Cleveland and Atlanta are both all right?" I said.

"Yep," he said. "Same as always. I'll meet you at the hotel after practice on the days of the games."

The discovery of the checks in the dead man's briefcase was a major and deeply personal humiliation for Jordan; of that there was no question. The checks were for gambling debts. He had lost an enormous amount of money during a golfing and card-playing weekend in South Carolina the previous fall, and the photocopies of the checks told the world just how high the stakes were. His choice of the people he gambled with was bad enough; in a rugged national economy, the disclosure by police of the amount of money he was gambling may have been even worse. It was one thing for the public to know that, as America's most prominent athlete, Jordan was making millions upon millions of dollars a year. It was another thing for people to pick up their morning papers and read that he was throwing that money away. Add to this the implication that some of the money was presumably lost during golf games at a time when he could have been at the White House.

He understood better than anyone the ramifications of this. It didn't matter that, if any person could financially afford that kind of gambling loss, he could. He recognized that many people were going to think less of him because of the news about the gambling, and he accepted that there was little he could do about it. This wasn't something that had been drummed up—he had done what he was accused of doing.

The NBA summoned him to a meeting in New York. Present at the two-and-a-half-hour session were Jordan; NBA deputy commissioner Russ Granik; league security chief Horace Balmer; and former federal judge and United States attorney Frederick B. Lacey, who had been brought in by the league to investigate the gambling story.

When the closed meeting ended, NBA Commissioner David Stern issued a statement to the press. Stern, said to be incensed at Jordan anyway because of the money the league stood to lose by Jordan's withdrawal of the rights to sell clothing with his likeness on it, began the written statement:

> This situation has been investigated with complete cooperation from Michael and his attorneys, and Judge Lacey has assured us that there appears to be no reason for the NBA to take action against Michael. We've also been advised that Michael is not the subject of investigation by any law enforcement agency. . . .
>
> Michael has advised us that he understands the gravity of the situation and that if he is not more careful about his associations it can reflect adversely on his fellow players and the entire NBA. He has assured us that he will be more careful about these associations in the future.

Stern said that there was no evidence, indeed no allegations, that Jordan had ever bet on basketball games.

Jordan, speaking to the press in New York, was contrite and muted. "I knew that at some point they had to look into the situation, which they did," he said, "and I just tried to be as straightforward as possible. . . .

"Sometimes you tend to forget as a public person the things you have to take into account. Naturally, it's an embarrassment for me, my family, the organization, and the fans as well . . . and hopefully they can understand that mistakes will happen. The embarrassment is something I don't want to encounter again. The letting down of people is something I don't want to encounter again."

I could only imagine how he was feeling about the exposure of his weaknesses; I wanted to talk to him and find out how it was affecting him. The part of his public comments about the embarrassment of letting people down . . . I read those words, and I thought of a couple of things I'd run into without seeking them out.

One was at a church the previous summer. I had been attending a funeral, and after the services I took a walk through the church building. A corridor took me past the Sunday school classrooms, closed on this day. I looked on the wall of one of the classrooms. There, among the religious items and reprints of verses, was a poster of Jordan.

Even talking about something like that is a risky proposition; to mention it even in passing borders on sacrilege. People referred to the public response to Jordan in quasi-religious terms all the time, which was interesting if you didn't take it literally. But the fact that people would think to use those terms, however symbolically, was instructive as to just how lofty a plateau millions of people wanted him to occupy. I hadn't been overly surprised to find that poster in the church. In a world hungry for public men and women to respect and admire, Jordan had come along to fill some need many might not even have been aware they fostered.

The second thing I'd encountered was in an elementary school I was visiting. It was a passage cut out of a newspaper, mounted on the schoolhouse wall. The language was purposely tongue in cheek, but the words were there nonetheless:

On the first day, God created the night and the day.
On the second day, He created the sky.
On the third day, He created the land and the sea.
On the fourth day, He created the sun and the moon.
On the fifth day, He created the fish and the birds.
On the sixth day, He created the animals and man.
On the seventh day, He rested.

Then, a few thousand centuries later, He came up with Michael Jordan.

That was precisely the kind of thing that made Jordan squirm, and justifiably so. No one can live up to that kind of adulation, no matter how whimsical, if questionable, the parodying choice of Old Testament language. And no one can escape the inevitable letting down of people who want to believe that a man can be without human flaws. That was why Jordan seemed to carry inside him the unrelenting and unforgiving vigilance: in preparation for the day when he knew he would disappoint the people who wanted to believe in him.

In New York he was asked by reporters what, in light of the revelations about his gambling, he would advise young people.

"Be very, very cautious of your actions and people that you don't really know very much about," Jordan said. Already his words were taking on the sound of a man who has found himself in the entranceway of the place he always feared going.

I flew to Cleveland on a Monday night. Out at the Stadium, the Bulls were playing a game; when it was over they would fly to northern Ohio in their charter after midnight. Because I had to be there in time to meet Jordan in the morning, I had to catch a commercial flight while the game was still in progress.

At O'Hare I passed one of those travelers' taverns in one of the flight concourses and saw people watching the game on television. It was the type of airport bar that has few seats; most of the patrons were standing and drinking. Some were cheering loudly for Jordan, a few were calling insults toward his image on the screen, one man was cursing him. I went to my gate.

Just before we were scheduled to board an announcement was made that the flight had been changed to another gate, on another concourse. I took my bags to the new gate, waited fifteen minutes, only to be told that we would be leaving from still another gate. On my way to the third gate I passed the stand-up tavern again. The one man at the bar was still cursing at Jordan, seemingly angrier and drunker than he had been before.

Because of the flight delays, it was close to midnight when I arrived at the hotel in Cleveland. I checked in and the desk clerk, who seemed a little unhappy, said, "A phone message just came in for you," and handed me a pink message slip. Before the flight to Cleveland I had called an old friend from high school, Gary Herwald, who lives there, to see if he wanted to have lunch or go to the game with me the next night. I assumed that the phone message was from Gary, telling me where to meet him, and I slipped it into my pocket without looking at it.

When I got to my room I threw my suitcase onto the bed, hung my coat in the closet, and took out the note to read it. It wasn't from Gary. It was from John Diamond, calling from Chicago.

The desk clerk had written down this message:

"John from Bulls called. M.J. will not be in Cleveland due to minor knee problem. Not decided till after game."

I was too tired to do anything but laugh. What good would it do to be frustrated or chagrined? Assuming that Jordan's knee problem was indeed not a serious one, there was something undeniably funny about this: hustling like crazy to get to Cleveland on time, only to be greeted by that note. No wonder the desk clerk seemed so disappointed. Working the late shift, he had to have been looking forward to the one bright spot in the night's routine: checking Michael Jordan into the hotel. He didn't have to be a CIA agent to figure out who the M.J. in Diamond's message was, and to realize that his duties behind the front desk had just become a little less exciting.

And if he was feeling deprived, there would be close to twenty thousand ticketholders at the Richfield Coliseum the next night who would feel just as bad and worse. Suddenly the hottest ticket in town wasn't quite so hot. I called downstairs and left word for John Diamond to call my room whenever the Bulls arrived. The phone rang around 2 A.M.; Diamond said Jordan's knee had started feeling sore during the game, an apparent recurrence of a tendinitis problem, and that the decision that he wouldn't travel was made in the locker room afterward. Diamond said he had called the hotel and left the message for me before getting on the charter in Chicago.

The way I figured it, that little pink message slip itself would be a good souvenir someday. Right now I might be thinking about all the time I'd wasted getting to Cleveland. Some year far in the future, though, the message slip about "M.J." and his "minor knee problem" might be as valuable a memento as a faded old note from some American League hotel in the 1920s saying that Mr. Babe Ruth was sorry, but he would not be able to keep his scheduled appointment because of an unanticipated stomachache.

* * *

In the morning I flew back to Chicago to get some work done. Diamond had told me that Jordan would almost certainly be going to the next game in Atlanta; the knee flare-up was nothing serious and would not keep him out of two games in a row.

So I went to the office the next day, and the day after that I was back at O'Hare, waiting for a Delta flight south. I was curious about what kind of mood Jordan would be in and what he would have to say about his recent travails, and I also made a mental note to check the newspaper coverage in Georgia on the day after the game against the Hawks. I'd been noticing something: Even when Jordan had standard, unspectacular games on the road, the local papers the next day often reported his exploits with "the greatest exhibition in the history of the arena" phrases; people wanted to convince themselves they had seen what they had been expecting to see. It was an interesting fillip, and I found myself looking for evidence of it.

I thought about those things as I waited for the flight to board, and just before getting on the plane I called my office to check for messages. I was told that Carmen Villafane had called, which struck me as highly unusual. Carmen had never called me before, and I didn't know whether she was even able to dial a telephone without great difficulty. From a pay phone near the door that led to the plane I called her back, and she told me that Daniel Spikes was dead.

She was distraught. Daniel's condition had dramatically worsened in the last few days, she said; he had begun to suffer massive internal bleeding, and had been in constant pain. Medical machinery had been all that was keeping him alive. Carmen was there at the end, she said; Daniel's family had called her, and her own family had hurried her to Presbyterian–St. Luke's to be with her friend from all those nights at the Stadium, and she had made it in time. She was with Daniel when he died. He was nineteen.

I didn't know what to say to her. We talked until right before the flight attendants closed the door to the plane. Carmen told me she had just wanted me to know, and I promised her we'd talk again when I got back from the trip.

At the Ritz-Carlton in Atlanta I went to Jordan's room. The

first thing I said to him was, "I just heard about Daniel Spikes. I'm very sorry."

He turned to me, and on his face was that expression you see on so many children's faces, the expression that just for a flash of a second you mistake for a look that is intended to make you laugh—a wild contorting of the mouth and the eyes, the look a child has on his face just before he cries.

"I thought he was going to be all right," Jordan said. His voice contained more despair than I had ever heard him allow himself to reveal. It was very slow, with a pause between each word. "I thought he was going to be all right."

"I know that you went to see him recently," I said.

"He was okay when I saw him," Jordan said. "He was talking to me. He had just watched our game when I saw him last. He'd seen it on television. He said he couldn't wait to get back to the Stadium again."

Jordan banged his hand softly on the top of a table in the hotel room. "He was such a good kid," he said. "He tried so hard. When I left that night I had no idea it would be the last time I'd see him. I had no idea at all. I told him I'd be back to see him soon, and I asked him what he needed. He said he wanted some music CDs, and some T-shirts, things like that. I told him I'd bring them to him the next time I saw him."

There was a newspaper in the room. Jordan picked it up. "They write about us every day," he said, his voice rushing now. "About what we do on the basketball court. We do nothing. We do nothing compared to someone like Doc. Do you know what he did last summer? I saw him, and he was in his wheelchair like always, and he had this look in his eyes. He didn't say anything, but he was looking at me like he wanted me to watch him.

"So I did. And he got up and he took two steps toward me. I never knew he could walk. I had never seen him do it. But he'd been practicing. It was just the two steps, and it was the bravest thing I've ever seen. I didn't cry. He didn't want me to cry. I smiled and I told him how great it was. But I wanted to cry, because I have never seen anyone do anything so impressive.

"Sometimes when there were people around Doc would ask me to buy him a car. Some of the people who heard him thought that he was trying to take advantage of my money. Didn't they understand? He didn't think I was going to buy him a car! He was saying it so they could hear him and think that he could drive a car. He just wanted to be regular. He just wanted people to think he could be regular. Didn't they understand that? That's why he was asking for a car. So that people would hear him say it and would think that he was a person who could drive.

"I don't know what to do now. I always thought I was going to see him again. You think about your own problems, and then you're ashamed of yourself for even thinking about them. A person like Doc, knowing every day when he opens his eyes in the morning that he won't be able to do the things that everyone else takes for granted. He won't be able to pick a girl up at her house and take her on a date, he won't be able to take a shower by himself. . . ."

His voice trailed off.

"Have you talked to his family?" I said.

"Yes," he said. "That's who called me to tell me. I asked if there was anything I could do. They're not wealthy people, and they need some help taking care of the funeral. I told them not to worry about that, I will take care of the funeral."

Jordan's voice was straining, suddenly rising, quavering. "He went through his whole life, and he never had anything good happen to him," he said. "He just wanted to be a person who was regular . . ."

We sat there for a minute or so. I wasn't sure whether I should excuse myself and leave the room, or ask him if he wanted me to come back later, or what. Finally Jordan shook his head vigorously, as if trying to cast out some thought, and then he said, "I'm okay. Let's talk about something else."

"I haven't really had a chance to talk to you alone since your meeting with the NBA," I said.

"The gambling meeting?" he said. "Boy."

"The papers said that it lasted two-and-a-half hours," I said.

"It did," he said. "It was two-and-a-half hours of like when you're a kid and they find out that you've done something bad in school and the principal calls your family in. And you have to go down to his office for a meeting and your parents are there and you have to sit there and listen. You have to sit there with your mouth shut and everyone's talking and you're the one who's being talked about. Everyone's there for one reason, which is to talk about you, and you have to sit there and take it."

"Did you feel the meeting was unjustified?" I said.

"No, it wasn't unjustified," he said. "They had to have the meeting. But you already know you've done wrong, you feel like driving a nail into your heart, you know what you've done, and you wonder what the purpose is of hearing it played back to you. I knew I made a mistake. I've already driven the nail. So why do they have to keep driving it in further? That's what goes through your mind."

"What was the meeting itself like?" I said.

"Two-and-a-half hours of making sure I knew how serious the situation was," he said. "I just sat there and listened to them talk. I was well aware of how serious the situation was. Every time things got quiet for a minute, they had this judge there who would talk."

"That was Frederick Lacey?" I said.

"Yeah," Jordan said. "Judge Lacey. It was like his job in the room was to go through all the different scenarios. What would happen to me if I did it again, what would happen to me if I was still doing it, what the repercussions would be. I'm sitting there very quietly. I'm not saying very much. Inside me I'm thinking, 'You guys, there's no need for this. We all know what happened. I've learned from this. I know what you really want to know. You want to know if there are other checks out there that are going to start popping up. No, there are no more checks out there. You won't be seeing this again.' But I'm not saying that out loud. I'm just listening to what they say and nodding my head.

"The meeting could have lasted half an hour, at tops. After they'd told me what they had to tell me, there was nothing more that needed to be said. I knew it, and they knew it. So we wasted the next two hours. I was angry to waste that time, because I knew exactly why we were spending so long. They wanted to be able to say that they called Michael Jordan in and talked about this stuff to him for two-and-a-half hours. Two-and-a-half hours sounds better than a half hour. So I sat there with them."

"Did you agree with anything they were saying?" I said.

"Yes," he said. "Except that I already knew it, so they didn't really have to say it. Was I gambling with goons who had bad reputations? Yeah, I was. Should I not gamble with goons anymore? Yeah, I shouldn't gamble with goons. But as they were talking to me, I was wondering: Are you telling me that I can't play cards with friends for a little money anymore? Is that what you're saying? Are you saying that if you hear that I've been in a card game with friends, you're going to kick me out of the NBA? What else is this meeting about?"

On one of those early Jordan videotapes marketed worldwide and produced through NBA Entertainment, I had noticed a brief film clip designed to show that Jordan's athletic skills were not limited to basketball. The film clip—promoted to the public with the full enthusiasm of the league—seemed more than a little ironic now. In the scene, Jordan had come off the golf course after a round with PGA tour professional Peter Jacobsen. The interviewer asked Jacobsen whether Jordan was a good golf partner. "I just really enjoy taking money from him," Jacobsen said.

"I also don't know why they made it a public meeting," Jordan said now. "I do know why, but I wish they hadn't done it that way."

"It wasn't a public meeting," I said. "It was private. It was closed to everyone but the people involved."

"It was public in the sense that the NBA made sure that everyone knew it was taking place," he said. "They had to make their point. And I'm sure that the people in the meeting are telling certain other people that they humbled me. So that's okay. That's part of my punishment for this, and I'll take it.

"But whatever I did, I was the one who made the mistakes. The fault was mine and no one else's. Why do people have to drag my family into it?"

"I wasn't aware that your family was a part of this," I said.

"They aren't," he said. "But all these newspapers are sending people down to Carolina to ask questions of my family and friends. It's embarrassing enough for me as it is, but to have people knocking on doors in the town where you grew up? I was told that's what's happening. I was told by people in Carolina that reporters are saying that they hear this whole thing really isn't about gambling at all, but that I'm trying to pay off some shady debts that my father has. Don't do this to me. Please. Deal with me, and say what you want to about me, but please, leave my family alone. Don't do this to my family."

The bell captain called from downstairs. Adolph Shiver wanted to come up to Jordan's room. Shiver and Fred Whitfield and Rodney Everhart, all of whom lived in the South and were taking the occasion of their old friend's trip to visit with him, were going to the Atlanta game tonight. Jordan was staying on a locked floor, so this was one of those hotels in which his family, friends, and even his teammates had to be escorted to his room by a hotel staff member.

When Shiver arrived he was carrying a big Federal Express box. "From Charles Oakley," Shiver said.

"Oh, right," Jordan said. "It's that basketball I said I'd sign for him."

Shiver opened the box and pulled out a ball. Jordan balanced the ball on one of his knees with one hand and autographed it with the other. "Will you send it back to him for me?" Jordan asked Shiver.

"Yeah," Shiver said. "He wants it Federaled back."

"Wait a minute," I said. "Charles Oakley wants your autograph?" Oakley was a forward for the New York Knicks.

"It's no problem," Jordan said. "I told him I'd be glad to do it."

"But that's not the point," I said. "He's your opponent. He's a player in the NBA just like you are. You don't think it's a little odd that he wants your autograph?"

"It's for a charity benefit or something," Jordan said. "I said I'd do it. I like Charles."

"Doesn't that affect the balance of power a little bit?" I said. "I mean, this is a guy you play against. You may be playing against him in the playoffs. What's he going to think as he's playing against you, knowing that he's asked you for your autograph?"

"Charles is a good guy," Jordan said, seemingly not finding anything all that unusual about the situation.

Fred Whitfield came into the room, said he was going out for a while and would see Jordan later in the afternoon, and he and Shiver left for the elevator. With any other group of three friends, the automatic offer on the part of two who were going out would be to say to the third, "Want to come with us?" Not with Jordan's friends; they knew that he was not free to do that. I continued to be struck by how the littlest things, things that the rest of us take for granted, became altered when he found himself trying to do them. I had been in the lobby, for example, when the team's bus had arrived at the hotel from the Atlanta airport. The Bulls were preregistered; all each player had to do was step to a special position at the front desk, say his name, and be given an envelope with a room key in it. I saw Jordan standing behind Cliff Levingston and Bobby Hansen; the woman working the desk listened to them say their names and handed out the keys, and she looked up, and even though she must have known this was going to happen her head jerked back a little when she saw who was next and when, identifying himself to her so that he could get his key, he said: "Michael Jordan." The look on her face would have been no different had be just stepped out of a spaceship from Pluto. This was the moment that the desk clerk in Cleveland had missed out on when Jordan had injured his knee the other night.

I'd been in the Macy's department store across Peachtree Street from the hotel before the Bulls arrived in town; on one floor was a display of clothing with Jordan's name and photograph on it, and the area around the display, along with most of this Macy's store on a weekday mid-afternoon, was deserted. Macy's was in Chapter 11 bankruptcy, and I'd stood there looking at the Jordan shirts and Jordan jerseys, thinking: He's in much better financial shape than Macy's. Ten years ago he was a North Carolina teenager, and now the Macy's department store chain would be delirious with grateful joy if it could make as much money as he did. At the Ritz, the desk clerk told me that two local teenage girls had tried to linger in the lobby, hoping they would catch a glimpse of him; when hotel personnel had told them that only guests were permitted to stand around the lobby, they had persuaded their parents to rent them a room. So here they were: newly registered guests in a luxury hotel, not even interested in their room, interested only in that they were now permitted in the lobby—and they didn't even know whether Jordan would ever come walking by, and not knowing was all right with them. At least there was a chance that he would.

He hadn't, not yet. On the locked floor we were talking about Magic Johnson. When Johnson had retired from the Lakers, he had seemed to be on the verge of changing his mind almost as soon as he made the announcement. Later, in the nationally televised ceremony from the Forum during which his number was retired and his jersey was put on permanent display up near the rafters, he had hinted that he might be back, and he had pointedly thanked the NBA, saying that if there had been no NBA, there would be no Magic Johnson.

"That's exactly backwards," Jordan said. "The NBA made him? I don't agree with that. The NBA made Magic Johnson?

He made the NBA—he and the other players. It's the basket-ball players who make the NBA work. The NBA without the players is just a business organization. What makes it different from any other business organization is the players on the court. Without the players, the NBA doesn't have anything that people want.

"That retiring-his-number ceremony, which the Lakers and the NBA were in such a hurry to have—it was as if the league was trying to push him out as quickly as they could. It's a forty-five-minute ceremony and Magic stood up there and thanked a lot of people . . . and I don't know whether he realized at the time that the league wanted him to retire be-fore he could give it too many second thoughts, the league wanted him gone. Because all of a sudden he represented a big potential problem to them, and they had absolutely no idea how to deal with it, and the best thing for them was to just have this big retirement ceremony and have him be gone."

"You really think they felt that way?" I said.

"I know they felt that way," Jordan said. "I don't even think they thought it was anything personal against Magic. They're a business, and they perceived that the situation he found himself in was not good for them, so they hurried to have this beautiful ceremony and the main thing was to get him out before he could think too much about it."

"Have you talked to him about that?" I said.

"Not specifically about the retirement ceremony," Jordan said. "But I think he knows. If he didn't know it when it happened, he knows it now."

"One of these days, you'll be having your own retirement ceremony," I said.

"I don't think so," he said. "I don't want any ceremony. I don't want the gifts or the speeches. I don't want a last trip around the league with presentations in every arena. When the time comes, I hope I'll just say that I retire, and that will be it. I'll say that I retire and then I'll go."

"You know they're not going to let you get away with that," I said. "They're going to want to have a big evening for you in the new Stadium."

Of all the changes that had happened in the last year, the announcement by the Bulls' front office that a new Stadium was going to be constructed directly across the street from the old one had the furthest-reaching potential to change the way basketball felt in Chicago. The new building, to be erected at a cost of more than $175 million, would give the city a modern arena of the sort found in Charlotte and Orlando and Minneapolis and other NBA cities, a structure with skyboxes and restaurants and elevators and glistening, airport-efficient corridors. Ground had already been broken; if all went according to schedule, the Bulls would be playing in the new building by the 1994 season.

"I don't like the whole idea," Jordan said. "I know it's a business, and that they think they have to build it. Whatever decision I make isn't going to affect what happens—they're going to build it anyway. And if it's ready in two years, I'll play in it.

"But I love the old Stadium. I just love it. The sense of unity we feel in there, the sound of it, the feel of it . . . I walk in there every night and I feel the history. Other teams hate it. They arrive at the Stadium to play us and they hate being there, because the Stadium is a part of our team. There's no other place like it.

"I know that the new building will be physically attractive. But I'm one for sticking with the old gym. I like the old gym. I wish we could keep playing there. But even if we can't, don't tear it down. Please don't tear it down."

"They probably are going to tear it down," I said. No official announcement about the fate of the old building had been made; there were some vague proclamations that perhaps it could be used for college basketball games and concerts. That seemed unlikely, though—the old Stadium just sitting there empty across the street from the gleaming new building.

"I wish they'd keep it up," Jordan said. "I'd love to go back to it on my way to work at night. The new building, I don't think it will give us a home-court advantage. It will be as new to us as to the other teams. To the other teams, it will feel like their own arenas. All the little nooks and crannies in our old building . . . I just love them. Even when we're playing in the new building, I hope they give me a key to the old building. Just so I can let myself in and walk around the place when I want to."

"Some people think you're going to use the new building to your own advantage," I said.

"I know they think that," he said. "What have you heard?"

"That you'll threaten to retire before they open the new

building," I said. "That you know that without you, they'd have a hard time selling seats in the new place."

"What is it I'm supposed to want out of this?" he said.

"Your name on the building, for one thing," I said.

"I don't want the building named after me," he said.

"And a piece of the team," I said.

"I don't want a piece of the team," he said. "Besides, you know that's not going to happen. Piece of the team? They're trying to sell me a skybox."

I'd read that. It was pretty astounding. Mike Mulligan of the *Sun-Times* had reported that a Bulls front-office executive had approached Jordan's friend George Koehler with a business proposition. Jordan always had family members and friends in town to watch him play. Would Jordan be interested in purchasing a skybox in the new Stadium? For $450,000?

"Can you believe that?" Jordan said. "They want to charge me $450,000 to bring my own family to see me play. No, I don't think that making me a part-owner is something they have in mind."

"But I can't believe you wouldn't want that," I said.

"I don't want it," he said. "If I owned a piece of the team, I'd want to fire and hire people. I'd want to get involved in every area of the operation. I'd want to tell everyone what to do. The players and management and everyone else. I get accused of doing that too much as it is; if I was an owner, I'd really be doing it. There would be finger-pointing at me every day. It's probably better for everyone if I'm just a player."

"You've seen the sketches for the new building, right?" I said.

"The amenities will be great," he said. "A bigger locker room for us and everything else. I can't help it, though. I like the old. The old is home."

It was a warm April day in Atlanta; tonight's game against the Hawks in the Omni arena would be the last road contest of the regular season. The Cleveland game that Jordan missed earlier in the week had been a disaster for the Bulls. The Cavaliers had won 115-100, and Chicago had looked all but inept.

"Did you watch?" I said.

"The whole thing," he said. "I watched it on TV at home."

"What was that like?" I said.

"It was a little depressing," he said. "When the game got

out of control, and Cleveland was running away with it, I had this desire to pop right in there. I was sitting at home in Chicago looking at the TV set, and I thought, what if I could just pipe myself into Cleveland right now? Just make myself appear in the arena and go into the game?

"I felt sorry for Scottie a little bit. He was trying to do it all, and it wasn't enough. I was thinking, now he knows what I did for so many years. You try your best, and the help isn't there and you lose anyway."

"How frustrating was it to watch?" I said. "Was there a time when you just wanted to turn the set off and go to bed?"

"I wanted to, but I didn't," he said. "I watched every second. I didn't switch channels and I didn't turn it off. I was yelling at the screen. I mean, really yelling, like I was sitting in the stands. If Scottie wasn't guarding someone close enough I was yelling, 'No, Scottie, no! Don't leave him! Don't leave him!' When we started taking wild shots I was yelling, 'That's stupid! You guys are taking dumb shots! Hold up! You don't have to take every shot!' "

"Some of them were upset that you didn't make the trip," I said. "They thought that even if you couldn't play, you should have been there."

"I know," he said. "I know they were saying that to each other. I was feeling two different things, watching the game. On the one hand, I was yelling at the screen the entire game: 'You guys are just giving up! You're losing your heads! Stay calm! Stay poised!' On the other hand, though, I was thinking: Gee, is this what happens when I step away? They were losing, and there was a sense that they needed me. It was a good sense. I was watching them play, and I wasn't on the court, and it made me know that they needed me to be with them. And when Cleveland kept their starters in to run up the score —what were they up by in the fourth quarter, twenty-eight points, and they still had their starters in?—I got angry. I got angry they were trying to make my teammates look bad. I hope we play Cleveland in the playoffs."

I knew that Jordan would want to be getting together with his old friends, and I didn't want to stay so long that it cut into their time with one another. We talked for a while more, and I said I'd see him at the arena in the evening.

"Most people's lives, it's like the progress of them is a series of up arrows and down arrows," I said before I left. "They look back over the years, and they realize that there have been times when their professional fortunes were headed up, and times when they went bad, and then got good again, and then got bad for a while . . . but there's always the hope that the arrow can go even higher up. I just wonder about you."

"What do you mean?" he said.

"Well, among everyone, you're one of the very few people whose arrow went so high up near the beginning of your career, it's hard to imagine it going any higher," I said. "When you look to the future, I don't see how you can envision the arrow going higher than it's already been."

"It can go up," he said. "I don't know how, but it will."

"It's hard to think what you could achieve that you haven't achieved already," I said. "Most of us keep waiting for the big thing to happen. I don't know what it must be like for it already to have happened."

"If I had to say exactly how the arrow could go any higher, I couldn't give you an answer," he said. "But I really do think it will."

"I'm not talking about all the stuff that's happened this year," I said.

"There's nothing I can do about that," he said. "I didn't ask for this job. It's not like I campaigned for the position."

"But besides all this stuff," I said. "It's just hard to conceive what might be out there for you that's even better than what you've already accomplished. That's a little scary. Most people would take it in a minute, but it's still a little scary."

"At this point, I don't think I need the arrow to go up any more," he said. "I think I'd settle for it just staying even. Not heading down."

"Your friend Magic says that if people don't start to give you a little room and a little privacy, you're going to walk away from basketball before you should," I said. "He says they're going to drive you away."

"I don't know why he keeps saying that," Jordan said. "He doesn't know. It's almost as if he feels he has to be the savior of my career. I'm sure his intentions are good, but I don't quite understand it. I'm always hearing that he says I'm on the verge of quitting because the pressure is getting to be too much. I have no idea why he thinks that's the case, or why he's saying it."

"Have you asked him?" I said.

"No," he said. "He doesn't say it to me. He says it to other people."

"Maybe it's his sense of the up arrow and down arrow thing," I said. "That it would be hard for the arrow to go any higher for you."

"Is there any way that things could go any greater for me than what went before?" Jordan said. "I don't know. I'd be willing to stay right here. If you offered me a deal that the arrow would never go any higher for me, and in exchange for that you could guarantee me that the arrow wouldn't go down, either, I'd take it. I'd make the deal. Just let the arrow go straight across. Not up or down. Just keep it steady from now on."

John Paxson's room was right across the hallway from mine. The "Privacy" sign stayed on his doorknob all day. For him and the rest of the Bulls, afternoons on the road were merely a holding period before going to work. The afternoon wasn't vital; the nighttime was. His used room-service lunch tray was on the carpeting outside his door. Down the hallway I ran into Cliff Levingston filling his ice bucket at the machine. The place was as quiet at 4 P.M. as it might have been at 4 A.M. The day hadn't started for the Bulls.

When the team left for the Omni, the two girls who had checked in just to see Jordan were standing near the elevator. He emerged, last one to the bus as always, and they snapped photographs. When we'd talked he had been wearing sweat clothes, but by the time he came through the lobby on his way to the bus he had changed into the customary business suit, white shirt, and tie. He was aware that there were always going to be people who would only see him for fifteen seconds out of their lives, and he was aware that the impression they carried away from those fifteen seconds was the impression that would stick.

When I got back to Chicago I called Daniel Spikes' father to offer my condolences.

It had struck me, as I had talked with Jordan about Daniel's death, that Jordan's gambling troubles were being written up extensively in virtually every newspaper in the Western world, while Daniel had died in absolute anonymity. His death had not rated an obituary or even a mention in either Chicago newspaper. Jordan's voice when he spoke of Daniel was so much more agitated and hurt than when he spoke of his own troubles; when he talked about Daniel's death there was anger and grief and pain in his tone. When he talked about the things that were being reported about him, there was mostly weary resignation.

I got the phone number for Daniel's family from Carmen, and reached Daniel's dad on the first attempt. Robert Spikes was an inspector with the City of Chicago's Department of Water. I told him that I had gotten to know Daniel at the games during the previous season, and that I had heard the news, and that I wanted him to know how bad I felt about it.

"He was a very brave young man," Mr. Spikes said. "We loved him very much."

I said that Carmen had told me she was there at the end. I said that Daniel must have felt blessed to have friends who cared for him.

"He had wonderful friends, a lot of them," Mr. Spikes said.

"Did he have a best friend?" I said.

I could hear something catch in Mr. Spikes' throat.

"My son's best friend was Michael Jordan," he said.

I said I knew that Jordan had visited Daniel after the game against the Clippers. I said Jordan had told me that Daniel had been in pretty good spirits that night.

"Did Michael tell you that he stayed with Daniel for more than two hours that night?" Mr. Spikes said.

"No," I said. "He didn't tell me that."

"Well, he did," Mr. Spikes said. "You know how much Michael Jordan hates to sit still for even a few minutes. And for more than two hours he sat in that chair next to Daniel's bed, just talking and listening to my son. He didn't look at his watch, he didn't say he had to be somewhere, he didn't look for any excuse to leave. He sat with my son until it was time for my son to take the medication that would make him sleepy. Only then did Michael leave the hospital."

"It must have been a very good night for Daniel," I said.

"It was one of many good nights," Mr. Spikes said. "Did Michael mention to you about the other visits?"

"No, sir," I said. "He didn't."

"In the last three months of my son's life, Michael Jordan came to see him in the hospital five or six times," Mr. Spikes said. "We never had to ask him. We never had to call him and say that Daniel was feeling lonely. He always came on his own.

"One night Michael brought my son a pair of shoes. Daniel wasn't going to be getting out of that bed. He wasn't going to be needing a pair of shoes. But Michael came one night carrying a shoebox, and he handed the shoes to Daniel, because I think he wanted my son to think in terms of getting out of bed and getting out of the hospital."

Mr. Spikes said that while in the hospital Daniel watched all of the Bulls' games on television or listened on the radio. "Michael would always tell him that his seat was waiting for him at the Stadium," he said. "I bought Daniel one of those big life-size Michael Jordan posters—you know, the cardboard ones that stand up. The ones that are six-feet-six-inches tall. Over the time Daniel was in the hospital, I think some of the nurses didn't really believe that Daniel knew Michael. They'd just see the stand-up poster in Daniel's room, and think that's what Daniel was talking about. So on the nights when Michael would show up, the nurses would walk in the room, and there would be the poster of Michael, and there would be Michael."

"What did Michael do when he saw the poster?" I said.

"Well, we dressed the poster up," Mr. Spikes said. "We put a coat over its shoulders, and a tie around its neck, and we had it wear a doctor's stethoscope. Every time Daniel had something done to him, we'd do it to the poster, too. If the nurses drew blood, we'd put a bandage on the poster's arm right where the bandage was on Daniel's arm."

"And Michael saw this?" I said.

"He joked about it," Mr. Spikes said. "He came in and looked at it and said, 'That's an old poster. I had hair.' "

I told him again how sorry I had been to hear the news. I said it must have been tough on him every time Jordan had to leave his son's room; he must have felt a little sad that Daniel wouldn't be seeing Jordan again for a while.

"No, it never made me sad when Michael left," Mr. Spikes said. "I was just so happy that my boy was so happy."

The regular season ended with the Bulls having compiled a 67-15 record, the best in the team's history. I realized that I'd been around the Stadium for a long time now; it had been more than two years since that day I'd brought Cornelius Abraham to his first Bulls game and mine. The playoffs were about to begin. By the time they were over, Jordan and his teammates would either be repeat champions, or be former champions. Once again winter was turning to full spring.

26

"WOULD I HAVE TO STAY in the same place all day?" Jordan said.

"No," I said. "You could travel around. But only by the usual means of transportation."

"All right," he said. "Let me think about it for a minute."

I'd asked him what he would do if he could be invisible for one day. For some reason, I thought that might be a fantasy that would appeal to him. In a way, it was the only gift the world could present to him now—the promise of one day when he could walk anywhere he wanted and no one would know he was there.

"Maybe I'd go into meetings the president has," he said. "In the Oval Office."

"If I recall, you passed up your chance for that," I said.

"Very funny, very funny," he said. "I'm serious. I would like to observe the president in his office, to see how he reacts to the kinds of things that I have to react to, but on a much bigger scale than I do."

"What kinds of things?" I said.

"Bad mail," Jordan said. "Bad calls."

"You get a lot of bad mail and calls?" I said.

"Oh, yeah," he said. "And I'm just a professional athlete. I'd like to see how the president deals with all the pressures. Whether he has someone to deal with all of it for him. Or whether he has to deal with it himself, like I do. How does he deal with it on that bigger scale? I'd really like to know."

"What you're talking about is almost a learning experience," I said. "That's not what I meant when I asked about being invisible. I meant being invisible and doing something that would make you feel good."

He paused for a few seconds.

"I'd go for a walk in a mall," he said.

"Just a shopping mall?" I said.

"Yes," he said. "I'd walk through the mall invisible, and I'd watch the people all day."

"Is there any chance you can do that now?" I said.

"I can't," he said. "They watch me. I know it from the first steps I take inside the mall. I see everyone turning. When I would go to the mall with my friends when I was a kid, though, we'd have so much fun. We'd just watch the people all day.

"We'd ride our bikes to the mall, four of us, and we'd hang around. The four of us would just sit there and watch. I'd like to do that now to see if the camaraderie is still there among groups of friends, like it was with my friends and me. We'd walk up to the stores where all the grown-ups were shopping, and we'd just watch everything.

"Just observing. The people would walk right past us. We were little—we might as well not have even been there. They didn't even notice us. It was a lot more fun. You're with three of your best friends, and you're talking about anything, laughing about anything. Maybe someone will trip, or they'll drop their ice cream cone on the floor, and you'll be observing and watching and when you see the ice cream cone drop you'll laugh.

"Now, I have to find out in advance where the store is where I have to go. I find out the door of the mall closest to that store. A lot of the times I'll double-park by the door, knowing that I'll get a ticket. But I'll pay the ticket—the car has to be there, so I can get out as quickly as possible. I'll walk as quickly as I can to the store and I'll get what I have to get and then I'll walk in a straight line back to the car as quickly as I can and then I'm out of there.

"It was a lot more fun with my friends. I never dreamed that someday people I didn't know in a mall would know me, and I never wanted that. With my friends we went to the mall and we had a good day. We laughed and we had fun and we saw people drop their ice cream and we ate ice cream. And at the end of the day we'd ride on our bikes together, all the way home. We'd be tired, and it had been a good day."

"It had been a day when nothing had really happened," I said.

"That's right," he said. "Nothing had happened. I love thinking about days like that."

The Bulls' first opponents in the playoffs were scheduled to be the Miami Heat. During the regular season, the Bulls had defeated the Heat four consecutive times; in fact, Miami, in the history of its franchise, had never won a game from Chicago.

The drama that was building had nothing to do with this first series, though. A year before, as the playoffs had commenced, the Bulls were regarded as likable young interlopers, a team from a city that had never been to the NBA Finals, Jordan and his erratic playmates. Now everything had changed. The Bulls were considered to be the best basketball team in the world. They had everything to lose. If they got knocked off in these playoffs, the previous year would be deemed to be, if not exactly a fluke, then an aberration. The team would go back to being a curiosity. With Jordan they would still fill arenas on the road, but the special feeling that had followed them in the wake of the championship season would be gone. The 67-15 record during the regular season had been fine and commendable, but it would be instantly forgotten if someone showed them up now.

"I want to just play the games and get it done and forget about it," Jordan said.

"Is the hunger anywhere near what it was last year?" I said.

We'd talked more than once about the inevitability of a letdown in desire. A year before, no one knew if Jordan could ever lead his team to a championship. That question had been answered. Now, regardless of how much tension and world-wide focus there was on the playoffs, what exactly was there to prove?

"The funny thing is, after all that's happened this year, I want it bad," he said. "I want it worse than I did last year. I didn't think I was going to. But I do."

"Have you thought about why?" I said.

"Sure," Jordan said. "To prove to people that the assholes can't hold me down."

Then:

"To show the assholes what I think of them."

He said it matter-of-factly and with an almost intimidatingly level tone. All year long he had been saying that the outside distractions in his life weren't affecting his game; on the eve of the playoffs his public interviews were still relatively bland, centering on predictable statements about how much the team had to demonstrate about itself by going for back-to-back titles.

But inside he felt such rage, bordering on abhorrence, for people—some in the press, some on other teams, some in the NBA league office—whom he felt had taken unseemly joy all year in his troubles and his failings. He had been outwardly calm when facing the world and responding to all the questions concerning the various pieces of bad news about him. He had been deeply hurt, though, and he had never been quite sure about how to salve that hurt. He often talked in public about what a "maturing year" it had been for him, as if he had welcomed all the turmoil. The truth was that he remained furious at the people who had gloated and taken pleasure in his shortcomings. Now he was ready to answer them.

"To win the championship again would give me a great deal of personal satisfaction," he said. "Because it would prove that it's they who are lacking, not me. Not me. Nothing I could ever say out loud would answer how I feel about them more than winning a second championship would."

"Do you think your teammates have the same level of desire they had last year?" I said.

"I don't know," he said. "I see a little slippage in their hunger. I don't know how seriously they're taking it yet. We'll find out soon enough."

Before one of the Miami games, Ray Clay got on the public address system to announce that NBC was just about to go on the air live from the Stadium to a national audience. He urged the Chicago fans to show how loud they could be—and thus provide a frenetic background for the opening of NBC's broadcast.

The crowd wouldn't do it. There are things to love about Chicago and things to hate about Chicago, but the crowd's refusal to bark on cue for a television network is emblematic of one of the most admirable qualities of the city. Anywhere else in the league, when an arena full of fans are instructed to stand and scream for TV, they comply and act grateful for having been asked. It doesn't work in Chicago—it didn't work on this night, and it would not work throughout the playoffs. They might yell on demand in Denver or Dallas or even in

New York, but in Chicago when someone tells people what to do and when to do it, their automatic instinct is to say no. The broadcast went on the air in relative, almost sullen, silence. The place would have been louder had Ray Clay said nothing to the crowd at all.

Jordan scored forty-six points in the Bulls' first victory over Miami, thirty-three in the second victory, and fifty-six in the third victory. He seemed restless, eager to be finished with all of this.

Every night—not just during the playoffs, but all season long—when the scoreboard clock ticked down into the last minute of the game, the time began to be displayed in tenths of seconds. This always felt a little bittersweet to me. It was a sign the contest was ending, and that the building would be emptying out. It didn't matter whether the game was a keenly significant playoff confrontation, or a regular-season yawner against the Charlotte Hornets on a Tuesday night in February—the signal that the evening was ending made me want to watch more basketball. I asked Jordan whether he ever wanted to just stay on the court and play another quarter or two.

"When it's over, I'm ready for it to be over," he said. "There used to be times when I felt like playing some more. Not now. Now, the game at the Stadium is only my first basketball game of the night."

"It is?" I said.

"Yeah," he said. "My older son is three-and-a-half now. He waits for me to get home from the games, because he's watched on TV and he wants to play against me. When I walk into the house he's standing there with one of those miniature basketballs in his hand. First thing I see—Jeffrey standing there with the basketball. It's the best sight I've had all during the season.

"So he's waiting up for me, holding the basketball. He says, 'Where are you coming from, Daddy, are you coming from work?' He calls what I do work. He says he's been waiting so I can watch him play basketball.

"I get down on my knees. He likes me to be on my knees so he can shoot over me and I can try to block his shot. Then after a while he'll play defense—I'll shoot when I'm still on my knees, and he'll try to block my shots.

"I'm tired on a lot of nights, so after a few minutes of this I may say, 'Okay, Jeffrey, let's go upstairs.' But he'll usually say, 'I'm not ready to go upstairs, Daddy.' I'll try to talk him into it: 'Daddy's tired because he had to work hard tonight.' But it doesn't work—he wants me to stay downstairs and watch him shoot.

"So I'll lie on the floor and watch him. We've got these little backboards all over the house. Sometimes I'm so tired from the day that my eyes will close and I'll start to doze off. He'll cry then, because I'm not watching him. So I'll wake up and watch some more. It's so important to him that I watch every shot he takes. He wants to show me about playing basketball.

"Sometimes when he's shooting I pretend to be the fans in the stands. A lot of times he says, 'Daddy, this is how you shoot a free throw.' He knows I'm the person he's seen playing basketball on TV, but I don't know how much it registers at that age—whether in his mind there's a difference between me in the games on TV, and me in the living room. He looks over to make sure I'm watching him, and then he teaches me how to shoot a free throw. It's obvious he's learned from watching me. But I don't know for sure that he knows that. He spins the ball, which is what I do. He takes a deep breath. He bounces it. He shoots it. Then he turns to me and says, 'See? That's how.'

"No, I don't mind it at all when the games at the Stadium are over."

The sweep of Miami in the best-of-five opening series moved the Bulls into the second round against the New York Knicks. From here to the Finals, all matchups were best of seven. Chicago versus New York went the full seven games, with immense national attention being given to it because of the ferocity of play, and the fact that the Manhattan media thought they might have a surprise hometown champion on their hands.

They didn't. While the series was under way, the roughness of the Knicks—with John Starks, Charles Oakley, and Xavier McDaniel playing the on-court role of sneering enforcers—made every game seem ominous and full of portent. The writers and broadcasters had a good story on their hands—how Pat Riley had goaded or allowed his team to be brutal and mean-spirited in the hopes of knocking off the Bulls in the only way they possibly could—and for the length of the series it did, indeed, seem like the biggest sports news in the world.

But the moment it was over, with the Bulls burying the Knicks 110-81 in the Stadium in Game 7, the fact became evident once again that losers in the playoffs are forgotten almost immediately. Certainly the Knicks would be back again the next year, maybe even joining Detroit as Chicago's acrid rivals. For now, within forty-eight hours of the Bulls' victory the memory of the Knicks series had already begun to fade. The playoffs were still going on and the Bulls were still alive, while the Knicks were spectators just like everyone else in the country who had a TV set. The one thing the series did do was point out just how tenuous life at the championship level can be—it made you realize that had the Knicks defeated the Bulls, this edition of the Chicago team would have become an old story just as quickly.

But the Bulls didn't lose. And every time I saw the snarling preening of the Knicks' players on the court—Oakley in particular—I had to smile at the memory of the Federal Express box in Jordan's hotel room. Oakley might be flexing his muscles and giving Jordan and the Bulls the bad eye now, but his cold and steely pose became considerably less threatening when you knew that he wasn't above asking Jordan for his autograph, like some fan in an arena hallway. Which is it, sir? Do you want to take my championship away from me, or do you want me to sign this ball for you? Jordan scored at will against the Knicks in Game 7, hitting for forty-two points as the Bulls eliminated New York and moved on.

Cleveland was next. The Cavaliers came into the Stadium full of fire; they knew that if they defeated the Bulls, they would be in the NBA Finals for the first time ever, and would shake the stigma that Jordan owned them. Chicago won the first game easily, 103-89, in spite of the fact that Jordan was feeling ill and showed signs of having a cold or the flu.

Months before, my friend Jack Roth had invited me to a family function up in Minneapolis, a weekend event that was going to mean a great deal to him. I had wavered about saying whether I would be able to attend; I knew that the ceremony would fall in the middle of the NBA playoff season, and if the Bulls were still in contention I knew that I would be drawn to the Stadium.

As Game 2 against Cleveland approached, I thought about what I should do. On the one hand, the Bulls were now barreling toward the Finals again, with every game essential; the

Stadium felt like the core of the sports universe each night. On the other hand Jack had been my best friend since we were children, and this was going to be a weekend he wanted to share with the people who had been closest to him throughout his life. As always, he put no pressure on me at all; he said, "I know you may have to be at the playoffs that weekend. I'll understand if you can't make it."

I weighed the two. A basketball game that much of the nation would be watching. A ceremony in Minneapolis for Jack's family and friends. I thought about the discussion I'd had with Jordan in his hotel room the last time I'd been in Minneapolis—how he'd asked me about Jack picking me up at the airport, how that had led to our conversation about the nature of friendship, and about the rarity of having a friend in your life you knew you could always count on.

I booked a bedroom compartment on the Empire Builder to Minnesota. I had enjoyed the trip to Cleveland on the Capitol Limited so much back in January that now, in May, I was glad to have the opportunity to get on board another long-distance train. The journey was scheduled to be eight hours from Union Station in Chicago to the depot in St. Paul.

I brought a battery-powered radio with me. As we rolled through northern Illinois and up into Wisconsin, I looked out the window at farmland and streams, settling back in my room and taking in the late-afternoon Midwestern countryside. We were well into the rural part of Wisconsin when game time arrived; I turned the radio on and twisted the dial, trying to find the sound of basketball. There was a Milwaukee Brewers baseball game, and a lot of music stations, but mostly there was static. We passed through a small town where a family was gathered at an ice cream stand, and we rolled close to the shoreline of a lake, and I savored the scenery and kept trying to find what I was seeking on the radio. We were in LaCrosse, Wisconsin, with the sun going down, when suddenly through the dim electric buzz came the voice of Neil Funk, the Bulls' radio play-by-play man: "It's 71-47, and Phil Jackson doesn't like what he's seeing. . . ." I lost the signal for a moment, and then Funk was saying, "Time out, Bulls."

We kept rolling. I had to hold the radio directly next to the window and rotate it in various directions in an effort to get a clear signal. "B.J. takes the ball downcourt," Funk was saying urgently into his microphone in the Stadium. "He shoots . . ." The Bulls were losing badly. "Pass in to Michael," Funk shouted on West Madison Street and into my room on the Empire Builder. *"Michael* with the right hand . . ." We were on a steel bridge passing over a silent river.

The lights of lower Minnesota were coming on in the houses and service stations and taverns. "Pippen's got it," Funk called, the raucous sound of the Stadium crowd behind him. "He looks toward the basket . . ." Radio sometimes can seem even more amazing than television. We sped through a town where two cars paused for us at a railroad crossing, and all was quiet outside the window, all was quiet in my compartment, save for the sound of the 18,676 shouting their roaring encouragement as B. J. Armstrong launched a long jump shot.

Around 8:50 P.M. I lost the signal; we seemed to be in the woods somewhere, and I tried to get the game back. I found Jack Jones singing a ballad at one post on the dial, and I kept searching, and Sammy Davis Jr.'s voice came forth from another position singing "I've Got to Be Me." I continued my quest. A station that identified itself as KDTH informed me that it was sixty-nine degrees in downtown Dubuque, Iowa, and the next time I located the sound of the game it was 85-52 Cavaliers, with 13:51 on the game clock in the Stadium and 8:58 on my watch on the train.

I thought about what time Jack would leave his house to meet me at the train station. *"Michael,"* the voice on the radio called. *"Yes,* M.J. tips it in." As we traveled farther north I was finding two sets of play-by-play announcers: Funk and Tom Boerwinkle on the Bulls radio network, Joe McConnell and Bob Lanier on the NBA's separate network. I hunted around the dial for the strongest signal, looking at backyards and village parks as I listened to the sound of the scoreboard horn blaring in the Stadium.

A Minnesota radio station was playing an old Beach Boys song; Brian Wilson's voice bled into Joe McConnell's narration of Jordan driving toward the basket. There were red lights and soft bells at the small-town intersections we passed, and desperate cheers in the night from West Madison Street. Cavaliers 107, Bulls 81 as time ran out, tying the series at 1-1. We rolled into St. Paul just before midnight. I stepped off the Empire Builder, and over by the station house the first people I saw were Jack and his wife, smiling and waving as I carried my bags across the concrete.

* * *

If Jordan had, in fact, vowed to punish what he perceived as Cleveland's mocking treatment of his teammates during the regular season game from which he had been absent, he made abundantly good on his pledge. The Bulls defeated the Cavaliers in six games, with Jordan scoring sixteen points in the fourth quarter of Game 6 to beat Cleveland 99-94 and move on to the NBA Finals.

The Portland Trail Blazers came to Chicago for the first two games of the Finals. In the moments just before Game 1 started, and even during the opening minutes of the first quarter itself, the fans in the Stadium were distinctly unenergized. They got on their feet and screamed for the spotlight introductions, of course, but after that they settled into their seats, as if they'd been slightly spoiled by the team's success. This was before any of us in the building knew that what we were about to see was a performance people would likely be talking about as long as basketball is played.

During the warm-ups, referee Jake O'Donnell warned Portland forward Alaa Abdelnaby not to hang on the rim as he practiced his dunks; it was unusual for a referee to start telling the players what to do before the tipoff had occurred, but O'Donnell seemed to want to make sure of two things: that he establish his authority early on, and that the NBC telecast not be delayed because some guy had broken the backboard before the contest even went on the air. The two men had brief words, and mostly it felt not so much like an NBA star being reprimanded by a veteran official, but like a day-camp counselor telling a kid to quit screwing around or he wouldn't be allowed to play anymore.

Portland pulled out to an early lead, and then Jordan did something no one had ever seen him do.

He began firing three-point attempts at the basket. This was not part of his usual repertoire; he did not customarily try shots from back behind the three-point line. Tonight he did, and the balls started dropping in.

At first the crowd reacted as they always reacted when Jordan was having a good night: They cheered wildly and stood to honor him. When it became evident that no one in the building had ever seen anything like this before, though, the mood changed. If there is such a thing as secular reverence, that's what was happening. Jordan was hurling shots from anywhere he pleased, hitting everything, and the feeling in the Stadium was something close to communal bliss. It was as if time had been suspended—Jordan dropped in one long-distance shot after another, and neighbors in the stands and on press row turned to one another and asked if they were really seeing this.

The more shots that went in, the more confidence Jordan developed. He scored seventeen points in the first quarter, sat out for almost six full minutes at the beginning of the second quarter, then returned to the game and started up again stronger than before. It was as if some unseen motion picture director was doing this with animation; from wherever Jordan stood on the court he flung the ball, and the ball kept going in. The sound in the building transformed itself into a kind of rapturous keening; everyone understood the uniqueness of what they were present to witness. Including Jordan's teammates; they were on the court, but they were spectators, too, this was the greatest basketball show they had ever seen, and if they could have stood in place and cheered, they would have. John Paxson brought the ball down the court as he always did, but if in other games he at least gave the impression that he was looking for the best available open man, tonight he had an elated grin on his face and he was baldly looking around for Jordan all the time, not even hiding the fact that it was Jordan he wanted to pass the ball to, because it didn't matter, Portland couldn't do anything to stop this. Paxson was throwing the ball to Jordan—passing is much too dry a term to describe what Paxson was doing, he was hurrying down the court and ecstatically throwing the ball to Jordan, heaving it, really, just as soon as he could locate him on the floor.

Jordan scored thirty-five points in that first half—an NBA Finals record—including six three-pointers, and after the game he would try to explain to the assembled sportswriters how he had achieved it. He likened the feeling to shooting free throws: "It was like if you get in the gym and you're shooting by yourself and someone is tossing you the ball back."

As I watched him doing it, however, burying the distant-range shots as if they were layups, all I could think about was what he had said about proving himself in the Finals. His language may have been inelegant and uncharacteristically coarse when we'd had the conversation—"To prove to people that the assholes can't hold me down. To show the assholes what I think of them"—and for all the criticism Jordan had taken, he was still one of the most admired people in the country. So maybe he had some need to tell himself that people were out to diminish him in order to work his energy up; maybe it was part of what charged him.

Every time one of those flawless shots sailed through the air, though, I looked at him and I could almost hear him saying it to the people he felt misused by: "This is what I think of you." Three points. "This is what I think of you." Three points. "This is what I think of you." Three points.

There is a short passage by the poet William Butler Yeats that has always moved me. It speaks to what happens when a person feels that everything has been taken from him, and knows that he must turn to his very essence in order to lift himself. Yeats died in 1939, well before there was any such thing as the National Basketball Association. But as Jordan roamed the court that first night of the NBA Finals, proving something that perhaps only he knew the depth of, I thought of Yeats' words:

"Now that my ladder's gone, I must lie down where all the ladders start, in the foul rag-and-bone shop of the heart."

When you are challenged, you go back to the strengths that no one ever knew you had in the first place. When you feel that there are enemies who are trying to take from you that which is rightfully yours, you return to the only place you can ever truly be sure of: your own secret soul. To the place that has served you best all your life. To the foul rag-and-bone shop of the heart.

Jordan knew that, were he not so gifted with a basketball, none of these people in the building would ever have heard his name. He might not ever have been a visitor to Chicago, let alone to the Stadium. Now many thought highly of him as a person as well as a basketball player, but he knew that Jordan the man would most likely never have been given a chance had Jordan the basketball player not emerged out of Wilmington, North Carolina. What he had felt during the troubles of this season could not have been all that different from what he had felt the day he was cut from his high school team. Someone wanted to leave him behind. Now, as then, he recognized that the way to show them all was with the basketball. Everything else could come later. It always had.

Three points. "This is what I think of you." Three points. "This is what I think of you." A missed layup by Pippen and a shuddering follow-up dunk by Jordan, who had been trailing breathlessly behind all the way down the court. "This is what I think of you." Three points. "This is what I think of you."

The Bulls ran away with that first game of the Finals, 122-89, and afterward Jordan said that his performance would count for nothing at all unless his team went on to win the championship.

There were times when John Paxson was so unassuming and so untaken with himself that it was hard to believe he was a starting guard on the championship basketball team of the world.

An hour or so before Game 2, he was up on the court, as he usually was, to practice his shots, but this time he wasn't shooting. He said hello to me, and we talked for a minute or two, and the minute or two grew into five. Which was fine with me, I really liked Paxson and enjoyed his company, but I didn't know quite what he was doing.

"Are you just sort of here?" I said. "I mean, are you just hanging around up here?"

"Well, I came up to shoot, but the ball boys haven't brought any balls up yet," he said.

"Did you say anything to them?" I said.

"Oh, I'm sure they'll get around to it," he said. "I'm sure they got busy."

So here Paxson was marking time until the ball boys realized that he needed a basketball. With all the pressures of the imminent game on his mind, he was like the most pleasant customer in a restaurant, who wouldn't think to bother the waiter even though it had been an hour since he placed his order. We talked until the balls arrived, and then he shot away. Some nights I just wanted to stay here forever.

Trail Blazers 115, Bulls 104 in overtime, after Chicago blew a 10-point lead with 4:36 left to play in regulation. The Stadium was as quiet as I'd ever heard it as the game ended with the series tied 1-1 and on its way to Portland.

Less than forty-eight hours later, all the way across the country in the Portland Memorial Coliseum, Jordan came out of the locker room early to warm up.

This was something that no one had expected. Pregame practice for Jordan had become rarer and rarer. An NBC production assistant picked up his walkie-talkie and made an almost frantic call to a camera crew. For any other player to shoot some baskets on the court before a game was customary; when Jordan did it, the network wanted to get it on videotape just to prove that it had really happened.

Jordan spoke to no one. He and his teammates were embarrassed and infuriated about having lost the game on Friday night; now Jordan warmed up in silence, avoiding eye contact with anyone, just doing the work. He was joined on the court by Pippen, Grant, and Paxson, all of whom adopted Jordan's stony and wordless demeanor. Clearly they had talked to each other about this and had decided to abandon all frivolity. Grant was such an unfailingly friendly guy, though, that when a local ball boy told him a joke, he laughed and kidded with the youngster before remembering he was supposed to have his game face on; on it came.

There was an earnest hospitality to the city of Portland and its fans that belied the harshly competitive nature of the NBA Finals. It started with some of the scoreboards, which referred to the Bulls as "Guest." A number of Trail Blazer partisans stopped by the press tables to tell reporters from Chicago that they hoped the Chicagoans had a nice visit to the city, a genuine gesture that some of the Chicago writers nevertheless instinctively distrusted, wondering what the angle was.

There was no angle. Even the handmade signs in the arena purportedly insulting the Bulls seemed to be gentle. One boy, for example, held aloft a sign on which he had written: "My Grandmother Lives in Chicago, But I'm For Portland Anyway." Followers of the Bulls were perplexed about how to even react to something like that; back home in the Stadium, what passed for a polite hand-lettered sign was one along the lines of "Detroit Sucks."

Just as NBC was going on the air live with its broadcast, and as the signal from the Memorial Coliseum was being beamed by satellite to ninety-two countries around the globe, the main scoreboard began descending toward the surface of the court. At first it seemed like an optical illusion, but second by second it dropped lower on the cords that suspended it from the ceiling. So as large parts of the nation and large parts of the world watched and waited for the game to begin, the scoreboard settled all the way to the floor. It turned out that this was intentional; there was a malfunction inside, and it had to be repaired. Scottie Pippen stared at this whole process as if his worst nightmare was coming to life. If he'd been reluctant to stand under a scoreboard before, this might have the potential to drive him out of the sport altogether. He scrutinized the scoreboard every inch of the way as it was raised back up into position.

Bulls 94, Trail Blazers 84, a one-game advantage in the series again. After the game John Paxson and his wife, Carolyn, lingered at the Coliseum, and Paxson missed the team bus back to the hotel. Dan Roan, a sportscaster for WGN-TV in Chicago who was in Portland covering the Finals, offered to give the Paxsons a lift, and said that I was welcome to ride along. We somehow took a wrong turn, and soon enough we had no idea where we were.

"There are some police officers up there," Carolyn Paxson said. "Let's stop and ask them."

"I'll do it," her husband said.

We pulled up to a squad car that was parked near an intersection. Several officers were standing around talking.

"Excuse me," Paxson said, rolling down his window.

One of the officers, in no apparent hurry, turned around. "Yes?" he said.

"We're from out of town," Paxson said. "I think we're kind of lost. There's a bridge we're looking for? I think it's a steel bridge?"

We're from out of town. Less than an hour before, television viewers in countries and principalities Paxson had doubtless never even heard of had been watching him play basketball. Now, in an open-necked shirt, he waited for the officer to give us directions. If the officer had any idea who the traveler in need was, he didn't show it.

"Just keep going straight ahead," the officer said. "You'll run right into the bridge."

"Thank you," Paxson said, rolling his window back up.

But we couldn't get straightened out. A few minutes later, outside the left windows of the car, we saw that we were sitting in front of the Memorial Coliseum, the same place we'd left in the first place. We had been going around the block all this time.

"Oh, no," Paxson said.

"I think that may be the bridge up there," Mrs. Paxson said.

"I can see the Coliseum from my hotel room," Paxson said. "Maybe that means I can see the hotel from here."

* * *

The team hotel—which we eventually did find—was the Benson, a beautiful old place that had opened in 1913 and had been refurbished to its original elegant refinement.

Security measures at the hotel had been heightened; nonguests were not permitted inside, and whenever the Bulls were scheduled to enter or exit the front door of the hotel, barriers were erected to keep back the crowds. The hotel's switchboard was kept busy all day, local television crews reported live from outside the building, and people gathered on the street as if the Queen of England were in residence— except Michael Jordan's presence in the hotel was probably a much bigger draw than the queen's would be.

On the afternoon following the game, then, with people jamming together on the sidewalk outside the front door hoping for a glimpse of one of the Bulls, I was standing at the first-floor bank of elevators waiting to go to my room when I noticed a side door of the hotel being opened, and was startled to see Jordan walking in off the street all by himself.

Apparently the hotel's management had let him know about this alternate door, where he stood a chance of slipping in and out in relative privacy. We rode upstairs together. Before the playoffs had started, he'd told me that it would be fine if I wanted to get together at some point. That had surprised me; I had assumed that during these weeks, he'd prefer to keep his own company.

"Not really," he'd said. "I try not to make my routine any different than during the regular season. If you want to spend some time, just let me know."

In the elevator I asked him if he was still open to a visit. "Let's get together Thursday," he said. "Why don't we meet after practice."

Thursday would be the day following the next game. "I've got family in town right now, but I should be looser by then," he said. "I'll see you then."

We arrived at my floor and I left him alone in the elevator car. When I got to my room I could hear the sound of the people down on the street, waiting to see if Michael Jordan might come by.

Game 4 was a disaster for the Bulls. They began the first quarter by taking a 10-0 lead, and were never behind until the last four minutes of the game. Then they fell apart and allowed the Trail Blazers to go on a 13-3 run at the end, and to win 93-88. The Bulls were seething as they left the court, showered, and prepared to return to the hotel. In their minds the Finals should have been over tonight, 4-0 Chicago, repeat champions. Instead they had become sloppy and had let Games 2 and 4 get away, and now the series stood at 2-2, with one more game to be played in Portland before the Finals moved back across the continent to the Stadium. Suddenly the Trail Blazers had a very real chance to win two of the remaining three games and take the title.

In the press parking lot as I left the Memorial Coliseum, Quinn Buckner, a former NBA player with the Boston Celtics who now worked as Bob Costas' partner on NBC's "Showtime" program, was getting into a car driven by one of the network's couriers. I asked Buckner if I could hitch downtown with him, and he said to hop in.

As we rode, he said that he thought the Trail Blazers' coaching staff had made a mistake by flying the team back to Portland from Chicago overnight after Game 2. The Blazers had departed Chicago immediately after that game and had been tired from the long flight when they'd arrived in Oregon. The Bulls, on the other hand, waited until Saturday morning to fly to Portland for the Sunday game. Both teams had chartered jets at their disposal.

"You can misuse a charter," Buckner said. "Because the Trail Blazers have a charter, they were able to fly all night. But I don't see what that accomplished for them, other than making them exhausted the next day. They probably should have slept in their hotel in Chicago, gotten a good night's rest, and then flown in the daytime Saturday like the Bulls did."

He began talking about life in the NBA when he had been a player, in the years before charters, and we heard some loud screaming. We were on Broadway, en route to Buckner's hotel, the Vintage Plaza; the screaming was coming from in front of the Benson.

What had happened was that the Bulls' team bus had just pulled up to the front door of the Benson, and the throngs in the street were screaming for Jordan. It was that Beatles-concert sound once again; it had nothing to do with sports.

We rode past the Bulls' bus; I was going to get out of the car with Buckner at the Vintage Plaza on the next block, and then walk back to the Benson. As we passed the bus Buckner looked out the car window, saw the screaming mob, and said, as if the answer to a puzzle: "Michael."

He kept looking as we drove on. "This is the only team this happens for," he said. "You just don't see this kind of thing anywhere else."

The Beatles, of course, never had a scoreboard. They might give a good performance or a bad performance, but when the show was over there was never a winner or a loser. Not so with Jordan and his teammates. They'd lost tonight. They were incensed at themselves for having let the game slip away. The people in front of the Benson didn't care about that. They were there to see Jordan get off a bus. So the Bulls, in defeat, stepped onto the sidewalk and made their way through a crowd of shrieking, exhilarated fans even though there was nothing to celebrate. Each man on the bus knew exactly why the screamers were there.

I half-expected Jordan to cancel our plans to get together the next day. I wouldn't have blamed him; the loss in Game 4 had been so disappointing to the team, and the prospect of the Trail Blazers taking over the series so real, that I could see him telling me that he just wasn't up to having company right now. The next game would be perhaps the most crucial of the year.

The Bulls were scheduled to hold an early morning practice, and to break for the day at 11 A.M. Just after eleven I went down to the lobby to see what would develop. About twenty past the hour the team bus rolled up to the front door of the hotel; the Bulls, back from practice and flanked by security men, hastened through the lobby toward the waiting elevators.

Assistant coaches Tex Winter and John Bach were on the outside edges of the group, as if protecting Pippen and Jordan and Grant and the rest from the hotel guests and employees who had gathered to watch. Jordan had his head down as he walked; he looked totally wrung out. He seemed to be trying to shut out everything that was going on around him, but as he passed by he stopped briefly and said, "Come on up. Get on the elevator with us."

There was a scramble for the first elevator—anyone left behind would have to contend with the autograph-seekers in the lobby until the next car arrived—and because the hotel was so old the elevator cars were smaller than those in more modern buildings. We were packed so tightly that it would have been wise for two or three people to get off; all those people and all that weight seemed to be too much for the elevator car, but the door closed and there was no breathing room and the car began to lift.

It was so warm in the car and the quarters were so close that no one even made jokes about it. As the door opened on each succeeding floor, the players who had rooms there got off. Will Perdue left the elevator, and Bobby Hansen, and Cliff Levingston, and Pippen. As each man departed the car got a little less claustrophobic, and one by one they stepped into one hallway after another, and finally we were rising to the penthouse floor and the other players were gone and Jordan remained.

He took two quick right turns in the corridor, and we were at his room. There was a sitting area, and a set of half-opened glass doors through which I could see someone sleeping under the covers of the bed.

"My wife's pregnant," Jordan said. "She's really tired." In her sleep she was stirring beneath the sheets.

I felt I probably shouldn't be here. If she woke up, I didn't think she needed to look around the room and see some guy sitting a few feet away from her.

Jordan settled into a chair by the window. I thought he was going to nod off. It occurred to me that I had never seen him so obviously fatigued before. Every bit of vitality seemed to have been drained from him. It was all he could do to keep his eyes open.

"Are you sure I should be in the room?" I said, gesturing toward the bed.

"It's okay," he said. "She'll sleep."

"Look, I think I'm only going to stay for a few minutes," I said.

He leaned his head back and his eyes did shut momentarily.

"Are you all right?" I said.

"I'm just so tired," he said. He opened his eyes again and tried to take part in the conversation. It was an overcast Oregon morning outside the window, cool with the look of distant rain.

He had played more than one hundred basketball games since the exhibition season had started in October. All the late-night airplane flights, all the early practice calls in the hotels, all the commotion in his life . . . it had never seemed to catch up with him. Now, though, his voice was raspy and his carriage was sluggish. Because he had committed to playing in the Olympics, he would go virtually straight from the Finals to the Olympic team's training camp, then on to the Tournament of the Americas, then to Barcelona for the Olympic Games themselves . . . and then back to the United States for the beginning of another eighty-two-game regular season.

"I've got to shake this off by tomorrow," he said. A Portland *Oregonian* sports page in the room featured a headline about the Trail Blazers' victory over the Bulls the night before. Everywhere else in town, this was just a bit of highly interesting news. Nothing the readers of the story would have to do anything about.

"How are your teammates reacting to what's happening in the Finals?" I said.

"There is still a lot of complacency," he said. "Even now. It's surprising. There's a lot of relaxation on the bus—even last night, after we lost.

"It was a little surprising on the way back from the game, to hear some people fooling around and making jokes. I can't force myself to make a joke right now. Maybe that's how some of them deal with the tension, by laughing and joking around. I can't even pretend to do that. On the bus back to the hotel after we lost last night, I just sat by myself and listened to that and didn't say anything."

"Do you all talk to each other about what you've got to do now?" I said.

"Everything we could say we're already aware of," he said. "And besides, that's not my job. It's Phil's."

"Do you think you can win the series?" I said.

"I really don't know," he said.

In a way, it was the most unexpected thing I'd ever heard him say.

"I'm just so tired," he said. "I'm so tired that even when it comes time to push myself, I feel the tiredness. I need to play full force for the rest of the series. I need to play as hard as I can to win this. If we're going to win it, I have to leave everything that's in me on the floor."

"Can you get some rest between now and tomorrow?" I said.

"Rest isn't the answer," he said. "What I need to do is to get away from basketball on the days between the games. That's why I've been going out and playing golf."

There had been a minor controversy about that; apparently Jordan had told some sports reporters that he wasn't playing golf during the Finals, because he thought that to tell them he was would make him look as if he wasn't taking the basketball seriously enough. Then the reporters had learned that he'd been seen at a local course, and they questioned the wisdom of his squandering his stamina in such a way.

"On the golf course I can think about something other than basketball," he said. "It's the only way I know of that I can get rid of the mental part of the tiredness. I just want to get my concentration up and get this over and done with."

"Who do you want to win it for?" I said.

"For me," he said.

I'd heard all the standard quotes on television—how the Bulls wanted to win the championship for the team, and for their city, and for their fans.

"I know you're supposed to say that you want to win it for everyone else, but for me right now it's totally personal," Jordan said. "All the difficulties I've had to deal with this season —this is very personal for me. I need to win this one for myself."

Across the bridge was the Memorial Coliseum. Around the world were those tens of millions of basketball fans who would be watching the next time the two teams took the court.

In the room we talked quietly so as not to awaken Jordan's wife. I looked over at the bed where she was sleeping. "I'm going to get out of here and leave you alone," I said.

"I'm sorry," he said. "I never thought this season was going to take so much out of me."

He scored forty-six points the next night.

It was the most points he'd yet scored in a Finals game, this year or last; it was the most points any player had ever scored against any Trail Blazers team in any playoff game. He was all over the court—pressing on defense, out in front of the fast breaks, soaring toward the net as Pippen or Paxson launched a shot so that he could provide a backup should their efforts prove errant. It was a long game—two hours and forty-three minutes from tipoff to the final buzzer—and I tried to put his performance together with what I'd seen of him in his room the day before. There was no rational answer. He may have been dead tired before coming to the arena, and he may have become dead tired again as soon as the clock ran out, but when the game was in progress he was without any question at all the best basketball player in the world.

Some day this had to stop; some day he had to become bone tired and then not be able to do this the next night. Not yet. In the second quarter he stepped past the end line and twisted his left ankle when he landed on some photography equipment. He hobbled to the bench and rested and tried to heal for just over one minute. Then he returned to the game and, on his first shooting attempt after the injury, hit a three-pointer.

The Bulls won 119-106, giving them a 3-2 lead in the series as they headed back to Chicago. They needed one more for the championship.

It was going to be another of those quick turnarounds; Game 5 ended Friday night in Portland, and Game 6 was scheduled for Sunday in the Chicago Stadium. On my flight to Chicago I sat next to Phil Jasner, the basketball writer for the Philadelphia *Daily News*. Although the outcome of the Finals was still not decided, he had spread out on his tray table a sheaf of papers summarizing the prospects for the upcoming NBA college draft. No matter who won the Chicago-Portland series, the one thing that was certain for Jasner was that a week from now it would be history, sand into the sea, and he would be covering the draft. Jasner pored over the names of the top college prospects, dealing at once with their long-term futures and his immediate one.

Two hours or so before last night's game in Portland, I had stood on the floor of the Memorial Coliseum with Tommy Roy, who was as usual producing the game coverage for NBC. As we stood there talking, a panel of apparently angry women could be seen on the four huge video screens that were part of the Coliseum scoreboard. Roy and I looked up at the scene; who were these women, so animated and so exercised?

They were on the "Donahue" show, it turned out; some member of the arena's building crew had turned on "Donahue," which was currently airing on a local Portland station, and had thrown the switch that would put it on the scoreboard. So on the video replay screens that in two hours would be showing Jordan and Pippen and Clyde Drexler and Jerome Kersey, Phil Donahue interrogated his guests. There was no audio, but it didn't matter; the message to us was clear. Donahue was on TV right now, and in two hours Tommy Roy would see to it that Jordan and Pippen were on TV, and as soon as the game ended someone else would be on TV. What seemed so consequential to us at the moment—the specific course of these NBA Finals—was, in the long run, just another piece of entertainment.

"Donahue" on the Coliseum scoreboard; Phil Jasner charting the college draft on the jet bound for Chicago. We'd all be moving on to other things eventually. Jordan, too. This all would pass.

For now, though, he had a championship to win.

Sometimes you forget what sports are all about. At least you are tempted to.

The world of sports has become such a chilly-eyed conglomeration of finances and contract law and broadcasting rights; has become such an endless year-round cycle of licensing options and subsidiary equities and merchandising spin-offs; has become such a carefully timed and predictably coordinated vehicle for arousing the public's interest on schedule and then taking the money and moving on to the next event—sometimes all of that combines to make you forget what made you love sports so much in the first place.

Then something like the final game of the Bulls–Trail Blazers series comes along, and you remember. Even as the contest is unfolding on the court in front of you, you know: This is it. This is why so many people love the playing of games so much. This is why people who love sports always hold out hope—for a game like this one.

For the Bulls, Game 6 began dismally. The Trail Blazers took command early, building a 25-19 lead at the end of the first quarter, with Jordan getting only two points. At the half it was 50-44 Portland; at the end of three the Trail Blazers had extended their lead to 79-64, and Chicago's players, and Jordan in particular, looked depleted and weary. It seemed certain that the Trail Blazers would cruise to a victory, silence the Stadium crowd, and force a seventh game—a seventh game Portland now seemed eminently capable of winning.

Phil Jackson began the fourth quarter with what at the time seemed a bizarre lineup for the Bulls. Jackson put four of his stars—Jordan, Grant, Paxson, and Cartwright—on the bench, keeping only Pippen from his starting lineup on the floor. To play alongside Pippen he put in the curious combination of reserves B. J. Armstrong, Bobby Hansen, Scott Williams, and Stacey King. Many in the stands thought Jackson had merely given up for the night.

And then it began. It happened like a succession of frames from a movie:

Bobby Hansen, thirty-one years old, the twelfth man on the Bulls, the one who'd been a stranger to the others at the start of the season, pulling in a pass from Armstrong in the far left corner of the court and, not hesitating even an instant, taking aim and hitting a three-point jump shot, sprinting back on defense, not allowing his face to betray anything, but shaking his fist triumphantly in the air.

Then, seconds later, Hansen stealing the ball from Jerome Kersey at the other end of the court and firing it to Armstrong to start a break.

Stacey King getting slammed by two Portland defenders, missing the first of his two free throws, being reassured with a whisper from Pippen, then hitting the next one; Pippen thirteen seconds later taking the ball and twisting past Drexler and two other Trail Blazers to lay it into the basket and cut the lead to nine.

Cliff Robinson of Portland putting his team back on top by eleven with a running jump shot, but then King, pummeled again, hitting both of his two free throws. Scott Williams grabbing a missed Portland shot, then Pippen running downcourt, coiling and torquing and maneuvering until he finds some free space, banking in a jumper to move the Bulls within seven.

And at the bench Jordan on his feet, pumping his arm, yelling in encouragement like a thrilled fan in the stands.

Drexler seeming to lose his concentration, being called for a double dribble; B. J. Armstrong fumbling the ball momentarily, then launching a high shot that somehow drops straight through the net, Jordan jumping up and down on the bench, his face full of eagerness and the vision of a new chance.

The Bulls stopping Portland on defense again, the noise in the Stadium rising by the second, big Stacey King maneuvering like a guard, knocking in a fourteen-foot jump shot off the backboard to cut the Portland lead to three. Jordan not even trying to hide what he is feeling, bounding into the air on the sidelines, seeing the second team get close enough to put a victory within imagination.

Now, with 8:36 left in the game, Phil Jackson sent Jordan back in, replacing Hansen, the only man on the Bulls who had not been a part of last year's championship. I could see the two men stop and exchange a few words as Hansen left the court and Jordan walked onto it. Later, I would ask Hansen what was said between them: "I said, 'Take over, Michael, take us home.' And he just nodded and said to me, 'We're going to get you a ring.'"

No team in NBA history had come back from a fifteen-point deficit after three quarters to win the championship, but here were Jordan and the Bulls. Drexler scored for Portland, then Pippen dribbled the ball the entire length of the court, snaking between the arms of four members of the Portland team to lay the ball in and move the Bulls to within three. Jordan, in the din of the Stadium, saw Jerome Kersey about to make an uncertain pass, leapt toward the ball, grabbed it in midair, hit a running jump shot with the crowd shrieking and moved the Bulls to within one point of the Trail Blazers.

If you want to prove that you're the best basketball team in existence, this is how you do it. Portland got two more points; Pippen, with the illuminated numbers on the shot clock racing down to zero, hit a perfect pressure three-pointer from the left side to tie the game at 85. Terry Porter put Portland back ahead; Jordan, falling backward in the lane, launched a sixteen-foot jump shot to tie it once again. In the bedlam of the arena floor there was a succession of frantic turnovers and steals; Jordan chopped the ball out of Buck Williams' hands under the Bulls' basket, then wheeled and leaped in the same continuous motion to lay the ball into the hoop and put the Bulls ahead at last.

In the final minutes Portland caught up anew, then saw the Bulls retake the lead on a Pippen jump shot. John Paxson, back in the game for Armstrong, stripped the ball from Terry Porter. Jordan coolly shot over Drexler from sixteen feet to put his team ahead by four. Drexler closed it to 93-91 with two free throws; Jordan drove right past Drexler on the other end and powered along the baseline for a layup with thirty-five seconds left. The noise was ceaseless and palpable now, the noise was so thick you could feel it pressing in on you.

The game would be determined with 11.8 seconds on the clock and Jordan at the free throw line. The Bulls were ahead 95-93. If Jordan made the shots, he would give his team a four-point lead and a certainty of the championship. If he missed them Portland would have plenty of time to take the ball down the court and tie or go ahead.

Calm and excited at the same time, Jordan stood at the line. Calm and excited—like a man who is exactly where he was meant to be; like a child shooting free throws at a tiny basket in his living room and waiting for his father to come home from work to watch him—he spun the ball in his hands, then bounced it, then tossed it toward the hoop. Good. He was ready for the second attempt. Spin, bounce: good. The Stadium erupted, the clock ran out, and the Bulls were champions of the world again.

27

THE LAST TIME I SAW HIM that night, he was standing on top of the scorer's table with his teammates, swaying back and forth to the music.

They had gone downstairs for the trophy presentation from the commissioner, had doused each other with champagne, and were preparing to take their showers when they were informed that the fans were not leaving. The Stadium was still full; the people wanted Jordan and the Bulls to come back upstairs.

So they did. Carrying the trophy, they had run up those grimy stairs from the basement, into the lights of the arena again, and when the crowd caught sight of them it sent up a roar the likes of which the gray and antiquated building may never have known. The team climbed up on the scorer's table to greet the people in the seats; the songs that were blasting through the Stadium's P.A. system were cranked up full volume, and the players were dancing in place, so proud and filled with contentment they seemed ready to weep.

Jordan dancing was a rare sight. For all his acrobatics on the court, for all his fluid grace in flying toward the basket, when he wasn't playing the game he was usually rather shy and self-protective in the way he carried himself. He didn't posture; he didn't strut. So to see him up there flailing his arms as if he were in a dance hall was to see him letting down his defenses. He was one of twelve at that moment; he was one of the team, he had done his job, and he was free.

I was standing on the surface of the court. Tomorrow, I knew, everything would start all over again for him. The Olympics lay ahead, and the new season after that, and all the decisions he would have to make about his life. But for a few hours tonight he could breathe, he could let himself go, he could exult in this. He could stand on a table and dance.

As I looked at the twelve of them, I knew that some day they would stare frozenly out of a team picture in the pages of a sports history book, or framed on the wall of some sports bar somewhere, and people would look at the picture with nostalgia and say, "What a great team those guys were." This was not nostalgia yet, though; this was tonight. I looked at their faces: Pippen, wary as ever, but now a proven star; Grant, guileless with or without the goggles, a man at the top of his profession; Cartwright, dignified and stoic, a winner near the end of his career; Paxson, open and without artifice, clear-eyed and steadfast and exactly what he appeared to the world to be; Armstrong, still with the face of a kid, but a kid who was now a two-time NBA champion; Perdue and Hodges and Hansen and Williams and Levingston and King, all laughing and swaying together under the lights.

And Jordan, always and ever Jordan. He had been named Most Valuable Player in the Finals, for the second year in a row. He had also been named Most Valuable Player in the NBA for the year, the second time in a row for that tribute. No one in the history of basketball had ever done that: two world championships in a row, two NBA MVP awards in a row, two Finals MVP awards in a row.

I thought of the last two years. I hadn't planned it out in advance, but if ever there were two years more worth the having, it would be hard to imagine them. A lot of times you find yourself not really valuing a period in your life until long after it is over; you find yourself looking back and wondering why you didn't honor it more. Not for me, not now. I stood on that Stadium floor as the crowd called Jordan's name and I thought of the last two years and I knew: You will never see anything like this again. You will never spend time like this again.

"Are you going to Barcelona?" he had asked me in Portland, just before we flew back to Chicago. I said no; I said that I'd be watching the Olympics on television, along with most of the rest of the world.

"Then I guess I'll see you in the fall," he said.

And I said yes, I guessed I'd be seeing him then. One of these days it will be time to stop going out to the Stadium, but the time hadn't come yet. The world I wrote about every day had become no less grim, no less dismaying than it had been the first time I'd walked into the building. Nothing was going to change that; if anything this world of ours keeps spinning itself into crueler and more sorrowful shape. But there is more than one way to look upon that world. Of all the things I'd taken away from all those Stadium nights, maybe that was the most important: the knowledge that, if you look closely enough, amid the merciless and the bitter there's always the chance you may find comfort and the promise of something good.

The Stadium itself would be gone before too long; even as the Bulls were celebrating in the minutes after their championship, the new arena was going up, and no one could offer assurance that the old Stadium would not be torn down, leveled to rubble. So the prospect was considerable that everything that had ever transpired in this building would soon be not only a memory, but a memory without a home. Once the building was gone, all that had happened within its walls—all the noise, all the happiness, all the life—would seem like a lost illusion, like something in a dream.

He didn't dream about basketball. That's what he had told me all those months ago, when I had asked him what filled his mind as he slept, lost to the world, through the middle of the night. Not basketball, he had insisted. "I don't dream about basketball anymore," he had said.

But I do. I didn't used to, but I do now. The dreams are vivid and bright, and they are filled with some of the most incandescent and hopeful images I have ever known. The dreams I have take place in this old building, and they will stay with me forever, and I dream those dreams all the time.

Bob Greene is a syndicated columnist for the *Chicago Tribune*. His column appears in more than two hundred newspapers in the United States, Canada, and Japan. For nine years his "American Beat" was the lead column in *Esquire* magazine; as a broadcast journalist he has served as contributing correspondent for "ABC News Nightline." He is the author of thirteen other books, including the national bestsellers *Be True to Your School* and *Good Morning, Merry Sunshine*. Most recently he has written, with his sister, journalist D. G. Fulford, *To Our Children's Children: Preserving Family Histories for Generations to Come,* and has published his first novel, *All Summer Long,* which has been praised by reviewers as "the perfect summertime novel," "as refreshing as a tall glass of iced tea on a July afternoon," and "the literary equivalent of one more night's cruise through the drive-in, your arm around your steady while the Beach Boys sing about young love and endless summers."

BESTSELLING BOOKS FROM

ST. MARTIN'S PAPERBACKS

FLASHBACKS: On Returning to Vietnam
Morley Safer
_____ 92482-8 $5.95 U.S./$6.95 Can.

THE SILENCE OF THE LAMBS
Thomas Harris
_____ 92458-5 $5.99 U.S./$6.99 Can.

BORN RICH
Georgia Raye
_____ 92239-6 $4.95 U.S./$5.95 Can.

WEST END
Laura Van Wormer
_____ 92262-0 $5.95 U.S./$6.95 Can.

THE WESTIES
T. J. English
_____ 92429-1 $5.95 U.S./$6.95 Can.

HOW TO WIN AT NINTENDO GAMES #2
Jeff Rovin
_____ 92016-4 $3.95 U.S./$4.95 Can.

BESTSELLING BOOKS FROM ST. MARTIN'S PAPERBACKS— TO READ AND READ AGAIN!

NOT WITHOUT MY DAUGHTER
Betty Mahmoody with William Hoffer
_____ 92588-3 $5.99 U.S./$6.99 Can.

PROBABLE CAUSE
Ridley Pearson
_____ 92385-6 $5.95 U.S./$6.95 Can.

RIVERSIDE DRIVE
Laura Van Wormer
_____ 91572-1 $5.95 U.S.   _____ 91574-8 $6.95 Can.

SHADOW DANCERS
Herbert Lieberman
_____ 92288-4 $5.95 U.S./$6.95 Can.

THE FITZGERALDS AND THE KENNEDYS
Doris Kearns Goodwin
_____ 90933-0 $5.95 U.S.   _____ 90934-9 $6.95 Can.

JAMES HERRIOT'S DOG STORIES
James Herriot
_____ 92558-1 $5.99 U.S.

LANDMARK BESTSELLERS
FROM ST. MARTIN'S
PAPERBACKS

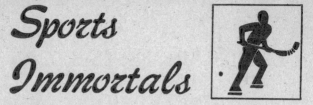